THE NEUTRALIZED CHURCH

THE NEUTRALIZED CHURCH

❖ IS IT WRONG FOR CHRISTIANS TO BE INVOLVED IN POLITCS? OUR FOUNDING FATHERS DIDN'T THINK SO!

❖ HAVE CHRISTIANS BEEN NEUTRALIZED POLITICALLY SO THAT SATAN COULD ACHIEVE WORLD GOVERNMENT WITHOUT OPPOSITION? ABSOLUTELY!

By
Gene Baldock

Order this book online at www.trafford.com
or email orders@trafford.com

Most Trafford titles are also available at major online book retailers.

All scriptural references are from
The King James Bible

All dictionary definitions are from
Webster's New Collegiate Dictionary

No part of this book should be considered as legal advice. Rather, it
is presented for the consideration that Christians have been purposely
deceived into abandoning our Godly responsibilities by satanic infiltration
into the church. Hopefully it will be considered a call to action.

Printed in the United States of America.

ISBN: 978-1-4269-5921-9 (sc)
ISBN: 978-1-4269-5922-6 (e)

Trafford rev. 03/03/2011

 www.trafford.com

North America & International
toll-free: 1 888 232 4444 (USA & Canada)
phone: 250 383 6864 ♦ fax: 812 355 4082

PREFACE

This book is designed as an introduction to answers. Scores of patriotic Americans and devout Christians have legitimate questions that they have long ceased to ask. Chief among them are: "What is happening to the America we once knew", "Why can no politician seem able to set this country back on a course toward prosperity or Godliness" and "Why, when the electorate replaces the party in power, is there no significant change in national policies"? Too many people have quit asking these legitimate questions because they went unanswered.

The fact is the answers have long been available! The answers have been right under our nose for generations. The problem is that we have been manipulated into ignoring the answer and dismissing evidence of its truth. We reject and ignore those who defy political correctness and speak the truth.

This book is designed for people with a foundational knowledge of The Bible and accepts it as the word of God. The purpose of this book is to show Christians how Satan has tricked them into promoting his agenda. Only by understanding what Satan has done to the church can we begin to understand why all efforts to bring about change fail. God works through those who willingly serve Him. Therefore the church is God's "change agent". God will not change His strategy just because Christians permit Satan undo influence over the church.

This book can only be an introduction to answers. The answers themselves require study on a variety of topics, however this book touches on many of these topics to show that all the problems we face in our society today emanate from a central source. This is the one fact that Christians have long ignored and must now investigate and embrace if we have any hope of being a positive influence on our generation. It is the evidence of this one fact that Christians have been too quick to dismiss without consideration.

This book is an overview of what is happening in America and how it is being done. In an effort to put proofs of some of the more controversial information at the reader's fingertips, I have provided many web site references. The information is developed in much greater detail in the books I have listed at the end of this book in a recommended reading list.

The information has long been available but truth lies dormant until one decides to investigate. This book will begin that investigation from a Christian perspective, with an emphasis on accurate scriptural interpretations, and will probably be the most controversial book you have ever read.

Acknowledgement

To Ed Darsow: This book is as much a product of your labor as much as my own. Without your encouragement, diligence and ambition this book would have remained a small series of Bible studies.

Thank you for your faithfulness and friendship

TABLE OF CONTENTS

PART ONE
Accepting Challenging Information

Chapter 1: Fertile Ground 10
Chapter 2: Rule One; Confuse And Mislead...............................24
Chapter 3: World Views 40

PART TWO
God Is In Control

Chapter 4: God Is In Control 55
Chapter 5: Calvinism Verses Free Will..69
Chapter 6: Neutralizing The Effectiveness Of God's People 85
Chapter 7: Neutralizing The Actions Of God's People 100
Chapter 8: The Church Infiltrated..114

PART THREE
Christians In Politics

Chapter 9: Christians And Politics...133
Chapter 10: Satan And Politics 150
Chapter 11: The Church And Politics 167
Chapter 12: Battles Abandoned 183
Chapter 13: History Of Christians In Politics............................198
Chapter 14: Prophecy And Politics 212

PART FOUR
Legislating Morality

Chapter 15: Authority To Legislate Morality 231

Chapter 16: Authority To Legislate Immorality 247

Chapter 17: Authority To Bind The Church 262

Chapter 18: Without Morality 277

PART FIVE
Government Is Of God

Chapter 19: God's View Of Government 293

Chapter 20: Satan's View Of Government 308

Chapter 21: Government And Party Politics 321

PART SIX
The World Deceived

Chapter 22: Introduction To Part 6 345

Chapter 23: Neutralizing Jesus 356

Chapter 24: Overwhelming Deception 373

Chapter 25: The Road We've Traveled 390

PART SEVEN
Options And Evidence

Chapter 26: Our Options Now 409

Chapter 27: Famous Quotes About NWO 426

Chapter 28: Recommended Reading List 433

PART ONE

*ACCEPTING
CHALLENGING
INFORMATION*

INTRODUCTION

Luke 19:13 "Occupy until I come..."

Recently several Christian novels depicting life during the Biblically prophetic "tribulation" period of The Book of Revelation proved to be extremely popular and every book in the series was a best seller. Christians love the topic of end time prophecy and always keep Bible prophecy classes and seminars well attended. We have several national ministries in this country that attempt to interpret current events as they relate to eschatology (the study of end time prophecy) and they are enormously successful monetarily even when they have questionable accuracy.

But on this topic there exists one field of study, containing an enormous quantity of factual information and incredible amounts of detailed documentation, which is curiously avoided by both pastors and laymen alike. This has become known as the topic of "the new world order". At long last, increasing numbers of Christians are beginning to explore and consider the information that has been ferreted out by brave researchers over a number of years. They are beginning to find that this research is quite true and quite well documented. The great masses of Christianity, however, are still significantly unaware or too skeptical to examine any amount of this information for themselves.

Unfortunately this is creating an even greater problem for the world we live in. Since we love prophecy we listen to news outlets that dispense this type of information. We become increasingly exposed to the problems but those dispensing this information do not provide any information regarding solutions. This serves to "desensitize" Christians to the evil that is growing in our midst but teaches no responsibility to address this evil. We come to view the growth of ungodliness as inevitable and we may welcome it to an extent, because we've been taught it signals the soon return of Jesus Christ. Additionally, the problem of unreliable sources does exist so many are not sure what to believe.

Students of eschatology are convinced that we are living on the threshold of a prophetic tribulation and some argue that this time period has already begun. The question is, does God desire that we complacently sit idle and do nothing as our world is conquered by satanic forces or does God desire Christians to stand against evil, even in these last days?

Repeatedly scripture says Christians are to have no tolerance for evil. We are told to resist it, meaning to "counteract or defeat". We are not to grow complacent and "wait out events" until the Lord's return. Exactly what we should be doing has become a subject of debate. Many Christians believe our sole responsibility is to spread the gospel and play no role in directly influencing events. Many Christians hold the opposing view that we have a responsibility to persuade our leaders and national policies toward Godliness. Few study the matter sufficiently to determine if there is some truth in both arguments.

Those opposed to political involvement correctly point out that political efforts made in the past have had little success. Just as frequently, the few successes achieved have not had long lasting results. Those making these points have not considered that Satan is using a strategy far more encompassing than they have been led to believe.

From his perspective if we spread the gospel only, not fighting evil and making no effort to train new converts to fight evil, he is free to pursue his agenda even while the gospel is being preached. If the gospel that we're teaching excludes verses on fighting evil then Satan has no opposition while pursuing his goals and new converts won't threaten his agenda.

Regarding our lack of success influencing society politically, today it is difficult to find the church having Godly results with anything that we undertake. We see new churches being built everyday, we see a host of new Christian movies and books widely distributed and we see more Christians home schooling or private schooling their children but these are internal.

What can we point to as an impact the church is having on society? Abortion is as popular as ever, the homosexual revolution is thriving, morality is nonexistent and pornography is everywhere. Instead of fighting these and many more issues, Christians are either coming to accept them as inevitable or embracing them as perfectly permissible. The Bible is no longer viewed as the first and final authority on these matters. Many churches, including entire denominations, view scripture as little more than a book of ancient wisdom.

Those who accept The Bible as God's word recognize that a one-world government is prophesied for the end times but far too many do not realize this government is completed to an alarming extent. Due to ignorance and false leadership Christians have actually played a major role in the construction of this government and this is a matter they must be made aware of. Christians should never find themselves in Satan's service and though this may sound offensive, Satan is a deceiver and if not familiar with his tactics anyone can be victimized.

Jesus said in Luke 19:13 "occupy until I come…" Some argue this should not be taken literally and is not a meaningful commandment to the church as it is given in a parable. To disregard it would mean Jesus was willing that we "surrender until He comes" which is what Satan wants us to do. Parable or not, why would He say it if He didn't mean it and since when do we disregard parables?

What has happened to the church? Why were they so formidable in generations past and so helpless against evil today? The church has been neutralized. Satan has long understood that a church living and working in the power of God would destroy his plans. If you take him seriously you must recognize that, by necessity, he had to develop a strategy to neutralize the once mighty church as a stepping-stone to building his coveted one world government.

Part of his strategy is to feed us false doctrine by false leadership, weak doctrine by weak leadership and confusion by confused leadership. Through the ignorance, apathy and confusion that are inevitable without good leadership we no longer fight evil and it is thriving in our land.

Much is known of Satan's tactics and strategies but not widely so by Christians and church leadership. We have been convinced it's not our fight. This is wrong. To achieve his ends Satan knew he would need an organization capable of much more than misleading the church. He would need an organization capable of misleading mankind to such a degree that they would choose him over God and destroy anyone who opposed his agenda.

He has worked to build such an organization. The church has been warned through God's word and has the duty to warn mankind, yet the majority do not heed the warning themselves. The devotees of Satan's agenda call themselves the new world order and today evidence of their existence and fruitful efforts are abundant.

Much of this book will be offensive and I trust the reader realizes that truth frequently is. We grow comfortable with our own beliefs and most of us are not looking for another battle to fight. Still there are two questions to be answered. The first is this; if I can prove scripture is being taken out of context, twisted and used to deceive, would you desire to know the truth? Do not answer in haste. Evidence has shown that few in any population truly desire to know the truth when it is offensive. The second question is what would God desire you to do? Most Christians hunger to be used of God but to be used of God we must be willing. To be effective requires understanding the deceptions that are being used against us.

There are primarily four lies that have neutralized the church. We can call them distortions of the truth so as not to deny a grain of truth in each one but they are taught and preached quite different from any original truth. We have embraced these concepts and teaching even though they are widely refuted in scripture. This book is largely a study of these four lies. They are: 1) God is in control; 2) Christians should not get involved in politics; 3) You can't legislate morality; 4) Government is of God. Again, this is not to say there's not a degree of truth in these statements. A half lie is more dangerous than a bold lie.

Every Christian should examine their beliefs from a scriptural perspective and prove them scripturally sound. This is what I will attempt to do here. I suspect most eyebrows were raised with the labeling of these commonly taught beliefs as lies and I suspect many readers will read no further. It is essential that Christians understand God's word. Too the extents Christians believe these lies we have been deceived and neutralized. Deceived into blaming God for what Satan has done, deceived into blaming God for what we've failed to do and deceived into blaming God for the natural results that stem from what we have not even attempted to do. By this method we have been neutralized from fighting evil and evil has naturally prospered.

We must understand God's view on these matters. In Matthew 12:29 Jesus says "how can one enter into a strong man's house and spoil his goods, except he first bind the strong man..." The church is strong in the Lord and we are surely being spoiled so we must conclude that we are bound. We may not recognize it and we may not wish to admit it but what else is there to conclude? If you believe that we are mighty in the Lord, and surely all must concede we're being spoiled, we have the wisdom of God to tell us why. The piece of information missing is in how we were bound. We are bound by deception and false leadership.

Then too, for Satan to build his new world order he must deceive the nations. There are many in every land that have not accepted Christ and yet through common sense and self preservation they would have no part of this satanic new world order. They too must be dealt with for this new world order to succeed. Part of this book deals with the lies that have neutralized them, all of which affect the church as well. The lies exposed in the latter part of this book are so staggering in their reach and scope it is difficult to accept that any rational person would be so gullible as to believe them but they are believed.

This book is not designed to expose a great many specifics about the existence of this new world order. Libraries full of excellent books exist on this topic and many are detailed concerning specific efforts by the new world order to promote and achieve their agenda. Concluding this book, I will list several books that I can recommend for those who are not aware of the new world order and the way it has come to affect our lives.

We should expect the church to be at the forefront working to expose any and all evil in the land. Quite the contrary, most Christians and most pastors dismiss this information because of either disbelief or apathy and inaccurately quote scripture to justify inactivity.

I am, of course, talking about a conspiracy. To a Christian this concept should not be disturbing since we recognize Satan is real and he operates in secret. These books I referred to almost universally stop short of exposing Satan as the main factor behind the host of threats that are destroying our nation. Irresponsible researchers want to identify an enemy but they frequently blame "The Jews", "The Masons", "The International Bankers" or some group. Satan will use anyone of any group, religion or ethnicity that is willing to serve him or be deceived into a single service. By placing fault on those in Satan's service without addressing Satan or his agenda we fail to properly equip the church. We become guilty of falsely accusing many who are not to blame and we aid in hiding Satan when we should be exposing him.

We as Christians should not allow ourselves to be caught up in hating or blaming those who are deceived. Rather we should be educated and involved in exposing the deception and the devil that's doing the deceiving. To war effectively we must be ready for an attack and we should be prepared to counter-attack. If we are effective we will surely be attacked.

We are at war and it is a war of deception. Christians are to be fountains of truth and warriors against evil. We want to believe we are safe in our churches and that our individual church is a good one. We also want to believe our personal pastor is good and he may be. Never the less, it is to underestimate Satan to assume he desires a one world government but failed to take Christians or the church into consideration as he plans how to achieve his dream. He would know he must do something about those with authority to destroy him. There could be no purpose in a battle of good verses evil without the church being targeted by the evil forces with full intentions to neutralize or destroy it.

To the extent we believe our church is involved is irrelevant. The proof exists that many involved in the new world order have great plans to use the church for their evil purposes. Infamous occult writer Alice Bailey has written, "*These ancient mysteries will be restored … through the medium of the church*".[1] Before they could do this they needed to infiltrate and redirect. The degree of success they have achieved should be of interest to us all.

Evil is in our churches. Apathy and complacency are predominating. Evil is disguised in a host of ways but most commonly as misinformation serving the purpose of keeping good people complacent. Each must decide to stand up in this hour or watch complacently as those that they love are led into a Godless tyranny that God doesn't wish on anybody. If you believe slavery and tyranny are

God's will or inevitable please consider the following arguments from scripture. It is not God's will or desire for us as a nation to be ruled by evil. It is a deception put to us by a clever subtle enemy who knows drastic results are frequently achieved by small measures.

It is an age-old deception achieving much success because God's warriors have been tricked into thinking it's not their fight. As Christians leave the political arena others rush in to do Satan's service! We should acknowledge their growth and success is due to our lack of action. This is a fight that God expects His people to be engaged in. An honest and diligent study of scripture will make this clear.

FERTILE GROUND

*Luke 8:12 "there by the way side are they that hear; then
cometh the devil and taketh away the word…"*

It has been said that in war, truth is the first casualty. This axiom should be expanded to explain that in war, truth is the first enemy. Typically when one considers war an infantry is probably the first thing to come to mind. Perhaps next we think of fighter jets or artillery. Three vital weapons of war that are seldom considered are intelligence, counter-intelligence and propaganda.

This is no less true in the warfare that the church is to be engaged in. Many excellent theologians have pointed out that Satan knows The Bible better than most Christians do. Satan knows that God's word is true and he studies it simply to gather intelligence that he can use to strengthen his efforts to destroy Godliness.

Furthermore, he couldn't pervert it or defend himself against it if he didn't know and understand what it says. This is simply the reasonable preparation of a warrior, to gather intelligence on an enemy; however, we do not see the Christian community gathering intelligence on what Satan is doing.

He is as likely to use propaganda against us as any enemy in a war. Propaganda by definition is the "deliberate spreading of ideas, allegations, facts or rumors for the purpose of helping one's cause or injuring another's". Satan's passion is to injure the cause of Christ. The propaganda he uses against us is engineered to neutralize our work for Christ but Christians no longer gather intelligence on our enemy so we have no concept what he's doing or why.

Most people make a quick decision to believe or to disbelieve something and they largely base this on assumptions or preconceived notions rather than research. We should remember we are in a war and information is valuable. We must also be willing to consider controversial arguments because we know that the truth is controversial. Knowing our enemy is the father of lies and confusion means we must be cautious and responsible to properly consider matters before we accept or dismiss them. We have a subtle adversary who desires to trick and manipulate.

The proper and responsible way to consider any and every matter is to turn to God's word and be clear what God said. We must conclude that God gave this instruction for our benefit, intending that we use it. We are not to be quick in assuming a matter is false or unimportant. We are commanded in 1st Thessalonians 5:21 "Prove all things; hold fast that which is good." This is as true for arguments and ideas that we allow to affect our actions and beliefs as much as those we allow to affect our inaction. Indeed inaction on the part of a Christian is dangerous!

We commonly associate the title scripture with spreading the gospel and rightly so as this is the context. However, we should recognize it has application to all the truth we hear. Information that challenges our comfort zone or deeply held beliefs, we tend to reject without consideration. We fail to allow these truths to take root.

It does not cease to be a truth at that point but we suffer for the ignorance. This is never more true than when we're dealing with satanic propaganda. Psalms 1:1 reads, "Blessed is the man who walketh not in the counsel of the ungodly…" Yet we do not stop to consider who is ungodly. Two aspects of successful propaganda are to place reliable information in the hands of unreliable sources and unreliable information in the hands of reliable sources.

An extension of this strategy is to create your own sources and have them promoted and accepted as "reliable". Frequently people are considered reliable simply by being on television or writing a book. God does not view success in the same manner men do. Being on television or on a best selling author's list doesn't automatically mean God put them in this position. This truth applies to the evening news and accepting what the anchorman is saying. There is no evidence God put them in their positions. All that they say should be carefully scrutinized.

A great deal of our evening news is propaganda. An example of this would be an anchorman telling us a certain politician is a Christian or that a politician is a conservative. How does he know? We have no reason to accept that this anchor knows anything about Christianity or that his definition of a Christian would agree with The Bible. As liberal as most in the major media are known to be, we should not be quick to accept his definition of a conservative either.

Plus, the politician he speaks of wouldn't be the first to hire a writer to do a book on their behalf telling how they were converted and how devout they are. Here too, we don't question the credentials of such a writer. We have a duty to examine each politician and government policy in accordance to God's word and hold that as the standard. Clearly this is not being done. We accept the counsel of the ungodly media and the unknown authors and decide which politicians to support on the word of these people.

The evening news is very instrumental in starting wars, setting trends, instilling fear, desensitizing us to immorality, causing depression, panic and generally creating emotional turmoil that is difficult for all to deal with. "Seeds" are being planted in our mind. We hear seeds of fear and seeds of lies. Fearful and ignorant people can be easily manipulated. Some seeds take root immediately through our acceptance, others are rejected, and some take root over time. Through the propaganda process these seeds are carefully nurtured for a purpose.

Only by knowing God's word and using the truth revealed in it can we protect ourselves from these deceptions. We need to consider those that don't know God's word. They deserve to be informed of these lies but who shall warn them if we sit silent? The Bible makes Satan's plan clear and Christians should be exposing his plan and his efforts to a lost world.

Consider the four lies that are the topic of this book from this perspective. First, God is in control. If we allow this seed to grow in our mind we are not in a position to fight evil as we regard all things to be God's will. No matter how horrific things become around us we accept that this is the way God wants them to be. We do not work to prevent anything because we do not want to fight God. We do not blame Satan. If we consider him at all it is from a perspective that he must be used of God or God would have stopped him. We are limited in our ability to minister God's love and grace to non-Christians because it is impossible to explain how a loving and merciful God would be so hostile and abusive toward His creation. Indeed this concept creates enormous confusion in our minds too.

Second, Christians should not get involved in politics. If we allow this lie to grow in our mind, Satan is free to pursue his agenda without opposition. Few Christians stop to consider that the definition of politics is "tactfully promoting or opposing a policy". It is primarily considered to be governmental policies. This lie is tantamount to saying, "let's allow Satan to do as he chooses". There can be no doubt Satan is behind this concept and greatly benefiting from this deception.

Third, you can't legislate morality. That the church has accepted this seed is incredible! Churches and Christian leaders have stood idle as law after law has been rescinded destroying morality and the great quality of life we have come to expect in our nation. As the church has come to accept this lie politicians have worked overtime to pass a parade of laws permitting everything from vile perversions to abortion. They've gone so far as to legislate against those who have attempted to stop the teaching of these vile perversions to our children. We don't consider that for some illogical reason "we" can't legislate morality while Satan and his hosts can legislate immorality relentlessly! They have achieved a dream of convincing their opposition to surrender the fight in advance!

Fourth, government is of God. Granted, structure is of God and a structure to manage the protection of lives and property is typically referred to as government but this does not excuse the governmental abuses and excesses we tolerate from our elected leaders today. Our government is completely out of control and nothing Godly is out of control. Our government does not regard God and does not believe it is accountable to anyone. By accepting this lie we no longer perform our civic duties. We stand idle believing that government is all-powerful and free to take whatever action it chooses.

These teachings should be examined according to God's word and not just accepted by Christians as true. These lies/seeds are all contrary to God's word and we will examine them in much greater detail but first let's back up and examine some of the strategies that come into affect in terms of how we can be made to accept or reject a seed.

There is a concept we should be familiar with called the "teach-ability index". It is "desire to know" and "willingness to change". We will easily disregard information because we fail to recognize it is important to us. The first step toward responsibility is knowledge but the first step toward knowledge is a willingness to learn and a willingness to learn begins with a desire to know.

An example of this is studying God's word. When we "desire to know" we research. If we don't have the desire to know our study time diminishes. The topic could be marriage, money, relationship, etc. but the principle is the same.

Willingness to change is one of the great challenges to human existence and one of the great promises of Christianity. We have a God who will change our heart if we ask Him to. We seldom have a willingness to change when the change requires sacrifice or a commitment on our part.

We forget that Satan can give our heart desires too. The new world order learned long ago that they will go further with their agenda by playing to base human desires. One way Satan has impacted our heart's desires is apathy. We no longer have a heartfelt passion to stop evil or stand up for righteousness. Most of us just want to be left alone. If the topic does not entertain us we have no desire to know. We certainly are not going to worry about changing our behavior when we don't know that there is error in our conduct but we suffer the consequences of our ignorance just the same.

Every patriotic American should be wondering what is happening in this country in terms of the growing Godlessness but because of the four lies most simply dismiss their concerns. Far too many church leaders have been neutralized through these four lies. They've embraced them with no desire to know if they're in error. They are not teachable on this topic and their resolve is so complete they will not even consider God's word on the subject.

This is not an attempt on my part to be mean spirited or disrespectful, this is a viable point! Many pastors are so committed to their belief that Christians should not get involved in politics that they will not even discuss The Bible on the topic. They have two, three or maybe four scriptures they quote out of context, like a bumper sticker. When they quote these verses they expect that to settle the matter. When you point out they are not quoting the verses in context or with proper application (something they probably would never do on any other topic) they refuse to listen or discuss it further.

If these verses are so absolute and conclusive as these pastors insist, why is no further dialogue permitted? Why is there no instruction or counseling? If I'm wrong, I want to know but I have legitimate questions and I don't want scripture misused and I don't want to be dismissed like I'm an idiot for asking. I have studied these verses and they are not being applied in their proper context. Most of these pastors would gleefully answer all the questions you had, with as many verses as you desired, on any other topic. The door to discussion and instruction is closed, locked, barred and guarded on the topic of political involvement.

With America in the desperate state it is in and with America's pastors refusing to even discuss Christian responsibility or lead the church toward any realistic solutions, what are we to conclude? Among the many possible conclusions exists the one that is the subject of this book; the church is neutralized by satanic deception. It is neutralized by leadership first and then laymen who have been seduced by subtle satanic lies to convince us to forfeit the fight and not concern ourselves about the Godliness of our country.

The New Testament talks more of spiritual blindness than physical blindness. This is a theme carried over from the Old Testament. The scripture in the title verse and the parallel verses in Matthew 13 are not commentary on the seed. Truth is always truth; the seed is consistent. The illustration is about the ground. We decide how much truth we will let penetrate our world by letting the truths we're exposed to take root or letting them die out, in which case we suffer the consequences of self imposed blindness or ignorance.

This is a battle that must be fought over every bit of truth as it comes to us. Too many of us are not fertile ground to receive information that challenges our current belief system because we've become comfortable with what we know. The most challenging information requires us to change our behavior. We have a responsibility to pass along the same freedom we inherited to the next generation as it was passed to us. The future of our country is at stake. The seeds of confusion have been sown in fields of truth that have long stood the test of time.

Every parent should desire to pass an inheritance along to their children. This is scriptural yet what value has an inheritance if we do not pass on our heritage of freedom? Luke 8:12 says, "The devil takes away the seed". How do you suppose he does that? Scripture explains he does it by tribulation and cares of this world. The Bible also lists deceitfulness of riches among his tactics and Matthew 13:23 adds that we need "understanding". A willingness to learn is an act of our will. If the question was asked of most of us, "do you want to know the truth?" most of us would hastily respond "yes" but looking around us today, we can easily discern that the truth is not held in high regard.

People consistently send their children to schools they know teach against the most absolute truths essential to a happy life and against a knowledge and relationship with God. People consistently get their primary information from a news media that is indisputably corrupt and dishonest. Staggering numbers of people who believe themselves to be Christians go to churches that have either abandoned The Bible as the word of God entirely or have relegated it to a book of poetry to be read and appreciated for it's poetic verse but it's relevance is to be "discussed" like a literary class and not properly revered as the word of God and the handbook to human happiness.

If in fact we were a people who demanded truth, none of this would be acceptable, tolerable or profitable. There are enormous profits to be made in the lies, false promises and phony threats of the new world order. We hear lies about a phony crisis and spend money to protect ourselves. We hear lies about phony promises and we spend money believing it's in our long-term interest. We are no longer in the habit of making God's word the source to verify and judge all information and therefore lack understanding, which leaves us confused and manipulated. We have heard that the Constitution is out dated and impractical for our modern age and we fail to recognize the implications of this argument. We see America in trouble but we don't turn to The Bible or the Constitution. These are both standards to live by and as Christians it is our job to see the standards are enforced yet we do nothing and don't even question our idleness.

If you love the truth, you must be willing to be offended. The truth is frequently, if not consistently, offensive. We read in Matthew 13:57 that "they were offended ..." at Jesus and we read repeatedly in the gospels that Jesus offended many and in John 6:60-70 we have a passage where many disciples left Jesus because they were offended at what He said but He let them go. The responsibility was theirs as it is ours to come to grips with the truth. We have the responsibility to speak the truth with disregard to whom takes offense. In this manner we can be certain that all will hear the truth. We do man a disservice to water it down or hold our tongue.

This is not to say that a purpose is served in deliberately offending people. We should also recognize principles of good communication such as building knowledge over time and not overwhelming people with unbelievable information at a rate beyond their ability to mentally process it but these are separate topics. The situation here is that the truth has been abandoned in exchange for what people want to hear.

If the topic is Bible prophecy, Christians will hang on every word and frequently non-Christians are interested as well. If that same topic addresses personal responsibility, the audience scatters fast. These are the reasons Christians are poorly educated on the horrors and accomplishments of the new world order. The churches have quit exposing the devil, those of us aware of this threat are not adequately building knowledge and far too many people don't want to step up and fight this very necessary war. As a result Satan goes forth unfettered. It is Christians that have the responsibility and spiritual authority to fight this battle and if we withdraw Satan wins. Those that do not have a personal relationship with Christ can do little and will desire to do little more than protect themselves, their family and possessions.

Additionally, because non-Christians are vaguely aware of Satan at best, they will be the more difficult to convince of the enormity of the threat. It has ever been so. The warnings have always existed and they have always been ignored by non-Christians. Now, in our generation we see the warnings ignored by Christians. The new world order could have been stopped scores of times. The Bavarian government produced a document in 1786 entitled *"The Original Writings of the Order and Sect of the Illuminatti"* and distributed it to the major governments of Europe. It was ignored. It should have been distributed to the churches. John Robison wrote a detailed account of the Illuminatti published in 1798 titled *"Proofs of a Conspiracy Against All the Religions and Governments of Europe"*. Here is a witness with first hand knowledge of strategies, tactics and other plans of this evil enterprise. He was personally invited into its membership and participated only to the extent of gaining knowledge of their plans and capabilities.

He was horrified at what he learned and risked his very life to give warning about this threat, yet he was ignored. His book is still available today but few care. As written in the introduction, there is no shortage of documented proof of this threat but too many don't care and Christians have been seduced into believing it's not their fight. We need a play on words here. "Responsibility" means "response ability". That is to say, it is Christians who have the ability to respond with authority to what Satan is attempting to do. The world has no ability to respond to Satan because such ability comes from God and is given those who serve Him.

Satan and his servants are busy with their agenda but Christians have stopped opposing them. This is not God's will, nor is it even necessary. It is simply the result of Christians being seduced into a complacency and not exercising their authority or pursuing their mission. Christians today are quick to tolerate all abuses believing they are "God's will" or "fore-ordained of God".

A child that is well fed and otherwise has his material needs met but at the same time is raised without discipline, respect for authority, a proper value system and work ethic will not be a productive, contributing member of society. This is not "God's will" and it doesn't happen because God "preordained" some children to be irresponsible. It happened because some irresponsible parent didn't perform their reasonable service.

The same is true with society at large. Christians are to be "salt and light" but what we have in society today is the natural results of no effective Christian influence. This is not happening because "God willed it" or "fore-ordained it". It's happening because this is what modern Christianity has become. That is to say we're not responding to the threat even though we have the ability. Today we have enormous access to the truth but few seek it out. When we hear something controversial we are quick to respond with "I don't believe that …" with a seeming conviction that what we choose to believe or not believe will somehow have an impact on reality. The real question is, is this too by design?

Why is so much information so readily available about this new world order if not to overwhelm those with authority to stop it? From the days of Pavlov's dogs there has been no doubt that one person can control the thinking of another through the use of a variety of techniques. Even those who are strong willed and more difficult to control can be greatly influenced. The key lies in what you get people to think about. Create a combination of the proper amounts of desires and stresses and you have essentially created a "carrot/stick" incentive. In this somewhat ancient analogy the farmer wanted the mule to pull the millstone pole in a continual rotation as it ground the grain but found it monotonous to lead the mule around and around the stone. He attached a carrot on a stick extending beyond the mules reach so it plodded away all day unsupervised trying to reach the carrot.

Much the same is done with us today. We have never ending promises of the great quality of life that will be ours. Free education, free healthcare, free childcare, safety, full employment that offers both personal satisfaction and monetary sufficiency, toys and entertainment (lots of toys and entertainment), if we simply go along with the agenda promoted by the self appointed masters of the universe. Few actually recognize that we have been harnessed to a pole and are going around in circles. We just keep chasing the dream.

Free education is not the impartation of vital information to make strong and independent individuals. It's brain washing our children into being good little subjects in the new world order, incapable of mounting resistance to authority. Free healthcare comes with the dangerous transfer of enormous authority of life and death decisions given to bureaucrats. Free childcare is a promise that requires we increasingly surrender our children to state control and the promise of safety requires we surrender everything else. On and on we can go. The only thing we are actually receiving is a dizzying amount of entertainment that far exceeds what any responsible adult should desire.

Satan's trick is getting people to "imagine" the promises are valid. By definition, the imagination is the part of the mind with the creative ability to form a mental image of something that may be real or may not be real or present to the senses. This is far more significant than people consider and The Bible has some important things to say about the imagination. The designated purpose of the imagination is great. It is with this that we are capable of gathering information from our memory and it plays a large role in enabling our memory to begin with. For example if your job is a cab driver you become proficient at your job by recalling the streets. That is to say you use your imagination to picture these streets in your mind. If you are an engineer you use your imagination to call forth the fundamental principles of engineering into focus as you work. The basic concept is the same.

We use the term "I'm thinking about the streets" or "I'm thinking about support structure ratios" but this process is actually the using of your imagination to search through your subconscious mind and draw into the focus of your conscious mind the current information needed. In modern computer language, think of your imagination as your "search engine" that races through the millions of files stored away in your subconscious mind (memory banks) to pull up the desired data and place in on your screen, which is your conscious mind.

The Bible warns in Proverbs 23:7 "as he thinketh in his heart, so is he". Genesis 6:5 says, "…that every imagination of the thoughts of his heart was only evil continually." It was this that caused God to bring the flood. In Genesis 8:21 God said that "I will not again curse the ground anymore for man's sake; for the imagination of his heart is evil continually from his youth…"

Satan knows that how we will use our imagination is opportunity for him. Unrepentant man fights no such battle. Deuteronomy 29:19 says "It come to pass when he heareth the words of this curse, that he bless himself in his heart saying "I shall have peace, though I walk in the imagination of mine heart, to add drunkenness to thirst: the Lord will not spare him" (verse 20). In other words he (man) disregards warnings that are given by imagining sinful pleasures but he suffers the consequences.

1st Chronicles 29:18 is a prayer that God would keep the imaginations of Israel toward Godliness. Jeremiah has seven verses warning that God will judge Israel because they follow the imaginations of their evil heart. There are many, many more scriptures that repeat this point that man uses his imagination to create evil desires which overcome any Godly desires he may have had. Satan knows how to manipulate men and encourage this process. Christians have been warned and we must warn others but to do this, we must be involved.

This then is the foundation strategy of the new world order, influencing us to imagine that we can have "much for nothing", to stifle understanding of Godliness and make our minds fertile to believe false promises. To have ever present in our thoughts these vain promises that we can have all these blessings and endless entertainment without labor, without expense and without God. To fill our minds with the promises, illusions and entertainment and all the while we are ignorant of their true agenda and indifferent towards their achievements.

We should be mindful too, that our imagination is constantly running. Unless our conscious mind is focused on a matter and using our imagination to either enter information into our subconscious or pull information out of our subconscious, our imagination is simply returning to "a set point". These are pleasant thoughts that each individual has trained themselves to revert to when mentally relaxing. This can be opportunity to Satan, however, if our set point is unrighteous. Such a person may desire to overcome some sin in their life and find it the more difficult because of what they have trained themselves to imagine when relaxing.

Consider public schools again. Students are exposed to a list of unrighteousness on any given day and not many pleasant things to consider. Neither are they taught to train their minds to focus "on that which is good". Hence the very urgent message of Philippians 4:8 "what so ever things are true, whatsoever things are honest, ... just, ... pure, ... lovely, ... good report ... think on these things." Satan would eagerly substitute his own list of things he would like us to "think on" if we permit him that authority and schools do just that.

School administrators would have us believe their curriculum is challenging, difficult and that they're graduating students better prepared for life than any generation previous. Students now need several math credits to graduate yet a hand held calculator can be purchased for one dollar all over America. Students need several science credits also. I needed one and unless it somehow helps me mow my lawn I fail to see how I benefit from that. An old saying goes that "all information is valuable but not necessarily useful". If a student desires a career needing math or science they will greatly benefit from this education. Most students won't. While there may be merit in the math and science they teach, there is ample opportunity to teach a great many other matters that are ungodly and this is Satan's opportunity to cultivate the soil and make it ready for his message.

Where is the education on civics so that they may be better citizens? Where is the education on sound economic principles? Where is the education of history, which teaches that corruption has long existed in government and in both political parties? Why have phonics, classes on sentence structure, comprehension and courses on critical thinking been abandoned? Where is the education on Jesus Christ without which no one will see heaven?

This is the ground that we must sow into. A ground smothered with seeds of lies, thrills, illusions, promises and every ungodly thing that man can imagine. Where shall the seeds of truth find good ground for root? Add to this that Christians imagine the second coming of Christ. We look forward to it and expect it so we question and reject any arguments of a need to get informed and address threats to our quality of life while we're on this earth.

The overwhelming amount of information has filled our mind with so much bad news that we now imagine losing our freedom as inevitable. Increasingly good people sit back and do nothing. This is the definition of complacency. We are to till our own soil. Each one of us needs to check our own minds and do the work necessary to insure we are receptive to truth. Not rejecting responsibilities hastily because we have been trained to do that. We must find the passion within ourselves that motivated the early church, serving God out of shear love of God, fighting evil because we hate sin and will not tolerate it and certainly will not allow it to prosper. We as Christians have a responsibility to insure that those who promote sin or regard it lightly are not elevated to leadership in our society.

As we move on to specifics about the four lies. I ask no one to let their guard down or receive this information casually. I ask only that you consider these arguments from God's own word. I ask only that you consider matters that you may not have considered before because you have been taught not to concern yourself. I ask you to consider if God's word is being taught to you accurately.

Finally, I ask you to consider your own heart in terms of do you really desire to know the truth and are you truly willing to let truth change you the way truth should?

Put the burden on me to prove what I am saying but if I can prove it then let the truth be our standard of conduct.

RULE ONE; CONFUSE
AND MISLEAD

*Isaiah 59:14 "judgment is turned backward ... for truth
is fallen in the streets"*

Whenever one broaches the subject of the new world order or a conspiracy, the first argument presented is that it couldn't happen "because 'somebody' would say something..." This is, in fact, a very reasonable point. A fact not considered by those waging this argument is that hosts of "somebody(s)" have been saying something for generations and they are ignored. Many would consider their research to be highly significant since it has such an immediate impact on our freedom and the overall health of our society, however, the majority of people are yet unwilling to examine these findings and important facts. Chief among the reasons for disbelieving warnings of this new world order is this argument "if it were true, 'somebody' would say something" yet when someone does say something their information is dismissed without examination.

"Somebody(s)" is laboring tenaciously to alert the larger segments of society concerning a very real threat. They are from all industrialized countries, they are from all major professions including government service, they are from a variety of religious affiliations but yet we lack the elusive "somebody" who's message will finally be considered. We have former prime ministers, presidents, cabinet members, businessmen, bankers, historians, educators, journalists, clergy (catholic and protestant), and the list goes on. Their evidence is known to relatively few because the majority dismisses them as not being "somebody".

The obvious purpose of the previous chapter was an effort to get Christians who are convinced that there is no conspiracy or "new world order" to consider some evidence for themselves instead of prematurely dismissing it out of hand because others have planted the idea in their mind that it's not quality research. This chapter is more specific, addressing some of the manipulation used to neutralize Christians and keep them from confronting the evil in our society.

Christians should readily accept that there is a battle between the forces of God and Satan yet staggering numbers of Christians do not consider this truth as relevant to their daily lives. Many regard that there is such a war but it exists only in a spiritual realm or that this is singularly a battle over the souls of men and our duty is only to spread the gospel.

Another huge misconception is that Satan occupies himself by enticing people into indulging sins of the flesh. Those who indulge these sins may do so from a spiritual attack or simply do to their own nature but scripture clearly reveals that Satan has an agenda that far exceeds simply causing men to sin. He wants a global government completely under his control and Christians take no interest in this revealed truth.

Christians have stopped challenging themselves on the question of whether God would desire them to do more for Him. As a result we no longer consider that the evil in our society is our responsibility; we simply are prepared to tolerate it believing that if God wants something done about it He will do it Himself. Christians agree that we are to serve God but fail to consider that serving Him includes having authority to right wrongs and battle evil. We no longer view the suffering in society from a perspective that our God loves those who suffer and would desire His people to intercede.

God has given us this authority but we do not use it. Instead we listen to those who proclaim our purpose is singularly to share the gospel. We give little thought to the fact that it is we who know of Satan and his agenda and, therefore, it is we who have a duty to watch for him and sound the alarm, warning our communities when we see him at work. Thus we can say if it is a lone responsibility to spread the gospel, than society is doomed because his own will not expose Satan. We can add that all who labored in the past to battle evil were in error.

Yet students of Christian history know this cannot be true. Books are filled with records of God's intervention to bless those who serve Him by "putting the evil away from among you" as commanded numerous times in The Book of Deuteronomy.

On such heinous acts as abortion many have simply come to accept it and have convinced themselves that their duty is but to pray for those involved. Others have gotten involved in a program assisting expectant mothers and consider this sufficient. While I applaud them for doing something, they too have come to accept abortion as inevitable and no longer work to solve the problem at its root source. Saving a few children in the course of a life's work is admirable but there are millions dying and we have a responsibility to them also. Christians will readily concede that Satan is the root cause behind evil; however, Christians have arrived at a place where we no longer fight Satan. Instead we've convinced ourselves that we do our duty by trying to lessen the impact he has on a few lives.

Christians accept the idea that Satan has legions of human laborers who promote his agenda simply for personal gratification. The suggestion that some part of these legions are strongly committed and organized to achieve a strategic advantage is difficult for people to digest. Many have come to find it is preferable to dismiss the evidence without a glance. We are advised constantly that any "so-called" evidence is circumstantial and those who possess such evidence are gullible and incompetent researchers. We hear the platitudes that "a conspiracy can't happen here" or "you can't keep a secret that big because somebody would say something".

We run into a predictable problem here. If we have not done any research then we have no foundation of facts to build on or draw upon to digest new information. To understand new information requires the ability to grasp the "reasonableness" of what we're being shown. With no foundation, it doesn't matter how factual the new information is, we naturally regard it as unreasonable and dismiss it as too improbable. This is simply a reaction made out of confusion when a more appropriate response would be to demand proof we can grasp. We do not demand proof because we have been manipulated into assuming all information of this type is not valid.

There is manipulation at work here; that of others who claim to be trustworthy and so we should grant them authority to determine what is truth and what is error instead of reading and thinking for ourselves. As long as we yield to this manipulation we will never know whether the information is valid or not and never establish a foundation of information to build on. We will continue to dismiss information because, with our limited exposure to the truth, the platitudes sound more reasonable. Furthermore, we can be manipulated into embracing new platitudes without proper consideration, such as "our only service is to spread the gospel". Manipulating us to accept these new platitudes is easy because this is where our foundation of knowledge is already established. Satan wants us to limit our service to God and deny our own authority.

With regard to Satan's view about our spreading the gospel, which is more to be dreaded from his perspective, a formidable enemy who is prepared to do battle in zealous pursuit of victory or an enemy who's convinced it's not their fight and content to limit themselves and their efforts to speaking of eternal truths but who will not actually get into the battle? Satan has neutralized the church by manipulating us into limiting our perceived duty. Satan may hate anyone accepting Christ but he's focused on his agenda. He knew that if he wanted Christians to leave him alone he would have to suffer them being busy doing something. He's willing to tolerate a church that recruits a few new converts as long as they're all taught to leave him alone. This is his "lesser of two evils".

Satan is not the all powerful, all knowing master strategist as Hollywood portrays him. There is a war going on and he is vulnerable to defeat. Those who accept Bible prophecy may take issue with this statement but Satan is defeated in thousands of lives daily. Similarly, throughout history he has been defeated scores of times in his attempts to establish his one world government. Satan is about his business and he is not patient. He has sought to control mankind from the beginning but as of this writing he is still short of his success because, from the beginning, good people came together to oppose his evil agenda. He has not won yet because he has been unable to win yet.

This is what we see lacking in our society today. No more do Christians feel the responsibility to fight evil and as a result evil is thriving. Our minds have been planted and nurtured with the idea that nothing happens without God's permission. Where previous generations accepted a responsibility to resist evil, we have come to accept that a satanic world government is inevitable and do not resist as previous generations have. We have allowed ourselves to be convinced that we have no duty in this war and no longer question what God would have us do. We have been assured He does not expect us to respond to the horrific evils growing in our land. Here we come to the heart of the matter.

This alone tells much about how we will react to information regarding Satan's agenda. Do we believe Satan can be defeated or are we just victims, hiding and hoping he won't find us? Do we want to defeat him in our life or has God left us helpless? From a purely logical perspective, whom do you believe would prefer we stand idle so that Satan may prosper, Satan or God? God certainly does not wish Satan to prosper in any of the torments he visits upon his victims. The Bible makes this abundantly clear!

The basic definition of "conspiracy" is "more than one person secretly working to achieve an evil act". Few would doubt this happens numerous times daily but find it difficult to accept a large-scale conspiracy could function in society. Yet The Bible makes clear that Satan is evil and uses people to achieve his agenda. Thus if you believe in The Bible you have been told of this conspiracy and, at minimum, should be open to the concept.

The Bible reveals that Satan uses people, even Godly people, in his service whenever he can. A good example of this would be 1st Chronicles 21:1 "Satan stood up against Israel and provoked David to number Israel" for which God judged the nation. The Bible is replete with other examples such as Satan tempting Eve causing Adam to sin, Satan provoking the Chaldeans in Job 1:17, Satan entering into Judas in Luke 22:3 and numerous additional examples ranging from Balaam to Saul of Tarsus. Satan has those who serve him enthusiastically but he also uses those whom he can influence to further his agenda. David is referred to more than once as "a man after God's own heart" yet Satan was able to use him.

A conspiracy is "two or more people secretly planning evil". This must, by word definition, be Satan's primary method of operating. It is applicable among all in his service and all of their efforts. Godly people can more easily be deceived into serving Satan if they are unfamiliar with his tactics and strategies. Godly people who refuse to consider a conspiracy are rejecting information about Satan's primary method of operation and are more vulnerable. Those who know of a conspiracy and remain silent serve Satan by helping him hide his existence, plan, efforts, successes and his strategies.

We need to examine some of the manipulations, which motivate people to prematurely dismiss this type of information. We should consider why so many people who believe in The Bible are so quick to embrace arguments that there is no conspiracy or that it's not our concern. We can readily recognize that most people with traditional values would not welcome Satan's agenda and, therefore, he would seemingly not desire anyone to make it known. His purpose would be to hide his agenda and those who exposed it would be against him.

Believing this is your first mistake. The first problem he would encounter here is the basic impossibility of having to accomplish the enormity of his agenda without someone discovering what he is doing and sounding the alarm. This is a problem easily solved by "hiding in plain sight". He simply needs to employ spokesmen to spread his message. His purpose is to influence the thinking of the masses before they can be educated. These spokesmen would not deny the obvious. Rather, they would openly discuss it.

They would announce the aspects of Satan's plans which could not be accomplished in secret and explain them in such a way as to make them sound beneficial although controversial. To do this most effectively requires him to have two spokesmen. One on the "left" and the other on the "right' who "debate" the merits and flaws of the proposal but always and only from their political perspectives. No mention of a larger agenda is ever permitted. The debate is limited to discussions of positive verses negative political impacts. When a researcher attempts to explain there is a larger agenda at work, we dismiss his comments believing we are already informed.

We can discuss the war in Iraq from the position of the left, which is the cost of the war and damage to humanity verses the right, which is stopping terrorism and bringing peace to the Middle East. Anyone who attempts to discuss this from the perspective of a new world order creating a military presence in strategic locations all around the globe is verbally attacked. We can discuss The Federal Reserve Bank from the perspective of inflation or raising interest rates but anyone who attempts to expose more about this is attacked. We can discuss The UN from the perspective of peace keeping to destroying national sovereignty but anyone who attempts to expose their growing global control is attacked. The list goes on and the public assumes they are educated since they hear both sides of the debate but they are manipulated into thinking anyone who speaks of a larger agenda is crazy.

A large part of the agenda of these spokesmen is to convince the masses that there is no conspiracy, there cannot be a conspiracy, no responsible and intelligent source is speaking of a conspiracy and, you can trust them, if there was a conspiracy they would know and be the first to tell you. These spokesmen frequently make a very handsome living because their service to the new world order is vital. They are promoted as intellectual and well informed and therefore are reliable sources for all-important news. The public is confident that if any such conspiracy were a viable threat these reliable sources would be first to sound the alarm yet their real purpose is to keep evidence of a conspiracy hidden when possible and distorted when it becomes known.

Naming names here will certainly cause enmity and resentment among those who are loyal to a particular personality but an example is in order. An excellent example would be the highly revered talk show host, Rush Limbaugh. He is universally recognized as one of the great conservative spokesman and never deviates from his staunch position that there is no conspiracy. He then spends a great deal of airtime talking of conspiracies by another name. Listeners are familiar with his use of terms such as "the liberal agenda", "the drive by media", "the ruling elite" and "the environmental wacko's".

If Mr. Limbaugh truly believes that two or more members of the media engage in a policy to dishonestly represent the facts, enabling others to gain power and inhibit the freedoms of the American people, then he is speaking of a conspiracy.

The same can be said of liberals and environmentalists. Whether or not he believes in a larger satanic conspiracy is a moot point. He may deny this argument from the perspective that he doesn't believe their agenda is evil but we know their agenda is the elimination of personal freedom under total government control. Even those who may not see the significance of this in Bible prophecy must still recognize it is an evil agenda.

Conspiracies are common and frequently thrive because the public has been manipulated into denial whenever they begin to recognize a conspiracy at work. A conspiracy could exist in a single publication if the management decided that certain news items would be withheld or altered. The question then becomes, is the above-described conspiracy included in all of the publications owned by a single group of businessmen. Those in journalistic trade groups and press clubs become complicit when they are aware of the editorial policy of this publication firm and accept employment consenting to cooperate with the deception. Next, do the investors and advertisers share this policy? Advertising is a very powerful control mechanism, as it will directly impact the profitability of a publication.

If the advertisers are aware that the publication has an editorial policy to distort important truths and they support the publication, they become complicit. They will always have deniability but if they knowingly support such a publication they are complicit. We can argue that the majority may be ignorant of the agenda but we suffer much harm in this country because we dismiss the possibility of collusion as we begin growing suspicions. Significant numbers of American's are aware that the truth is distorted in media. They are aware that facts are abandoned in certain fields of science in lieu of outright fraud. Yet these people are uncomfortable with the word conspiracy. This is due to manipulation.

Mr. Limbaugh recently closed a contract for a reported $400 million for services over the next eight years while his syndication boss "Clear Channel" is awash in red ink and (according to Media Matters) is moving ahead with another round of layoffs. He assures us this enormous salary is deserved, as it is simply a fraction of the revenue he earns for his advertisers yet Clear Channel is suffering financially. Where else may we see this standard applied to insure that this scale is valid? Mr. Limbaugh estimates his audience size as 20 million listeners per week while other sources put him much lower. Where is the talk show host with 10 million listeners who earns $200 million? Reportedly Sean Hannity was recently offered $200 million for eight years. These two hosts are paid on a scale including no others.

Every evening we see several talk shows on television with listeners ranging from 3 to 6 million daily. This would put them in the range of Mr. Limbaugh's reported 20 million weekly and far above him if his figures are exaggerated. Not one of these TV hosts is paid half of what Mr. Limbaugh makes. Is it possible that Mr. Limbaugh and Mr. Hannity are paid these enormous sums, not because of revenue they generates for advertisers but because of their accomplishment in keeping disgruntled Republicans continually supporting the party rather than bolting and starting another party? To one who is versed on the tactics of the new world order, this is an entirely consistent and reasonable probability especially when considered with other known facts. To one who rejects information about the new world order this would be regarded as absurd. Yet no more effort is made in explaining the disparity in salaries or the self-serving concepts Mr. Limbaugh has regarding conspiracies.

Not many people who describe themselves as Constitutionalists would take commentary to heart when it comes from a spokesman they know to be on the "left" and who has a value system they know to be contrary to their own. Yet if largely the same commentary were to come from one who they believe to hold similar values to their own they are far more likely to accept it. Satan would be neglecting a host of important opportunities if he failed to employ this very basic strategy of infiltration and propaganda. Mr. Limbaugh and Mr. Hannity are two examples but the strategy is used on a much larger scale and not simply radio.

Many will argue that Mr. Limbaugh and Mr. Hannity support values that are contrary to the liberal, socialist agenda. Yes on many issues but they promote two very important aspects of this agenda; 1) follow "do-nothing" leadership and 2) reject all information that a conspiracy exists. They, and numerous others, are extremely successful – not because they inform the public on a host of issues but because they misinform the public on what matters most!

This is why they are so valuable to the new world order. Am I suggesting that these two are Satanists or knowingly complicit in Satan's plans? Not for a second. I am simply saying that both enjoy their current situation and both know what topics are off limits if they hope to keep the money coming in. Whether or not they understand the long-term horrors they are helping to usher in is more a question of how self-deceived they are. As King David was deceived in 1st Chronicles, so too this may be what is motivating these two. In any event, it is our duty to investigate for ourselves. We must quit trusting that others know the facts and can be trusted with our future. Motivations and personal ideologies are not what matters.

As Christians, we know that evil is real and we are the ones with a duty to dispossess it. Anyone who tells us differently is not walking in Godly truth and authority. Mr. Limbaugh and Mr. Hannity are very guilty of misinforming the public about the true "conservatism" of some key national leaders. Had patriotic Americans known the truth of any number of candidates or political maneuverings they would have acted quite differently than they did under the influence of these two. After listening to these two advise us whom we should support for leadership, Americans are increasingly demoralized. It is increasingly difficult to get people involved since the best we can get elected does nothing when in office and this frustrates people. Even when we win an election we accomplish nothing. This too is part of the plan. Our duty is not to speculate as to their motives. It is to know the truth and act responsibly. We do future generations and ourselves a disservice when we afford these two and their confederates the authority to define what is truth and what is foolishness.

Consider for a moment why we even have evening news. Consider too why we see an explosion in the number of cable news channels. The networks have claimed for generations that they offer this "service" for the public even though they continually lose money from it. Yet most people do not suffer for lack of availability to a news source so why do the networks consider this service so necessary and why should they be so eager to lose money? Another good question is why are they so persistent when increasing numbers of Americans are abandoning them as a reliable news source?

We are led to believe there are two basic political paradigms where those on the "left" are committed to a system of government management of all matters while those on the "right" prefer a small government uninvolved in the personal affairs of the people. This is pretty straightforward stuff, either you believe the government should be involved in something or you don't.

If this were true, no major news "personalities" would be necessary. One would simply consider what the left or right are proposing and weigh it against your own value system. The problem with this is that Satan and his agenda would lose. Thus "salesmen" or, if you prefer, "spokesmen" are required, not to inform but to confuse the issues. Again, if salesmen (news anchors) were objective and honest they would be of no value to the new world order and of little value to the rest of us. We would simply make our personal choice for a news service and support the left or right position. The left would lose overwhelmingly according to most polling regarding the political allegiance of the American people. Yet the left is arguably winning if we base this conclusion on recent elections and the growth of the national government. The reasons why we find ourselves in this dilemma are predictable: 1) The lack of accomplishment on the right even when elections are won and 2) an enormous amount of confusion regarding major issues. Consider these factors with particular attention on whom we're told are conservative spokesmen that we can trust and how they advise and inform us.

First of all, I know of no "conservative" voice employed by any major news organization that failed to support one of the three "conservative candidates" in the recent election. John McCain and Mitt Romney have strong ties to the agenda of the eastern establishment and Mike Huckabee supports many of their positions. One wonders if Governor Huckabee has significant knowledge of this agenda but if he does he has voiced no opposition to it. If he doesn't he can hardly be expected to help stop it.

Any one of these three were pronounced acceptable by all of the pundits on the right while these same pundits denounced Ron Paul and Chuck Baldwin, if they mentioned them at all. Yet it is Rep. Paul and Mr. Baldwin who openly speak of out of control government growth and other issues embraced by average Americans with traditional values. This is one example (and there are many) where "spokesmen for the right" have assisted the left by helping them eliminate quality leadership on the right by discrediting or ignoring quality candidates.

Through the employment of this strategy we do not get quality leadership on the right. Time after time the public has dared to support someone professing traditional values because those we trusted assured us they truly held these values and each time they have been completely deceived or disappointed because so little was accomplished. The public was manipulated, by the perceived conservative pundits, into supporting candidates who had no sincere conservative agenda. At the same time these same pundits labeled those who truly hold conservative values as "unelectable".

The second point, regarding confusion, brings us to the issue of whether these pundits on the right are giving us the full range of options. Students of the new world order are aware that they are, in fact, failing to inform the public on several viable options. Again, they simply offer positions slightly to the right of those proposed by the perceived left. They do not inform the public of the larger agenda and they frequently applaud government involvement however they argue it should be done with some variation. This confuses true conservatives who want no government involvement in a specific area and cannot understand why a perceived conservative would accept government growth where it doesn't belong.

A significant amount of their efforts are contradictory, a part is true and a part is psychological manipulation. Few people have time to study issues for themselves so they come to trust a news personality. By promoting a news anchor as conservative many conservatives are drawn in. If this person is loyal to the globalist agenda for any reason they will not reveal important information and will "sell" aspects of the agenda to conservative listeners that could not be sold to them by a perceived liberal. Since they are overwhelmed and confused with so much contradictory information they rely on this news anchor and can be more easily deceived.

This anchor is more highly valued by the new world order if they are ignorant of the true agenda. All that is necessary is that they be willing to support the conservative mainstream. If they are ignorant of the greater agenda they will be more convincing and more willing to challenge anyone who attempts to expose a larger conspiracy. All spokesmen fit into a rather narrow interpretation of the larger political spectrum. Spokesmen like Limbaugh and Hannity are promoted as "being outside of the mainstream" because they are so far to the right but in truth they are very much in support of the agenda of the mainstream. Again, this aspect of the agenda is not to inform the public. Satan does not want the public informed!

Their job is to keep voters satisfied that The Republican Party, while not perfect, is the best realistic solution. This is done by defusing the anger and frustration of the people before they take effective action. Mr. Limbaugh and Mr. Hannity are as staunchly opposed to any effort to launch a third party as they are to any discussion of a conspiracy. Both decry it as extremely counter productive and this is a consistent attitude among hosts on any significant network. They argue against anyone who insists there are no significant differences between the two parties but this too is a tactic of deception.

When the Democrat Party has an opportunity to move the country to the left, they do it even to their own political detriment. Yet the Republicans never seize opportunity and The Democrats efforts are seldom reversed. When the Republican Party has an opportunity to move the country to the right, they compromise. The best that can be said about them is that they are slowing our nations move to socialism but this is paltry achievement. The Republican Party has a reputation for small limited government that they have not earned. It is not deserved but it exists in the minds of the American people regardless. We will address this in more detail in later chapters.

This entire argument of a difference between the two parties is an outgrowth of frustration when the question should reveal the answer. One wonders if we have ever heard this comment from a Democrat. The attitude of the two parties being virtually identical is made by conservatives who are tired and frustrated at having to watch as their party sells out or compromises again. To these people, there is no question because the question answers itself. Those who believe "politics is the art of compromise" and who expect a good party to do this are not upset and continue to support the Republicans.

Professor Carroll Quigley (whom I will detail later) was in a position to learn the precise agenda of both parties and he wrote.

"The argument that the two parties should represent opposed ideals and policies, one, perhaps, of the Right and the other of the Left, is a foolish idea acceptable only to doctrinaire and academic thinkers. Instead, the two parties should be almost identical, so that the American people can "throw the rascals out" at any election without leading to any profound or extensive shifts in policy"[2]

Another way of stating the question is if The Republican Party does not reflect your views then why do you continue to support it? A conservative is not going to support The Democrat Party so why should they support The Republican Party if it too fails to support your views? The answer is because most people do not regard they have another reasonable choice and this is the point! Diligent efforts have effectively stifled any third party and conservatives continue to throw their vote away on leadership that can only be relied on to sell out traditional values, all be it while denying this is what they're doing. Hope abounds that a good man will somehow rise to prominence in the party or the party will be reformed but these hopes have proven baseless.

The "Health Care Bill" is the most recent example. Olympia Snowe, a republican, saved this bill from defeat on October 13th 2009 in a Senate Finance Committee vote where it was expected to be killed for lack of support. Olympia Snowe is a good example of how the new world order operates. They do not make overt gestures to call attention to themselves. They do not boldly make demands. Like a wild beast they simply watch the herd and pick out the vulnerable target and they move in. In their case they may attack with money or promises of greater power but seldom with threats or violent acts, which would be too revealing whereas money and power are too appealing.

So this one person, a Republican, made possible this piece of legislation, which is widely regarded as the most dangerous and intrusive in our countries history. It is true that this one person could not have done this without the help of the entire Democrat Party but she is not a Democrat. Where the agenda was destined for failure she made possible its success. This is a pattern we see repeatedly. When the new world order needs votes from Republicans, they get them. When the bill is not of vital importance to them the Republicans are free to vote as they choose.

Yet The Republican Party has no incentive to punish her in any way since she is a valuable member of the party. Conservatives are frustrated and point to this as an example of cooperation between the two parties while others will argue this legislation was passed by The Democrats and won't blame the party for the actions of Senator Snowe. Yet the agenda of the new world order is coming to pass and they always find the help they need from those in The Republican Party.

Conservatives are told by the spokesmen who supposedly represent their values that this is the scenario they must continue to support because starting their own party will not succeed. By the same token, we are emphatically and repeated lectured that this is all circumstantial and not part of any larger strategy or design, satanic or otherwise. Insuring that this pattern continues is worth a great deal of money to the new world order and this is why they must have their spokesmen on both sides of an issue.

"NAFTA" is another good example. This is a massive shift to a globalized trade policy promoted by President Clinton and widely believed as the primary cause of our current immense unemployment rate. This passed with 132 Republicans supporting it in The House and only 102 Democrats. In The Senate the vote was 34 Republicans (many who were widely perceived as "conservative") to 27 Democrats[3]. This piece of legislation that has sent millions of jobs to foreign countries was promoted by a recognized leftist President (actually, NAFTA was promoted by President H.W. Bush as well) and passed through the Congress by The Republicans. This is not unusual, it is typical but it is not the way the two parties are perceived by the American people. Patriots get rhetoric and globalists get results.

This is the value of conservative pundits to the new world order. They may direct blame to Senator Snowe (in this case) but away from the party and away from viable solutions thus assuring that the establishment remains unthreatened. This is how the new world order functions on the subject of a third party and on the subject of discussing the known facts of a conspiracy. Anyone in the employment of any major news organization can be counted on to ridicule and mock anyone who manages to acquire some small platform and seeks to make known any variety of injustices that expose a larger "master plan". All of this sounds quite ridiculous to those who have not studied the new world order but the solution demands that we study the new world order, not dismiss information simply because it is from a field of study which we have never pursued before.

We must continually come back to the question, "if it were true, would you want to know?" Others were skeptical in their turn but wanted to know. Without a willingness to examine the evidence, the concept of a conspiracy will constantly sound ridiculous. Only by examining the evidence can you begin to build knowledge and understanding. No one should compromise his or her skepticism. It is reasonable for each person to hold on to their own standard of what they consider proof but no proof can be considered properly without investigation.

WORLD VIEWS

Matthew 24:26 "he is in the secret chambers..."

We need to understand the basic elements that comprise a conspiracy. First and foremost, they must operate in secrecy. This makes their existence difficult to prove and creates opportunity for false explanations regarding any part of their true agenda should it get exposed. The argument is proposed that a conspiracy cannot exist because it could not remain hidden and once revealed it's no longer a conspiracy. Those who make this argument fail to recognize they speak paradoxically of a word that disputes its own definition! Their rebuttal would be that conspiracies can exist but only until "someone talks" at which point the whole thing would unravel.

Where does that leave us from a Biblical perspective? The Bible tells us that Satan has a goal but many Christians haven't stopped to consider that he's created a plan with which to achieve his goals. The Bible also says he works through people, that he works secretly using deception, lies and "wiles" (trick or stratagem intended to ensnare). Hollywood has taught us to fear Satan and the church has taught us to ignore him. Satan has taught the world that good is evil and evil is good and the church is starting to accept many of these arguments. The Christians who are not quite ready to accept evil as good have come to accept it as inevitable or tolerable.

The church is not prepared to fight Satan, nor are we prepared to fight evil. We don't know who our enemy is anymore and failing to identify an enemy, we question whether or not we're really at war. We have such distorted and complacent concepts of evil that we can't bring ourselves to believe that our families and we are truly threatened by anything tangible.

Another point of confusion is the many religious leaders who have led us to believe that we can relax and enjoy life because Satan can only achieve success after "the rapture". It is important that we understand this point. I too believe in Bible prophecy but this is because I believe in The Bible. We are overwhelmed by would be experts who are making enormous fortunes "interpreting" prophecy and, in the end, they are only speculating. We must believe The Bible first and foremost. To the extent we enjoy reading these interpreters is a matter of personal choice but it is The Bible, which is true, and the accuracy of these people is, as yet, unproven. Therefore it is a very self destructive and dangerous thing to ignore scripture and place our future in the hands of those who tell us not to be concerned.

For those who are unfamiliar with "the rapture" theology, it is based on 1st Thessalonians 4:17 and particularly the two words "caught up". In the Greek this is the word "harpazo" and in The Latin Vulgate St. Jerome translated this word into "rapturous" (Latin) which literally means "snatched away". There are other verses that support this theology and there are varying theories on when this rapture is to take place. Most commonly this is taught in association with a "seven year tribulation" period and the teaching assures us the rapture will happen prior to this seven years, hence, the no need to worry; no matter how bad things get, we won't be here. Our friends in the "Bible prophecy business" have offered so much input, conjecture, speculation and counter-speculation that one comes away poorly educated and simply chooses to believe one source over another.

The great cost of this theology, however, is that Christians no longer see a need to fight against evil anymore. We need not refer to some "crusade" or holy war but there is certainly abundant evil in our society and it is unaffected by the church. A great many history books record Christians taking a stand for God and holding back the ambitions of evil but not in our generation. The church does not reflect on this tolerance of evil or consider that Satan is strongly influencing our agenda. We should keep in mind that it is far preferable for Satan to neutralize a group of believers above all other options. Blatant attempts to destroy Christians have resulted in the unintended consequences of massive growth and increased loyalty.

If I said that Christians have a duty to be good citizens, no one would challenge me yet if I comment that simply paying taxes, obeying the laws and voting is insufficient to qualify as a "good" citizen I would have many confront me. Paying taxes and obeying the laws are largely done out of a sense of self-preservation so we do not go to jail. Voting in our modern age is done far differently than envisioned by our founding fathers and increasingly recognized to be a complete waste of the few minutes it takes. We do not prepare or study, we just show up. We do not regard an employee as "good" just for showing up or for doing the bare minimum tasks associated with a job description. Sadly, we are not good citizens and what's even more sad is that we don't even know it or we don't care.

Many will regard this as offensive but when we look at our society today, I don't see how it can be denied. Rather than deliberately offending people, my purpose is to encourage each one to take a hard look at what we have come to believe and challenge you to consider that we may well have been deliberately misled. It is scripture that should be the standard of good citizenship but verses on government are not researched with the same vigor as other verses and not taught correctly.

We are taught submission to government; we are taught that even the churches are to submit to government. We are told that the church of the living God must submit to man (man's rule) and we don't question this or consider that Satan is influencing the church for his purposes … incredible!

In the last chapter I addressed some of the arguments concerning those who make their living decrying the existence of a conspiracy and promoting "do-nothing" leadership. I will refer to them as "professional scoffers". In this chapter I want to address the mindset of so many Christians to dismiss information they should analyze. Many do so because they have long heard others scoff at the idea of a conspiracy and choose to accept their conclusion. Still others will go so far as to set themselves up as experts on this topic. I will refer to theses as "volunteer scoffers". These are scoffers who have the zealousness of religious loyalty to their beliefs and fervently argue extensively but when they are questioned several things become apparent. They have done little research and what research they may have done was not intellectually honest. This is to say they were so firm in their beliefs that they did not give the research due credit but were merely looking to find fault with it and the ability to claim they had viewed the research with their "superior intellect" and we can take their word that it is inaccurate.

One more consistent attitude among them is, virtually all of them are fiercely loyal to one or more of the professional scoffers and (like the professional scoffers) they would hope to advise the rest of us what to believe by encouraging us not to investigate for ourselves. They can easily be identified by how consistently they quote the professional scoffers and will repeat much of the information from the days broadcasts. It is their devotion to these professional scoffers, which gives them their boldness and they will live or die by their firm belief that if any talk of a conspiracy were true these reliable anchors would be broadcasting the information. They simply will not allow themselves to see the bigger picture. All they are truly capable of is incessant arguing. They are firmly committed to their beliefs and will not consider the facts or any new information.

Am I suggesting that if they disagree with me they are automatically wrong? I have only two matters in which I disagree with them. The first is that I trust you and your judgment! I highly recommend you do your own research and make up your own mind. Where they encourage you to trust them and not bother investigating, I say do not trust them, anyone or me but investigate for yourself. It is your responsibility and there is too much at stake to let anyone tell you what is fact and what is fiction. Decide for yourself.

Secondly, I say the time to debate is over. They will seek out those who disagree and have their argument in spite of no desire to argue among those of us who have studied for ourselves and have long since grown tired of talking to those who refuse to listen or read. It is not a question of believing me or being automatically wrong. It's a question of examining the evidence and drawing your own conclusions.

These are possibly very well intentioned people but they have nurtured within themselves a passion to challenge anyone they perceive as believing that a conspiracy exists or believes that information about the new world order is valid. They do not seek information and they are not willing to consider any. They simply enjoy the argument. Their ability to seemingly win arguments has convinced them that they have a superior intellect and have gathered the more accurate facts. In this chapter, we will explore some of the reasons for this attitude. These are not to be applied to those who simply don't care and don't want to hear any facts proving or disproving a new world order but only those who love to argue about it.

The topic of "World Views" is a common one today and this is a very important area of discussion in association with the idea of a new world order or any attempts to discuss a conspiracy. A worldview is basically defined as a person's foundational beliefs from which they will interpret and react to information and events. A worldview contains any number of basic beliefs that the person regards as logical but many are, in fact, theoretical. It is from this worldview that a person applies their logic to theoretical information as well as provable facts. It is important for each one of us to realize that we each believe in a host of matters, which are not provable.

Another important point is that worldviews change. Typically this is called an "epiphany" or "revelation" defined as "a sudden grasp of reality (possibly intuitive) due to some event". The event could well be the gathering of information. Satan's trick in operating a conspiracy is to develop core beliefs in people, which encourage them to dismiss all information without consideration. The point here is not how you prove or disprove a conspiracy. It is how can he convince people to prematurely dismiss an entire (and substantial) body of evidence even when they should know better. All of the absolute evidence in the world is worthless to those who will ignore it! The answer is the same in this field as it is in any other field of study.

If you want people to learn, you must provide teachers. If you want people to dismiss information prematurely you must provide revered teachers admonishing that this is the appropriate standard of behavior until this thinking becomes a strong core belief. Some would argue that Christianity is a strong worldview; it is not! It is a single core belief that helps comprise an individual's worldview. Other core beliefs held by any individual will have an equal influence on how this person receives and reacts to information. An individual who has long sat under the teaching that a Christian's only responsibility is to spread the gospel will react to information about the new world order from the perspective that it does not mandate any action on their part. Even here we may find one who accepts the information and regards it as prophetic while another dismisses it entirely.

A Christian who has sat under the teachings of a "social gospel" may welcome this information and regard it as good news while one who has been taught more specifics about Satan and his agenda would receive this information much like a general receives an intelligence report before battle. This is really the point here. In the end, for a Christian it's not a question of a conspiracy or new world order. It's a question of your core beliefs, whether you have been taught to accept evil as inevitable or have been taught a responsibility to fight it. The reader can see that Satan has a vested interest to insure Christians are taught anything over a belief in a responsibility to oppose him.

From Satan's perspective, he can succeed as long as you believe anything except that you have authority and responsibility in the name of Jesus to dispossess him of all his evil gain. Any other beliefs neutralize the church. From this point the reader can recognize that it was necessary for Satan to provide teachers before he could expect his ambitions to be accepted by any number of people. Christian worldviews vary. Some believe government should play a large role in helping the less fortunate members of society, others believe these events are inevitable and welcome them as evidence that the end is near and still others hold a view that we have a civic responsibility to pass liberty to future generations as it passed to us by previous generations. This means we will not try to predict the future but serve God and leave the timetables up to Him.

A relationship with Jesus Christ will not, in itself, determine your worldview. A strategy is employed to convince Christians to disregard the information, which would cause this much-needed "epiphany" or "revelation". It is important to consider that to teach indifference to Christians one need not be a valiant laborer for the occult; one simply need hold this worldview. The most passionate teachers simply teach what they believe. One core belief addresses responsibility and another service to God but a third would be how one views evil. To many evil has become so non-threatening it's widely viewed as personally inconsequential or inevitable and this has a major affect on their worldview.

This may be viewed as a surprising statement because many people consider themselves aware of the horrific consequences to evil, however, human nature has one thing in common to a Godly nature; a natural aversion (or empathy) to human suffering. If we truly understood the consequences of evil we would take action to hinder its growth and alleviate the suffering, yet we remain idle. Satan has been successful in altering our worldview, giving us the core belief that it is government that is responsible to negate suffering and not an individual responsibility.

We have been convinced that it is no longer necessary for us to take action since there is some government program or international charity to step in. The real consequence of evil is its appetite. It grows until it is stopped. You cannot understand the consequences of evil and not labor to hinder it because you understand if it is allowed to exist it is allowed to thrive and will soon be at your door. Here is where the church has lost its focus. Due largely to this rapture worldview we do not believe evil will affect us. We've come to believe we will suffer no consequences and this has become a huge part of our worldview.

This hinders our taking action or responsibility. This defies both human nature and a Godly nature. All of society seemingly works to thwart evil. We go to war, create laws, finance massive educational systems which include programs to "reform" those who commit crimes, have a variety of oversight groups as well as checks and balances in our systems and the reason for it all is to squelch evil. It is an inherent belief among good people that evil should not be tolerated but aggressively stopped to the full extent of our ability. Yet what does the church do to stop evil? This organization with the power and authority given by God to fight evil has opted to ignore it. We accept the teaching that we can define our relationship with God with a focus on a single verse or teaching which defines our duty as spreading the gospel and ignore all others duties and responsibilities.

With this worldview, we have come to tolerate many things Jesus spoke against. John The Baptist spoke against Herod's affair with his sister-in-law. We seldom hear sermons about sexual immorality and if we do, few speakers dare point a finger at elected officials. Because of the decay that society is experiencing we are facing many evils that Jesus did not name specifically like pornography and NAMBLA. We are accustomed to corrupt officials, filth on television and we've even stopped taking offense at the blatant blasphemy against Jesus while other so-called spiritual leaders are revered. The simple fact that Christians no longer hate evil or feel a responsibility to do something about it is very telling and reason to question those in church leadership but we do not question them.

In many ways talking to people about the new world order is much like talking to people about God; they either get it or they don't. There is an old axiom that some people "can't see the forest for the trees" and old axioms remain due to their concise truths. People do not, however, busy themselves decrying that forests are mere fantasy, imaginations and superstition. An interesting truth about both God and the new world order is that scores of non-believers have appointed themselves "experts" and strive most diligently to argue that neither truly exist. Those, they inform us, who believe in God are superstitious and unscientific. Those who believe in the new world order are paranoid and gullible.

With unabashed condescension those who would be our spiritual advisors lecture us about eternity and the supernatural proclaiming there is no God. Yet what are they willing to do to earn our respect that we should recognize them and accept them as an advisor? Who's life have they blessed or improved at their own expense? Who have they counseled to any success? The ability to ridicule is a fool's achievement yet we are awash with these people in both religion and on the subject of the new world order; professional and volunteer scoffers; one highly paid, the other highly motivated.

Just as the self-appointed spiritual advisors claim superior knowledge from which they desire to teach us, so too the self-appointed experts on history and politics insist we listen to them. We need to consider where conspiracy theories come from and why some insist they are the studies of simpletons. Conspiracy theories generate from reasonable questions asked by practical people about important matters. These people have become aware of a possible fraud and want to know the details and see the guilty brought to justice. When these questions go unanswered on major issues we frequently see independent research done.

It is telling that the major media insists that throughout the entirety of world history, absolutely no independent research is valid or credible. They alone can determine fact from fiction. Others are always "conspiracy theorists", "paranoid", "gullible" and certainly "unqualified" and "inexperienced".

These independent researches range from those with integrity to the sensationalists who simply love an audience but why should everyone among them be judged incompetent without a hearing? The answer to this lies in the framework of the deception. As written previously, the major media does not exist to inform but to misinform. If just one independent researcher is legitimate then the whole media structure is in jeopardy of not being able to accomplish their purpose. That is to say, everyone who proves the major media wrong is informing the public of something the new world order desires the public be kept ignorant of.

We can agree that people increasingly distrust the major media but the fact is that Satan's plan is working. As the Internet grew with alternative information sources so did we see an increased avalanche of misinformation sources. Bogus news channels are all over cable television and they misinform and confuse staggering numbers of people daily. All researchers who are not controlled by those who manage the agenda must be discredited. The single largest factor in their being discredited is establishing the worldview that a conspiracy is not possible.

Conspiracy researchers are simply people that ask questions that major news sources have decided not to answer. Rather than address the issues they "shoot the messenger" as a vital part of their strategy. Conspiracy researchers are simply in the pursuit of information. All theories begin with attempts to connect the known facts. This means there are reasonable facts including varying amounts of proof. This doesn't mean all theories or conclusions are accurate but neither has it been established that they are all wrong and not worthy of examination. This is not to argue that skeptics aren't entitled to proof. It is an argument that honest skeptics should examine evidence before they can accept it or reject it as proof.

Worldviews are at the heart of the matter. The belief in a major media having a purpose to deceive rather than inform, also requires a belief in a conspiracy. If you recognize that a conspiracy ceases to be a conspiracy when it is exposed and recognize that the first task to be mastered by conspirators is to hide themselves, you will understand they could not succeed without a controlled media of substantial magnitude. When we factor in that to be conspirators they must be working to accomplish something deemed evil and, no-doubt, something for which they could be prosecuted under the law we must take note that they have all of their hopes and dreams limited to their ability to remain obscure. Indeed, being vague and nebulous has proven to be part of their success structure.

Had they labored to remain invisible and completely undetectable they would be much more vulnerable. They would be susceptible to exposure because the enormities of their ambitions require a certain amount of public awareness. It is impossible for global government to be accomplished in secret. It is far more difficult to talk to someone who believes they already know the facts than to speak to someone interested in your point. The media became a vital asset to misinform the public of certain people, organizations and agendas since if the public did not have this illusion of understanding they would be much more interested in hearing facts and evidence that explains much of why we are facing the problems we are.

With this illusion of understanding and a confidence in an anchor who is withholding information the public rejects sound and vital information. By functioning in a seemingly tenuous manner behind some discordant effort and a host of organizations, they will only suffer the risk of exposure by those who have the tenacity and commitment to do the research. Those who have labored investigating their agenda are then tasked to convince a skeptical public that their research is valid. It is at this point (not during the investigatory process itself) in which the researches must go "toe-to-toe" with the conspirators.

This means conspiracy researchers must go "toe-to-toe" with the agents the new world order has in place tasked with hiding the truth, the media. The conspirators are committed to their agenda and the need for accomplishment demands a certain amount of risk in terms of possibly being exposed. They have planned carefully and are prepared to take these risks, however, what they are not prepared for is the success of the investigators revealing the confirmable information they have laboriously documented.

The need to breed cynicism cannot be overstated; their agenda requires it. They could achieve only limited success in an all out effort to remain hidden. Someone would talk, someone would rebel and the possibility exists that someone would simply research and learn the truth. The ultimate success of their agenda depends on this element of the strategy, not on hiding a conspiracy but to give the public prejudice to examining the very proofs of a conspiracy. It does not matter to them if their actions are discovered by intrepid researches so long as these researchers are mocked, ridiculed and stifled in the market place.

The secret in hiding a conspiracy is not in denying its existence but in convincing the public to reject all such information without consideration. They are everywhere and they are nowhere, they achieve by influence not coercion, they manipulate instead of educate, they deal in ambition and not integrity and they succeed by patient diligence and not aggressive actions. They are always behind a veil. Let researchers do their best since you're not going to stop them anyway but be ready when they're done researching. Have their audience prepared in advance, not just skeptical and contemptuous but confident that it is they (the audience) with the better compilation of facts.

This is done by giving the public a partial awareness of these front groups so that they recognize the names and have every assurance that they are familiar with who and what they are. It is more difficult to "re-educate" than "educate". If you've been led to believe an organization stands for certain principles it is far more difficult for me to convince you this is a fraud than for me to educate someone about this organization who's never heard of it before. The former requires that I overcome your preconceived notions, assumptions and beliefs. The latter requires only that I lay out my information to someone who is far more open-minded.

Acts 5:29 says, "Satan himself is transformed into an angel of light." Satan is behind the light. He will not reveal himself in his true state but only function behind some right sounding cause or seemingly beneficial purpose. There is always some organization to protect him from exposure by drawing any attention. It is Christians who have been warned and must examine the light and sound their own warning.

Satan's success hinged on his ability to convince Christians that he is not their concern but this is not what The Bible teaches.

In the Federalist Papers, number 51 James Madison questions *"What is government itself but the greatest of all reflections on human nature"*? We can see human nature changing and becoming much more base. We can see government changing and we're told this must be done in response to changing human nature. As a result we are seeing far more government than ever before in this country.

We see the church changing and taking less of an active role in society. Currently churches are spending enormous amounts of time helping people work through problems but not going on the offensive and dealing with the root source of these problems. Now even churches are calling for new and larger government programs.

To question all of this is not wrong. To consider Satan as the influence behind all of this is a reasonable possibility and deserves to be examined and not just on a general level as the author of evil, it should be considered on a political level as previous generations have done. It is on the political level that reasonable efforts to sustain a civil society suitable for raising families can be maintained. The likely examiners are Christians who hate evil and wish to see it hindered at all costs and if possible stopped. There are many Christians laboring to expose evils in our land but we do not see other Christians responding to their alarm in any significant numbers.

Why the church, and Christian, have ended efforts that came naturally to previous generations has much to do with our world view today, which is quite different from that of previous generations of Christians. This is what we will examine in the following sections of this book. We are being deceived and it is being done purposely so that we will not step up and achieve what God has asked us to do.

In Matthew 24:5-28 Jesus talks about His second coming and in verse 24 He comments about the many false messiahs that will arise. It is not strange that in verse 26 He warns us not to believe the messiah is "in the secret chamber". This is one of the verses the church has failed to appreciate. The secret chambers are real and it is where Satan dwells and meets with his cronies. Jesus points out in this verse that the real Messiah is not in the secret chambers. He does not close the door to the false messiah being there or argue that there are no secret chambers. Christians cannot afford to blind themselves to this truth.

We serve no purpose in arguing with those who will not believe, be it about Christianity or the new world order. We have a duty. It is not a duty to argue or debate and it is not a duty to submit to the conclusions and assumptions of others. It is a duty to be salt and light. It is a duty to preserve Godliness and shine light exposing the evil that Satan is working in our land. It is a duty to serve God and resist Satan. It is a duty to know God's word and abide by its truths and teachings.

Here then we leave the topic of human nature and Satan's tactics to manipulate the thinking of those who are to be on guard. We now begin the study of scripture to see for ourselves what God has to say in addressing these four lies.

PART TWO

GOD
IS
IN CONTROL

GOD IS IN CONTROL

*Isaiah 46:9-10 "I am God and there is none like me,
declaring ... the things that are not yet done."*

Perhaps the greatest constant of the church today is this teaching that "God is in control". There are some Christians who attempt a debate to what extent that this is true because they do not want to accept the implications associated with making God responsible for all of the evil in the world but still, this teaching is so universal in Christianity today it is taught as commonly as the fundamentals of the faith.

All Christians should accept the basic premise that God is real and we can know Him. This is an important point as there are many religions and even some Christian denominations that argue that man cannot truly know God. As Christian this point that we can know God should be obvious because we have scripture. The final Book of our Bible is "The Revelation of Jesus Christ" but it is important for us to recognize that our entire Bible is a "Revelation of God". It is through the study of scripture that we come to know Him.

Any matter that arises in the church or in our lives could and should be resolved by a study of scripture and in this manner we will come to know and understand God more. If scripture is vague or silent on a matter it should not be taught as doctrine. A mature Christian will regard God's word as absolute and recognize the key to better understanding of God is more study and prayer.

This is never more necessary than when a doctrine is introduced that may be supported by some verses but contradicted by others. Confusion also arises when some doctrine is taught which scripture and experience reveals to be contrary to God's nature.

The God is in control debate is the most confusing on the question of whether or not God created evil. Another side to this argument is if God preordained evil how can God judge those who do evil? Many Christians cannot mentally reconcile God with evil so they refuse to accept these arguments but neither do they study sufficiently to refute them. Without study we lack understanding. This lack of understanding does not, as a stand-alone reason, explain the success of this God is in control theology. There are many issues that need more study but none that have reached the level of acceptance of this teaching. This teaching is promoted specifically because of the affect it has on Christians.

This debate has existed since the passing of the original Apostles so I have no illusions that I will settle the matter but this point is central to the plight of Christians and patriots today so it must be addressed. It is precisely this "God is in control" teaching that has neutralized the greater part of the body of Christ and has made us so complacent and tolerant of evil that we resist nothing.

Not too many years ago this teaching was rejected by the majority of Christians as "extreme Calvinism". Calvin adopted this theology from Augustine and heavily promoted it. Calvin arrived on the historical scene about a hundred years after the invention of the printing press and about twenty years after The Reformation had begun. Today he is credited for ideas which he promoted rather than originated.

The more extreme of Calvin's followers not only insist that God preordained who would go to heaven and who would go to hell but they say every vile act of man or Satan is God's will. When pressed how a loving God could ordain abortion or child abuse or the never-ending list of horrors we see in our society they typically shrug with a vague argument that we can't understand God's ways, which is a type of excuse not to study (why study if you can't learn).

The more determined among them will pursue an argument based on what they call "the revealed will of God" verses "the secret will of God" with the obvious argument that we can't understand what God has determined to keep secret. As Christians we should not be willing to accept this. If we believe the purpose of scripture is so we can know and understand God than we have to use scripture for that purpose. When someone comes with some confusing theology it must either be proven in scripture or abandoned.

Logically, if there were a secret will of God it could not possibly disagree with God's revealed will or God would be double minded. We that are made in His image have been warned by God not to be double minded so it's foolish to accuse Him of being that way.

The extreme Calvinists insist that God is sovereign and this is spoken as a conclusive, indisputable affirmation of their point. In their mind, to continue to disagree with them is to argue the sovereignty of God, which is an argument lost since we all agree that God is sovereign. The disagreement comes in how they define "sovereign". The definition they use is that not one atom can exist or function aside from what God has ordained or God is not sovereign. They vehemently deny free will, personal duty, circumstance or Satan. Their extreme position of sovereign is that God has predetermined millenniums ago how every piece of matter would function eternally.

It may shock many Christians but there are two words that do not appear in the original King James Bible. That is to say, they are not used one time in any deviation or context. These two words are "sovereign" and "control". Already we can recognize these are two words that God did not choose to use to define Himself. Today newer translations of The Bible are replete with these words. The New International Version uses the word control over fifty times and the word sovereign is used over three hundred times! I should point out that in context these are not all references to God but obviously newer, Calvinistic Bible publishers have embraced this belief and are heartily promoting it.

The idea of God being in complete control may be comforting to some but they fail to recognize some implications. One example is as the church accepts every horror as God's will and fails to fight evil believing all things to be God's will Satan becomes completely unrestrained. Another implication is that non-Christians are not drawn by the goodness of God as they should be (Romans 2:4) but become wary that God may be unforgiving. Many Christians also come to resent God for some of the bad things they encounter and are mistakenly taught that God was responsible. They are confused wondering what they've done to deserve such "judgment" or what God is "trying to teach them". This entire concept is not supportable in scripture.

The debate is over Calvinism verses what some theologians refer to as "Arminian Theology" named after James Arminius, which emphasizes freedom of choice or free will. Arminians argue God's will is consistent with God's sense of justice. Calvinists argue everything God wills is automatically just simply because He willed it since God is sovereign.

Christians can agree on a definition of sovereignty, which is applicable to God. He is the one and true God and creator of all things in the natural world and the spiritual world. He is all power, all present, all loving and His justice is perfect. He is the final and ultimate judge and all will account to Him.

We are in error, however, if we discern from this that God can do anything He wants to or that God's will automatically comes to pass because God is so powerful. Scripture is replete with examples of God's will not being manifest. Here is just a short and incomplete list:

➢ Genesis 3:6 Adam eating the fruit in the garden
➢ Exodus 1:16 Pharaoh killing the male Hebrew children
➢ Joshua 9:15 Joshua making a treaty with the Gibeonites
➢ 1st Samuel 8:5 Israel wanting a king
➢ 1st Kings 3:1 Solomon rejecting God
➢ Psalms 78:41 Israel limiting God
➢ Matthew 18:14 people perish without salvation
➢ Matthew 23:37 Jesus weeping over Jerusalem
➢ Matthew 26:40 disciples falling asleep in the garden

And there are many more.

The real question is not about God's will as if it is some force in its own right but about God's desire. We agree that if God desired to create men and angels that had no free will He could have done that (with a lot less aggravation)! God desires to love and be loved and He desires to be loved by free moral agents that can choose to love him as a decision of their free will. Obviously this debate would have died centuries ago if there were not some scriptures for the Calvinists to base their argument upon. Most common among these are scriptures using the two words "predestinate" and "predestinated" which is used in scripture twice in Romans 8:29-30 and twice in Ephesians 1:5 and 1:11, a total of four times. Admittedly this would be sufficient for doctrine if they were quoted accurately and in context but they are not.

A casual reading of these verses will support the Calvinist argument but many vital truths are missed in a casual reading of scripture. The focus of this chapter is the teaching "God is in control" taught as an extreme belief that God has ordained all actions of men. This includes the idea that nothing is truly subject to free will and subsequently we can take no action of our own choosing but rather, any action we take would be only because God preordained this and all actions before creating man.

We need to start with the idea of predestination concerning salvation and examine it according to scripture since Calvinism teaches that it is God who has ordained some to eternal life and some to destruction. There are numerous verses that declare man has a free will to make decisions for himself and that God will hold each of us responsible for our decisions but the vast majority of these scriptures deal with salvation. We need to examine the question in terms of salvation but also in terms of our responsibilities as Christians in all areas of life.

The Book of Romans is considered to be Paul's great revelation of God's grace toward all of mankind and Chapter 8 is assertion after assertion of God's great love and grace to all of mankind. *If Paul planned to introduce a doctrine that it is God who determined in advance who would be saved and who would be lost, this would be a strange place for him to do it!* It would be a complete contradiction of several points expressed in Romans - especially Chapter 8 as well as contradicting a great many of Paul's other writings.

If it truly were God who appointed some to salvation and some for loss Paul could have (and would have) shared this vital information in a host of other writings. It would be as clear as any fundamental truth of Christianity and not the single biggest disagreement in the church today, possibly in the entire history of the church!

We must remember that the Book of Romans was written to Jewish and gentile believers at Rome. The early church had more Jewish converts than gentile for a good many years and while Paul was the "Apostle to the gentiles" he never failed to take opportunity in trying to win his fellow countrymen to Christ. Indeed we read in the last chapter of Acts that Paul was still reaching out to Jews and in Acts 28:24 he is winning some. Problems arose, as it was frequently the Jewish believers who had a stronger foundation in scripture but lacked the understanding of grace.

Additionally, many Jews were completely immersed in this concept of predestination. They were taught from an early age that Israel was God's chosen people but they were not taught what God chose them for and why. Frequently the belief was taught that they were chosen because the patriarchs were righteous, hence, predestined for eternity in heaven. Paul had to explain that God had not chosen them because of their righteousness and this was truly a revelation to many Jews. The teaching that they too face hell was highly offensive to many.

The concept of a "Savior/Messiah" was lost on many Jews as they regarded the Messiah would be an earthly ruler and reestablish their earthly kingdom. This led to many disputes concerning gentile believers having to convert to Judaism since they believed God's promises were to the Jews as "the chosen people" and they had not been properly taught what they were chosen for. Again, this concept of a new work among the gentiles was just as beyond the understanding of many Jews as was salvation by grace. Paul had to make the point from different perspectives that no one, Jew or Gentile, is predestined for salvation by God but all must accept Jesus as their Savior. This is what we read in Romans.

First of all, examine the Book of Romans in terms of how frequently Paul assures us that God's grace and salvation are offered to all of mankind. This theme is consistent throughout Romans:

> Chapter 1:16 "I am not ashamed of the Gospel of Christ; for it is the power of God unto salvation to everyone that believeth; to the Jew first and also to the Greek"

Paul said "the Gospel of Christ is the power of God unto salvation", not predestination for Jew or Greek but only to those that believe.

> Chapter 1:18-20: "For the wrath of God is revealed from heaven against all ungodliness and unrighteousness of men, who hold the truth in unrighteousness; because that which may be known of God is manifest in them; for God hath showed it

unto them. For the invisible things of Him … so that they are without excuse"

Here Paul makes several important points. When he says that God's wrath is revealed against "all ungodliness and unrighteousness of men who hold the truth in unrighteousness" he was writing to the Jews. The Jews recognized themselves as the "holder of the truths of God" as they were given the scriptures but they did not know they were unrighteous. Paul was teaching them that all men are unrighteous without Jesus as their Savior. Paul goes on to explain that God has a witness in each man's heart so all men are without excuse. Each could judge his own heart and recognize he needed a Savior and God had this witness in the hearts of Jews and gentiles equally.

> Chapter 1:26: "God gave them up unto vile affections…"
> Chapter 1:28: "they did not like to retain God in their knowledge, God gave them over to a reprobate mind…"

Here Paul clearly makes the point of every man having a free will to choose Godliness or unrighteousness and God will not violate it. No part of this can be interpreted to put God at fault. The people that Paul referenced had rejected God and suffered the consequences, as will all that reject Jesus Christ.

Chapter 1 does not mention salvation but makes a clear point that man can decide to reject God. This is consistent with all of scripture including Revelation 3:5 "I will not blot out his name out of the book of life" which indicates everyone born is listed in the book of life and those who decide to reject God then have their names removed. This is proof that God does not will that any perish, 2nd Peter 3:9.

> Chapter 2:1 "thou art inexcusable o man whoever thou art who judges"
> Chapter 2:5 "… thy hardness and impenitent heart treasurest up unto thyself wrath"
> Chapter 2:6 (God) "who will render to every man according to his deeds"
> Chapter 2:7 "To them who by patient continuance in well doing seek for glory and honor and immortality, eternal life:"
> Chapter 2:8 "But unto them that are contentious, and do not obey the truth, but obey unrighteousness, indignation and wrath"

> Chapter 2:13 "For not the hearers of the law are just before God, but the doers of the law shall be justified…"

These are a continuation of the points made in Chapter 1 and Paul makes it clear that it is man who is responsible for his actions. Paul has been making arguments to the Jews who believed being Jewish was all that God required to be saved (predestination). They had been taught that God would not hold personal conduct against the Jews.

Verses 13 through 15 are parenthetical, as Paul makes known God will judge gentiles by the same standard. In verse 17 – 29 he is again making the point that being Jewish won't save anyone.

Chapter 3:1-4 Paul is making the point that God's purpose for which He had chiefly chosen the Jewish people was that His word was committed to them and the Savior/Messiah of mankind would come from their race.

> Chapter 3:9 "all are under sin" (no one predestined)
> Chapter 3:22 "righteousness of God which is by faith of Jesus Christ unto all and upon all them that believe for there is no difference"
> Chapter 3:23 "all have sinned …"
> Chapter 3:24 "being justified freely by His grace through the redemption that is in Christ Jesus"
> Chapter 4:13 "promise … not to Abraham or seed … but through the righteousness of faith"
> Chapter 5:1 "justified by faith"
> Chapter 5:6 "Christ died for the ungodly"
> Chapter 5:7-8 "scarcely for a righteous man will one die … while we were yet sinners Christ died for us"

These are all radical teachings to the Jews who were immersed in life long teaching that they were God's chosen people due to the righteousness of the patriarchs. Jewish theology no longer taught that they too were sinners in need of a Savior. Now Paul had to teach them the error of believing in salvation by the predestination of Jewish nationalism and accept the belief of salvation by God's grace. He then had to teach them that Jesus was the Messiah and salvation was an individual choice.

> Chapter 5:18 "… the free gift came upon all men unto justification of life"

Which is another way of saying God does not offer salvation to the Jews alone.

Paul continues throughout the next few chapters to teach the Jewish believers that their salvation rests in believing on Jesus and not on their ancestry. He also makes clear that their feeble attempts to keep the law do not impress God. Chapter 8 continues this theme. With all of the confusion on this one word, we could ask why Paul chose to use this term. The reason is that he was talking to Jews and it is a term they were familiar with. We must understand that Paul's use of the word "predestinate" has nothing to do with salvation, as Christians understand it but is more about righteousness, as Jews understand it. They'd been taught that they were preordained for righteousness as a Jewish birthright. He then uses the term in reference to God's plan for those who choose to accept His plan of salvation.

Paul explains that God's plan from before the foundation of the world is that those who believed on Jesus Christ were "planned" or "predestined" to conform to His image which is the image Adam was created in, sinless, pure, innocent, holy and perfect righteousness. Verse 28 is vital in understanding who and what we have in Christ! In understanding what we were predestined for we come to understand what a fantastic and enormous work God did within us when we were saved.

By putting our focus on this argument (some being predestinated for salvation and some being predestinated for loss) Satan has stifled a vital instruction within the church. God's plan was that when anyone accepts Jesus they are conformed to His image. This is to say, they have returned to them that which was lost at the fall! After one accepts Jesus, he is no longer viewed by God as a sinful or rebellious man. God views them in the image of Jesus. If we quit arguing and come to see ourselves in this way, as we should, it will revolutionize how we think and act towards each other and the evil in our world.

If Satan can get us to argue about semantics we will not come to know God's plan for us. Satan gets us to focus on our problems and we lose focus on who and what we are in Jesus and this lack of focus changes how we deal with our problems. The Gospels record that Jesus had problems and issues to deal with and they also reveal how He dealt with them. He took authority over them and overcame! This is information Satan would prefer to keep hidden from Christians.

According to God's plan from the beginning, we are conformed to His image when we accept Him as Savior. God holds nothing back. Yes we have problems to deal with and God planned that we deal with them the way Jesus did and through Jesus He has given us the power and authority to do that, to overcome! God predetermined those who accept Jesus would walk in the fullness of who He is from the beginning of the relationship. We limit ourselves by a lack of faith and an unrenewed mind but God is not limiting us.

This is made clear in verse 29: "For whom He did foreknow, He also did predestinate to be conformed to the image of His Son, that He might be the first born among many brethren." This is what the debate is about, two words amidst such glorious revelation and because we argue instead of study we are robbed.

The Calvinists argue that "foreknow" equals "control". No one argues that God has foreknowledge but the Calvinists fail to consider one vital implication of their argument. If foreknowledge equals control then God has no control either! Their argument has no merit. Yes God has foreknowledge but foreknowledge does not equal control. He gave us free will to decide whether to accept Jesus or reject Him and since we had to have free will to make this decision we had to have free will to make all decisions and we're responsible for our decisions.

➤ Verse 30, "Moreover whom He did predestinate them He also called and whom He called, them He also justified and whom He justified, them He also glorified"

Do words have a meaning? Rather than being confirmation of the Calvinists argument, verse 30 disproves it. What else could this verse mean? The eighth word "also" is the proof. God has a plan and He will follow that plan and allow no exceptions. This verse clarifies that even those God foreknew would accept Jesus still had to be called and be given the opportunity to make their own decision. No one is saved without making a personal decision to accept Jesus. The only predestination God did is in what will happen to those who have made this decision. He also has predestined what will happen to those who reject Jesus!

By grace, when we are saved, we are conformed to the image of Jesus and this is why we can have the relationship with God that He wants us to have. All are required to decide for themselves and are responsible for a personal decision.

Ending Romans 8 Paul explains the confidence we have in our salvation since God establishes it and once established by God, it is eternal. We should not be surprised that Satan has chosen to introduce so much confusion in a context so rich in God's promises to those who accept Jesus as their Savior.

The other two times these words are used in scripture is Ephesians 1:5 "Having predestinated us unto the adoption of children by Jesus Christ to Himself, according to the good pleasure of His will…" Verse 11 "In whom also we have obtained an inheritance, being predestinated according to the purpose of Him who worketh all things after the counsel of His own will." These too are references to God's eternal plan and have nothing to do with a chosen people.

There is no end to those who teach these verses according to the Calvinist doctrine and how anyone can accept their interpretation and not get increasingly depressed is beyond reason. Not only can you never be certain of your salvation but also you are powerless to seek God's favor and all the while God's love seems remote and not personal. Why would God create people just to suffer in hell with no hope of redemption? Why, if God chose who would be saved and who would not, did He have to send Jesus? If He's going to exercise the degree of control over mankind to determine who would be saved and who would not, He could have simply created certain people who would not sin in the first place.

While the Calvinist interpretation certainly seems to fit the modern context, it doesn't fit God. Predestination is no more than a carry over from Judaism where they believed they were predestined for righteousness because God chose them. This same concept existed among the Greek Gnostics who believed some were born with a divine spark and others were not. Those that subscribe to this belief today frequently refer to reuniting with their "divine source".

We can find some scriptures that indicate God, as sovereign, predestined some people for certain actions but we have no evidence this was forced on them against their will. Mary being chosen to birth

Jesus, the choosing of the twelve and Paul, in The Old Testament Samuel, Saul and David are a few examples but in each case we see them consenting to be used.

There is an old analogy that may prove insightful. If I'm in New York City and desire to travel to Los Angeles I can take advantage of any airline that offers this route. Therefore when I use my free will to purchase a ticket and board the plane I am predestined to arrive in Los Angeles. If it happens, however, that the plane must stop in Chicago and Denver the airline will take no responsibility if I use my free will to disembark the plane. I have altered what I was predestined for by choice. We have the choice of buying a ticket to heaven by accepting Jesus as our Savior but it's our choice and responsibility to "buy the ticket and stay on the plane".

I have already listed several scriptures where God's will wasn't realized because the people involved have a free will of their own. There are several other arguments that can make the point as well. For example, The Bible documents several times where God has made a covenant with people just as He offers to make one with each of us. This too is telling. A covenant is an agreement between two that can each keep or break the terms of the covenant. You can't make a covenant with a plant, a pet or a robot. A covenant requires a free moral agent otherwise what's the point? Why bother making a covenant if one party couldn't break it, in fact, couldn't even want to break it?

All of this is not so hard to understand. Every loving parent gives their child perimeters. A responsible parent will not let a toddler out of sight. As the child grows he may exercise more free will but he still has perimeters and not many parents of two or three year olds doubt the existence of a free will in their child! A child of High School age wouldn't be allowed to take the family car on an extended journey. It's not uncommon for children in college to meet some requirement of their parents, work part time, come home on major holidays, etc. A great many laws we regard as necessary in society are to stifle free will such as traffic laws.

The fact that God gave us perimeters is proof of free will. Because of our free will we may indeed get ourselves into trouble, which we certainly did! If we had no free will we would face no danger of taking action contrary to God's purpose. Because of free will man could rebel against his Creator and thus needed a "Mediator" to reconcile their rebellion. If we had no free will we could not rebel and wouldn't have needed a Savior.

Scripture is the best resource to refute the God is in control lie but another argument is that Satan's workers obviously don't believe it. What a wonderful world it would be if those in Satan's service believed that God had predetermined everything that was to happen and therefore there is no point to serving one's master. What a wonderful world it would be if Satan's workers believed that they shouldn't be involved in politics because government is of God and therefore it is no place for them or all effort is futile because everything is preordained. Sadly, they don't believe it. Many of them are diligent, industrious and dedicated workers.

The confusion comes in when we choose to believe a theologian rather than scripture. God said in Joshua 24:15 "choose ye this day whom ye will serve". We too have a choice, to believe scripture or believe what have become more popular teachings. We are God's ambassadors on earth and we need to represent Him more accurately.

It is interesting that the Latin word "religio" from which we get our word "religion" has a verb which influences its meaning, "religare" which is to "bind as in placing an obligation upon."[4] Satan had mankind under his bondage until Jesus broke his stranglehold. We must oppose a return to bondage even if it comes from our own leadership. It doesn't come from scripture and true leaders will respect that. It's up to Christians to insure men are not deceived into bondage again.

In the end it's all about Jesus. The more we get to know Him the more we understand how much we need Him. Those who desire to serve Him can easily learn the truths of free will because it is a learning process to seek Him first. It is the unrenewed mind of man, which will launch out on some enterprise with the best of intentions only to have to live with the results of our decisions.

In the end this is more than proof of free will. It's proof of the nature of God. Jesus didn't die a quick painless death. He suffered a lengthy, painful, and humiliating death. How can anyone conceive He would have done this if other options were available? I'm referring to the option of God creating a sinless man who wouldn't require redemption. God didn't do this because His purpose was to have a free will being who could choose to love Him back.

Those who argue He created a split population, so those predestined would know how blessed they are, miss the point. If God would have created a split population, Jesus still wouldn't have needed to die and those predestined wouldn't care how blessed they are because they were never in danger of losing their blessings anyway. This is similar to the attitude Paul had to battle among the Jews who believed in predestination.

We reward the love of God by accusing Him of all the vile acts our sinful hearts can conceive. We blame Him for not moving in our lives when it is we who stand idle and allow evil to prosper in our midst and destroy our homes, our lives and our society. We are neutralized by deception but we do not need to remain that way. Our study is just beginning.

CALVINISM VERSES FREE WILL

1st Thessalonians 5:21 "prove all things, hold fast that which is good"

Of all the delicate balances in the human mind, none is more easily manipulated than whom we choose to trust. This seemingly small and obvious truth has served Satan well over the years and has long ago become a pseudo-science in its own right. Many understand this principle when it involves sales or marketing but fail to consider it is also true in the church. It has always been true in the church. We read the popular book and assume it's accurate, we go to the big church and we let the popular television evangelist impress us even though we have no clue of his credentials or knowledge.

We allow for human error but staunchly refuse to believe we are being manipulated or deceived. We have come to use these popular books and speaker as our guides for truth and proper conduct but this is not God's plan. We have scripture and this is to be our guide. God expects us to use scripture as the final authority and in Acts 17:11 Luke compliments the Bereans for their diligent and daily search of the scriptures. All of the books we read and sermons we hear will not replace personal study time!

John Calvin is an example of a man who has been raised to Apostle status by reputation and history has been very kind to him. Few among us have researched this man or his teachings and judged him by scriptural accuracy or the evidence of his works. Indeed, many that accept the "God is in control" theology probably don't even realize it is Calvinism. It is so widely taught and believed today it is considered scripture.

To put Calvin in his era, there was much dissention rising against the Pope and the abuses of The Catholic Church. These abuses are not to be understated. They too are the topics of many books and quite horrific in their own right. We must understand that such dissention is opportunity for Satan. Never in the human experience is there a shortage of men who will strut into the limelight and make stimulating speeches to delight and arouse the crowd. Satan is able to take full advantage of dissention and if those listening don't search the scriptures for verification they will assume the articulate, stimulating speaker is anointed of God.

This harsh statement may not be entirely applicable to John Calvin but we see this type of adulation toward charismatic speakers very common today and few study their teachings against scripture. I wish to make no personal attack on John Calvin. I have no way of knowing his heart or his relationship with God. We can recognize that many important truths were brought to light through his efforts in a most difficult time. Still, he was not infallible and all teachings of all instructors are to conform to scripture.

Calvin, as a man, is no longer an issue for us today. Calvinism, as doctrine, has the duty to conform to scripture. My effort is to reveal that the God is in control theology is contrary to scripture and very possibly taught today to an extreme Calvin would disagree with. Calvin had every opportunity to search the scriptures for truth and while we may assume he labored in scripture, he is also known to have relied on other sources for parts of his theology. God in control is the theology of St. Augustine,[5] which Calvin adopted and taught to a people who were hungry for God's word. Other parts of Calvin's theology led to the excesses and abuses we commonly associate with "Puritanism" here in America.

He was referred to as "the Pope of Geneva" and one fact is indisputable. At a time when many sincere Christians were seeking freedom to know and worship Christ, Calvin worked diligently to insert himself as a "Pope substitute" for his personal benefit and ambitions. Perhaps the worst action of Calvin was the burning at the stake of those who refused to accept his teachings and dared to criticize him openly.[6] We need to remember that a primary doctrine of his theology states that Paul's use of the word "predestination" makes God responsible for deciding who is saved and who is lost. What is to be said of a man who believes and teaches this and then publicly tortures and kills those who will not be coerced into accepting his doctrine?

Even today we can question why Calvinists work to defend their theology or spread the gospel. If God predetermines salvation, we can have no impact. Calvin insisted that it was his teachings that were taught by the early church fathers. The implication is that he was referring to the twelve Apostles as well as Jesus Himself. This is a distortion of scripture. Approximately 190AD St. Pantaenus founded a theological school at Alexandria. This was significant for "developing of Christian theology" which we wouldn't think needed to be developed beyond the teachings of Christ and the Apostles by The Holy Spirit.

Now that the church had a "school", the concept of "discipleship" that Jesus taught was increasingly abandoned. Now church leadership became a passion of "the intellectuals" and formalized credentials were increasingly esteemed.

Pantaenus had not been discipled by anyone qualified. Rather, his background was in the teachings of Plato and Stoic philosophers. He declared a conversion to Christianity but his pursuit was not in knowing or teaching Christ but to introduce Greek philosophy into Christianity. Clement was his most accomplished student and took over the school upon the death of Pantaenus. Clement is known for very little aside from being the instructor of Origen who, in his turn, had much hunger to unite Christianity with Greek philosophy.[7]

Origen introduced the term "Gnostic" into Christianity, which he used to describe Christians who had attained special "deeper" knowledge like himself. For Bible believing Christians, not much good can be said of Origen. He didn't believe in taking The Bible literally (what little scripture he used) and had many beliefs that were contrary to the teachings of Christ. He believed himself to be an intellectual but his knowledge of Hebrew is suspicious at best. He assumed leadership of the Alexandria school at the young age of 18, plus he openly disrespected Christians who lacked formal education regardless of their relationship with Jesus.[8]

Some hundred years later Augustine arrived on the scene. He too had not been discipled according to the scriptures but embraced the teachings of Origen and the Alexandria school. Augustine, too, had many beliefs contrary to The Bible. None of these men had done anything to demonstrate a commitment to Jesus Christ and all of them were students of Greek philosophy, especially Plato, and Gnosticism.[9]

These then are the "early church fathers" that Calvin revered and followed. These are also the sources he quotes and used for his instruction. It is true that these men suffered along with discipled Christians from Roman persecution but this is not evidence of their commitment but rather evidence that Rome didn't concern itself with the difference between one professing Christian and another.

There were many church fathers that Calvin could have studied who had better credentials and quite a different view of free will than the sources Calvin used in his theological teachings. Here are a few examples:

Ignatius of Antioch is believed to have been discipled by both Peter and John. He died a martyr's death in the Coliseum. He left seven letters still available today and wrote, "If anyone is truly religious, he is a man of God; but if he is irreligious he is a man of the devil, made such, not by nature, but by his own choice".

Polycarp, a disciple of John, was martyred in 155AD by being burned at the stake. He had a disciple of his own named "Irenaeus" who has left us a large and significant body of writing. Irenaeus was Bishop of Lyons and spent a great deal of his writings addressing heresies in the church. He wrote, "Men are possessed of free will and endowed with the faculty of making a choice. It is not true, therefore that some are by nature good and others bad". In another of his writings, "man is endowed with the faculty of distinguishing good and evil so that without compulsion he has the power by his own will and choice to perform God's commandments by doing which he avoids the evils prepared for the rebellious."

Justin Martyr is credited with the earliest surviving writings of significant size. He wrote "man acts by his own free will and not by fate" and again "we have learned from the prophets and we hold it to be true that punishments, chastisements and rewards are rendered according to the merit of each man's actions. Otherwise if all things happen by fate, then nothing is in our own power. For if it be predestined that one man be good and another man evil, then the first is not deserving of praise or the other to be blamed. Otherwise, if all things happen by fate then humans do not have the power of avoiding evil and choosing good by free choice, they are not accountable for their actions whatever they may be... For neither would a man be worthy of reward or praise if he did not of himself choose the good but was merely created for that end. Likewise if a man were evil, he would not deserve punishment since he was not evil of himself, being unable to do anything else than what he was made for.

God, wishing men and angels to follow His will, resolved to create them free to do righteousness; possessing reason, that they may know by whom they are created, and through whom they, not existing formerly, do now exist; and with a law that they should be judged by Him, if they do anything contrary to right reason: and of ourselves we, men and angels, shall be convicted of having acted sinfully, unless we repent beforehand. But if the word of God foretells that some angels and men shall be certainly punished, it did so because it foreknew that they would be unchangeably [wicked], but not because God had created them so."

Archelaus wrote, "All the creatures that God made, He made very good. He gave to every individual the sense of free will, by which standard He also instituted the law of judgment.... certainly whoever will, may keep the commandments. Whoever despises them and turns aside to what is contrary to them, shall yet without doubt have to face this law of judgment.... There can be no doubt that every individual, in using his own proper power of will, may shape his course in whatever direction he pleases."

Methodius wrote: "Those (pagans) who decide that man does not have free will, but say that he is governed by the unavoidable necessities of fate, are guilty of impiety toward God Himself, making Him … cause and author of human evils."[10]

These are the teachings that Calvin chose to ignore in favor of Origen and Augustine. The earliest evidence of Augustine's activities in Christianity date some 400 years after the first apostles. Calvin's reasons for choosing these as his sources and calling them "the church fathers" is speculation but we can agree that the sources closest to Jesus and the Twelve are the more accurate and are better sources to use in guiding us into scriptural truths.

Our focus here is to question whether or not his teachings are scriptural to the extent of being doctrine or supported by a few out of context verses. Here is a necessarily incomplete listing of many scriptures that refute Calvin's doctrine:

- ➢ Genesis 4:7 "If thou doest well, shalt thou not be accepted"?
- ➢ Deuteronomy 30:19 "…I have set before you life and death … choose life…"
- ➢ Joshua 24:15 "… choose you this day whom ye will serve…"
- ➢ 1Kings 18:21 "How long halt ye between two opinions? If the Lord be God, follow Him but if baal, then follow him …"
- ➢ Psalms 106:29 "Thus they provoke Him to anger with their inventions …"
- ➢ Ecclesiastes 7:29 "God hath made man upright but they have sought out many inventions."
- ➢ Isaiah 65:12 "when I called, ye did not answer; when I spake, ye did not hear but did evil before mine eyes and did choose that wherein I delighted not."
- ➢ Ezekiel 18:23 "Have I any pleasure at all that the wicked should die? Saith the Lord God and not that he should return from his ways and live?"
- ➢ Jonah 2:8 "They that observe lying vanities forsake their own mercy."

- Zechariah 7:12 "They made their hearts an adamant stone, lest they should hear the law and the words of the Lord of Hosts…"
- Luke 13:3 "… except ye repent, ye shall all likewise perish."
- John 3:16 "For God so loved the world that He gave His only begotten Son, that whosoever believeth in Him should not perish but have everlasting life."
- Acts 20:21 "Testifying both to the Jews and also to the Greeks, repentance toward God and faith toward our Lord Jesus Christ."
- Romans 10:9 "That if thou shalt confess with thy mouth the Lord Jesus, and shalt believe in thine heart that God hath raised Him from the dead, thou shalt be saved."
- Romans 14:12 "So then every one of us shall give account of himself to God."
- 2nd Corinthians 5:15 "He died for all…"
- Ephesians 4:19 "… given themselves over unto lasciviousness, to work all uncleanness with greediness."
- 1 Timothy 2:5-6 "… the man Christ Jesus; who gave Himself a ransom for all …"
- 1 Timothy 4:10 "… who is Savior of all men, specifically of those that believe."
- Titus 2:11 "For the grace of God that bringeth salvation hath appeared to all men"
- Hebrews 10:10 "… through the offering of the body of Jesus Christ once for all."
- 2 Peter 3:9 "The Lord … not willing that any should perish but that all should come to repentance."
- Revelation 3:20 "… if any man hear my voice and open the door, I will come in…"

I repeat, this is an incomplete list; a comprehensive list would be a sizeable portion of The Bible. The majority of verses I quote have to do with free will in salvation but this is sufficient to disprove Calvin's doctrine as he includes salvation above all things as being predetermined by God.

Calvinists use Romans 9 as their "proof text" so to fully address their arguments we must focus on these scriptures. To completely understand Romans 9 it is vitally important to keep in mind that it was written with specific consideration to the Jewish Christians. Those that fail to recognize this cannot deny much of it is about the Israelites so to understand Romans 9 we must understand certain beliefs of the Israelites.

In Paul's great love for his kinsman he goes to great lengths to convince them of their need to accept Jesus as Savior. One of the initial difficulties of the early church is that Christianity was viewed as a Jewish sect or offshoot. The obvious question put to them was that "if Jesus is truly the Messiah why did the Jewish elders reject Him"?

This is a reasonable question for gentiles to ask but more so for Jews. They firmly believed they could trust their elders because of their devotion to The Torah. Having been taught they were the chosen people from their youth, Christianity was extreme, offensive and contrary to all the religion they knew. All of this both explains Romans 9 and calls attention to the fact that if we do not understand Jewish culture and thinking we will not understand Romans 9. If we take Romans 9 out of its context and not do the research we will get a completely distorted view of God, which we call Calvinism.

The first point to be made here is that Romans 9 has nothing to do with salvation as Christians understand it but rather it's questioning predestination, as Jews understand it. Paul begins Romans 9 by professing his love and devotion to the Jews. In verse 4 he acknowledges they were chosen of God as the only nation He agreed to adopt, give glory, have covenants, give the law, reveal how to serve and in verse 5 he acknowledges that it was through Israel's patriarchs that the Messiah came in the flesh.

Having brought Jesus into the topic Paul writes in verse 6 "Not as though the word of God hath taken none effect for they are not all Israel that are of Israel". In other words, the promise of God is not nullified simply because some (elders) do not believe but rather will be fulfilled in those who do believe whether Jewish or gentile. Verse 7 "Neither because they are the seed of Abraham are they all children but in Isaac shall thy seed be called". Paul makes the point that Abraham had other children, which emphasizes that Jews are not predestined simply because of Abraham. This was a familiar point to the Jews, as they too believed that Abraham's other children were unrighteous but righteousness flowed through Isaac to Jacob. Paul applied the logic that righteousness didn't flow through flesh at all.

Verse 8 "That is, they which are the children of the flesh, these are not the children of God but the children of the promise are counted for the seed". Remember, the Jews had been taught to believe that as God's chosen people they were predestined for heaven to the point they recognized no need for salvation. Verses 6 through 8 were common arguments made by the Jews and Paul refutes them to create understanding that the Jews must accept Jesus as their Savior as must the gentiles.

Verse 9 "For this is the word of promise, at this time will I come and Sarah shall have a son". This is a very meaningful verse to the Jews as it affirms that Isaac was a miracle baby, which would not have been born without divine intervention. This is significant to the Jews as it affirms that they and their beliefs are founded on God and that God did a work through Abraham, it was not Abraham in his own power doing anything. Ultimately many Jews came to believe that the covenant Abraham had with God was eternal including salvation and that God had done this in recognition of Abraham's righteousness.

Paul is explaining that God chose Abraham and his descendents but not because they were more righteous. In verses 10-11 Paul points out that righteousness had nothing to do with the twins as they hadn't even been born yet so neither of them had committed good nor evil. Modern theology attributes this to God's foreknowledge but this is not accurate. This passage concerns the two nations, not the boys themselves. Verse 12 speaking of the older serving the younger is clearly a reference to the nations of Israel and Edom as Esau never served Jacob.

Verse 13 also reveals this passage refers to the nations and not the boys as the first part of the verse "Jacob have I loved" is a quote from Genesis 25:23 and the second half of the verse "but Esau have I hated" is a quote from Malachi 1 made after Edom had spent centuries in rebellion to God.

I should point out that this word "hated" is not what we understand as hatred today. It simply means "a stronger love". "Jacob I had a stronger love but Esau have I loved". The same word is used in Luke 14:26 "If any man comes to me and hate not his father and mother ... he cannot be my disciple." Hating your father and mother, as the word is used today, is a violation of The Fifth Commandment. The Jews understood all of this but it is lost in modern theology.

In verse 15 we also see another reference the Jews would have understood. The quote is from Exodus 33:19 when God agreed to go with Israel to the Promised Land. God told Moses he would grant his request because Moses had found grace in His sight (verse 17). In other words, God would show mercy on Moses and grant his request to accompany them and show Moses His glory. Again, this passage has nothing to do with who goes to heaven or hell but rather it speaks about God's nature in that God is free to interact with each of us differently. He does not owe one the mercy or a blessing He bestows on another. Today this verse is very twisted portraying God as a harsh, angry master who deliberately created some for hell. If you want mercy, ask!

Verse 16 "So then it is not of him that willeth nor of him that runneth but of God that sheweth mercy." These passages have nothing to do with salvation. The question in verse 16 is what is the "it"? "It" is not salvation but must be tied to verse 15, which is God's mercy and compassion, but in the context of the quote of Exodus 33 "it" is that God may grant a request of those who serve Him, in this context Moses was allowed to see God. In other words, yes God is sovereign, yes God may choose to supernaturally bless someone and yes God is above the reproach or challenge of any man but these truths do not dispel free will and do not prove predestination. The application is that God blessed Israel in the various ways listed previously but that didn't mean He automatically owed them anything more.

The point is that God is free to interact with each one as He chooses, relating to both people and nations. These verses should not be taken out of context and applied to salvation. As for predestination, Paul is simply trying to get Jews to recognize that God doesn't owe them anything. To further clarify this point Paul returns to an example the Jews would clearly understand but is lost on us today; that of Pharaoh.

Thus we come to the great Calvinist stronghold. If God created Pharaoh for destruction and if it were God who hardened Pharaoh's heart the Calvinists would have an argument. It cannot be denied that there are scriptures here that do make this argument. We must understand principles of good Bible study to understand this portion of scripture. It is always dangerous and wrong to take a scripture or a passage of scripture out of context and use it for doctrine. All scripture must be in accord. Additionally it is necessary to study the context and historical application of appropriate verses.

First of all, Pharaoh never expressed any interest in God or had any repentance for any of his actions and subsequently destined himself to hell and this would be equally true if the Israelites had never gone to Egypt. Secondly he was strongly influenced by the magicians and sorcerers of the Egyptian mystery religion and this is no small point. There is a deceptive power in the occult and one who embraces this evil with zeal has contempt for Godliness. From the tower of Babel, as men migrated towards Egypt they experimented with evil and increasingly embraced ungodliness to a degree that was not duplicated any where else on earth.

To say God "raised them (Egypt) up" (Ex 9:16) is only to say God tolerated this evil to grow and prosper and pursue their own lusts for a purpose. God destroyed other nations for this behavior but He tolerated Egypt for a purpose. He satisfied His purpose when He demonstrated that even when the full extent of evil is manifest in a man's religion it is still no match for His power! This is a truth the church should stand on today! We must search the scriptures for understanding of God's purpose.

The first obvious purpose is stated in Exodus 3:8 to bring Israel out of Egypt as He'd promised Abraham, Isaac and Jacob. This is repeated in verses 6:3-5. Additional purposes are listed in verse 3:21 "I will give this people favor in the sight of the Egyptians", verse 4:5 "that they (the elders of Israel) may believe that the Lord God of their fathers ... hath appeared unto (Moses)", verse 6:1 "Now shalt thou see what I will do ..." and verse 7:5 "The Egyptians shall know that I am the Lord."

As stated before, all scripture is a revelation of God and it is God's desire to be known to His creation. When we read Exodus we are not dealing with a creation that knows God. The Israelites have little or no faith and the Egyptians are in total disbelief. True worship and relationship with our creator had ceased and "gods" were spooky and mysterious. Remember, this predates The Priesthood, the law, the prophets, and the wondrous miracles that we have recorded for our benefit or the relationship we can enjoy today. All the Israelites had were stories of unfulfilled promises made to their Patriarchs and stories of the creation, the garden and the flood. This was four hundred years into slavery with ever increasing horrific conditions.

Conceivably, there were more of them that had long since abandoned any faith in the promise made to Abraham than those who still held hope. How much faith would we have in a God who had not yet fulfilled any of His promises to rescue His people from the burdens of Egypt or the power of Pharaoh? God still had His remnant, to be sure, but He also had the need to reveal His faithfulness and power to all of Israel. They were, at the time, a nation of slaves with a slave mentality. They were not warriors with any boldness or aggressiveness capable of freeing themselves. Neither were they equipped with weapons and knowledge of warfare. They were not free people with a determination and resolve to be treated with respect or even the knowledge of how to launch a nation or challenge Pharaoh.

We can recognize that it was necessary to build up the faith of the Israelites with an emphasis on building the faith of the tribal elders. We also read that, to an extent, it was necessary to build up the faith of Moses as well. What we read in Exodus is a revelation of the power of God. To Israel it was confirmation of God's faithfulness as well. God allowed Egypt to prosper in spite of the evil work of the Egyptian occultist magicians which were so accomplished that the occult of today traces it's knowledge to "the Egyptian mystery religions'. God's purpose was to show that the occult could never stand up to Him and make that truth absolutely clear in the minds of the Israelites. In short, His purpose was to prove that He is the one true God.

We read how Moses and Aaron had increasing courage to stand up to Pharaoh and the elders and people had increasing courage to follow their leadership. God was building up their faith. We read later, when things got challenging, many wanted to return to bondage because they were still thinking with a slave mentality. Many would have refused to leave in the first place without such a wondrous and fantastic show of power because of the fear they had of the Egyptians. The Israelite slaves were accustomed to watching the Egyptians exercise enormous power. God, through Moses, had to overwhelmingly defeat the Egyptians and all their power and force to prove the Egyptians were no match for Him and His power.

Also, you realize, Moses was asking these people to abandon everything they knew and follow *him* out into the desert with only what provisions they could individually bring. The trust factor was huge! Parents who loved their children would not be likely to simply take their families and follow this guy into the desert just because he "said" God had sent him to rescue the people. A show of force was necessary to prove that God really was with Moses and too, that God was powerful enough to sustain them in the desert.

Still we must address the matter of Pharaoh's free will. The Calvinist's interpretation is taken from Exodus 4:21 "I will harden his heart". The presumption here is that had God not intervened to harden Pharaoh's heart he would have let Israel go free simply upon request. Immediately we recognize the Calvinistic double-mindedness. Had Pharaoh been created with no free will and for the purpose of this stand off with God, no "hardening of his heart" by God would be necessary at this point as Pharaoh would simply act as preprogrammed.

Setting that argument aside, we must review the actual record of events. In verse 5:2 we read that Pharaoh has no reverence for God what-so-ever. The pattern of events begins in verse 7:13. Here the presumption is that the "he" ("he hardened Pharaoh's heart that he hearkened not unto them") is a reference to God. That this was God is not clear from this verse and 7:14 says "he refuseth to let the people go," indicating he, as Pharaoh, still had the power of choice. This is repeated in verse 16 "... hitherto thou wouldest not hear". 7:22 says simply, "Pharaoh's heart was hardened" and verse 23 "neither did he set his heart to this".

The point is that Pharaoh had numerous opportunities to yield to the voice of the Lord but through a combination of faith in his magicians and stubbornness he had no interest in God's will. Many things harden a man's heart against God like pride, arrogance, anger and in this case false teachers.

This subject resumes in verse 8:8 where, even though the magicians were able to duplicate the frogs they could do nothing about the frogs God sent. Here for the first time Pharaoh agrees to let the people go and as a matter of his free will he is allowed to determine when the plague is lifted; verse 10 "be it according to thy word that thou mayest know that there is none like unto the Lord our God". Was Pharaoh permitted to name the time so that he could yet understand that God would hear his voice?

To a Calvinist, why would it be important to Moses that Pharaoh "knows" this if the information could be of no benefit to him? Verse 9:15 clearly indicates Pharaoh hardened his own heart and changed his mind breaking his promise to Moses. In verses 18 and 19 we arrive at plagues the magicians could not duplicate and even they recognized this was the work of a God more powerful than their own. Verse 19 states Pharaoh's heart was hardened but it, again, does not state that this was because of God. Verse 22 repeats "... that thou mayest know that I am the Lord ..." By verse 29 even Moses had figured out that Pharaoh could not be trusted. Verse 8:32 is quite clear "Pharaoh hardened his heart at this time also ..." Verse 9:2 clearly speaks of free will "if thou refuse to let them go ..." and once again in 9:7 we read "the heart of Pharaoh was hardened".

At long last, in verse 9:12 do we have the fulfillment of verse 4:21. For the first time, here five chapters and a host of opportunities later, do we read that it is God that hardens Pharaoh's heart. Not only is it obvious at this time that Pharaoh had numerous opportunities to repent but also verse 9:20 clearly states that many Egyptians had come to know that the God of the Hebrews was God indeed. Fourteen times we read of Pharaoh's heart being hardened or his having an opportunity to repent and he does not. The Calvinists argue this was God all along but this cannot be found in scripture.

Still, we need to further examine this idea of God hardening Pharaoh's heart. In verse 9:27 he reflects, "I have sinned this time: the Lord is righteous and I and my people are wicked." By verse 9:34 he changed his mind again, "he sinned yet more and hardened his heart, he and his servants". This was not God. Pharaoh knew what he was doing. He was challenging God. With each reprieve he convinced himself that God was now exhausted and finished to the point his magicians could finally overcome. A man with no free will cannot change his mind with each change in events. Neither was he willing to fully recognize that God is God. So mired in deception was he that he constantly turned back to his false gods.

We must know specifically what is meant in verse 10:1-2 "the Lord said … I have hardened his heart … that I might shew these my signs before him: and that thou mayest tell in the ears of thy son and of thy son's son what things I have wrought in Egypt … that ye may know how that I am the Lord".

There is a particular verb used here and in verses 10:20 "the Lord hardened Pharaoh's heart…", verse 27 "but the Lord hardened Pharaoh's heart…", verse 11:10 "The Lord hardened the heart of Pharaoh…", verse 14:4 "I will harden Pharaoh's heart …", verse 14:8, "the Lord hardened the heart of Pharaoh, king of Egypt" and verse 14:17 "I will harden the hearts of the Egyptians…"

The word "harden" in its various forms appears nineteen times in the book of Exodus stemming from three Hebrew verbs, which mean quite different things. The most common, and the one used in the above contexts, is "Chazaq"[11] which means "to strengthen", "to make courageous" or "to urge". This word is used *twelve times* and consistently with regard to God "hardening" Pharaoh's heart. It is inaccurate to use the word "harden" as we currently understand the word. God did not violate Pharaoh's free will. He simply gave him the courage and determination to follow his heart's desire against Israel.

To illustrate why this was necessary, forcing the Israelites to make bricks without straw is no personal threat. Following them down into the sea with walls of deep water on either side is significantly more intimidating so God strengthened his resolve to do it.

Pharaoh was not a kind, benevolent dictator who would have freed Israel if only they would have asked politely. He was a cruel, murderous taskmaster but he had the same sense of self-preservation that we all have. Pharaoh wanted to enslave the Israelites or see them destroyed. His free will was to be relentless and cruel toward Israel. God simply gave him the courage to follow through. If we learn anything from this passage, we come away knowing that Pharaoh had to be destroyed as he'd proven quite absolutely that he, by an act of free will, would not restrain himself and would pursue Israel continually or until one of them was destroyed. God is not the harsh judge here except from the perspective that Pharaoh wanted a fight to the finish and God finished it so that Israel could be free from this relentless tyrant. Ultimately it would have come to this anyway as we have no reason to believe Pharaoh would ever have willingly quit the pursuit to enslave Israel.

The second Hebrew verb is "Kabad"[12] which means "to become difficult or grievous" as in 8:15 "when Pharaoh saw that there was respite he hardened his heart".

The third verb is "qashah"[13] which means to "be cruel". Why would God, through Moses and Aaron, tell Pharaoh to let the people go if he had no power of choice to do it? If Calvinists are correct God wouldn't have needed to harden Pharaoh's heart, he would have simply done what he was created to do. 10:3 why would God ask Pharaoh to humble himself if he were predestined and couldn't?

What about Moses' free will? In Exodus 4:13 Moses made it quite clear he did not want to do this. How could he make this decision and arguments if he had no free will? God did not remind him he has no choice, rather he calls for Aaron as a helper.

Back to Romans, 9:21 is further illustration that Paul is reaching out to the Jews. "Hath not the potter power of the clay, of the same lump to make one vessel unto honour and another unto dishonour?" This is an Old Testament reference the Jews would have understood. It is taken from Jeremiah 18:6 "O house of Israel, cannot I do with you as this potter ..." but the Jews understood that the passage continues in Jeremiah 18:8 "if that nation, against whom I have pronounced, turn from their evil, I will repent of the evil that I thought to do unto them." This is a wonderful promise of God that is lost to Christians if we fail to refer to the quote in original context.

The answers can be found in scripture if we seek them out. If predestination is true then how many scriptures are false? Predestination in terms of salvation is not true. God is the same yesterday and today. If we turn from our evil we are predestined for awesome unimaginable things. These truths have been hidden from us by design. The purpose these and so many other truths are twisted and misapplied is to neutralize the church. God is awesome. When we serve Him we do not need to fear and fail. We do need to step up, which is Satan's worst nightmare!

NEUTRALIZING THE EFFECTIVENESS OF GOD'S PEOPLE

Matthew 7:15-16 says "Beware of false prophets, which come to you in sheep's clothing but inwardly they are ravening wolves. Ye shall know them by their fruit ... "

Christians are the natural enemy of Satan and his forces; therefore Satan has a vested interest in neutralizing Christians if he hopes to achieve his goals. Christians may well recognize this but those who desire to be active in the Lord's service fail to consider that their effectiveness will be hindered if they are not knowledgeable of Satan's tactics. Scripture reveals what Satan's strategies are but they are not commonly taught in the church today. Christians are taught that Satan is a liar but repeatedly scripture warns us that Satan uses false prophets. We expect Satan to lie but we are not on guard that the teacher in our church may be insincere or poorly educated.

Other chapters deal with other specific attacks that we should expect. This one deals with neutralizing God's people. While the word neutralize is not in scripture the definition of this word clearly applies to Satan's agenda. To neutralize means "to counter act the activity or to make ineffective." Christians expect Satan's forces to oppose our efforts but they are not prepared for the strategies he uses. One very successful strategy is to create a debate. People that debate do not take decisive action and as Christians, if we hold God's word as our standard the debate is over. This may sound strange to people in our society because we are encouraged to debate as a form of research. This is largely a deception.

Virtually everything learned in this process is learned in prior study preparing for a debate. We cannot afford to be confused here;

it is the study that is important. Those who lack the will to study will come away from hearing the debate with little learning and more confusion. Even here the difference depends on what they knew prior to hearing the debate. One who may enjoy debating may develop superior verbal skills and those listening may hear a fact or argument that they immediately embrace but much more can be learned from one who knows their topic and can lecture and teach as opposed to the confusion created by two who constantly go back and forth with competing arguments.

The point here is that we can be tricked into debating the word of God. If we know God's word the way we should (or if we're willing to study for ourselves) and stand on that word we will be effective. If we allow ourselves to debate relatively pointless facts and word meanings we will be robbed of our effectiveness. How can we teach the world to revere God's word if we indecisively argue among ourselves and Satan's oldest trick is to ask, "hath God really said"?

Satan can neutralize the church simply by getting us to debate God's word instead of standing on it at which point we will be ineffective. Satan desires to destroy our effectiveness and therefore he must address our strongest weapon. Additionally, we can expect Satan to take actions against the actions of those taken by the church or individual Christians. We are in a war of truth against deception. If we are active and effective we will do immense harm to Satan's agenda. God is awesome and His word is no less awesome. His word is the revelation of Himself as well as guidance and direction regarding a quality life. This means God's word tells us how to build and maintain a quality society in addition to spiritual happiness.

Satan must, therefore, offer instruction on how to build a "counterfeit quality society" in addition to "counterfeit spiritual happiness". This is an important point, as Satan knows he cannot substitute nothing for something. He knows he can't take the greatness that was once America and replace it with total chaos and crime and expect the people to be content. The same is true of spiritual matters. He knows he must have some system to offer those in his service that will afford them both happiness and hope. We must know God's word to recognize the counterfeit.

Satan has much to be gained by separating us from God's word and toward that end we would underestimate him if we fail to consider all the various ways he will employ to separate us from it. He has made attempts to destroy God's word outright, he has attempted to limit its availability and he has made numerous attempts to modify God's word with weak translations that slightly alter vital truths. There is, perhaps, no end to the list of tactics he will employ to separate us from God's word but high on this list is the stresses of time, which takes us away from personal study.

Debating and endless lectures will not replace this personal study time. We live in a fast paced society where we expect everything to come rapidly and this can make study all the more tedious but God is not governed by the pace of our society. Rather than attending churches where we are expected to study, we are encouraged to buy tapes and listen to them as we drive. We buy books believing the author will impart some greater truths than what we would have received directly from The Bible if we'd read that instead and we leave church having learned nothing, but guilt free because we showed up. These things are all good in their place but all combined will not replace personal study time and prayer.

It has been proven that your mind does not grasp as much information from a tape as from something you read and choosing to read other books at the expense of the Bible says a lot about what we expect to receive when we read something. The argument can also be made about what you expect to receive from church when you attend. The most anointed leaders can't help those who physically attend but have their mind on the golf course. The God given purpose of the church is to disciple people. To teach people to grow in knowledge and faith so we will live in the "abundant life" Jesus promised. Far too many churches have no discipleship program.

Many people that have been Christians for decades have no stronger or more effective prayer life now than when they first accepted Christ nor do they have a closer relationship with God. We have become accustomed to a church that offers entertainment and a motivational message, not life changing truth and instruction. The Bible study in many churches may have no greater impact on us than a poetry club. We attend these churches and keep silent even when we're not learning scriptural truths or growing in the knowledge of God. We don't question whether they're effective spiritually or if they're even involved spiritually.

We have an Americanized concept that we owe an hour to God every Sunday morning and we go where it's convenient. We accept that these pastors are qualified spiritual leaders but we really don't expect anything but entertainment. Some pastors are accepted as spiritual leaders for having done nothing more than being a local businessman who has organized a network of volunteers to put on a show every Sunday morning, a show that climaxes with his motivational speech. If we like the show, we come back. We've become so accustomed to receiving nothing aside from entertainment that entertainment is frequently what we seek when searching for a new church.

If we are not being trained up in the ways of the Lord then what is our spiritual advisor doing for us and why are we satisfied with him as a spiritual leader? There can be no doubt that Satan has a high priority on deceiving us into following a spiritual leader who is ineffective for Christ and will fail to disciple us the way God intended. Satan must provide these leaders in order to offer "counterfeit spiritual happiness". For this reason we must use all caution in choosing a spiritual advisor just as we would a financial or legal advisor. We must know them with regard to their motives, their knowledge and their relationship with God. We have a duty to them, and ourselves, to verify their teachings, not simply and complacently believe what we're told.

Someone should earn the right to be our spiritual advisor, or any advisor. They should minister to us personally in such a way as to prove they are able and willing to disciple us. This means they can teach us Godly truths from scripture and in application so we grow in spiritual knowledge and ability and not just an emotional boost. The fault is not necessarily on the pastors, however. Many wonderful pastors are frustrated at how rapidly the crowd thins when the challenges get stronger. Here is where Satan's "counterfeit quality society" comes in.

If government meets all of our needs and protects us, we see no need to change our behavior and accept challenges from a pastor to deepen our relationship with God. We need to examine what has happened to Christianity and the modern church. We need to ask what happened that we have such a small impact on our society and the best leadership the church has can offer no solution to regaining influence. We need to ask why so many Christians and pastors are content with the current situation.

The desires of most Christians are very basic. First of all we want to go to heaven and not hell. Secondly we want to be blessed and not cursed. Thirdly we want fun and recreation more than we want responsibilities and labor. We can conclude that Satan is well aware of human nature and knows how to manipulate Christians just as he knows how to manipulate non-Christians.

Let's consider what Satan wants for a moment. Many Christians believe Satan wants to keep them from going to heaven and will do anything he can to accomplish that. While this may be true on a basic level, Satan isn't so stupid to limit his ambitions in such a way. My point is that Satan can't keep you from heaven if you are committed to serving God and he knows that. Satan is focused on a much larger agenda than an individual salvation. He is focused on deceiving the masses. He has successfully deceived many into no longer believing hell is even a threat.

While this strategy would seemingly accomplish little among most Christians it has been very successful on two levels. The first being that we do not mourn for the lost as the church once did. We have grown somewhat complacent to their fait believing they had a choice and they get what they deserve. We have little passion to evangelize as the church once had. Secondly, modern Christians are a very distracted people. We do not rely on the Lord the way previous generations did and this hurts our relationship with Him. An example would be a farmer's mentality. When you need rain to fall and seed to flourish you need a God that can deliver those blessings. When you are accustomed to receiving a paycheck regardless of the corporate profit earnings it affects your thinking by giving you a false sense of security.

We begin to rationalize that our career is more in our own hands and we can advance our career if we focus on education or pleasing an employer instead of God. We focus on our earthly investments and no longer prioritize the things that we are commanded in scripture to be of chief concern, like Bible study and prayer. When we have only a shallow relationship with God we grow no spiritual roots that we will need in hard times but if we are to be effective for God we will need these roots in prosperous times as well.

By the same token, if it is Satan's counterfeit system that we have come to rely on, it is his system we'll turn to (and trust) in hard times. This means that even in hard times we will ignorantly seek Satan's solution to problems instead of God. Equally important here, it is Satan's leadership that we will follow, not God's.

Neutralizing the church requires neutralizing both Christians and the pastors. This is what was described above. This is done by a combination of influences. Changing the expectations that a Christian has about responsibility while promoting false and shallow leaders that fail to disciple, teach responsibility and who simply appeal to human nature will produce a contrary system to the one Jesus instituted. We do not notice because we don't questions the system. Pastors that preach Biblical moral standards and work to disciple new converts watch helplessly as they go across the street to view the drama club presentation.

These pastors naturally grow weary and disillusioned and if they continue in the ministry at all they simply copy "what works" and abandon what Jesus taught. I want to acknowledge that we have many pastors who are fighting this deception and are holding the line in their small congregations. I salute them and thank God for them because it is they that are holding the line in this spiritual war. I further want to emphasize that if we as Christians have set our ambitions at the low level I've listed (avoiding hell, being blessed and having fun) we have simply failed to consider what God would have us do.

Other Christians want to be discipled but consider themselves forced to settle for entertainment as the only option available because they can't find quality leadership. This too is not scriptural! 1st John 2:27 promises that if you are willing, The Holy Spirit will teach you. It is a matter of free will and we must be willing in this as with all of our responsibilities. We must step up and get engaged in the war if the war is going to continue. I look forward to the return of Christ but I do not believe we will hasten His return by a premature surrender on our part.

Whether they know it or not, most people don't have a spiritual leader they have an entertainment director. One whom they've given a ridiculous amount of influence over their life! This is Satan's counterfeit system and has neutralized the church. If you find this offensive, take a short quiz. How is your relationship with God stronger than it was when you first started attending where you do now? Do you have a relationship with God or just with a local group of Christians? How much more effective is your prayer life now? How has your life changed? These are reasonable questions and a qualified spiritual advisor would be asking you these questions himself.

Christians that are fortunate enough to have a Godly spiritual advisor need to recognize what they have and be ready to assist them. Those who are unsure owe it to their pastors to communicate their desire for the church to have an impact on society. Your pastor may be just as frustrated and concerned about society as you are. In the event you are rebuffed and told Christians should not get involved, you must seek God and perhaps become a spiritual leader in your community. America will not survive without Godly spiritual leaders; it's just that simple.

One matter all concerned Christians should keep in mind is that many Godly churches are struggling simply because they cannot compete with the entertainment offered by the larger groups. We cannot afford, as Christians or patriots, to have entertainers in charge of our agenda. Church leaders who encourage their members to ignore the key issues of our time may do so by ignorance, duplicity or self-serving convenience but it is certainly not scriptural. No one wants to believe their spiritual leader is corrupt, misguided or lazy but we have a duty to challenge what they preach (1st Thessalonians 5:21 "prove all things").

Part of this problem is of not being able to teach what you do not know and many whom we recognize as spiritual leaders today have never been anointed by God or discipled themselves. Additionally, far too many leaders have come to enjoy the comfort, respect and benefits of a pastorate. They will not tolerate anything that threatens the Sunday morning attendance because this is their measure of success. This is a problem of the spiritual health of the church and the spiritual health of our nation. We must recognize, as a nation, we'll not survive amidst so much spiritual decay. America cannot survive without an effective church. Satan cannot succeed in the presence of an effective church so he has worked hard to neutralize it.

He has succeeded in stopping the church from demanding a Biblical moral standard be respected for society as a whole and certainly among our leaders. He has succeeded in stopping the church from protecting the sanctity of the home and family. He has succeeded in stopping the church in the fight to maintain a Biblically based judicial and legal system and even in the defense of our God given rights. This is a seed that has been nurtured for a long time. The result is that our churches have become cathedrals of complacency.

Pastors feel like they do great works for God when they have a couple people make a public confession for Christ on a Sunday morning. Even a complacent person will run to the street when their house is on fire and as the complacency in the church spreads these too grow lukewarm, Revelation 3:16. From Satan's perspective it is preferable to have an ineffective church as opposed to destroying the church entirely. By allowing a neutralized church to exist Christians have the illusion of serving God.

A neutralized church is no threat to Satan or his agenda of a new world order! Actually, it's become quite beneficial! How much easier to deceive Godly people from the pulpits and Bibles studies than simply from politicians and the media! Jesus said in Matthew 7:15 to "beware of false prophets … in sheep's clothing but inwardly they are ravening wolves." What is this "sheep's clothing" He referred to? Could it be a pulpit, a $1000.00 suit and a big smile? Ravenous wolves are starving for something. Could it be fame and fortune and the notoriety of pasturing a huge church?

The tolerance of evil that Christians have today must be questioned. Again, as Christians we must know the strategies and tactics of our enemy. Who benefits from Christian apathy if not Satan? We could propose that the problem lies in the seminaries, schools or television evangelists. I submit to you that the problem is Satan and the solution is personal commitment to God and determination to stop evil. If we tolerate evil because our church leadership tolerates evil we are as guilty as they. Scripture is very clear what happens when the blind lead the blind (Luke 6:39).

Keep in mind that we have two examples here, false prophets and blind leadership. Many who would never consider themselves susceptible to the deceptions of a false prophet consistently attend the same inactive church every Sunday, waiting for the day they are led into a ditch. Spiritual leaders who have blinded themselves to the consequences of allowing evil to prosper have blinded their congregations to the results that will impact us all. A pastor who ignores evil simply because it's "official government policy" (abortion, punitive taxation, tax money sent to foreign governments, leaving our children's education to the state, policies breaking down the family, etc) are not holding to a scriptural standard.

Christians that have been neutralized by these false teachings need to stir themselves up and recommit to God and the truth. If we abandon God's word we really leave ourselves with nothing. This means we have nothing to offer the world, nothing to sustain our own relationship with God and nothing with which to fight evil. If we are following leadership that has abandoned God's word, what credibility do they have?

It may serve us well to examine our local pastor by a Biblical standard but the greater duty is to examine ourselves. Yes its reasonable to ask if we're getting what we really need from our local church but too, are we really ready to step up and serve. How many have asked themselves if they are truly serving God to the extent they feel they should be and are they serving Him effectively in what they are doing. I have asked pastors how I may serve and most frequently the answer is teaching in the children's department, being an usher or security guard in the parking lot during services. When I have agreed and served in these areas I have been very much appreciated.

When I have desired to proceed to what I regard as the next step and made suggestions on how I believe the Lord would have me serve I have been turned away with vehemence and unbridled hostility. I have worked in the children's department and know first hand the challenges and difficulties there. I have ushered and worked security. I have never had it explained to me why when I aspire to move out of the children's department I am relegated to the parking lot.

I was not questioned about why I was certain it was God leading me. I was not counseled about some doctrinal error. Neither have I been questioned about my teaching ability. My heart's desire is for the church to make an impact on society by being knowledgeable patriots who take an active interest in their community. This is an area many pastors consider off limits and they are not willing to discuss it. I have had my experiences with teaching outside of the church and have my successes but my field of study is not welcome in the church.

Those that were honest enough to give me a reason frequently mentioned 501c3, which they have never bothered to educate themselves about but they were certain I knew less about it than they did and quite offended when I suggested they had been mislead. Aside from 501c3 the biggest argument was how I would offend people and bring division to the church. Remember, this is an assumption on their part. I hadn't offended anyone but the pastors I spoke with and in truth, I didn't offend them either. They were offended at this idea long before I met them.

I have attended churches that teach classes on financial planning, cooking, exercise classes even foreign languages but the one thing that is not welcome in the church today is teaching about what is taking place in our government. Any other topic may get a fair hearing but not Christian civic duty. We can agree that the purpose of the church should be to disciple people but I've even seen a church program to teach skiing so I recognize that it is civic responsibilities alone that are singled out and not welcome in the church.

This is a historical change in our country. We have a mental disconnect considering that the people we're trying to invite into the next world currently live in this world. There is a need for them to know the truths that have the greatest impact on their daily lives. One of these great truths is that Satan is determined to destroy everything that draws men to God. There is an obvious double standard when we're fine with the church teaching people tips on reducing their "carbon footprint" or foreign languages in our church but we staunchly resist teaching them vital truths about how their government functions.

At the same time that we fail to teach our fellow Christians the truth about government we teach them that God is in control so He gets blamed for the horrors we see rising up among us. We are led to believe that Christians should do nothing and we're falsely told that

God has preordained everything that happens. It is quite obvious that we cannot be effective if we feel no responsibility to try.

Neither is it a defense to argue that it will cause division. Division is simply the separation of one from the second. In all aspects of life we welcome division. For one example, we typically count ourselves among the moral having divided from the immoral. This is not only the way we want things to be but this is the way in which we feel happier and more secure. We separate ourselves from others for a host of reasons.

A common reason is that those of us who love truth tend to separate from those who lie. If we tell the truth about government we can reasonably expect that lovers of truth will appreciate hearing it. Far too many people accept the lie that "all politics is a matter of opinion". This is tantamount to saying "all religion is a matter of opinion". Admittedly, they are both heavily immersed in lies but there is much truth that needs to be taught never-the-less. It is precisely because there is so much truth immersed under so many lies that the church needs to speak the truth instead of running from it out of a fear of offending someone. The likelihood is that the one offended at hearing political truth would be equally offended at hearing many spiritual truths. Trying to accommodate these people has led to many problems.

If we are so anxious to avoid division we will be anxious to avoid differences. No truth can be adhered to in such an environment. There exists in the church today an illusion that if we avoid talking of matters that "may offend" we create an opportunity to "share Christ with many more." The reality is that while we may preach the gospel of Jesus Christ to some degree, we cannot teach Biblical morality in such a politically correct atmosphere. John the Baptist openly declared the adultery of Herod to be a sin. Jesus spoke against harming children, which would certainly include abortion. Many are quick to get offended when they hear something they don't want to believe. It is the church that is to stand its ground.

We hear so much these days about hate speech yet we must consider, truth becomes hate speech when people hate the truth. Where does that leave the church? People will never mature and be able to accept the truth if we continue to pander to them. We should keep in mind that no one ever came to Christ without hearing the truth. Yet in today's church the emphasis is on building large crowds and it is agreed this requires modifying our message so as not to be offensive.

Subsequently the goal today is a "feel good" message with an emphasis on humor and entertainment. Gone are the days of the two-hour sermons or even one hour. Now it's thirty minutes from which you learn nothing. The important point here is that Satan is working hard to destroy our society and reasonable people would expect the churches to be on the front lines working to protect society.

Yet all Satan had to do was three things: convince Christians that they are wrong to get involved in politics, put his people in government as the Christians leave, then pursue his agenda by making all things "political". Suddenly marriage, abortion, education, and a host of other issues are no longer moral issues, they are political issues and Christians are not allowed to voice an opinion. The morality of these issues is ignored and they are discussed solely as matters of public policy. All of these matters were viewed as moral issues to previous generations and the church demanded that Biblical morality was observed by society. No more! The government dictates policy on all issues now and Christians do nothing.

Since this strategy has started taking effect Satan's agenda is seldom mentioned in a church! The topic is neutralizing God's people and the point is that God's people are ineffective if they are not properly trained for the warfare at hand. It is wrong that they cannot be trained properly in the church because the church leadership doesn't want to offend anyone.

We can become neutralized by developing a complacent attitude concerning other people going to hell, we can become neutralized by becoming affluent and not seeking God and we can become neutralized by seeking too much entertainment when we need to labor. In short, we become neutralized if our focus is not on developing a relationship with God and serving Him.

We fail to appreciate that God really gave us an advantage when He revealed Satan's battle plan! Surely we cannot believe He did this so we would help Satan become victorious! He did it for the same reason He exposed other aspects of Satan's plan, so that we could know the wiles of the enemy and be better prepared for battle. It should not be wrong for lies to be exposed from our pulpits. It should be considered vitally important, given the lack of confidence we justly have in today's media! Many pastors who know the bias of today's media refuse to offer corrections to their lies. We cannot survive when truth is willingly suppressed and lies go unchallenged.

Lies pertaining to the proper authority of government are decidedly tolerated in our churches today. Court after court has made rulings against the church and many Christians have been hauled into court and prosecuted for their adherence to some Biblical truth. The vast majority of churches do nothing to remove these bias judges who continually violate the limits of their proper authority.

We see that the courts, as all government bodies, are accepting and tolerant of any religious beliefs so long as they don't speak of Jesus Christ. We recognize this whole argument as an attack on Biblical based Christianity and still we stand idle. If people cannot hear the truth in American churches, what confidence do we have that they will ever hear it anywhere? Psalms 1:1 reads, "Blessed is he who walks not in the counsel of the ungodly". Yet our churches leave those who attend services no other choice but ABC, NBC, FOX and the like for news. Surely we can recognize these sources as ungodly counsel.

The churches have quit exposing lies as the schools, media and government shape peoples thinking in the fashion they prefer and even Christians are being deceived by misinformation that goes unchallenged or unexposed. One who believes in absolute truth must accept we can know it and teach it. Those afraid of division have simply not made known the level of truth they will compromise to keep so called unity. Satan's lies go virtually unopposed in America today and too many Christians are lost for lack of knowledge.

We are warned of this in both Isaiah 5:13 "my people have gone into captivity because they have no knowledge ..." and Hosea 4:6 " My people are destroyed for lack of knowledge: because thou hast rejected knowledge, I will also reject thee that thou be no priest of me..." Both of these reference are to God's people. God wants His people to have knowledge. Scores of verses in Psalms and Proverbs declare God's demand His people be given knowledge.

During America's founding era many awesome and inspiring teachings came from the pulpits in this land. That has changed now.

To let someone live in deception and lose all they hold sacred through ignorance is not a Godly love. We should not all be forced to lose our God given rights simply because a few can't accept the truth when it's presented. We could not be sure that those few were interested in the truth in the first place. If we're so easily manipulated, Satan could plant a few whiners in each church to keep the church silent and no truth would be taught. Quality leadership would see through this foolishness.

The gospel itself is divisive since there are those who prefer to walk in darkness. If we don't speak the vital truths of our time those who would chose to know it will be left in ignorance. Romans 16:17 reads "mark them which cause division contrary to the doctrine you learned … and avoid them." It goes on in verse 18 "by good words and fair speeches deceive the hearts of the simple".

Scripturally, it cannot be argued that division is bad when Paul commands us "to avoid them" which is the act of separating ourselves. These verses are about those who challenge the truths of Christianity and are not saying that we are to divide over every difference. Neither are they saying that it is wrong to speak the truth even though it's divisive. It is ironic that Satan can control what's preached in our churches simply by having some protest that it's political. Many churches work to accommodate these protesters when filling seats has become the measure of success and preaching the truth has become secondary. It has become common to hear "good words and fair speeches" from the very pulpit that is to represent Godly truth; nowhere does scripture tell us to compromise the truth.

There certainly are those who will argue the truth when presented but they are not to be given authority in our churches, which is to say church leadership is not to abide by their commentary. We are not to customize our message so we won't offend them; we are to avoid them. We are to tell the truth and not compromise and let those who attack us for it separate on their own. Let them hear the truth, accept or reject it as they choose but let us continue preaching the truth to those who desire to know it. Let every man hear the truth!

This is the scriptural standard; the standard is not to be entertaining and inoffensive. Godly pastors serve a vital role in God's plan for the body of Christ. Churches cannot be effective if we fail to speak, preach and stand for the truth, all truth. To do less is to tolerate lies to flourish in our midst. The church has been neutralized and rendered ineffective because we have too many leaders that no longer hate evil and willingly condemn it from the pulpits for truths sake. American history is filled with political truths being preached from pulpits by bold pastors. Lacking leadership Christians have lost their focus and purpose. We no longer take responsibility for our world and evil is thriving.

Some people will argue with this, of course. They will insist that the fact that someone is building a church on every corner or that churches are building larger buildings is proof we are having an impact. This is deception. Free entertainment always draws a crowd and clearly the people are coming to be entertained. Clearly they do not attend to find life changing truths that demand sacrifice. This is not the church we read about in the Bible.

God has given us the authority, His word and The Holy Spirit but the decision is ours to get involved or stand idle. He did not give us these things so that we would suffer at the hands of a defeated enemy. They are ours to use. This chapter may appear to be an attack on the "super-churches" but it is supposed to be a call to action. We may love our drama clubs and the golfing programs at church but we are loosing our society and we are distracted by these diversions into thinking we are doing our Christian duty. We are a very blessed people and to whom much is given, much is required, Luke 12:48. If we were doing our duty and if our churches were truly having an impact America we wouldn't be in the mess it's in.

We blame God and say it's His will but it's time to take personal responsibility and stop blaming Him. We, as Christians are not exercising the power and authority we have in Christ. We need to look to scripture and let scripture be the final guide.

The next chapter expands on this point and deals directly with action on our part and that of the new world order. This deception to neutralize the church has been a strategy of theirs for a long time but in war strategies must be hidden from enemies. They know this world needs God and their strategy includes creating a "God substitute".

NEUTRALIZING THE ACTIONS
OF GOD'S PEOPLE

*1ˢᵗ Corinthians 3:13 "Every man's work shall be made
manifest, for the day shall declare it"*

After writing about Satan's ambition to destroy the church's effectiveness, we now move on to the topic of Satan's ambition to neutralize the actions of Christians. This includes spreading the gospel but it is important to Satan that he destroys the actions of Christians from being a blessing to society as a whole. If God or Christians are a blessing to society it is a powerful incentive for people to seek greater knowledge of God. By the same token, if someone is in desperate need of a blessing they may seek God. If a large group of people is in need of a blessing, they may seek God. Satan cannot permit this because he knows that if people seek God, they will find Him. Therefore Satan must bless them first so that they will not seek God.

When people think of Satan they don't typically think of him in terms of being a blessing to anyone but we should consider this; Satan deceives people for a living. His job is to convince those who will believe it, that he does not exist. There are many who know he is real and he must have a strategy to deal with them. One tactic would be to keep a low profile. Another would be to keep them from asking too many questions. A third would be to alienate people from the source that is most likely to educate them about Satan and his true agenda. A fourth would be a public relations campaign to plant the idea that radical Christians have him all wrong and they're just trying to scare people. You don't go to war with a single battle plan and neither does Satan. He incorporates all of these ideas.

There are many in Satan's service that enjoys what we would typically call blessings. They are quite financially affluent, they have awesome healthcare, they seem to be happy, etc. It may be true that these people do not recognize Satan as their benefactor but neither do they recognize any need for God. Satan has much to be gained by keeping people content and ignorant of his true character and agenda. It is the job of the church to expose Satan and his agenda but this job is made all the more difficult in a society that has no interest.

A society that effectively has its material needs met is content. In generations past it was common for churches to run charities to feed, clothe and house needy people. As the people sought assistance they were given spiritual direction as well. Today the government has largely taken over these benevolent efforts and, in the process, eliminated any spiritual guidance to those in need. Many large charities are active in assisting these people but they do not necessarily minister to their spiritual needs and frequently are legally prohibited from doing so. These programs and charities have seemingly lessened societies physical need for God and the church.

In effect, they have alienated qualified spiritual counselors from those in the greatest need. You can see where Satan must supply these needs if his deception is to succeed. There is the added benefit that the ability to administer these programs requires unconstitutional government growth. Government growth is very important to Satan because that's his power structure and his ambitions are always unconstitutional. The task of destroying the Constitution is accomplished most easily through benevolent programs since many will hesitate to confront a program that helps those in need. The irony is that Christians are frequently taxed to pay for these programs and frequently welcome them. Christians, too, no longer understand the need for these programs to be run from a church.

The long-term effect is the abuse and fraud from a lack of accountability, which has created multigenerational families in need of assistance. A greater problem than this is that the church has lost its influence in society. People are having their needs met without making any lifestyle changes or sacrifices. The greatest problem of all, however, is the impact this has had on preaching the gospel. We seldom see people coming, seeking answers and Godly wisdom, that they might be ministered to. The church's response to this is organizing door-to-door programs to distribute Bible pamphlets. This is what we're reduced to and we don't even question what happened!

It is important that we focus on the lack of influence we have in society. Where political leaders once revered the church, it is now dismissed. Where the church was once recognized as the halls of truth, where evil would be exposed, they are now inconsequential. Where the church was once a force to be reckoned with because devout, committed, patriotic people gathered, learned, talked, planned and worked together to bring forth (and maintain) a Godly society, it is now politically correct where we don't want to offend anyone. Where the church was once Godly, active and diligently promoted Godly values, we now put on shows. Where the church building was once known and respected as "the house of the Lord" we are now viewed as just one among many religions and no longer considered an asset or have service to a community.

Not so long ago, the church recognized a responsibility toward what was called "the cultural mandate". This was a reference to Godly people being "salt and light". Only Godly people will promote the Godly values necessary to preserve a society. The obvious fact is that we fulfill no part of a cultural mandate without being involved in society. We have chosen to abandon attempts at influencing the elected leaders of society and this is the biggest mistake we could have made. This has played right into Satan's hands and a review of history reflects his success.

We look back in history and we see a series of events and the more we learn of history the more events we should question and take note of. For the purposes of this chapter we can begin with the lie of a "separation of church and state" which The Supreme Court arbitrarily started using to decide a variety of cases in 1947.[14] Then The Bible was removed from public schools in 1962. Then in 1963 The Supreme Court ruled to ban prayer in public schools, this from a case that the atheist Madelyn O'Hare lost at the local and at the Court of Appeals level. Not one church bothered to file a brief in the case – not one!

The Sexuality Information Education Council of the United States (SIECUS) was founded in 1964. They justified their existence and agenda by telling us what a noble service they had to offer mankind, the teaching of *value neutral sexuality* among young people. They insisted this was needed to "address the growing sexual revolution" of the 1960's and to address the spread of sexually transmitted diseases. Planned Parenthood had long been a primary supporter for sexual education in the schools and the first Executive Director of SIECUS left the staff of Planned Parenthood to take the position. The NEA passed its first resolution endorsing sexual education in 1966 and in 1970 the first Title X funding of Planned Parenthood programs was approved.

There were those who worked opposing this agenda but they were not prepared for the fight and they lacked organization and strategy. This proposal wasn't launched as previous programs had been. It was strategically brought into being through a seemingly limitless amount of funding and exceptional organization. Here is one of the examples where we can clearly see the new world order at work if we have the foundational knowledge. Otherwise we are left wondering where SIECUS got their funding and clout.

This topic was highly offensive to the majority of parents as well as a very emotional topic. They had passion but were not equipped and ready to battle the massive forces organized against them. This one topic has hurt society astronomically but it has hurt the church to a greater degree because now the forces promoting an evil agenda had defeated the church. Satan chose a strategic target, the school system, he chases the church out and comfortably moved in to set up his hellish, life destroying agenda with no further opposition. It all happened with military precision. Since that first victory, Satan's forces have gained momentum and now proceed at a staggering pace.

Ultimately their adversary, the church, left the field of battle. All that remains now are mop up efforts that, essentially, fall into two categories: controlling the population and reducing the size of the population. Implementing the means to control the population require identification cards (even healthcare identification cards will suffice nicely) and making the public increasingly dependent on government programs. Reducing the population to manageable levels can be done with wars, diseases, starvation and natural disasters. Most immediate, however, is not reducing the population in numbers. It is more about reducing their ability to resist the agenda of total government control.

Other mop up efforts would include getting control of armies, police departments, law making authority, courts, food supplies and all of this seems well under way today. Moving all laborers to massive international corporations rather than small family owned businesses is an example of his type of accomplishment.

Satan has taken steps to replace the services and duties that have traditionally been performed by the church. We now have a new generation that fails to recognize any benefit of a church and views it as the superstition of a small minority. Convincing the public to trust government was the first step. Next they will be taught to love it. To a people who trust government, government growth is no threat. For Satan to accomplish this in a free society he must not visibly raise alarm, call attention to himself or arouse suspicion.

This is why the church must get involved. It is the responsibility of the church to expose Satan and his agenda. His entire agenda is not alarming or suspicious to a society that is entertained, has its basic needs met and hold the church in low regard. If the church continues to stay inactive untold millions will fall prey to this deception. The fact that we have lost a few battles and may loose a few more is not important. Making our voices heard and exposing the enemy and his agenda is our duty.

We have been neutralized from holding government accountable and those who acknowledge a Biblical standard for society have withdrawn from the arenas where the issues are discussed and decided. We have come to accept the argument that all problems are best solved by another government program. An example of this would be the arena of healthcare. To read modern scholars, you would come away with the idea that nothing has hurt the advancement of health and medicine as much as Christian beliefs. Now with Christians out of the arena the system is based on the three "C's"; "cutting, chemicals and chemotherapy" none of which offer healing. They are simply very profitable ways of treating diseases. Here again, Satan moved the church out and he comfortably moved in.

Perhaps this is an appropriate place to mention the concept of "unjust profits". The Biblical standard of profit is based on moral truth, integrity, stewardship and respect for our fellow man. This obviously excludes greed, attempts to burden one man for the benefit of another, oppressing people, fraud, theft, force, violence, coercion, and (debatably) centralized control. When an unjust system is allowed to prosper there will be serious repercussions.

The best example here is our currency. Man has long recognized the benefits of using a currency instead of a barter system. Currency by definition is "a medium of exchange." This is the way our system of currency has developed because it is obviously impossible to deal in actual goods. Still, the paper in our wallets is just that – paper. The figure on our bank statement is simply and electronic entry. They represent our wealth and this system works because the majority of people are willing to tolerate the system. We have no such good fortune on a global scale. Many currency traders in other countries have begun questioning the reliability of our currency. If it collapses they do not want to be holding a bunch of worthless paper. Increasingly the global market will not accept paper as a medium of exchange because it's proving to be a bad investment.

There are four items, which have risen to take the place of our paper. These are tangible items that have an intrinsic value even if the markets collapse. These four items are oil, precious metals, pharmaceuticals (legal and illegal) and munitions. Consider the unjust profits to be made in any one of these industries. Each has a higher demand than ever before and it continues to rise. There was a time when oil was believed to be the property of whomever owned the land over the oil deposits and they were free to contract with any interested party to drill wells for a royalty. Now we live in a world where seven corporations own virtually all the oil deposits. They got them through political malfeasance and coercion but they now have the political force to threaten any competition.

Most people don't stop to consider that the costs of pumping oil, shipping and refinement are all relatively fixed. Once the oil is discovered and the well is productive, it is virtually all profit. When a mere seven corporations sell oil at $100.00 per barrel when the cost to drill, ship and refine is ten percent of this amount and the volume exceeds twenty million barrels a day the profits are astronomical. Since the initial costs were the larger costs, any increase in prices renders increased profits more than an offset to higher costs. When you consider these profits must be reinvested you can calculate that at some point these investors will own or control everything that money can buy.

The same principle is true when you consider a pharmaceutical company that has a per pill production cost of a few cents and they sell this pill for anywhere between a dollar and hundreds of dollars a pill for some of the more radical medications. In time, as this unjust wealth is reinvested, a handful of corporations will have reinvested their wealth to sufficiently control the entire marketplace.

We are left with worthless paper and they are permitted to amass the wealth of the planet. All of this is done in an unjust way by Biblical standards. Many Christians don't regard this as a vital concern for the church but this ignores the evil that can be accomplished with these enormous profits. It is time to take note of where the world is headed; who is determining our direction and what (if anything) are we going to do about it? Satan has a plan and these corporations are in Satan's service. These unjust profits are used to create an ever-increasing power base for Satan and his agenda.

Today it takes mere minutes to do some research into corporations and the information that is available is staggering but only to those who investigate it. Corporations, for the sole purpose of greater unjust profits, are tampering with the food supply with total disregard to human health and well-being. A vast amount of information is available on genetically altered foods and the conceivable side affects. The debate over vaccines has come at the price of permanent mental damage done to hundreds of thousands, if not millions of innocent children and undocumented numbers of deaths. Most who read this and disagree will not do a few minutes of simple research to verify their position or challenge mine. We no longer want to know if we're wrong in our beliefs. Everyone must consider that our entire healthcare system is based on evolutionary theory and these researches have no quandary with mixing animal and human blood or organs.

The problem we've created is that the church has become accustomed to being inactive so we no longer regard a duty to address any issue. We've come to believe we must only spread the gospel and we have left ourselves only three options to tell others about Jesus; one is sending money to missionaries, two is continually bearing witness to the same people we see day after day and third is some church door to door program trying to recruit strangers with a one time contact. At least those engaged in these are doing something but if the church stood for truth and exposed lies and unjust profits in the market place it would stifle Satan and his agenda and have those seeking truth coming to us.

Who among us wants to face Jesus and have it eternally recorded that we did nothing to fight evil in our time? If one applies Matthew 25:21 some may get a greeting of "well done thou good and faithful servant.' This implies that we "did" something. Will there be lesser greetings for others? I'm not trying to be radical or mean spirited here. I'm simply making the point that America needs the church. If the church isn't doing anything, it's the same as not having one. At minimum the church needs to take up the abortion issue and stop these premeditated murders.

We need to expose immorality as a cancer on society. Few Christians stop to consider that immorality is being thrust upon us through a number of organized efforts including sex-ed in the schools, pornography and perhaps the best organized offender, homosexuality. Homosexuality is a disease ridden, depressing lifestyle that must sustain itself by recruitment. It can be argued that not every homosexual is depressed or has a disease but statistically their average far exceeds heterosexuals. The point is that this is not a harmless, somewhat controversial, alternative lifestyle decision that some prefer. In many cases, especially among the more radical groups, it is unbridled sexual passion that feels license to go fourth and consume all that can be brought into its sphere of influence.

As Christians grow more tolerant its sphere of influence has become our children. They aggressively pursue new conquests with the abandonment of all moral restraints just like a cancer must continue to attack healthy tissue to survive.

Homosexuality is simply one element of the cancer of immorality. Whenever and however immorality is permitted to spread it will destroy society. We must be aware that immorality is also revealed in unjust profits. Christians have a calling to stand for truth and that includes fraud and unjust profits in the marketplace that threaten the health of the nation. Those who make these unjust profits are certainly well organized. This is why Satan and his minions had to get the church out of the picture before they could hope to make substantial progress. The church of earlier generations was sufficiently organized to be a threat capable of exposing all of Satan's evil schemes.

The Christianity we're taught today is to "love" them, which is a convenient way of saying we don't want to offend anybody. Once again I remind you, if people are offended at the truth so be it. It is our responsibility to insure they hear the truth. Christian consumer buying power would have an impact on the direction corporations take if we even took that small step to stand for truth.

There is an old axiom that if you don't stand for something you'll fall for anything. The deception that we as Christians have no responsibility in our society is very prevalent in the church today. We can agree that some of these topics are very controversial but there are many that are not. Many Christians desire to be of some service to God and the opportunities abound. No one of us could tackle the overwhelming majority of issues we face in our society today but we all have God given ability to do something.

Some will focus on abortion because God gave them a heart to be passionate on this issue. Others will be as passionate on education, corporation fraud, government corruption or some issue that I may not even be familiar with. The point is that if we stand up for truth we will show the world that we stand for something. We will win far more to Christ if we stand for something and expose the evil behind all these man made or satanically inspired god replacement programs. We must expose this lie that the solution to all problems is a larger government program. The solution is God and we need to act like we believe it.

The government does not have a history of solving problems. They have a history of expanding their own programs. If Christians don't get involved and insist that some of these problems legitimately get resolved our days are numbered and the collapse is not too distant. Anyone who is paying attention knows that America is on the verge of collapse. Our money is worthless with the best estimates being that the buying power of a one dollar bill is equivalent to three or four cents of the 1910 dollar and this before the recent bailouts. Our educational system has lost ranking among industrialized countries, as mentioned our food has so little nutritional value we require supplements, our foreign policy has made us the most hated nation on earth and the list goes on.

America needs the church. America needs a body of people that are selfless, productive, honest and of moral virtue. These people must step up and make their lives matter. We must reenter the arenas we've abandoned and let no one force us out again. We must expose the lies that throwing money at problems is a self-serving motive with no hope of positive results. We must insist on the reduction of government power and reestablish the God given rights our country previously recognized.

The new world order always follows established patterns of conduct. When a movement is started they will try to stifle it. If they cannot stifle it they will seek to discredit it. If they cannot discredit it they will move to gain control of it. If they are unsuccessful of gaining control they will start their own movement, which will be financed and promoted with all of their substantial assets. They will use churches and false prophets to achieve their means. They will seduce and misdirect leadership at all levels. We must develop a Godly resolve to stand for righteousness. We must develop respect for Christian leaders based on what they do for Jesus and no more simply because they are on television or promoted by the major media. If we argue amongst ourselves it must be an argument about how to get more done, not on whether we should be active in promoting a Godly society.

The most frequent argument I have heard on this last point is the subject of Bible prophecy. Many believe that Jesus may return any second and therefore there is no need to concern ourselves with this world. If these people truly believed what they say they would be out evangelizing ferociously. Few of them do this at all. One of the largest debates in the church deals with whether or not we should expect a "pre-tribulation rapture." This one theological teaching has done more to neutralize the church than any other. The only teaching that compares in its degree of neutralizing people is the teaching of "God is in control" so all effort is futile.

Many who consider themselves experts at Bible prophecy are clueless about the agenda of the new world order. The new world order promoters are not stupid and know they must take prophecy into consideration if they are to deceive the church.

Voltaire, who was committed to destroying the church, and his associate D'Alembert had made efforts to start a nation of Israel and rebuild Solomon's Temple as far back as 1763[15] and their sole purpose was to deceive Christians.

How easily our founding fathers could have adopted the thinking of today. They read the same Bible we do. With Great Britain ruling half the globe they could have reasoned that nation would be the one world end time government. This would lead to the conclusion that the antichrist would ascend through the office of King of England. They didn't jump to conclusion and assume they had prophecy understood correctly based on current events. They stood for righteousness and opposed evil in their time, as we should in ours.

Our current era is not Satan's first attempt to build a worldwide government. History records many attempts that he has made to achieve his goals. The difference is that in times past Godly people opposed evil. Now we embrace it with some misguided belief that it is evidence of the soon return of Jesus. I too believe the return of Christ is near but if the church doesn't get active now and Christ doesn't return for several more years, these will be horrific years for all of us. We should keep in mind that the Bible does not authorize us to stand idle and let evil prosper based on our assumptions of prophecy.

God's will is not made known by the ease of the task at hand. We have much work to do because we have let the problems fester and we have given Satan enormous footholds in our society. It is a reasonable question to ask how important the rapture teaching is to God when so little space is given to it in scripture. We're not called to be so heavenly minded that we're no earthly good. We have responsibilities to our fellow man while we have opportunity to serve here on this earth.

God explains why He gave prophecy in Isaiah 46:9-10: "… I am God and there is none like me, declaring the end from the beginning … saying my counsel shall stand …" Isaiah 45 and 46 are worth studying in their entirety but the point here is that God makes plain He gave prophecy to prove that He is God. No other religion has a God that can tell the end from the beginning, only Christianity. His stated purpose for telling us the future is to prove we can trust Him because His counsel will stand. His purpose was not so that Christians would take these verses as a license to stand idle and let evil prosper on the earth.

As the spiritual decay increases in our nation we see more people openly and enthusiastically embrace immorality and government policies that are beneath the dignity of a Godly people. We can recognize that not many years ago self-respecting non-Christians would have shunned the conduct of many Christians of today. One example to prove this argument is the way many Christians accept immoral behavior on the part of church leaders as well as political leaders. We cannot hold the standard for society if we are tolerant of ungodly behavior among our church leadership and we have a duty to hold the standard among political leaders as well regardless of party.

It is by design that Christians have been neutralized from being active in the world we live in. Once our influence and we have been removed there is no longer a struggle for control. There is simply the enemy advancing at as rapid a pace as he can accomplish while maintaining his covert posture. Remember, even non-Christians will oppose this satanic new world order if they truly understand the horrific implications so all of his efforts must be disguised.

It is simply good judgment to prepare for the future but what point is found in preparing for a future of ungodly violence, fraud, deception, hunger, disease and hopelessness? America needs Christians to be active participants in society and determining society's future. Thank God we live in a country where we can fight immoral, carnal and ungodly leadership. Thank God we live in a country where we can fight these battles with political involvement. We are a blessed people.

The sad situation is, however, that we are not fighting these problems and we are not fighting to make or keep a Godly society. The new world order has neutralized the actions of the church by replacing these actions with government programs which has, in the mind of many people, called into question why we even need a church. In losing this purpose we have lost credibility. With no appreciable purpose and no credibility we have lost influence. Politics is the art of influencing government policy. By convincing Christians to stay out of politics we are kept from organizing and taking decisive action. Our actions are neutralized by policies of government to do our charitable work with no accountability.

With Christians out of the picture government is free to satisfy the basic physical needs of society, which affords them a substantial amount of acceptance from the public. People are not likely to protest a government that is housing them, providing meals and educating their children, even if it does occasionally do something they find alarming. Since the public has become accepting of new and expansive federal laws the government is free to create a few laws that are self-serving and strategically purposed. With no alarm sounded in the church and no reliable media to warn the people we can only hope for an occasional "whistle blower" which is typically neutralized easily.

Leaders of the church have, willingly or not, joined the chorus promoted by the new world order when they claim Christians shouldn't be involved in politics. The message is "let the ungodly be in charge of your future". Recognizing the bluntness of this statement and the reality with which the church has embraced it, it is obvious that the church has been neutralized before they would accept such a foolish notion as letting the unrighteous be in charge. There is no way to interpret this mindset except that it allows evil to prosper unopposed.

As we choose to stay out of politics we choose to tolerate immorality. We choose to tolerate leadership that cannot and does not lead. We choose to tolerate attacks on the sanctity of the home. The most significant aspect of this is that the church is no longer sounding the alarm to warn people of Satan's counterfeit system. Our society no longer seeks God as the solution to problems since we've been taught a government program solves all problems. Then we don't hold the programs or the politicians accountable to achieve their stated purpose. All the while government keeps growing in power and becomes less accountable to the people.

We tolerate the expansion of power and do not consider what politicians have in mind with what they have gained. We do not know history so we are grievously unaware of the dangers consistent with an all powerful central government. Many dangerous programs have been arranged, authorized and established but not yet implemented so as to cause undo alarm among the public. Like a skilled chess player, pieces are arranged for future use and when the time comes to strike powers and mechanisms are in place to stifle all opposition.

Being salt and light was not supposed to be a vacation. You cannot preserve a society and offer Godly leadership to a society if you are not involved with society. Only salt and light can secure Godly leadership.

We will shortly move on to lie number two but first let's take a closer look at Satan's work to control the church by infiltration. It was leadership from within the church that did the most labor in convincing Christians to sit idle.

THE CHURCH INFILTRATED

Acts 20:29: I know that after my departing shall grievous
wolves enter in among you, not sparing the flock"

As stated before, the unjust profits of the new world order have afforded them incredible opportunities to invest money. We need to be aware that they have invested substantial sums of money into the church. They have had a variety of reasons for doing this but the obvious and primary reason was to gain control. This is not something recent but has been part of their strategy for quite some time. This chapter can be but a brief accounting but it is vital for Christians to understand how we were deceived.

While we have been led to believe that circumstances were taking place because they were God's will, the fact is that the vast majority of circumstances were taking place by the design of the satanic new world order. Christians did not oppose these circumstances because those they had come to respect as leaders in the church had embraced these new concepts. Other ideas spread rapidly, only because they were encouraged, not because they were scriptural. In reality these concepts were the agenda of the new world order.

There is no point in trying to determine when infiltration of the church began. We read examples in The New Testament of those who hoped to take charge of the church, even Jesus' ministry, for their own benefit. Our focus here is more directed toward those who have had substantial success in infiltrating the church and misdirecting it to idleness, confusion, false doctrine, and misguided service.

As mentioned previously, Voltaire was aware that he must make provision for those who were fully committed to Christ. To go head to head with them would spell certain disaster and expose his agenda. Even prior to Voltaire there is evidence that many who supported Martin Luther had questionable motives. Some supported him because they sought freedom to serve Christ beyond what The Catholic Church permitted but others desired to weaken the church and they saw Luther as an opportunity to divide the church and loosen it's grip. For the purpose of brevity we must look at a more modern chain of events.

Christians that hold The Bible as the "inspired word of God" will have enormous disagreement with an organization called "The World Council of Churches" This very socialist leaning organization came into being from a series of conferences that were held.

"Between 1890 and 1899 to promote the idea of state and local federations of churches. During a meeting at the Union Theological Seminary in 1894 the suggestion was made to create a "Federate Council of the Churches of New York City." This Federation passed a resolution in 1900 calling for the formation of a "National Federation of Churches."

Next they organized a National Federation of Churches in Philadelphia, which met in 1901. During preparation for this event a letter was prepared and sent to the leaders of the larger churches in the nation encouraging federation. The letter was signed by each member of the federation's committee. These signers were well known liberals in the field of religion and not committed to Biblical truths or traditions.

They had no authority to represent any church but they did have money. Money to print and distribute literature (staggering amounts of literature), rent halls and conference space, hotel and travel expenses but most important of all, attract notable speakers. By the time of their organizational meeting in Philadelphia several local federations that had been built (with financial help) attended in sufficient numbers. This created credibility, which was promoted by friends in the newspaper business that falsely create the impression of overwhelming approval to this meeting and its agenda among the greater church membership.

Well-informed clergymen knew that those who were promoting this federation would not be interested in promoting the cause of Christ. These were shut out of any major newspaper exposure and ignored. The Federal Council of Churches was formally announced in 1908, however the Council had actually existed in New York City since 1905. Among the resolutions passed in 1908 were the formal support of a The National Education Association, support for an International Court of Arbitral Justice, opposition to The United States increasing its armaments and promotion of treaties of arbitration".[16]

Those who have accepted the teaching that Christians should not be involved in politics will look at this list and have no doubt that this Federal Council of Churches was founded with the full intent of being involved in politics. There can be no doubt, either, that those who created this organization and were in full control of its agenda had every intension of using all available political influence toward big government social programs. For the success of their agenda they needed to be recognized as the spokesmen for all Christians across the country.

All of this organizing did not come cheap. Nor did this concept of using churches to promote a social gospel through big government programs originate in 1890. Wherever organizations are found promoting the cause of big government, the name Rockefeller is sure to be found high and frequently on the list of donors. Finding it amidst movements to merge denominations and spread a social gospel is to be expected and we can note the family has spent vast sums toward this end.

We can consider the amount of money that was necessary to successfully launch this organization and immediately recognize it didn't come from the offering plate at a local church. When we examine the biographies of those who have long promoted strong intrusive government for their own benefit we regularly read their biographers bragging of their generosity directly to The World Council of Churches or to foundations who then support The WCC. When reading The WCC's list of donors we see "The Moravian Church in South Africa", "Province of the Anglican Church of Rwanda" and many more that we can suspect donate little! Only the smaller amounts of funding came from their member churches.[17]

The point here is that the pressure they brought to bear on elected leaders was illegitimate as even though they claimed to represent all Christians and the larger Christian denominations of America they did not. Over the years their agenda has called for approval of The League of Nations Treaty, recognition of Soviet Russia, Rights of illegal aliens, cancellation of foreign debt and basically promoting the Socialist agenda down the line.

Nor was The WCC the single effort to obtain control and influence of America's churches. Among other less successful groups there were "The World Alliance for Promoting International Friendship Through The Churches" and John D. Rockefeller Jr.'s "Interchurch World Movement" of which he said

> "I know of no better insurance ... for the safety of ... investments ... than this movement affords..."[18]

Then too there was Andrew Carnegie's "Church Peace Union" which he funded in 1914 after some disillusionment that his "Endowment for International Peace" would never function as envisioned. Carnegie, it will be remembered, denied the basic tenants of Christian beliefs and is much heralded for his book "The Gospel of Wealth". The names of the trustees of the "Church Peace Union" are the familiar names that are constantly encountered when one investigates the abandonment of Biblical Christianity in favor of this social gospel. The first effort of Carnegie's new creation was to draft

> "Two peace and disarmament resolutions which were sent to each sovereign, president, prime minister, minister of foreign relations, president of legislatures and other high officials of the world powers and to

the clergy of Germany, Great Britain and the United States".[19]

All of these organizations promoted the idea of a social gospel achieved through massive government intervention and even before they had achieved notable success in The United States they began efforts in other countries.

In the previous chapter I created a shortlist of activities that I believe the church should take an interest in and Christians should regard as their responsibility. After reading about the agenda of The World Council of Churches you must find my list petty as compared to what they have been busy working on.

There is an obvious point here; they are absolutely committed to the primary point of this book, they do not want Christians involved in politics. Let me clarify the point that The World Council of Churches by any name is not a Christian organization. Satan's servants who were promoting the new world order worked to get Bible believing Christians out of politics so that they could move in.

Many of the primary promoters and donors to create The Council have extensive and verified communist affiliations or shared beliefs. A primary provision of communism is atheism. No Christian would desire to promote communism and no communist would desire to promote true Christianity. These activities are not Christian activities and their positions on the issues are not Biblical positions. They are the activities and agenda of the new world order.

Their dual purpose was to neutralize true Christians from having an influence on society and use the vehicle of the church to promote their communist, atheist agenda through the medium of the church just as Alice Bailey foretold in the 1920's. When Mrs. Bailey wrote these words she was not being prophetic or overconfident. She knew precisely how her satanic associates were implementing their agenda. Satan and his minions had already made substantial advancement into infiltrating the church and were well on their way of accomplishing their goal. Only an awakened church and Christian commitment could stop them and they didn't worry about that.

"As far back as 1883 John D. Rockefeller used missionaries to gather information that would benefit him financially, first in the western United States, then South America and across the globe. In the 1880's Rockefeller used missionaries to the various Native American Tribes to inform him of uprisings that would threaten his mining operations.

As this proved successful further efforts were made to cultivate relationships between the family's business enterprises and various denominations. Frederick Gates, the son of a Baptist minister worked with a few associates to convince John D. into funding The University of Chicago as a seminary in the west. John D. had no interest in a seminary that taught Biblical truths but did fund this University in 1887 "for influencing the religious development of the new states being added to the Union".[20]

That is, influence them for his advantage. For those that dare read between the lines, this would be to teach John D's views of religious development.

"Gates was recruited to head Rockefeller philanthropy. By 1924 Pastor John Stratton who served as a leader of the Baptist Bible Union and Pastor of Manhattan's Calvary Baptist Church said, "Rockefeller money is the greatest curse that rests upon the Baptist denomination. Through the Infidel University of Chicago and the unbelieving Union Theological Seminary of this city, it is doing more to blight us and blast us than all other forces combined".[21]

Many men of this era that history defines as "captains of industry" were faithful to one denomination or another and most of them were avid about tithing. Men such as John Wanamaker of Philadelphia department store fame was a devout Presbyterian, Swifts of the meat packing business were Methodists, Armour who were also in the meat packing business supported Dwight Moody and even the infamous Jay Cooke was an Episcopalian.[22] This kind of philanthropy buys a lot of devotion among church leaders who have a stronger desire to build elaborate buildings and head great ministries than their desire to serve God but any Bible believing Christian in the pew can tell when the church changes direction.

The term new world order was not in common usage at that time but there were many laymen and many committed leaders who knew the business practices of these philanthropists and were determined to hold fast to Biblical truths. Many humble pastors bravely stood in their pulpits and renounced and exposed the evil they witnessed taking over the churches. The way John D Rockefeller had built Standard oil, the way Andrew Carnegie had build U.S. Steel as well as the business and labor exploitation practices of the others was well known. They were openly accused of trying to take over the church the way they had taken over various industries. These sermons drew enough attention to make life unpleasant and embarrassing, for the Rockefellers mainly, but others were named occasionally.

Even then these tycoons employed strategies, which would ultimately become the standard method of operation for the new world order. Their first efforts were to buy loyalty or at least silence. When this failed they tried discrediting their adversaries. As they moved their selected speakers into the more influential positions they used what media they controlled at the time in attacking the fundamentalist preachers for their lack of formal knowledge, old-fashioned ideas and referred to them as "extremist radicals". All the while they were assuring the public that their chosen people were indeed devout men of God.

Then came the event history records as "The Scopes Trial". Many people may yet be unaware that this entire circus was created by The ACLU in a blatant attempt to use the courtroom as a forum to attack Christian beliefs. The ACLU was founded in 1920 with a political agenda most people would agree to be far to the left. Thinking it would be a comical way to stimulate local business, the town of Dayton Tennessee accepted the ACLU's challenge.[23]

With all of the money Rockefeller and his associates were putting towards creating the fallacy that fundamentalist Christian beliefs are ignorant and irrational the publicity generated by this trial sealed the deal. Many zealous pastors felt they had to tone down their attacks on this movement against Biblical Christianity since the public was overwhelmed with information about the new, enlightened Christianity, which we know today as the "social gospel". At the same time all of this was happening efforts were made to secure teachers in America's seminaries that firmly believed in the new social gospel.

This is a brief view into the efforts of a small group of people to remove Biblical beliefs from our churches and remove Bible believing Christians from politics. A similar story can be told of their efforts to control other arenas of influence. Outlaws do not create great nations or civilizations; men who understand the Godly principles of civilization build them. I can argue that the Bible is the best source to outline how a civilization should be built but we have the benefit of history and all history now recognizes certain absolutes for the benefit of a strong civilization. They center on a strong family and a strong moral culture. America has abandoned these strengths over the last fifty years and a short reflection reveals we are suffering many ill effects for it.

This is why the church must be salt and light. Indeed this is why Jesus gave this message of salt and light to the church. Satan has his own agenda and no part of it is concerned with the betterment of civilization. The new world order is an illusion. One with teeth, to be sure, but an illusion never the less. The new world order promises all things to all people but they have no intention of fulfilling these promises. It is power Satan is after and it is power his minions are after.

They do not covet civilization; they covet chaos. They do not covet peace; they thrive on war and senseless bloodshed. They do not covet benevolence; they are indifferent to human needs and suffering. They do not covet Godliness; they are evil. Christians had to be removed from the scene to make room for this new world order church, a church which itself is an illusion. This is a church that truly has no concern for the spiritual needs of a lost world or truly has no concern for people and their suffering. A church that is an illusion because Jesus Christ is nowhere to be found in it and neither is He welcome.

Yes, they use his name to perpetuate the illusion and for the good will associated with it but they have done much to destroy that good will and this too suits them just fine. Many parts of the world are blind to the true love of Jesus and they're not interested because the "so-called" Christians they've been exposed to have no admirable qualities including compassion.

If God were in control the way this teaching is exaggerated in the church today He would have no need that His church be salt and light. We would not be commanded to take the actions that are associated with these verses. Today the church is not in a position to be salt and light because we have been immersed in deception so deeply and for so long we have lost the ability to discern truth and offer leadership. This is a situation that we can change.

When has salt lost its savor? When has light been placed under a basket? When it no longer seeks to serve God and fight evil. When the only objective of a church is to "wait out the clock" and dismiss all concern for mankind it has lost its savor. This is not a Godly attitude. God would end all of this today unless there is some objective yet to be gained. There is. There are millions of souls on this planet that God loves and desires to come to a saving knowledge of Jesus Christ before the time of judgment begins. These will only have that opportunity if we who have that knowledge spread the gospel. Satan and his new world order are heavily involved in stopping us by any means necessary.

We are in a race, not over time but over the flow of information. We must get the truth to the people that Satan's promises are all lies and the end thereof is death. History shows that ignoring Satan has been the biggest mistake Christians have made. We live in a land abundant with freedom and we have the freedom to battle Satan where he has achieved his greatest success, the arena of politics. Only salt and light will bring Godly government but it will be a fight, a fight that can only take place when the church arises to do battle and take back what Satan has taken from us.

Paul warns us in Acts 20:29 that false leaders will arise from within the church. He warned us to be on guard. He did not admonish us to follow their leadership simply because they had a position of authority. We have a duty as Christians and patriots. Anyone who tells us to ignore this duty has exceeded their authority.

Esther 4:14 says " if thou altogether holdest thy peace at this time then shall their enlargement and deliverance arise to the Jews from another place … who knoweth whether thou art come to the kingdom for such a time as this". The fact is, with Satan on the loose it is always "such a time as this". When Satan desires to kill it is "such a time" for righteous people to stand up and stop the killing. When Satan desires to destroy families and the sanctity of marriage it is "such a time" for righteous people to stand up and demand that God's law be revered over man's law and over the desires of any special interest group.

When Satan and his forces seek to enslave mankind with lies, treacheries and a parade of illusions promoting the idea that a utopia can be had without God it is time for righteous people to stand up and "cast down imaginations and every high thing that exalteth itself against the knowledge of God", 2nd Corinthians 10:5. At no point is this commandment more significant than when we see and hear Satan raising vain imaginations that God is the problem and his new world order is the solution. Ironically, this vital verse is one that Satan has twisted and uses to keep Christians out of politics so we will address it in detail in a later chapter. The point here is that mankind will suffer the illusion of the vain imagination Satan has set before them if Christians don't expose the lies.

These "captains of industry" were committed to changing the thinking of the American public in their time and they have likeminded laborers currently working towards the same goal. While they focused a great deal of time and money on the church they also spent fortunes influencing the direction of public education. Their goal was to create standardized education with a heavy emphasis on social sciences. This would be their strategy to influence future generations and the impact on these students of these social sciences would be predictable.

Social Science is defined as "a branch of science that deals with the institutions and functioning of human society and with the interpersonal relationships of individuals". If you spend twelve to sixteen years in government indoctrination centers learning that government has the role, responsibility and authority to oversee all relationships and organizations, you naturally assume that includes the church and the family.

That the church was a strong influence upon previous generations that Satan's servants must dominate is evident from their efforts. This was necessary to cement the teachings of public education.

Had students gone to government schools and been instructed one way and then to church on Sunday and instructed a different way would have let to unmanageable conflict. The churches had to be remade so as to reaffirm what the social scientists taught.

This would serve the equally important objectives of putting the religious passions of the public to work achieving Satan's goals and stop the church from teaching and pursuing the Godly principles needed to perpetuate society. This, in its turn, would bring forth the chaos that would ultimately demand the force of government to bring about resolution and the public would welcome it.

In July of 1953 The U.S. House Committee on Un-American Activity investigated the National Council of Churches. Reliable witnesses gave testimony that Communist leaders in Moscow had infiltrated American religious institutions including the Christian churches. The stated objectives were to change the thinking of the clerics away from spiritual matters to material ones. Dr. Harry F. Ward was named as the communist's chief architect to infiltrate and subvert the church. Mr. Ward has a long history of involvement with The Federal Council of Churches as well as numerous communist organizations. He is known for not taking the Bible literally or believing in a personal relationship with Jesus Christ.

Testimony was also given at the House Committee sessions regarding plans to "revise" The Bible according to "contemporary scholarship". Those involved in these efforts were known to have no knowledge of Hebrew or Greek.[24] They did, however, have extensive knowledge regarding the agenda of the new world order.

Mr. Ward is the author of such books as "The Social Creed of The Churches" in 1914 and "The Gospel for a Working World" in 1918. Mr. Ward is credited with drafting the official creed of the Council. Throughout these years his writings (books, magazine and newspaper articles, pamphlets, speeches) did not deviate from the public rhetoric of the communist party and focused largely on promoting labor agitation. He had created some controversy for The Council with his public endorsement of Bolshevism. In years 1924 and 1929 Mr. Ward traveled to Moscow to meet with Soviet Premier Stalin to discuss the use of churches for the benefit of the communist agenda. In 1925 he traveled to China to speak on the merits of communism there. A man believed to be Mr. Ward's mentor, Dr. Rauschenbusch had been active in socializing the church for decades and had links to the infamous "Fabian Socialist Society" of London.[25]

This would link The Federal Council of Churches to The Fabian Society whose strategy is to infiltrate and patiently take over governments from within. This would also reveal much about the intentions and strategies of The Federal Council of Churches. In 1914 The Fabian Society organized an "International Fellowship of Reconciliation" to protest the war. A year later Mr. Ward helped organize a branch of this organization in The United States, which further links him, The Federal Council of Churches and The Fabian Socialist Society.[26]

A point to be stressed here is, while some conclusive evidence exists that communists labored to infiltrate the church in America additional evidence is equally conclusive that those who appointed themselves to be the ruling elite of our planet regarded communism as an opportunity much like they viewed the church. Several sources, such as "Origin and History of The Federal Council of Churches of Christ in America" by Elias Sanford written in 1916 documents a parade of efforts to socialize the churches and unite them under controlled leadership going back into the early 19th century, predating any serious communist activity. Presumably other sources could take the movement back to earlier history.

It was not the concept or ambition that was new with The Federal Council of Churches in 1908, it was the available funding. This funding did not come from zealots promoting the cause of Christ. It came from greedy arrogant men whose accomplishments deceived them to believe they had a right to rule other men and whose ambitions singularly determined this to be their life's sole purpose. To rule they first needed to control arenas of influence and to control these arenas they first needed to remove those who, for whatever reason, had influence in these arenas.

People are not suffering from this illusion because God wills it or preordained it. They suffer because we sit idle. We hold our tongue and Satan has many voices and they go unchallenged. We have served Satan long enough. We have served him with our silence, confusion and idleness. We cannot indulge our own illusions any longer. We must stand up, stand together and serve God.

Those sold out to Satan and his new world order knew politics to be what it is, an effective non-violent way to influence those whom we entrust with the authority of government. Knowing this, they have used the political process to make great strides in bringing forth the government their master desires with no opposition from Christians. Proverbs 23:7 says, "As he thinketh in his heart so is he". All they had to do was to get us to think that politics was not for Christians and we quietly left everything up to them. At the same time they gave us something to think about – that we will soon be raptured out of here, and we focused on this. If we choose, we could also focus on the "social gospel" to keep us busy.

We should also keep in mind that those sold out to Satan and his new world order knows the passion Christians have for prophecy. Periodically, in this study, we touch on prophecy and we need to touch on it here. Because Christians are so uninformed politically most fail to conceive how the new world order manipulates prophecy, staging supposed prophetic events and masquerading their own as devout servants of the Lord, to deceive Christians.

The new world order crowd knows The Bible foretells of "a new Jerusalem" and they are well along on their "New Jerusalem Covenant Project". Briefly, this is a plan to open a portion of Jerusalem (not the temple mount) for Moslems, Christians and Jews to worship together. The idea has been put forth that since the Pope is head of the body of believers most united in their beliefs, management of this area would be best left to the Catholic Church. Self serving as this sounds, it certainly puts the Pope in a position to be recognized as a spiritual leader by adherents to all three major religions and Hindu and Buddhist teachings include reverence of other religions. It is now common to see the Pope welcomed into Moslem countries and heralded as a great spiritual leader.

The new Jerusalem Covenant Project will sound ridiculous to those unfamiliar with the new world order. They will base this assumption on the propaganda they have been taught regarding animosity between Moslems and Jews. They fail to understand the influence the new world order already has over leadership in the

Islamic and Jewish communities. A good example would be 9-11. After the attacks our evening news carried numerous stories about the celebrations in the Islamic countries. Word went out from Yassir Arafat to stop and these celebrations stopped immediately.

A worthwhile historical study will prove that the events bringing forth World War I and II were the manipulations of persons and organizations affiliated with this new world order agenda. It stands to reason then, that a third World War will be brought forth the same way and Christians with no knowledge of politics or current events will believe the propaganda. The Bible says, "When they shall say peace and safety, then sudden destruction cometh upon them" 1st Thessalonians 5:3. The specific context of "their saying peace and safety" isn't given but we are told to not be in darkness so this day will overtake us as a thief in the night.

Some conclude that they say peace and safety out of a sense of security believing they have ended war. This shows poor understanding of the new world order, as they have no part of their agenda to end war. War is a very necessary element to them. It is more likely that they say it to deceive and create a false sense of security among people of all nations, perhaps so they will disarm. If we can believe in a false peace, why can't we believe in a false war? Especially since we have a dozen false wars going on right now!

The point here is that, whatever their reason, it will be affirmed by leaders of Satan's false religious system. They will have events staged exactly as Jesus warned us in Matthew 24:24, "there shall arise false Christs and false prophets and shall shew great signs and wonders insomuch that, if it were possible they shall deceive the very elect". How many of the very elect today are deceived by evangelists claiming fantastic powers to heal or pray you into prosperity, for a donation as well as "self help" gurus masquerading as ministers of the gospel. We must consider that the most dangerous among all of these are those who tell us to sit idle and embrace satanic government.

A simple "you tube" search will expose strange things going on today in many churches, things that have roots in occult practices. We have abandoned disciple ship as a strategy and grown bored with teaching as a practice. We have sought and enjoyed entertainment to such an extent that it is now difficult to find new and interesting amusements to draw us into church. Now it has become necessary to pursue strange new things in order for church attendees to feel some rush of excitement or thrill which is really what they came to church to experience.

God knows there is a deceiver and he will lead men to a belief that they can serve God any way they choose. Numbers 3: 4 "Nadab and Abihu died before the Lord when they offered strange fire …", 1st Samuel 6:19 "because they had looked into the Ark of the Lord even He smote of the people fifty thousand and threescore and ten men …" and 1st Chronicles 15:13 "because we did it not at the first, the Lord our God made a breach upon us, for that we sought him not after the due order", all document people put to death for thinking God's ordinances didn't matter and they could serve Him any way of their own choosing.

God did not give these rules to burden or hinder. God's rules are astonishingly easy. Still, if there is no penalty for serving God falsely, how can we ever be certain we serve Him correctly? If there is no certainty that we serve God correctly how can we even know with certainty that we serve the one true God? God gave his word so we could know conclusively that we have found relationship with the one true God. So long as we hold fast to His word the deceiver can't lead us into his lies and His word is absolutely clear that there are consequences to error. If we are not taught His word when we attend a local church and if we make no effort for personal study, then how shall we be safe from the deceiver?

Church leadership would, theoretically and figuratively, stand at the church door and bar Satan and his minions access since they would be knowledgeable and on alert. We do not see this happening in the church today. Rather, we have seen certain "celebrity evangelists" elevated in stature by the media and politicians who disarm the masses as they speak of tolerance and compassion for that which God has called evil. We have seen others elevated, perhaps while being ridiculed, for their supposed "miracle working power". As we watch on "Christian television" we are led to believe that they have such a fantastic manifestation of God's presence at their meetings that we begin to judge our local churches as if we're missing something or our pastor is less Godly than the celebrities.

We should be judging our local pastors to insure they are teaching us the true word of God and that they are ministering so as to make these truths applicable and understood by all members that all may grow in their understanding and relationship with Jesus Christ. Are they theological or theatrical and theoretical?

As these celebrity evangelists make way that evil be tolerated it becomes all the more difficult for local pastors to stand against them. In this manner the church has lost so many battles against evil that I have had to continue this chapter on "The Church Infiltrated" into a second chapter "Battles Abandoned". Battles that are made clear by the word of God but not confronted by the church today, as they once were, since we have been convinced these matters are now tolerable.

Setting this aside then for now, we must move on to the next deception that has made it easy for Satan to neutralize the church.

PART
THREE

CHRISTIANS
IN
POLITICS

CHRISTIANS AND POLITICS

Matthew 5:13-14: "Ye are the salt of the earth ... light of the world"

If my research is any indication, a tremendous number of Christians have a deep felt desire to get involved in politics. The question is being asked in all arenas and schools of thought, "Should Christians be involved in politics and to what extent"? Almost universally they are discouraged from doing so by church leadership. Yet when some movement is began by some patriotic Christian it is heavily supported by a scores of Christians. I'm referring to "Operation Rescue", "The Moral Majority" and "The Christian Coalition" just to name a few of the most popular movements.

Then there are churches that have an entire agenda that is quite political. These are churches that lean more to the left and support programs such as "Gay Rights", "Human Rights", "World Unity", etc.

This chapter will focus on Christians who attend Bible believing churches and why they are virtually always discouraged from getting involved. There are certain scriptures that are universally used to support this admonition to such an extent we no longer hear them applied in any other context, as if The Holy Spirit spoke them forth specifically to instruct Christians not to get involved in a political system that wouldn't be an option for most of them as it wouldn't be developed for nearly 1800 years! Equally important, we do not hear them quoted in context but merely stated like a platitude or bumper sticker.

Many who have the desire to get involved view politics as a natural opportunity to assure a more Godly society in addition to being a civic duty. It is necessary to examine why so many church leaders have adopted a position contrary to the desires of so many Christians and the scriptures they use to support their positions.

The church has been seduced into accepting many positions on a variety of issues that are contrary to God and most are adopted for the sake of expedience or lack of understanding. In this chapter I hope to prove that the reasons given against involvement are wrong and the reasons given for involvement are shallow and inadequate to addressing the truths and falsehoods that are common in this debate. I will attempt to prove that being involved in politics is very much a part of God's will and a Christian's responsibility.

One wonders where today's Christians think our current liberties came from. It's easy to take our freedoms for granted if you don't know your history and what price was paid by previous generations for the liberty we enjoy today. No one should believe that these great blessings were bestowed by non-Christian politicians. Nor can it be argued that God directly bestowed this great blessing of freedom. If God bestowed blessings on The United States alone, that would be showing preference and The Bible makes it clear that God is no respecter of persons, Romans 2:11. This is to say His blessings are equally available to all peoples of all nations who diligently seek Him.

Many believe we are losing our freedoms because God is judging America. They simply refuse to connect the facts that as Christians increasingly withdraw from the process, or are increasingly ineffective in the process, we are getting the government that non-Christians desire. This is another example of reaping what you sow.

Still, the real question is what does scripture say? On this topic, as much as any other, Christians have five or six scriptures that have come to be their favorites. These are quoted to substantiate the position of those discouraging others from participate in politics but always quoted as stand alone verses and never studied to clarify if they are being applied accurately and in context.

Here, as with all scripture, it is vital to keep the context and be mindful of the historical application of the scriptures. We forget that politics as we know it was not an option for most of those in The Old or New Testaments. It was only an option for a handful of people who were next to the king and scripture records many occasions where

Godly people next to the king were used by God to influence him and avoid judgment on the nation.

Let me begin this chapter by saying that this question of whether Christians should be involved in politics that we've wrestled with the last few decades is only a question because they got uninvolved in the few decades preceding that! A study of American history reveals an enormous involvement of the church in politics. The one indisputable reason this nation had Godly government for so long is because of the involvement of Christians. This will be addressed in much more detail in the chapter on "Christian History in America" and other chapters as well.

This chapter is dedicated to what I have termed "lie number two that has neutralized the church" which is the argument that Christians should not be involved in politics. This chapter will deal with the scriptures used to support this position.

First, I must address the argument that for all of our increased involvement in the last few decades nothing has been accomplished which is said because the major moral issues of our day remain unchanged. This is true, however, losing a war does not render the cause unjust. Rather than moving directly to surrender we should examine why we are losing. We are losing because we no longer understand how the enemy operates. We are simply "outsmarted" and "out maneuvered". We lose because we are simply unprepared to do battle with the enemy due to his superior organizational structure and financial recourses. We lose because our leadership has failed to properly assess the enemy, fight the important battles and count the cost of defeat. We lose because our leadership has encouraged us to surrender. We lose because winning is no longer important to us. We no longer consider active patriotism a Christian duty.

Those that are quick to make this argument that politics is futile are frequently the same ones who feel "we will bring about a Godly society by leading more people to Christ" and they come back to the point that our responsibility is to spread the gospel. There is no question that a Christian's primary responsibility is to spread the gospel but this is not our only responsibility.

Christians do many things like having a job and supporting a family and they do not view these responsibilities as a threat to their responsibility to spread the gospel. So too should we spread the gospel as we're being good citizens. We should not have to choose one or the other and previous generations understood this. They did all that was required. Voting is frequently the extent of a modern Christian's involvement in politics and I'm not encouraging people to stop voting, plus I certainly don't want to encourage anyone against spreading the gospel. My point is that civic responsibilities are far greater than just voting and voting alone will not bring about Godly government.

Indeed, those who argue that political involvement is futile and that the church needs to focus on sharing the gospel exclusively to bring about a more Godly society need to consider this point; leading people to Christ, while eternally important, has not proven to have a positive impact on society either. Support for the argument that Christians only need to spread the gospel emanates from the point that a Christian is certainly a better, more law abiding citizen than a non-Christian and will, presumably, vote for more law abiding candidates.

I do not dispute this as a basic argument but it ignores the fact that we face a satanic plan that is very strategic, well organized and determined to destroy everything we hold sacred. Part of this plan includes deceiving Christians into believing a candidate is a Christian when he is not. Every Christian has bought into this by supporting a professed Christian in an election only to see a parade of disappointments.

Neither can we afford to believe that Satan's people will be voted out of power. They're not stupid and have planned strategies to eliminate that threat. How formidable would Satan be if accomplishing his goals hinged on winning an election? To succeed politically we must understand the enemy and his tactics.

We must be prepared to meet and overcome him organizationally. Please read that again. We are involved and we're losing. It is not a question of whether we should be involved in politics because as long as we live in this country, under our current system, we are involved. We simply fail to do our duty strategically.

Leading people to Christ is of paramount importance in terms of their personal salvation but this will be no threat to Satan's agenda unless these new converts are educated about Satan's agenda by someone familiar with it. There are matters to be learned and understood before you become a better citizen. You do not automatically know principles of good government, principles in sound economic policy and history simply because you accept Christ. If you didn't know how to repair a car before you were saved you still had to learn after you were saved. It is the same with matters of civics and economics. It is also helpful to understand the enemy, which means understanding his agenda, goals and how he operates.

Our founding fathers gave us a "participatory system" of government. To participate effectively we need understanding. Christians can be involved and do their part to influence our leaders and stand firm for Godly government or stand idle as corruption reigns.

There is one truth that the church needs to become aware of; Satan is using the political process to build his new world order and to be involved in politics without knowing this, in addition to his tactics and strategies, leaves us unprepared for the battle. It is Christians who have the authority in Christ and the responsibility to fight evil and expose Satan so here we have a legitimate question, do you want to fight Satan as the Bible commands? We can agree that spreading the gospel is priority one but scripture commands us to resist Satan and expose evil and it does not restrict us to non-political matters. Resist means "to withstand the force or effect of" and "to exert oneself to counteract or defeat in opposition".

Far too many Christians argue that Satan battles in the spiritual realm and ignore what he's doing in the physical world. The Bible makes it clear that Satan desires a one-world government and we happen to live in the one world he wants. Many Christians believe very devout Godly men founded our nation. If we believe this, then we acknowledge (and should be grateful) that in previous generations, Christians were involved in politics. If we appreciate what they did then we should emulate their work.

Government will inherently work to increase its own influence over the lives of men. This means it will inherently work to decrease God's influence over the lives of men. Christians have a duty to oppose this work. We're told political involvement is futile since we are a two party system and neither party changes our nation's direction when in power and both have much to be ashamed of. This argument is certainly valid but it is also part of the deception. We are not a two party system. Our system is open to as many parties as the people choose to have.

It is due to the success of the ungodly new world order that another party can't get support and this is also why both existing parties are so similar in their policies once elected. A great bumper sticker reads, "If America is a two party system, we need a good second party!" The only real difference is the extent to which each party has deceived the churches. This topic I will detail in the chapter on political parties but this is not a good reason to give up on the process. It simply means we need to pursue more successful solutions to the problem.

The dictionary defines politics as "shrewdly promoting a policy". We can agree that the policy of the church is spreading the gospel and having the word of God revered as a moral standard for society. This is no more than recognizing what churches used to call "the cultural mandate" which is the command Jesus gave that "ye are salt of the earth ... light of the world" in Matthew 5:13-14. Salt is a preservative and light is leadership shining toward the Godly path. If we are not to do these things politically, just where are we to do them? We can do nothing but tell ourselves we're "letting our light shine" by the way we live and act, as one option. This is a minimum contribution to the cause of Christ!

In our great nation we have the opportunity to do so much more and to whom much is given, much is required according to Luke 12:48. Voting alone does not overcome the threat. Compared to what Satan's forces are doing in the political arena getting more Christians to vote is like putting salt on dirt or light on a white wall. In spite of what we believe, this is having no impact and if the objective is to fight evil this token gesture is insufficient to accomplish the task at hand. Satan is using politics to promote his agenda and what could be more shrewd that to convince his enemy, the church, to surrender without a fight? We're under attack and those who are under attack do not have the luxury of choosing the battlefield.

Politics is the arena in which decisions are made and Satan is using it for his maximum advantage. It is irresponsible of us to ignore that. Another definition of politics is "the science of influencing government policy". It cannot be disputed that this is exactly what satanic forces are doing! With this definition we can see that God's people who had opportunity were involved in politics from the establishment of government.

Beginning in Exodus 5, this is a good description of what Moses was doing with Pharaoh. He was influencing him on behalf of the people and what God wanted to do in their life. 1st Samuel 14:33 relates the story of righteous men informing Saul of a sin of the people so that he could correct their action. Also in verse 45 the people interceded for Jonathan and saved his life. Samuel was constantly influencing Saul in the name of the Lord. These are all examples that fit this definition of politics but they are not taught this way in churches today.

Those that dispute this as a reasonable definition of politics choose to accept a very limited view of the duties of salt and light. Not only does this limited view fail to fully serve God but also it must be examined for scriptural accuracy. Our system of government wasn't known in Biblical times. The Old Testament was written first under patriarchal governments and later under a monarchy. The New Testament was written under a dictatorship.

Our system of government is far superior and should be appreciated, not abandoned simply because its opportunities are more recent than when scripture was written. Yet another definition of politics is "the system of perpetuating a system of government". If Christians don't get involved we are not perpetuating a Godly system but rather are failing future generations as Satan perpetuates his! We will not get Godly government from people who do not esteem God. If we believe government and freedoms were created by God then we should embrace these things and protect them for future generations.

So let's take a look at the scriptures that are commonly quoted to Christians who desire to be involved politically. I remind you of a quote from Pastor Jonathan Mayhew, a pastor who stood to be counted during America's War for Independence. He preached: "If all scripture is profitable for doctrine, reproof, correction and instruction in righteousness why are verses on civil government not examined and explained as well as the others?"

2nd Chronicles 7:14 is one I hear frequently, "If my people which are called by My name shall humble themselves and pray and seek my face and turn from their wicked ways; then will I hear from heaven and will forgive their sin and will heal their land" In context this is clearly dealing with Israel as a nation. To take it out of context and apply it to our country is to abandon the covenant we have with God and apply the covenant God had with Israel.

We have a superior covenant where we don't relate to God as a nation through priests, rituals and ceremonies. We can have an individual relationship with Him and can boldly approach the throne room of heaven through Christ as written in Hebrews 4:16. We, individually, can have a relationship with God that includes blessing, prosperity and avoid judgment. The way this verse is commonly applied is that God will only deal with us as a nation. This is the old covenant God had with Israel. We each can humble ourselves and seek God now. So the question becomes, "what are we willing to do, individually"? If we are not willing to work, we have no promise from God that He will provide food. If we are not willing to work for our freedom, we have no promise He will provide our freedom.

We read in Matthew 5:39 "… resist not evil…" which obviously requires study as it would seemingly contradict other passages. This is a scripture commanding us not to have petty fights between us. The parallel verses in Luke 6:20-38 list nothing but petty offenses. These passages are not referring to spiritual warfare with Satan but rather immature battles of the flesh. We have other scriptures telling us to fight and resist evil. This is not a contradiction; it's a question of application. We are to fight Satan and satanic evil; we are not to get offended and argumentative when others insult us over petty matters.

Another example of this misapplication of scripture is John 18:36 where Jesus said, "My kingdom is not of this world". Jesus went on to say "To this end was I born and for this cause came I into the world, that I should bear witness unto the truth." These verses are about the fulfillment of prophecy and the sacrificial death of the Messiah for the sins of the world. It is not logical to take these verses and apply them to political involvement. What Jesus is saying here is that He came into the world to die for the sins of mankind. Simply because there is a spiritual purpose here is not reason to give this passage a physical application. We live in a physical world and should, therefore, be mindful of making this world a better place through all reasonable efforts.

We should keep in mind that Jesus is "Lord of Lords", a spiritual title, and "King of Kings", a political title. He is both. To take a verse like John 18:36 and imply that Jesus has no concern about this world but only the next is improper application. We have to live, work and raise families in this world while we look forward to the next. There is nothing against the cause of Christ in attempting to make this world more Godly. We must apply the verses to their context.

We also see this misapplication in 2nd Corinthians 10:3-4 "For though we walk in the flesh, we do not war after the flesh (For the weapons of our warfare are not carnal but mighty through God to the pulling down of strong holds)" Just prior to this, in verse 2 Paul makes clear he is referring to those who accuse him, "think of us as if we walked according to the flesh." Are we to suppose some accused Paul of being involved in politics? If not then why do we suppose he suddenly began talking of politics in verse 3 and 4? If we read the context, Paul was responding to some who had taken issue with him, not concerning politics, but concerning his authority as an apostle (verses 8-10). It is not proper to pull verses 3 and 4 out of context this way and claim this has to do with political involvement.

If we read on we see Paul list the "weapons of our warfare" that are carnal, which he was referring to; "commend themselves, measure themselves by themselves, comparing themselves among themselves, are not wise, boast without measure" and Paul moves on in chapter 11:3 expressing concern over their (our) being deceived by Satan. This is all the same context as he goes on to list his credentials as an apostle. It has absolutely nothing to do with politics or our desire for Godly government. It's about pettiness, jealousy and slander and should be read and applied in context. To add politics to Paul's list of "warring after the flesh" is completely outside of the point he was making and contrary to the way he conducted himself when he had cause to stand up for his rights.

Ephesians 6:12 "For we wrestle not against flesh and blood but against principalities, against powers, against the rulers of the darkness of this world, against spiritual wickedness in high places." Far too many Christians are not wrestling against anything. We seldom realize this verse lists four things we are to have engaged in battle: principalities, powers, rulers of darkness of this world and spiritual wickedness in high places. Today we are taught that all warfare is spiritual warfare and this "we wrestle not against flesh and blood" is used as a proof text and specifically proof that we are not to be engaged in politics. If you accept this argument, then how are you engaging the enemy? I'm sure you're praying but if you've closed your mind to getting involved, what is prayer aside from you asking God to do something He may have asked you to do? Or perhaps you're praying that God will raise up someone to do something you're not willing to do? God works through people but once God's people pray they must be willing to take action.

Christians forget that we have three arenas of battle. Yes, we have spiritual warfare, second we have our own flesh and thirdly we have the world and its influences. This third arena of battle must be fought or surrendered just as the other two must. Our society is structured in such a way that political victory goes to whoever is most knowledgeable, organized and active in the political realm and they will have the greater overall influence. We should not leave this opportunity unused. There is no good reason why Christians should not take advantage of this system to do good works just as Satan's forces hope to do for evil. It is a battle to convince Godly people that they have been deceived into surrendering vast opportunities in politics. It is a battle we must fight with prayer, Bible study and action.

Ephesians 6:12 does indeed refer to spiritual warfare; however, we take those first eight words out of context and apply them to all warfare. Again, politics is singled out for special treatment. Imagine if we had an unruly child and instead of discipline we simply prayed about his disobedience. Imagine if we had a neighbor who was known to be a violent thief. We know who he is and what he's doing but we choose only to respond with prayer. Imagine if we had an elected leader who refused to abide by the limitations of his office and greatly abused the public trust for his own benefit at our expense. These are all examples of worldly influences, which, if left unabated, will negatively impact our quality of life.

In any of these cases prayer would be the best beginning but in scripture man is commanded to raise his children in the ways of the Lord and punish them when necessary. We are also given instructions on the treatment of criminals. In these cases we can refer to scripture and note that God does not tell us to pray for criminals to cease in their crimes and consider this effort as our sole duty. He has listed crimes and punishments and he expects men to exercise their authority and punish criminals and in our system this would include politicians who commit criminal acts. Indeed many of God's crimes and punishments have been thwarted by Satan's use of our political system while Christians have stood idle and let him.

Today we suffer enormous harm in our communities due to this neglect of God's word and our responsibilities. Our system of government isn't mentioned in scripture but that doesn't make it ungodly. If we refuse to take the obvious action needed and tolerate ungodly leadership and ungodly government policies we will suffer the consequences of our idleness. We, for whatever reason, tolerate the election and conduct of evil people in government but we pray for God to bless us with Godly leaders. This is a violation of spiritual law and God will not violate the law. If we want Godly leaders we should pray that God would raise some up but then it falls to us to support them and insure they get elected because Satan will surely be working to defeat them. For us to pray for Godly leaders while we're idle or supporting ungodly leaders is simply to ask God to violate the principle of reaping what we sow and bless us in spite of what we've sowed with our irresponsibility.

The point is often raised that after Israel possessed the land they still had scores of battles to fight. This doesn't mean they were not mindful of better things to come, nor does it mean they were always indifferent to God. Their largest victories were direct results of God being with them but God still expected them to field an army. In The New Testament we are somehow led to believe God is going to do it all Himself. Without God we will surely fail but what makes us think God will succeed without us? Obviously I would not disparage the power of God, I simply argue that God's plan for us is not to pray and ask Him to do everything.

A verse we commonly hear quoted is 2nd Timothy 2:4 "no man that warreth entangles himself with the affairs of this life; that he may please Him who has chosen him to be a soldier". Again, to argue that Paul was considering politics, as we know it, ignores the fact that politics, as we know it, wasn't an option for Paul. He lived under an emperor and could not possibly be talking about politics.

How can we be so quick to believe politics is the "affairs of this life" that Paul was referring to? If working so that my children will grow up in a country with a Godly government is an affair of this life, and thus to be avoided, why then would marriage or having children not be an affair of this life? Are we equally prohibited from starting a business or furthering our education? Clearly all of these things are "affairs of this life". It's always and only politics that is singled out as an "affair of this life" to be avoided. Under our system, if we refuse to use politics as a means of influencing our leaders we play right into the enemy's hands! If wanting my children to live in a country with a Godly, non-oppressive government is an affair of this life it seems to me we have a host of other passions to abandon first, like sports maybe?

Clearly we see this scripture applied with a double standard engineered exclusively to keep Christians out of politics and the church doesn't question it. We're not faulted for watching football or having a passion for golf. We focus on our careers and involve ourselves with building elaborate churches. All of this is fine but somebody has decided "politics" is "the affair of this life" to be avoided above all. No longer do we view politics as an investment in our future.

Then there are those who would argue "scripture is inspired by The Holy Spirit so even though Paul could not envision our system of government, The Holy Spirit could"! Sure, but this is exactly why we need to use scripture as a foundation.

We constantly hear (half of) 2nd Timothy 2:4 quoted as a stand-alone scripture. I dare say this is because Paul next references a "soldier", which was common for Paul to do, but Christians seldom think of themselves as soldiers in combat. Rather we want to be "stay at home prayer warriors" and not miss a meal or a football game while having full enjoyment of family and friends.

No one can doubt a soldier in combat wants to be singularly focused on a single mission but soldiers have other commitments aside from combat. If we leave this verse in context, we read in verse 5 that Paul references athletes and in verse 6 he references farmers. Linking verses 5 and 6 with 4 brings serious questions to modern interpretations of this passage.

Any reasonable person must (perhaps unhappily) admit that sports are an affair of this life and certainly no priority to God. Farming is simply a reasonable way to earn a living and since Paul worked as a tent maker we can conclude he was not encouraging anyone to quit working in order to spread the gospel.

The problem here is that we commonly interpret the word "entangle" to mean, "involve" which is an accurate definition. Additionally, however, this word can be defined as "complicate" or "confuse". If we use this definition Paul is simply saying don't confuse or complicate your life. Thus there is nothing wrong with holding secular employment, enjoying a sport or working to maintain a free society. Just keep your priorities straight and never miss an opportunity to share the gospel. We must keep our focus on God but there is nothing unscriptural about working to build a Godly society in which to raise our families.

This passage of scripture begins with Paul lamenting over some who "turned away" (all those in Asia) and encouraging Timothy in 4:2 to "focus on faithful men" in terms of training up disciples. When we read the entire passage in context we return to Paul's constant theme, not politics but the gospel of Jesus Christ.

Paul's reference in 2:5 regarding sports "if a man strive ... he is not crowned except he strive lawfully" is a point that those who teach another gospel will not be crowned. This scripture has no more to do with politics than it has to do with a Christian's attitude towards a car repair. Paul's reference to "affairs of this life" is clearly dealing with the message taught by former associates and is clearly defined in 4:14 "... strive not about words to no profit but to the subverting of the hearers". He continues about profane and vain babblings and those who teach the resurrection has occurred. All of this is the same context.

The Holy Spirit has not told us to avoid influencing our leaders to be more Godly. The Holy Spirit has not told us it is bad to influence our neighbors to seek more Godly leadership. This is man's interpretation of an "inspired scripture" that is obviously misapplied. Again, who decided politics is an affair of this life and who benefits from this thinking? Concern for our family and a neighbor is a Godly attitude. This is how scripture is applied to politics, always taken out of context and twisted so that Christians will be taught politics is wrong; it is not!

Freedom would never have been passed to this generation if previous generations had the attitude the church has today and if we hold to current thinking freedom will pass no more. Agreed, we should prioritize the word of God but only recently have we adopted this concept that it's "either one or the other". We do not understand that our nation's founders combined serving God and man by being honest and true with both. Most of us view our major priorities as "God, Family and Country". From where comes this seed of thought that serving God means we cannot be active citizens? If ever Satan would want to steal a seed, the best one he could steal would be a seed about serving God! We read in Acts 22:25 that Paul demanded his rights be respected as a Roman citizen. For us to do as Paul did is not ungodly. Yet we tolerate a parade of abuses to our rights as citizens and parents because of some confusion that to protect our rights is ungodly. Evil will destroy our rights through the political process if we remain idle.

If we seek support from a local church we're reminded that Jesus didn't get involved in politics with the Roman government. Scripture reveals that Jesus didn't do many things we do naturally today. He didn't get married, buy property, go to college, start a business, go into debt, join the army, volunteer for His local Boy Scout program, have a church drama club or bake sale. He didn't regard entertainment as a necessity or spend all Sunday afternoon glued to a football game. The deception in the 21st century church has insured the only thing we don't do in planning for our future is planning to be free in that future!

Thirty-year mortgages, going to college, taking care of our health, getting married and having children, these are all planning for the future. We vote (thirty minutes every two years). Has freedom ever been so cheap? Perhaps we were partially neutralized by the lie of a separation of church and state. This teaching that such a clause exists in The Constitution is as bold a lie as the church has ever been told, yet it worked. It is an easy matter for any Christian to get a copy of our Constitution and read The First Amendment for them self. You will see these words do not appear. Nor is a separation of church and state possible. It is an obvious attempt to silence Christians and it's worked brilliantly. The fact that the church is victim to such a blatant offensive lie with such horrid consequences and yet does nothing about it should remove any doubt the church is neutralized.

As Christians withdraw from politics we see two immediate results. First, a government not concerned with the will of God and second, a government not concerned with the will of the people. Not having to concern itself with the will of God or the will of the people, only the will of the state remains. This is significant when one recognizes that there are people who covet the ability to rule their fellow man. Removing constraints on the power of the state simply entices these people to run for office at which time their agenda is to increase and solidify their power.

In this fashion it is merely a matter of time until a ruling elite, who recognizes only a self-serving agenda and cannot be removed from office, runs all "states". This nation was founded by "Christians in politics"; it will only be preserved by the same. Their view was that God created all men with certain Godly (unalienable) rights of life, liberty and the right to pursue the ownership of property. If Christians believe this then they must take responsibility to maintain these rights.

Yes we should all prioritize spreading the gospel. Whether our current church leadership acknowledges it or not, politics and religion are interlocked. Israel was involved in politics when they rejected God and demanded a king even though God warned them what a king would do to their freedom. Moses was involved in politics when he demanded Israel be released from Egyptian slavery. We should thank God that through His light that was revealed to His servants in previous generations we were given the most limited government in the history of the world. With government limited we were free to pursue the full extent of our potential. As the church withdrew from politics we have seen the limitations on government increasingly removed and the effectiveness of the church immediately impacted.

We are commissioned to preserve Godliness and lead people in and toward Godliness and The Bible does not restrict us in any way from doing just that. We have the best system of government ever devised by men because it is the most restrictive toward government but to be effective requires participation. Imagine how we can use our system of government to be salt and light. When we ponder the opportunity to install Christians in state legislatures and congress it immediately becomes obvious why Satan told Christians they should not be involved in politics. To desire a Godly government cannot be evil but it is completely contrary to the agenda of the new world order.

Their strategy was to get into our imagination. That is to say get us to imagine it is not our arena of battle and we would vacate. It has worked brilliantly but we have the power to reverse this course. One basic principle of war, spiritual or otherwise, is when you are attacked you can fight, surrender or run. Ignoring the enemy is really nothing more than another way to surrender. It may be hard for some Christians to accept that the new world order I refer to is actually the threat I describe. It may be hard for some Christians to accept that Satan is fighting his war for global government in the natural world because you have been taught he is fighting in the spiritual world. The proof of Satan's work is prevalent. If you as an individual are not aware of this threat it is either because you have not looked or have prematurely dismissed proofs as they were presented to you.

For a Christian to challenge the concept of prayer is highly offensive. Let me be clear; I firmly believe in prayer. Never the less I must challenge a comfort zone of many Christians that I believe has become a stronghold of Satan. This is the teaching that we have no obligation aside from praying. Currently, we are deceived into believing we should pray for those in authority. This is scriptural but we need to consider that those in authority are sold out to Satan's agenda. Praying for them now is like praying for a guy who's robbing your home. Perhaps praying doesn't hurt but neither is it logical to stop there. We may pray and ask for God's protection on our home but we also lock our doors and take other reasonable precautions.

We have local police departments (with extensive investigatory assets) and courts to insure that our fellow citizens do not abuse us in any criminal manner. We want all local criminals caught and punished. Yet when the criminal is a politicians and the property stolen is our rights, we are persuaded to tolerate the abuse! Who can doubt that it is Satan behind this persuasion and if you do not doubt it, why are we allowing it? Even worse, when a true man of God steps forward for government service, we let Satan's media destroy his character by persuading us he's an extremist, unqualified or unintelligent and we fall for this trap repeatedly. We also continue to fall for the trap of letting Satan's media persuade us that a phony running for office is really a man of God.

In short, we're doing all the wrong things and this is why we have accomplished nothing in the political realm. We pray for people who are not responsive to God and believe we are doing a Godly work, we vote for who the world tells us to vote for and satisfy ourselves with only the two candidates selected for us by the "two" parties. We fail to support a Godly candidate when we have the opportunity by listening to Satan's media tell us they're "unelectable", "they can't win" or "too extreme". We fail to hold our elected leaders accountable to a Biblical standard or even to the commitments they made while running for office and all the while we believe it's God's will or God's judgment that our country is deteriorating before our eyes.

It is time to fight the war we're in and stop pretending that our battles are for another place and time. The enemy is in the camp and it's time to stop pretending that he can be trusted. We have duties and responsibilities. Scripture tells them to us. The war is upon us and our duty should be clear.

SATAN AND POLITICS

Ephesians 4:27 "neither give place to the devil"

For some strange reason modern Christianity does not take notice of Satan's efforts to accomplish his goals. If one studies church history it is not unusual to find times when the church was over-zealous in thinking Satan was behind every illness and misfortune. This is quite a change from today when the church ascribes everything as God's will. Trying to inform Christians that Satan is alive, well and focused on his business is met with blank or confused stares along with arguments that God is in control as if Satan is no factor at all.

The belief seems to be that Satan may cause someone to get an illness or some financial trouble but if you're not suffering from one of these "attacks" then he's leaving you alone and it's best to leave him alone. As long as we leave him alone he'll focus his efforts in The Middle East. To the extent Christians recognize a world government taking shape they shrug it off as fulfillment of prophecy and do not view it as a personal threat to be concerned about.

The purpose of this book is to address four deceptions Christians have embraced which limit or eliminate their effectiveness in serving God and their fellow man. It is due to these deceptions that Satan is achieving so much success in our time. To further make this point, it is worthwhile to consider what those in Satan's service have said about this topic. In The Introduction I'd referenced a book called "Proof's of a Conspiracy" written in 1798 by John Robison who was invited to participate but instead, he used this opportunity to do his own investigation.

Those familiar with the new world order are familiar with the term "Illuminatti" which is considered to be the hub around which all secret societies revolve and get their direction. The founder of the

Illuminatti was Adam Weishaupt and Robison reports Weishaupt's instructions as:

"We must win the common people in every corner. This will be obtained chiefly by means of the schools. We must acquire the direction of education – of church – management – of the professorial chair and of the pulpit".[27]

We should be mindful that God works through people but Satan does as well. The Bible makes it clear that Satan has desires to both rule the entire earth as god and be worshiped by men as god. The church, having chosen to avoid politics, has lost sight of the fact that it is government that rules the daily lives of men. It then stands to reason that to achieve his goals Satan will seek to control government.

Hence the government should be a primary focus point of Christians to insure Satan does not amass power or influence over the lives of men. Some governments vary from others as to the extent with which they can actually control the lives of the citizens but Christians should take note that we live in an age where all governments, including our own, are rapidly increasing their control over the people. Satan is accomplishing his goal of controlling the lives of mankind through a strategy of increasingly moving his servants into higher government positions from which they constantly work to increase their power as they increase the power of government.

Towards this end, Satan is left with a dilemma. He must achieve his long dreamed of one world government covertly so as not to alarm those who would work against him. This would certainly include Christians but we can reasonably conclude that no small number of non-Christians would fight against living in a satanic tyranny. To achieve his goals secretly Satan must become the master of several arenas. This strategy is typically referred to as "the long march thru the institutions". Primary targets would be arenas that influence the thinking of people such as churches, media/publishing and schools/ universities. This is Weishaupt's plan. It would be impossible in a Godly culture for Satan to get control of government. Satan's plan is not so brilliant that it cannot be learned and exposed by those who are anxious to serve God.

He consistently focuses on three arenas; education to get the youth, the church – not to eliminate his opposition but to mislead and control them and the third arena is secret societies so that he can always remain hidden and only suffer minimally in the event his agenda is discovered and exposed. Lest you think this strategy died with Weishaupt, Lenin said, "the best way to destroy your opposition is to lead it". Once he had established substantial influence over education and the church (total control may come in time but is not immediately necessary) he invested some time to alter the public's thinking through these institutions.

Next he could move on to secondary targets which do not have as great an influence on the masses but afford control on the daily lives of individual people. This would include banks – Satan's world system is based largely on borrowed money and the borrower is slave to the lender; major corporations - Satan's world system is based largely on people employed by big corporations verses being self-employed or working for a small company.

To examine this point a little further consider, controlling the people is easiest when you employ them. We have a work force in The United States of approximately one hundred and fifty million workers. If we figure (arbitrarily) that a large corporation has twenty-five thousand domestic laborers employed, this would only translate to six thousand corporations. Six thousand is certainly more easily controlled than, say, one hundred and fifty thousand private business that employ one hundred people each. It may be more reasonable to double the number of employees per corporation, which leaves us with three thousand corporations.

If the three to six thousand corporations have one or two percent of their directors which have been enticed into a private agenda, then it becomes the passion of this group to have a subtle influence upon the rest. We can add to this an additional two to five percent of the managers who may lack understanding of the agenda but completely grasp what is necessary to benefit their own careers. Do not underestimate that these paltry percentages can have an enormous influence when they work between themselves, afford each other substantial advantages (such as insider information) and receive preferential treatment by government and lending institutions.

The key to success is subtle perseverance over a long span of time. When we consider that our government is now our largest employer and about fifty percent of the private workforce is employed by large corporations you can see that corporate America has an incredible influence on the voting public. When added to the number of government workers who are similarly influenced we can note that the new world order goes into each election with a substantial base.

Seldom do we see a government employee who braves to fight improprieties and as corporations merge the pressure to maintain a good relationship with an employer and managers will create ever-increasing pressure upon those in the private sector to comply against their own values. This strategy has become so successful that we commonly see corporations acquiring one another creating ever-larger corporations which leaves ever fewer corporations outside of the immediate influence of those committed to Satan's agenda. These corporations are not overtly influenced to embrace Satanism but they are directed toward supporting larger government and increased government controls over the lives of individuals.

They support increasing government control over corporations to their detriment since this stifles their competition. They support increased global regulation over business because this ultimately achieves their desire of global government. They support the "dumbing down" of America's youth in a worthless school system because it creates generations of "servants" instead of capable people that do not need their system. They support a military presence all across the globe because it protects their foreign investments including their greatest investment of all - the system they are creating.

We are no longer a nation of small patriotic and independent minded businessmen. Our country now has a completely different system and this new system is one where the only means of supporting yourself (and a family) is by maintaining a good relationship with your employer and not making any waves.

It should be recognized that "employees" in The Bible are called servants, defined in six different ways. We have become accustomed to the concept of being "employees" not recognizing that in God's system we should at least desire and strive to become "employers". This too is a form of bondage and control that God would not wish His children to suffer. This is how Satan works to get control over all people, including Christians.

Another secondary target to note is police/military. Satan's world system is based largely on force and this is the ultimate non-spiritual force. As government assumes more power it becomes a police state with the police charged, not with protecting lives and property, but enforcing the dictates of government (will of the state). As this new world order government grows it must increasingly force its will on innocent people. This requires "peace keepers" (military) to protect the interests of the new world order (government) against exposure and resistance.

Police must be convinced that local patriots, upset about losing their freedom are, in fact, criminal enemies of the state. They must be convinced that military assault procedures against innocent citizens are "what they deserve" as well as a "safe, reasonable way for them to perform their duties". All resistance must be broken before it can threaten the system. Police must be armed and equipped with military type weaponry so that it is poised and ready to put down any and all resistance to the agenda. Police must be alienated from the community as much as possible to develop a useful "us against them" war like mentality instead of the prior attitude of "serving the public". As Christians, perhaps the highest priority we should have is befriending and supporting law enforcement so they cannot be corrupted and turned against the public.

The next arenas Satan seeks to control would be transportation, communication, energy and the basics to a daily life. This would virtually eliminate all efficient means of organized resistance. Without the ability to travel one obviously becomes quite limited. No organized resistance of consequential size can be accomplished without communication tools. Energy and communication puts people "on the grid" which is to say makes them traceable. The people need not be "sold out" to an occult agenda; they simply need to be prevented from opposing it.

The threat of losing your job would do much to intimidate people into silence but in this modern computer age, the threat of establishing a "permanently documented work history" which would follow you everywhere and render you "unemployable" (as a dissenter) would certainly be a matter of consideration for all who have children to provide for. Many would be intimidated into staying quiet.

Last would be the people themselves. This would include both those who believe they would receive some personal benefit from informing on their friends, family and neighbors but it also includes intimidation. There are two types of applications here. The first are people who are too afraid to face life without "big brother" to take care of them. The second are those too afraid to suffer the consequences of doing the right thing. Fear is a powerful manipulation tactic.

These are the targets but the goal is complete "government control". Once Satan has government control he has control over the lives of men. The greatest part of this effort is to insure secrecy of the real agenda. Satan knows he must accomplish all of this without rebellion or exposure of his true goals so it is done covertly behind false causes and promises. If people realized their government is satanic they would take steps to establish better government; if they recognized the media lied to them, they would seek out better sources for information, if they understood the purpose of schools is to keep students ignorant they would pursue other educations systems.

They must never be permitted to learn this truth while Satan is yet vulnerable. 2nd Corinthians 11:14 states "Satan is transformed into an angel of light". He makes his progress by making promises to do a service but to keep these promises requires increased power to government, but the true agenda only serves him. Schools are for his benefit, government programs are for his benefit and an increased military and police power are for his benefit. All new government programs are sold to the public by the promise of protection and benefits seldom delivered.

It is the job of the church to expose Satan as he hides behind these right sounding movements and good sounding causes. As we move toward global government we hear the deception of how it will be a benefit to mankind yet the common denominator is always more government power in the hands of a chosen few. Another way of stating this point is that the common denominator is always less pursuit of

God's solutions to problems (they won't work in this enlightened age) and more pursuit of government to solve all problems.

Christians should know the error of this concept and act on their knowledge. Typically when Christians say they are not involved in politics they mean they will not volunteer for a political party, a candidate or work for or against any specific legislation. It is also reasonable to say that the majority of them do not make an in depth study of the major issues or candidates that appear on a typical ballot. God wants us to be a Godly society and He wants us to have Godly government. This will not happen to any degree if Christians continue to withdraw from the system and continue to be largely uninformed of the major issues of the day. We will not be informed properly when we get our information from sources under satanic influence as written in Psalms 1:1 "Blessed is the man who walks not in the counsel of the ungodly ..." We should be hearing truth from our church pulpits.

We need to recognize that the strength of "the new world order" is in creating an illusion, a very dangerous illusion. Those promoting this agenda do so with false promises and creating the illusion that they will take care of us in harmony, peace and contentment. They have us imagine that if we give up the "Bill of Rights" they will protect us. They have us imagine that if we give up our parental authority they will educate, protect and guarantee our children will have a better life. They have us imagine that if we give up our private property they will house us. They promise to provide health care, child care, elderly care, better food, clean water, clean air, job opportunities and everything else that comprises "cradle to grave" security and happiness.

Please keep in mind, these are the "can't" people. They "can't" do anything they promise to do. They can't patrol the border, they can't improve education, they can't create jobs, they can't balance the budget, they can't cut spending and so forth. It is incredible that they have convinced so many people that, if given enough authority over the daily affairs of men, they "can" deliver a utopian, secure, high quality of life for all! All good patriotic citizens need to do is give them more power at the expense of individual liberty and all needs will be met.

Recognize that only God could fulfill all of these promises and this is very telling as it becomes obvious they want "godlike control over the lives of men"! Make no mistake; they have *no intention* of keeping these promises! It's all an illusion. It's the power and control they want and they will promise anything to get it. Even today they provide these services only to perpetuate their illusion so they can amass more power. Once they have satisfactorily destroyed all means of resistance the blood bath will begin.

The only option will be to completely submit in despair, "Who can make war with the beast" Revelations 13:4. Christians are commanded in Ephesians 4:27 "neither give place to the devil". The seat of government is a place and control is the prize. Giving government over to Satan is not only wrong and ungodly but the repercussions are extraordinary! This is giving the ultimate "place" to the devil. Through government Satan can increase his control and have his seat of power.

Another arena where we should not "give place to the devil" must include "our thinking". The Bible makes a connection between our imaginations and evil. We can give Satan "place" in our imaginations and we should recognize why he desires to have that "place". The new world order desires we imagine a wonderful world with peace, safety and contentment and without realizing it we begin thinking this is attainable if we cooperate with their agenda. We quit thinking about what God has told us and grow further away from Him and His word.

This is precisely why Christians need to be involved in politics. Satan can easily get non-Christians to imagine his fantasy world and never suspect it's a fraud. Christians are to be alert to the lies of the enemy and are to expose these lies and false promises. This means Christians must expose this illusion, of a "coming global brotherhood of man where we all live in peace and harmony side by side," as a satanic deception told only to hide his true agenda. It is in exposing these lies that salt and light can and must be applied. Salt and light are going to have an impact whenever and wherever they're applied.

Their lies are designed to eliminate opposition as they amass power, not to improve the welfare of mankind. This leaves two truths that must be addressed. The first is the subject of "manipulation" by the new world order and the second is the consequences to each of us for allowing them to succeed. Proverbs 23:7 says "as he (any man) thinketh in his heart, so is he". The desire to control the thinking of mankind has become "big business" and this is very much a part of Satan's control of the institutions. The goal is to get us thinking like we're helpless, confused and facing danger on all fronts instead of focusing on God and our proper authority.

We have a major media, which is heavily controlled by a very small handful of people. One has but to switch channels during the evening news to recognize that the only difference between them is the order of which they air their various news items and all appear identical to what appeared in the daily newspaper. What are the odds that three networks would have three independent staffs which were free to gather and air whatever news items they regarded as important and aside from a human interest story or two their conclusions are identical day after day. Sure, if there is a major event one expects all networks to report it. Yet when events are minor to insignificant all three networks independently and consistently air identical items. This clearly reveals the existence of a common determining factor between all three networks and their subsidiaries.

We have an educational system in this country that is controlled by the government but yet is promoted as "public" education and not "government" education. Public education is a travesty that parents are required to support but an entire subculture of institutions has been spawned by parents who know their children can't be educated in the schools. They are well aware that the education their children receive in the schools is inadequate but they stop short of considering what the children actually do learn there. The subculture I speak of is tutoring programs, Internet education sites, private schools, home schooling and many more. Yet nothing is done about the government schools. The agenda of our educational system is to create generations of socialist thinking citizens that do not challenge authority.

If they dare challenge authority in the school they are hindered from a good college education. Challenging authority in college is encouraged as long as they challenge only those authorities the professors want challenged. Any individualism or freethinking and the student may be hindered from getting a good job with a major corporation. This system is now called "education". The previous system of reading, writing and arithmetic has been abandoned. It is a system of manipulation to destroy individualism.

Book and magazine publishers are most commonly promoters of the same socialist, pleasure and entertainment seeking agenda. The effectiveness of this is apparent to us all when we consider that virtually everything we worry about is what we're told to worry about. As the media prioritizes an agenda, be it sports, global warming, some Hollywood airhead, healthcare or which ever they choose on a daily basis these are what people are talking about. Thus our thinking is manipulated and controlled. Perhaps not completely but sufficiently to affect our imaginations as needed to insure we do not challenge the system because we live in a world where few even imagine challenging the system.

Since we do not think about challenging the system we do not think about what life is like in the system we're creating for ourselves. We only imagine what it will be like in the system we're taught to anticipate, either the new world order or the one promised in scripture. This is very dangerous as the one the new world order is promising is an illusion and it is the one we will all have to live in temporarily.

John Adams said that our system of government was "inadequate for any other than a moral people". We think of morality pertaining to sexuality and choose not to remember that theft is immoral too. This is what Adams was speaking of. We control the vote; we control the ability of government to steal. Far too frequently, if we benefit from that theft we stand silent. A world in which government can take anything it chooses from the people is a world where government is in total control and beyond reproach. A government that is empowered to steal is a government empowered to sustain its own promises and illusions aside from truth.

Up to this point I have referred to the new world order and those in Satan's service in general terms. We should examine those who have helped Satan accomplish what he has and just who the people are that have been of such devoted assistance. The first group to be mentioned is The Council on Foreign Relations. There are four things every American should know about The CFR. The first is with regard to the people who founded this organization. This is no secret. Their beliefs, aims and ambitions are well documented. In short they are the ones who brought about The Federal Reserve Bank, entangled The United States in World War I, attempted to destroy the sovereignty of

The United States by having us join The League of Nations, brought about The IRS and The Sixteenth Amendment which is the income tax amendment and several other anti-American objectives.[28]

Perhaps their two most harmful achievements was The Seventeenth Amendment, which did away with state legislatures appointing senators in favor of direct elections. Arguably the most important purpose of The Senate, and the purpose for each state having two Senators, was that they protect "states rights" against encroachment by the federal government. Since The Seventeenth Amendment, the Senate has failed to protect states rights under The Constitution and we've seen a steady flow of power shifted to Washington.

Possibly the second worst among their list of horrors was the concept of "treaties" having superior authority over The United States Constitution. With this we have seen The Constitution gutted line by line under a variety of treaties. The senate is charged with ratifying treaties but more importantly with preserving, protecting and defending The Constitution as the supreme law of the land and subsequently any treaty should be conditional on The Constitutional authority of government. This legal principle has been abandoned.

This is a short list as substantially more is known of these men and their agenda. They were internationalists with no devotion to any country. They bailed out the failing Bolshevik revolution creating The USSR, manipulated events to create the wars of the twentieth century, assisted Mao Tse Tung in bringing communism to China, created the infamous World Council of Churches and ultimately ensnared our country in The United Nations.[29]

I suspect many will find these statements impossible to believe. Then don't believe it but research it! The proof of all of these statements is quite easily verifiable and I ask no one to simply take my statements as proof. Again, the real question is "if it is true, would you want to know"?

The second thing every patriotic American should know about The CFR is that since their incorporation in 1921 they have called and worked for world government at the expense of national sovereignty. They have never deviated from this agenda. Thirdly every patriotic American should be aware that every successive Presidential Administration from

Herbert Hoover to William Clinton had an increasing number of CFR members working in their administration.[30]

Americans should know that The Executive Branch of their government is run by people who do not respect The Constitution and are working to create global government at the expense of national sovereignty. Many patriotic Americans wonder why no change occurs in national policy after an election even when a new party takes over and The CFR influence is the answer.

It should also be noted that the pattern of CFR members running The Executive Branch of government continues. The established pattern of growth was slightly interrupted only because President Clinton went wild with CFR members at 687 serving in The Executive Branch. President Bush had about 450.[31] The fourth matter regarding The CFR that everyone should know is that, aside from serving in government, they are the power people of our time. Both private membership and corporate membership lists are available. When consulted we note that most heads of the major banking institutions are CFR, many of the heads of the big eastern foundations are CFR, CEO's of international conglomerates are typically CFR and one can usually find CFR members heading the major publishing firms, media outlets, even leaders in many mainline denominational churches are members. And yes, the power people in America's institutions of education are frequently CFR. This is not to say that every member of The CFR is a sovereignty-hating globalist but the fact remains that they willing joined an organization whose function is to bring about world government. While it is common for candidates of both major parties to be a CFR member to insure that The CFR wins regardless of which political party loses, it is sometimes acceptable if the candidate is not a member himself so long as his key Cabinet Secretaries are members. This helps hide The CFR influence.[32]

Aside from The CFR other organizations exist such as The Buildebergers. This group of globalists meets at some secluded location annually to strategize global monetary policy and other efforts to promote world government. Buildeburg watchers report that it is now common for both candidates to appear at Buildeburg meetings prior to receiving their party's nomination for President. Another group is The Trilateral Commission, which has expanded beyond its original purpose of entangling The United States, Japan and Western Europe economically to such an extent that they would be entangled politically. Currently their purpose is to do the same for Europe, Asia and The Western Hemisphere.

There is a lengthy list of additional groups but one worthy of note is The Federal Reserve Bank, which is not a government agency as many presume. Some shares of the stock in The Federal Reserve are owned by the member banks and stockholders. A controlling percent is owned by private holding companies and as they are private it is not known who owns these investment firms.[33] Thus the specific persons who own controlling interest in The Federal Reserve Bank and control our economy are unknown. The name of this institution was chosen for its deceptive potential. Today we have many companies with the name "Federal" in their title like Federal Express but in 1913 this was not so. Additionally any idea that this institution is holding any reserves has become very doubtful.

At this writing attempts are underway for Congress to audit "The Fed" however the current Fed Vice-Chairman has threatened to increase interest rates if they try, yet President Obama has reappointed the Chairman and taken no action against The Fed for this threat! Lastly this is no bank under any reasonable definition of the word. It is a private organization that has been given unconstitutional control over our nation's money supply and raids the public treasury for the benefit of an unknown few.

It is true that The President "appoints" the members of The Federal Reserve Board including The Chairman. It is also true that once these appointments are made neither The President of The United States or the Secretary of the Treasury for The United States is permitted to attend Federal Reserve Board meetings or look at the state of its accounts. Neither can The Congress, The President or Secretary stop The Fed from raising interest rates if it chooses to do so.

Then, of course, we have The United Nations. Many Christians view this organization as a harmless debating society. This is exactly what the new world order wants you to think. A man named Edward Mandell House drew up the first draft of The League of Nations Treaty. Perhaps no name is known of a single individual who's had more to do with altering the course of our nation.

This is the man who won The Presidency for Woodrow Wilson. He had hand picked him for the job and guided Wilson's career from his days as a Princeton Professor. House's loyalties were to International Bankers and he served them with devotion. It is a matter of public record that the same people who funded Wilson in 1912 also funded Theodore Roosevelt of The Progressive Party. Roosevelt, having formerly served as a Republican, predictably caused The Republican Party to split its vote between Roosevelt and Taft insuring Wilson would win the election. The men who financed this fraud had Edward House in their service. [34]

House had Wilson appoint a committee known as "The Inquiry" to give the appearance that The League of Nations Treaty had been formulated by the best minds available when, in fact, it was a private draft and The League was designed to serve a small handful of people rather that the world population as promised.

Historians write positively of The CFR "volunteering" to provide "an overworked" State Department with assistance at the outbreak of World War II. They came with their own agenda, however.

A group of CFR members were organized within The State Department as an "Advisory Committee on Post-War Foreign Policy". The committee's Director of Research was a Russian born man named Pasvolsky. When Pasvolsky died in 1953 Time Magazine eulogized him as "the architect of The United Nations Charter". The same strategy had been followed, the same outline had been used, some of the individuals were involved in both groups but this time the plan worked. This begs the question of how much negotiating and formulating of The UN Charter actually took place in San Francisco in 1945? It was virtually complete when the delegates arrived.

On August 14, 1941 (some four months prior to Pearl Harbor) President Roosevelt and British Prime Minister Winston Churchill signed "The Atlantic Charter". On January 1, 1942 the nations at war with The Axis countries signed an agreement called "A Declaration of The United Nations" pledging their combined adherence to the policies of The Atlantic Charter. The United Nations organization that we know was formulated at a meeting in Dumbarton Oaks in 1944 and the final details agreed upon at Yalta in 1945.[35]

The first Secretary General of The United Nations was a former Roosevelt advisor and CFR member named Alger Hiss. Hiss was later exposed as a Soviet spy but, believe it or not, we have a statute of limitations on espionage in this country. This saved Hiss from going to jail for espionage but he was sent to jail for forty-four months for perjury before a Grand Jury regarding his being a Communist. This is an example of the type of people that entangled The United States in The United Nations and an example of what happens when the senate allows treaties to supersede our Constitution. Trygvy Lie, a known henchman of Joseph Stalin, replaced Hiss at a UN election in October 1945.

Today the nations that sit on The UN Security Council sell about eighty percent of the global munitions market.[36] This is very revealing about this "peace" organization. These weapons are sold to third world countries on loans, which force the countries into debt, and then the increased violence requires The UN to send in "Peace Keepers" which increases its military power. Then these peacekeepers confiscate the weapons so the countries are indebted to pay for weapons that the sellers steal back from them! The globalists can't lose! The significance of all of this is that Christians must understand two things. One is that the truth is frequently hidden and must be researched. We are of no service to God or humanity if we are uninformed and ignorant of the enemy's tactics.

We do not have the luxury as warriors to determine for ourselves when and where we will fight. We have a duty to meet and overcome the enemy when and where he attacks. Additionally, Christians must understand that Satan and his minions are busy. Christians must understand that these events were planned long in advance. The very situations that come about and create the need for expansion of government beyond what God has revealed are the situations we are to be involved in stopping.

The United Nations has become the foundation of a satanic empire. From this foundation we have The World Bank, which may deal with a world currency at some point but is currently involved in enslaving the nations of the world to a satanic system of economics. This is expanded in The World Trade Organization, which claims authority to determine trade policy for all member nations. The WTO has ruled against United States policy on several occasions and The United States Congress has altered our policy to conform. We have even had lawsuits, won in The United States, appealed to international courts such as the "NAFTA Courts" which overruled our court and these judgments are respected and complied to. [37]

Aside from these attacks on our national sovereignty there is The World Health Organization, which uses U.S. taxpayer money to perform abortions and sterilizations in poor countries. There is UNESCO, which promotes teaching globalism, evolution and sex education in the schools and has been given authority to alter public learning in The United States to conform to international standards. Most visible on this front is the 1994 legislation of "Goals 2000". Originally called "America 2000" by the H. W. Bush administration, it was widely feared to be a takeover of education by the federal government with no regard to parental or state's rights. A chart can be viewed at http://www.crossroad.to/charts/UNESCO-Goals2000.htm,[38] which reflects that this law conforms to 1973 UNESCO objectives for global education. Another UNESCO document, "Education For All"[39] published in 2000 was greeted with The G.W. Bush administration passing "No Child Left Behind" in 2001conforming to the new changes.[40] President G.W. Bush rejoined UNESCO which President Reagan had withdrew from during his administration.

This is not yet the entire tip of the iceberg. Glancing at the UN's list of subsidiary organizations appears much like several spider webs super-imposed one on top of another. Their ambitions to reach into every life and establish control have become so exhaustive as to give them several avenues into each life, which are largely unknown to most Americans. Currently it is largely done with the full cooperation of our own government. This is all ungodly and un-American and is only possible because Christians have withdrawn from the battle. With the UN in charge of our education our children are no longer being taught truths of American heritage, the greatness of free enterprise or the simple need for morality. Satan has insured that future generations will increasingly embrace his entire agenda.

Ponder for a moment the stupidity in which we are now entangled. As we went to war in Korea, Vietnam and Iraq we did so, not by our Congress declaring war but through the authority of

The UN. These "wars" were called "UN Police Actions". In the cases of Korea and Vietnam our Congress was well aware of the fact that The Soviet Union was supplying arms and at times manpower to the North Koreans and North Vietnamese yet who sat on The UN Security Council with The U.S. as strategies were developed, troop strengths and locations openly discussed and plans made? The Soviet Union, as a fellow member of The Security Council, was right there at the table. We find ourselves having to fight wars while inviting our enemy to sit at the table with us during planning sessions. All of this because The CFR has successfully perpetuated the lie that treaty law can overrule our Constitution.

Our leaders are not this stupid! They know what they are doing. It may be that many in Congress lack understanding of the full intent of the agenda but they cooperate nonetheless. Satan is involved in politics to a degree Christians are woefully ignorant of. His success has an incredible and dangerous impact on our lives and our future security. We have no good reason to sit idle and let him and his agents destroy our country and the world. We have given him this place and now we must dispossess him of it.

THE CHURCH AND POLITICS

Ezekiel 3:18 "Thou givest him not warning nor speaketh
to warn the wicked ...
his blood will I require of thine hand"

It is vital that we all understand that this single concept of Christians avoiding politics has come at a very high price. This thinking has done more to destroy our national heritage than any single matter the enemy has successfully rooted in our land. It is due to this philosophy that we no longer take responsibility against the growth of evil in our land and do nothing about the plantings and lies of the enemy. We allow all immorality and corruption to thrive when the enemy uses the machinery of politics to work his fields and promote his agenda.

Here we must examine how the church could be so easily out maneuvered. We were told in scripture that the responsibility is ours to speak to the wicked and warn them of their wicked ways. We are aware that civilizations that lived by God's standard thrived. We are aware that these cultures (our own included) were created by devout men who sought to build a society on Godly principles. We understand that Godly societies do not happen without Christians "being involved" to build and maintain them. Yet we have allowed ourselves to be convinced that building and maintaining a Godly society is not what God wishes Christians to do. We have watched as our own great civilization has degenerated into a dangerous, vile place to raise a family and we still remain idle.

It is a strange world we have made for ourselves. We know our schools are dangerous, counter-productive and perverted yet we continue to send our children and decrease our involvement there. We know television is the all important distribution system for piping Satan's values, lies and priorities into our home yet rather than take offense, we pay good money to have a greater selection of channels to watch. We do nothing more than complain when sexual predators are released from prison and housed (at our expense) in our neighborhoods.

Furthermore, we have little alarm when we learn that government is expanding its own powers to a dangerous level and is becoming a significant threat to the family unit God has ordained. These are not political issues they are moral issues. Yet because we are told they are political we do nothing. It then becomes reasonable to ask who is leading Christianity down this road that we obviously do not belong on. It is reasonable to ask who is advising us so effectively to take no action when our country and family so desperately need us to get involved.

We know we are needed but we placate ourselves and follow these leaders. This makes it all the more important to examine who is leading us into premature surrender and what their agenda is. The central issues of this chapter are the argument that Christians don't belong in politics and that this argument is encouraged and promoted by Satan and his minions, not God. Satan has simply established his people in key positions, promoted them as more intellectual and has achieved extraordinary influence over the church. They have been successful in planting many false seeds from many false teachers but their greatest achievement was in altering the church from fighting evil. While this may be offensive I remind you that the new world order has, for centuries, focused on three entities. They are the church, education and secret societies.

For Satan to control the church does not require that he control every Christian or any significant number of them. Only that he would have a strong influence on those regarded as church leaders. This influence would not require that they be wholly sold out to the occult but only that they had lost their passion to serve God. Neither is it important that their passion is substituted.

We read in Matthew 24:42 and Mark 13:33 that we are to be watching in connection with the second coming of Christ. However if you read these passages of scripture in context you will notice another point. We are to be watching for the second coming of Christ but we are to be watching to insure we are found about His work when He comes! The implication here is that we are not to be just waiting for time to run out.

Indeed those with such an attitude are accused of "sleeping". The church frequently interprets those "sleeping" as those who have not accepted Christ as Savior. While aspects of this interpretation are reasonable, here the passages speak of a personal relationship between the master and servant. Jesus was clearly speaking to those who had accepted Him as Savior. Mark 13:34 repeats the same point, "his servant" once again defining that He is addressing those with whom He has a relationship. Luke 21:35 says "as a snare shall it come … on the whole earth" which clearly is a reference going back to the unsaved but goes on in verse 36 "watch … that ye may be accounted worthy…"

Matthew 24:46 "Blessed is that servant whom when his Lord cometh shall find so doing". We read in verses 43 - 45 what they were "so doing":

➢ Watching so the thief does not come
➢ Protecting his household
➢ Ruling and providing for his household

God created a system putting men at the head of the household with certain responsibilities. Men have abdicated this role to government and that's ungodly.

This has allowed a satanic system to take over the home and it was not sufficiently resisted. It was accomplished through the political process after Christians had been deceived into having nothing to do with something labeled "political". The trap was set by a two-step process. First leadership teaching Christians shouldn't get involved in politics and secondly by politicizing a host of family and spiritual issues.

Parental rights over their children are not political, marriage is not political, and morality is not political. Very few things are political in a Godly society but we're told that everything is political in our society today. We've come to accept all things as tolerable as long as we can "vote" for or against those who attack a Godly standard. While the Christian home was under attack the Christians were placated by their leadership instructing them that all God wanted them to do is spread the gospel. This argument was accepted and the home was lost to a satanic system.

False leadership played an instrumental role in creating this change. Acts 20:29-31 is an instruction by Paul to watch for false leaders. This is a duty that God expects from every one of us. It is also a requirement beyond simply spreading the gospel. If our sole duty is to share Jesus with our family and friends we no longer test church leadership. This was an ongoing concern of Paul and in Acts 20:30 he is very specific that the false leaders he feared would come from within the church, "of your own selves shall men arise speaking perverse things to draw away disciples after them" and "not spare the flock". "Of your own selves" is far more deadly to the church than a satanic attack from an outside source.

This reference of not sparing "the flock" is another clear reference to a duty beyond spreading the gospel as "the flock" refers to those already saved. "Not sparing" can easily mean both not protecting and misleading. "Not protecting" would be to fail in guarding against evil as well as tolerating its growth in our midst. These are not unreasonable interpretations but they do challenge the position of those who insist we are to limit ourselves to spreading the gospel.

Need I point out that the more we limit our activity the more easily we are controlled. Furthermore, the more we limit ourselves the greater the opportunities for evil and where evil is allowed to grow the more difficult it is to spread the gospel.

It would serve us well to consider the subject of "the church" and the appropriate authority God gave it over our lives. We will address this more in another chapter but the church, like the government, is prohibited from violating the sanctity of the home and has no authority to change God's laws or duties He has given to believers. In scripture the church is mentioned in quite a different fashion than what we picture as the church today. Today many churches strive to be the center of the family as a combination of recreation center, community college, a selection of social clubs/ dating services and hopefully a Bible study.

I'm not arguing that all of this is a bad thing, who's to say. I have no doubt it meets the needs of many people. Still, we read of none of this in the early church and much of this change is necessary due to the break down of the family and educational system. If the church wants to add activities for the benefit of the parishioners, most would probably welcome that but the church still has an obligation to follow scripture.

In most cases when the church is mentioned in scripture it is used in a generic sense, "Lord added to the church", "Persecuted the church at Jerusalem", "Herod vexed the church", etc. Then there are scriptures where Paul and Barnabas ordained Elders in some churches, Paul preaching in the churches and "when you come together in church", etc. Today we frequently use the terms "church" and "Christian" as interchangeable, at least when discussing issues like politics. The argument "the church" shouldn't be involved in politics" is considered the same as "Christians shouldn't be involved in politics". This is not a scriptural position. I point this out as an argument illustrating how we are manipulated; I firmly believe that both Christians and churches should be involved in politics.

Even aside from organized denominations there is a notable effort to develop standards of conformity in Christianity. One seldom encounters a church that meets on Saturday or deviates from the standard Sunday morning agenda to any degree. We simply accept predetermined activities as "the way it's supposed to be done" and continue the pattern. This too is a forfeiture of significant control to a system. Again, I have no issue with this; I simply point out we are manipulated into following a prescribed pattern and it may be that God would like to do something a little different in a few places.

A Christian involved in politics is frowned upon as promoting disunity in the church. God works through people so the more widely this concept is embraced the more ungodly our government will become. When a layman attempts to bring an important matter to the church's attention, something that will have a detrimental effect on the greater congregation, he is frequently discouraged from doing so. Subsequently we loose the input of Godly watchmen and church members must rely on Satan's information system for their news.

I believe God has blessed every nation with what it needs to survive and thrive. Two things a nation needs are watchmen and warriors. In today's America we think of our warriors as our military or police. To an extent they may well be, however, for them to be Godly warriors they must be anointed by God and in His service. This is an important distinction. This is not to say that they cannot be in

God's service while in government service but if our government is not abiding by God's law or promoting Godly policies then those who are working promoting government policies cannot be said to be in God's service. Rather, they are in the service of our government.

Those that have studied the matter and understand how our government has been co-opted by the new world order can detail how our military does much service for Satan by fulfilling the objectives of the new world order. This may be highly offensive as there are many devout Christians in our military who sincerely believe they are serving our country. This is not to impugn their character or voice any lack of appreciation for their commitment. America needs a strong military but I am not talking about our military needs. I'm talking about a belief that God wants every nation to have warriors that are in His service and help sustain Godliness in the land.

It was (and is) the duty of Godly warriors to sound the alarm when God's laws are being violated, even when government violates them. This is something our military cannot do and it is not their responsibility or that of the local police. We need watchmen to sound the alarm when the nation's leaders are violating God's laws or His system. It is unrealistic to expect those in any government service to fulfill this role.

By silencing the watchmen in our churches we have forced Christians to rely on Satan's information system, which would not be reliable for our purposes. It is curious how we came to a state of being where we demand the watchmen be silenced from sounding the alarm. This too is something we have come to accept as "the way things are supposed to be done"; the watchmen are to be silent in church so they do not create disunity. Watchmen would naturally be the first targets of a satanic attack.

The first objective in any attack is to be as covert as possible for as long as possible. Therefore a high priority is to take out the communications. In this case, Satan would want to take out the watchmen. The most effective way for him to do that is through church leadership who, rather than respond to an alarm, assist in silencing the watchmen. There are different ways to silence them; they are constantly telling the watchmen they are carnal and divisive, they work to diffuse the message by assuring the membership all is in God's hands so we need not react, our responsibility is singularly to spread the gospel and the ever popular argument that we shouldn't combine church and state. The watchmen are ignored and grow discouraged since nobody wants to hear their message. Satan is in the camp with few even aware of it.

The enemy rarely deals in facts; he deals with emotional arguments. This is how manipulation works. Satan must be able to manipulate Christians in order to influence them. Christians and non-Christians alike are emotionally manipulated today as never before in world history! We are manipulated into being afraid of diseases, crime, Islam and a host of other matters. With the watchmen long silenced Satan is no longer suspected as the root threat behind these issues in any direct sense. Since Satan is not regarded as the immediate cause he is not fought in the way an immediate threat should be.

Thus if Christians are involved in fighting anything they fight a disease, crime, etc., focusing their energies on symptoms and not the root cause. Since Satan and his cohorts are never under attack they are never hindered or threatened. They are free to continue an offensive fight since nobody puts them on the defensive. The watchmen are no longer free to inform people what Satan is doing and how he is doing it. We believe Satan's minions when they tell us the desired solution is more government to solve these problems since we have eliminated the vital information source that would have exposed the real cause, strategies and solutions.

It may be true that in other countries there was little that could be done but in our country, with our participatory system of government, there is much that can be done and we should be doing it. We are losing because we are ignorant of the enemy's devices and have been tricked into thinking it's not our fight. The obvious point here is that Godly warriors and watchmen are going to be Christians. Non-Christians are not going to be concerned with serving God or doing His will and they wouldn't know what that is anyway. If church leadership discourages Christians from stepping out and fulfilling the Godly duties of exposing liars and frauds in our government then what hope have we as a nation? I repeat, God would not call upon non-Christians to do this.

I have met scores of people who have a sense about government that frequently exceeds their knowledge. For example, they may not know many principles of economics but they instinctively know there is something wrong with The Federal Reserve System. They may not know many principles of good government but they instinctively know that there is something wrong about America constantly going to war and The United Nations. I know of no way to consider such people except to recognize they have a calling from God, an anointing. I can consider no purpose for such an anointing except that these people are to be watchmen and when they instinctively sense trouble approaching – and can research it and verify the threat, they are to wake the town and tell the people.

These people are eager to research and verify these threats but they cannot be expected to overcome these threats on their own. It is the people united that will overcome the threat and not the watchmen doing battle alone. The watchmen are the first line of defense but all are to be prepared to stand up for what we know is right and do battle when needed. The threat to the people is obviously increased when these watchmen have been silenced. In our world a need for watchmen is not given any consideration. We have grown to trust Satan's informational system in spite of Psalms 1:1 "Blessed is the man that walketh not in the counsel of the ungodly ..."

When a watchman sounds a warning regarding a candidate we've decided to support, we don't want to hear it. When word comes regarding some new proposed legislation, we dismiss it. When we are told of an organized, evil threat to destroy Godliness and enslave mankind we react the way we've been trained to react, we refuse to examine the evidence. Many would rather remain asleep and placated by Satan's media than have the responsibility to take action.

Additionally, everyone gets busy with their daily business and routine. The Godly watchmen will surely be the first to sense and be aware of an approaching threat. Let's consider the matter from another angle. Why must the church be salt and light and why must the church endeavor to fight evil beyond spreading the gospel? Scripture gives us Satan's plan so it is Christians that know him and his agenda, the world doesn't! God wants them warned. There is no other purpose in God having given us this information aside from His desire for us to use it. Satan wants to remain unexposed so he must obstruct the church before it exposes him.

Satan knows how to accomplish the building of his one world government. He must amass staggering amounts of control over the masses such as the world has never seen. While doing this he and his true agenda must remain hidden. The world is ignorant of Satan and his devises. They can be easily deceived into believing the changes really are for the promised good but Christians should be on the alert and warn people.

The ability to warn people from the scripture gives us a powerful opening to begin teaching the world about Jesus Christ. As we turn to scripture and show people how many of these things were prophesied we have opportunity to share the gospel. As God defeated pharaoh so too should we expect to be triumphant in our day and what a message this would be to the world! As God intervenes through His people and Satan is defeated the world would be left no conclusion aside from the one we want them to have, OUR GOD REIGNS! We don't send this message and we don't give God opportunity because we've already surrendered!

Satan's efforts are completely contrary to the word of God. The greater his success the more unbearable life becomes for all of us. For example he must control all property because in this way he can control the people that live or work on that property. His strategy, then, is to do away with private property. It is not necessary that he and his minions own it; only that government can regulate its use through regulations or government ownership. Satan has his minions propagandizing the masses against private property but it is Christians who are to intercede exposing that private property is a God given right that government is prohibited from abridging. It is the watchmen that will be first to take note of this attack and understand the threat because they have studied concepts of Godliness and good government.

As the watchmen are silenced fewer people are warned of the consequences of losing private property rights. The well understood principle is that if you do not own your property you will constantly be subject to the dictates of whoever does own it. Additionally you will be robbed of the opportunity to build personal wealth. The need for watchmen to sound the alarm and expose satanic frauds is as valid with a host of issues misunderstood by Christians today such as immigration, government education, treaties and innumerable other topics. These matters have all been corrupted to create an advantage for Satan but the church is not warned.

Another example is money and The Bible has much to say about honest weights and measures. Yet under our current paper system our money is corrupted, honest people are cheated and the church doesn't suspect a thing. It is the church that is to be salt and light and warn people that they are being defrauded of their wealth under this satanic system. Poverty is increased with all the suffering and disease associated with it because the church has failed in this duty. At the same time many in Satan's service have attained incredible amounts of wealth that they are reinvesting to gain even more control. Christians are robbed of their God given ability to create wealth because they have silenced the watchmen who were to warn them of Satan's evil schemes and Satan's agents are getting this wealth.

Imagine what a blessing the church would have been to the world if we had interceded and stopped Satan's counterfeit money system. Imagine what a testimony we would be to the world if Christians refused to join Satan's system and thus gave God an opportunity to bless them for their faithfulness in following His word. This would be opportunity to test the two systems side by side and God could show the world that Satan's path leads to destruction.

Another example is medicine and this is probably the largest and most controversial topic in this chapter. Battle lines are being drawn as Satan and his forces are working to steal even greater control in this arena. Basically the two schools of thought are "homeopathic" medicine verses "allopathic" medicine. Homeopathic medicine is the treatment of ailments and diseases by natural cures. Natural cures are vitamins, nutrients, minerals, herbs and so forth that experience has taught have a positive impact on certain ailments or parts of the body and subsequently provide healing.

"Allopathic" medicine is described as being the three "C's". These would be cutting, chemicals and chemotherapy.

The first thing you notice is that none of these should be considered healthy. We've come to accept cutting as beneficial to eliminate an organ that is a threat to the greater health of the body but many researchers challenge modern medicine with covering up substantial information about harmful side effects that lead to prolonged and dangerous health problems from surgery. As Christians we should recognize that God gave us those organs for a reason and cutting them out may not be healthy just because that's what we're told, especially if some natural cure will stimulate these organs back to functioning normally.

The next point is chemicals, which can never replace proper nutrition, but evolutionists believe that chemicals are an effective way to treat diseases. They also promote the belief that animal tissue, which is used in many vaccinations, is inconsequential and this too is based on evolutionary theory.

The very basic and obvious point that we no longer cure diseases but "treat" them should be a matter of concern to everybody and evidence that those in charge of the acknowledged medical establishment do not have our best interests in mind. Cancers, heart disease, diabetes are just a few of the diseases that are spiraling out of control while we're told there is no cure but scores of independent researches have had impressive results through natural cures. Yet we're told to dismiss their claims and run to a doctor who admits he doesn't know how to cure us.

We're constantly told "it's our fault, we don't eat right, we don't exercise", etc. We are not to question the system. The system is good, we're bad. Meanwhile the system is working to significantly deny people access to common vitamins and minerals, which, by any logical standard, will exacerbate the problems! Those that are unfamiliar with this agenda should research "Codex Alimentarius" for a bit of an "eye opener" on just how much the medical establishment cares about our health. This is a blatant agenda to destroy an individual's ability to protect their health through vitamins and minerals, something that would have no purpose in a system concerned with good health. [41]

The evidence that laetrile, as just one natural treatment, should be considered as a treatment due to a track record of positive results is information seldom made available to cancer patients. The only solution that the larger health care industry is willing to acknowledge as legitimate conforms to the "three C's" policy. Those that oppose Satan's system of healthcare are considered fringe and ignorant.

Thirdly, it's quite a feat that, we have all been educated about the dangers of radiation yet we pay huge sums of money to be exposed to it at a time when we're already seriously ill! Few people are aware of how controversial this topic is because the major media no longer regards it as controversial. They singularly promote it. We have been robbed of the opportunity to maintain good health by a culture that has moved us away from natural, Godly treatments of disease and healthy diets to a diet of chemicals and hazardous treatments.

We must consider the food supply too. The Bible reveals how soil is to be treated so that it will yield the maximum nutrition into the food. With the abandonment of small family farmers to farming corporations these practices have been abandoned for profit and now we have a food supply with very little nutritional value, full of chemicals and toxins from fertilizers. Now we are seeing both the standardization of "GMO's" (genetically modified organisms which include food's) and laws being passed to protect GMO producers by prohibiting consumers from knowing if their food supply is genetically modified.[42] Is it any wonder that killer diseases like cancer, heart disease and diabetes are skyrocketing? Other countries employ a variety of homeopathic cures that should be explored due to their success.

The common denominator in Allopathic medicine is profit. There is no profit for pharmaceutical companies in a healthy society that is free to grow their own cures in their backyard or pick them up at the supermarket. When one can consult a matriarch for treatment instead of a doctor there is no one to sell the chemicals for the pharmaceutical companies, which is a service currently performed by your local doctor.

Revelation 6:8 speaks of the fourth seal "power was given unto them over the fourth part of the earth to kill with the sword and with hunger and with death and with the beasts of the earth." How do you kill with death? Trying to survive, physically, with a food supply that does not have the vitamins and nutrients the body needs is a problem. To replace these vitamins and nutrients with chemicals to the point we are developing a biological dependency on them means we become slaves to the chemical manufacturers and live only by their continued supply.

Revelation 6 does not list natural phenomenons; these are horrors against a world that has turned its back on God and Godly instruction. Many think these are judgments from God but we read in Revelation 6:10 "how long Oh Lord … dost thou not judge …" and this is after the first four seals. These are not judgments from an angry God. They are the culmination of years of ambitious planning by this satanic new world order. How can Christians consider ourselves salt and light when we fail to give Godly instruction and sound the alarm as Satan is building his new world order?

Many are too quick to argue that since it is prophesied we should just accept it and not work to expose the evil growing in our midst. Again, site me a scripture telling Christians to stand idle and let evil prosper. Site me a scripture that salt and light are to run and hide when evil approaches. Who among us wants to stand before our Lord and brag that we were among the first to surrender? We have been deceived into the belief that all matters are political and we have no duty aside from voting. As a result Satan has succeeded in dominating all arenas of our daily lives. We do not view his attacks as cause for alarm because his strategy is to influence instead of destroy.

If we truly understood that we are at war we could immediately recognize that we have been infiltrated and are being destroyed from within. We have embraced this teaching that Christians shouldn't be involved in politics to the point that we no longer consider the impact that all of this is having on our families and freedoms.

The curious aspect of this is how easily we surrender our responsibilities and freedoms. Previous generations got angry when they saw evil rising in the land and they reacted to threats far less alarming than those we tolerate today. One would question if the current generation of Christians have the ability to get angry anymore. If they do, what will it take for them to get angry to the point where they are willing to step up and get involved?

In this study we examine many scriptures in context and compare this to how they are commonly taught today. Perhaps the most brazenly misquoted is Ephesians 4:26 "Be ye angry and sin not; let not the sun go down upon your wrath". Today this is taught most commonly as dealing with marriage, admonishing spouses to make peace before the day's end. There is simply no way to conclude this analysis from the context.

Paul does not begin discussing marriage until chapter 5:22. Between 4:26 and 5:22 Paul addresses a long list of various issues so there is no reasonable way to connect the two thoughts as one. The context here becomes a specific focus in verse 4:20 to the change in attitude one should have when he becomes a Christian. Here he lists some matters that are appropriate for Christians as well as some that are inappropriate for a Christians.

In Ephesians 4 we see the words "wrath" and "anger" used twice; in verse 26 (quoted above) and verse 31 "Let all bitterness and wrath and anger and clamor and evil speaking be put away from you with all malice". We note immediately that these two verses are contradictory. We can either labor to study and understand them in context or accept what has been done here, which is the twisting of the first verse to conform to the meaning of the second. Simply put, there are different types of anger and wrath; there is a Godly anger and wrath and there is a carnal anger and wrath.

To know God is to know that sin makes Him angry and that He will vent His anger in an appointed time of wrath. Wrath can be used in the context of "vengeful indignation of an offense" or "divine chastisement". Man is created in God's image and just as God has the ability to get angry at sin, so too man has the ability to get angry at sin but we seem to be losing this ability. If we read the complete sentences we note that verses 26 and 27 go together just as verses 31 and 32 go together. The first two are dealing with evil and the second two are dealing with Christian relationships. With regard to verses 26-27, if we are not going to "give place to the devil" we had better get involved and if we expect to please God we better start getting angry at the matters that anger Him.

These would include lying (or tolerating liars) theft (or tolerating theft) violation of Godly mandated jurisdictional authorities (or tolerating these violations) or as Paul put it: "that we henceforth be no more children, tossed to and fro and carried about with every wind of doctrine by the sleight of men and cunning craftiness, whereby they lie in wait to deceive: but speaking the truth in love ... walk not as other gentiles walk, in the vanity of their mind, having the understanding darkened, being alienated from the life of God through the ignorance that is in them because of the blindness of their heart … to work all uncleanness with greediness", verses 4:14-19.

God is not pleased that we have become so idle and complacent that evil is thriving in the land. We have a duty that was recognized and accomplished by previous generations and if we fail to recognize this duty it is because we have been deceived. Verse 4:7-18 "Be ye not partakers with them. For ye were sometimes darkness but now are ye light in the Lord … have no fellowship with the unfruitful works of darkness but reprove them (some translations say "expose them") … but all things that are reproved are made manifest by the light: for whatsoever doth make manifest is light. Wherefore He saith, Awake thou that sleepest and arise from the dead and Christ shall give the light. See then that ye walk circumspectly, not as fools but as wise, redeeming the time, because the days are evil. Wherefore be ye not unwise but understanding what the will of the Lord is …" Reproved "by the light", by Christians.

It is a simple matter of duty. One of the sources our founding fathers revered and studied was Dutch statesman Hugo Grotius. He had written, "What God has revealed of His will we call law". He was speaking of Biblical law and the need for them to be incorporated into the laws of society. The more we, as a society, accepted sources other than The Bible as the basis for our laws the more we moved away from God's will. Had God ordained that Godly people should not be involved in politics He could hardly have called King David "a man after His own heart" or sent Paul to witness to Caesar. Godly men have been involved in politics throughout history and we must accept this responsibility as they did.

Hebrews 11:6 says, "He is a rewarder of them that diligently seek Him". Now as never before in our history, America needs Christians to be salt and light. America needs us to be informed and involved. We have been seduced into believing God will bless America if we pray for this without changing our behaviors or that it is meaningful to put a scriptural bumper sticker on our car. Our problems are serious because the enemy is entrenched. He is entrenched because we tolerated the deceptions encouraging us to stand idle.

Satan may be able to deceive the masses but we should not tolerate his efforts and we surely shouldn't adopt them as our own. Our God is God and we need to declare that it is He whom we will serve. He has made known to us the rightful duties of government and the responsibility is ours to take back the place given to Satan and return this nation to its Godly heritage. There will always be many who dispute this responsibility. Let them speak for themselves and let them remain idle if they insist but do not let them convince you that they are qualified leaders. A leader will obviously take you into battle, not into leisurely entertainment when the battle is raging on all fronts. We have too much at stake to tolerate idle leadership any longer.

BATTLES ABANDONED

2ⁿᵈ Corinthians 6:14 - 18 to "come out from among them"

The attitude that Christians should not be involved in politics has resulted in some mighty satanic strongholds in our society that are strategically used to influence and manipulate the thinking of the masses. The purposes are to do Godliness the most harm while promoting their own agenda as a reasonable (and preferable) alternative. Many Christians may be uncomfortable with inflammatory terms like "war" but it is naive and inaccurate to substitute politically correct terms such as "political differences". The majority of issues at stake wouldn't have been considered "political" by previous generations and this may well be the most important battle abandoned by the church, keeping government out of the business of defining morality when it is the responsibility of the church.

Two generations ago, a sodomite coming to a public school and openly discussing their sexuality would have been cause for such public outrage as to bring about the dismissal of all officials involved as well as possible criminal charges. Similarly, the blatant and blasphemous attacks on Jesus would have been openly opposed by a good many of the instructors. Today these things are promoted openly by the schools and tolerated by Christians with little objection.

We are at war and The Bible makes this clear. It is not a war fought with bombs and bullets. It is a war fought with false leadership and lies. Where wars are typically fought over the right to dominate a piece of ground, and subsequently control the people who live there, this war is fought over the right to dominate the major entities of influence in our society. The objective is really the same, the right to control the people. The enemy thinks in terms of future generations.

By dominating the influences that our children are exposed to (schools, media, entertainment, church, etc) the enemy can manipulate the thinking of our youth and create a welcoming environment for his agenda. Rather than realizing this, the church has abandoned the battlefronts of influencing these entities and today they are firmly in Satan's grip.

Schools are, perhaps, the most important entity for Christians to be involved in. It has been said of America's government schools that if parents desire a place to send their children that they may learn to sin, they have their desires met in the school system. The government sets the curriculum and like it or not, that's what your child will be taught; even those that "home school" are required to battle and meet federal controls. There are a few opportunities for excluding a child from one program or another but very few by comparison.

It is common for a child to return from school having been indoctrinated with some political belief contrary to what they learn at home. It is becoming increasingly common for school children to be used as stage dressing at political rallies and marches opposing traditional values.

Predominant among all that can be learned at a government school is the teaching on evolution. This teaching has currently expanded far beyond science and is taught (subtly) in literature classes and even used in the dialog for algebra equations. "Inherit the Wind" was a very popular script used by high school drama classes for three decades. Christians no longer feel compelled to remove their children from government schools in spite of the ungodliness they know is prevalent there because it's easier to tolerate the schools than "teach a child in the way he should go" (proverbs 22:6).

Many churches have now joined "the environmental movement" on some level. Some are pushing recycling while others endorse some misguided energy program. Recently efforts were promoted to bring the environmentalist's "Ark of Hope" to schools across the country. The majority of churches that were aware of this did nothing. This was a very elaborate hoax promoted and designed by the extreme environmentalists to introduce young minds into earth worship. Now churches yield to these kids as they dutifully propose some environmental program. There is no basis in scripture for this it is all political. Our children have been taught earth worship at school, reinforced at church and never questioned at home. The result is increasingly less protests about increasingly more environmental laws. These laws have no impact to actually improve our environment but actually increase the power of this satanic world government over the daily lives of people.

Another example is Halloween. Many churches "celebrate" this satanic un-holy day in some fashion and believe they are doing a good work. Children are not stupid; not even when we wish they were. We convince ourselves that it's wrong to leave our kids out of "the celebration" so we come up with some compromise and never question what message this sends to the children. How can it not be viewed as a double standard or a compromise to celebrate a satanic holiday? In the end, do we believe it matters to God how we celebrate it?

Again, the issue is not whether your children costume up as a Bible character and go to a carnival at church, the problem is that nobody is explaining to these kids just how evil Satan really is. Church "haunted houses" perform mock abortions, illustrate the affects of drug addiction and commonly have a "hell room" to dramatize what these kids can expect if they die without Christ. Perhaps some good comes from some of this but who is sitting these kids down and teaching them how to be on guard against Satan and his wiles?

Inherent in growing to adulthood, children will naturally learn to oppose evil or to tolerate it. They are exposed to no leadership teaching them to oppose it and taught tolerance at school, home and even church. The affects of all of this tolerance are a host of satanic movies, games - including role-playing, and music that comprise the majority of our children's entertainment. They have been taught to tolerate those of differing views and desensitized to evil. Books like "Harry Potter" among a host of others have intrigued them with the occult.

The growth of these satanic tools is a clear example of how the church has lost influence over society to satanic influences. The church no longer speaks of Satan and no longer takes responsibility to fight any issue if it's proposed through political channels. The children are taught at school that Satan is basically a "misunderstood party animal" and what's wrong with having a good time?

God has been kicked out of the schools and traditional Christian Holidays are celebrated with no mention of Christ. 1st Corinthians 10:20-21 makes it clear we're deceived, "...I would not that ye should have fellowship with devils. Ye cannot ... partakers of the table of The Lord and the table of demons..." The parents don't fight for what they believe in so how deeply committed can they be from the child's perspective?

We're teaching our children our beliefs are not worth fighting for and they see Jesus losing on all fronts, while the enemy is winning and having a good time too. Schools will not allow mention of Christ at Christmas, Thanksgiving or Easter but Satan gets an entire day dedicated to him with schools sponsored festivities. You are welcome to attend these events dressed as Satan but you can't even wear a "Jesus" "T-Shirt". The school libraries have any selection of books on the occult and witchcraft in addition to occult themes that have been strategically worked into the curriculum but no Bibles are allowed.

Imagine what would happen if children were taught the historical horrors of Halloween and Satanism. What would happen if we quit celebrating this day with carnivals and candy and used it to educate people about the ruined lives of satanism and the inevitable suffering that comes from evil? What if we taught our children to identify the subtleties of witchcraft as they're secreted into the classroom? If done effectively, the first and immediate result would be that Satan and his minions would demand that Halloween be taken out of the schools because they would not wish to suffer even this limited exposure!

It would be a fight; Satan won't give back ground without a fight. If Jesus can be kicked out of the schools why can't Satan? Toward kicking him out we could at least expose him! We have truth on our side and we should employ that truth on this unholy of days, if on no other, to expose Satan's true agenda. If they can bring in members of the gay rights community, why can't we bring in former members of the occult? Why can't we even bring in former gays?

We can no longer imagine accomplishing a victory such as this and thus we are defeated. We can only imagine defeat and this mindset makes victory unattainable. The Bible has much to say about raising children, yet today we ignore these verses and tolerate the new world order influencing (through the school system) our children to become the first generation of American's that can't rationalize right from wrong, traditional values from situational ethics, Christianity from superstition or the value of a virtuous life over a bleak existence.

Increasingly children grow to adulthood with no hope or structure. The church must accept responsibility; we have failed to be salt and light. We have abandoned the battle over schools and lost the ability to influence the next generation. Yet we leave our own children in this system.

Another battle abandoned by the church, which has significant implications for our youth is that of music, including "Christian rock and roll". When at first Christian leaders preached against rock and roll, and in its turn "Christian" rock and roll, now they book concerts in some of the larger churches and have them as guests at some of the larger crusades.

Jimi Hendrix is quoted as saying "you can hypnotize people with music and when you get people at the weakest point you can preach into their subconscious whatever you want to say". In the book "The Psychology of Music" Dr. Schoen writes, "Music is the most powerful stimulus known among the perceptive processes". According to Dr. William Sargent, at one time Britain's foremost expert on brainwashing, the continual playing of loud rock music can create paradoxical brain activity where bad becomes good and good becomes bad".

No more than a generation ago, those popular in the music industry were frequently interviewed to assure us all of how harmless it was; just clean fun. Now we just as frequently hear and view abundant evidence that satanism is a constant theme of many groups and labels. We hear lyrics that are the only evidence needed by reasonably intelligent people to correctly judge what spirit this music is promoting. We live in an age where the leading voices on raising children make an effort to rapidly put as many on psychotropic drugs as possible. Yet after these children are drugged to make them pliant for hypnotic suggestion we do nothing as they listen to endless hours of this music and we still "blame the guns" and ask why when one of them becomes violent as they've been trained to do.

In America today we have many voices (seldom Christians) demanding that the cold impersonal corporations that exploit people for profit be held accountable by government. Factories are harassed for environmental concerns, munitions manufacturers including gun and ammunition makers are hassled and sued simply for involvement in a profession others do not approve of, automobile companies are under threat by every special interest group with a creative lawyer as are toy manufacturers for "safety" arguments and the list goes on. However those same people that demand all of these corporations be regulated are amazingly quick to cry "censorship" when the suggestion is made that the entertainment industry be regulated. These same people are quick to scoff at the mere suggestion that evidence exists that this music does have a negative impact on young listeners.

It is the church, which is to know better and neither does the church fight this battle anymore. Many churches have now embraced this music and hold concerts as an outreach to attract younger people in a confused belief that if they draw them in with this music they create an opportunity to reach those they otherwise wouldn't. Nowhere in scripture do we have an example of this compromise with evil in an effort to spread the gospel. The saddest part is that the music is no longer considered to be evil so long as the words "sound" Christian or at least talk of love. We have chosen to forget that words are but one part of the equation.

The list goes on but all battles are abandoned today. Where once the church fulfilled its duty of salt and light in a host of areas, these areas are now simply dismissed as not having anything to do with preaching the gospel. Areas such as respectable clothing, respectable television programs and commercials, promotion of homosexuality as simply a choice, birth control to children, abortion, strip tease bars, selling liquor on Sunday or even having a business open on Sunday, fraud in the market place as well as in government. All of these things have to do with the quality of our communities in direct relationship to how Godly our society will be for ourselves and raising children.

What should be a Christian's involvement in politics? Twice the involvement of Satan's! We should be promoting the word of God and Godly standards for society like it matters! The word "church" is from the Greek "Ecclesia" which is commonly interpreted as "the assembly" or "the assembled". Being assembled together with like-minded people makes the church a very powerful organizational entity with far reaching ability to influence the larger community.

This serves a variety of purposes such as simplified training, education, support, encouragement, standards and accountability. Problems arise when we undergo training but are never led into battle. The entire army develops a complacent "what's the point" attitude. Another old axiom is "education without action leads to frustration". Many are exposed to the problems but are never given assistance when they want to become part of the solution. The organizational structure that God ordained to assist Christians has become counter productive as it is now used to create a "universal mentality" of idleness. This mindset of Christians and the church being synonymous is dangerous when we allow ourselves to be controlled and neutralized as a group instead of fulfilling individual responsibilities.

The church, as an organization, has its support and training duties but when we permit church leadership to have an ungodly amount of control and influence over our lives we have created an institution which can mislead Christians corporately. Satan hungers to control everything including powerful organizations and the church would be no exception. The church was never to be organized in such a way as to control the individual Christian. It was to train them in righteousness and support them as needed.

Even though we are led to believe Christians shouldn't be involved in politics, let me list a few ways the church is involved in politics in such a way as to neutralize our effectiveness:

First of all 501c3 laws and laws of incorporation are so burdensome to the church and are destroying our effectiveness to such a degree that they will be addressed in an entire chapter devoted to this subject alone.

Then there is the fact that we all pay taxes. There is tremendous deception here that could not stand if the church sought to expose it. The ability to tax has created opportunity for the government to examine the families financial business, burden the family financially and use the money for satanic purposes. It has been used as an excuse to number every American, enslave them with debt at birth, monitor their employment, charitable donations, bank accounts and severely penalize those who they determine to be troublemakers.

Whenever federal policy allows for expansion of the debt we all suffer the affects of inflation. This has an impact on our family budgets in everything from the food we can or can't afford to purchase up to where we live or where we vacation.

We are so proud of our sons and daughters that join the military that we have forsaken our duty to question the motives of our leaders who send them around the world to kill others whom God loves (Luke 6:27). This too is an abandoned battle. Grotius (sighted earlier as a source revered by the founding fathers) makes an interesting point, "Christian leaders have a Christian duty to avoid war". He was not a pacifist; he did not dispute the need for certain wars. He did believe that God had no partiality between people and Christians need to respect the sanctity of life.

Therefore this modern day concept of killing anyone our President chooses for whatever reason he choose is an affront to God. Our founding fathers put war-making powers in the hands of The House of Representatives who were accountable to the people. Now this has been abandoned and we see constant war, singularly determined by the President, and this tolerated by the Congress and seldom questioned by the people and certainly not Christians if the President is of "our party". To the extent people do question a war, they seldom have tangible reasons, it's more political rhetoric. Christians never step in and insist we have no God given authority to cross the planet killing whomever we desire.

Control over the family has been forfeited to government; control over the money supply, soon the government will have control of all retirement funds and health care. Churches have never had this degree of control and now have been pushed out of the process. Currently we see churches lining up for money under the program of "Faith Based Initiatives". They are not aware that The Supreme Court has ruled that what the government finances, it has a right to control.

The churches no longer consult the word of God when our political leaders announce a new policy. If our churches no longer consider the word of God, why should our leaders? Groups from The ACLU, People for the American Way, NORAL, NOW, NEA and a long list of others lusting for an anti-God agenda all influence government but churches are told it is not our business. These groups have a satanic agenda and Christians need to confront them.

We are commanded in Ephesians 4:27 to "give no place to the devil" and in 2nd Corinthians 10:5 to "cast down ... every high thing that exalts itself against the knowledge of God..." This would include government and politicians when they violate God's law and this is our warfare. This is our duty. We were never to sit idle and give Satan the seat of power that is government.

Those committed to Satan's agenda of a new world order strive for control of all the entities from which we get our information that they may control what we know. America's pulpits and seminaries are a source of information. They would be guilty of a major oversight, never corrected, if we believe they have not sought control of our pulpits. When we recognize how our churches have followed the leadership of our politicians and submitted themselves to what our political leaders desire, it is quite obvious who is influencing whom.

We are commanded in 2nd Corinthians 6:14-18 to "come out from among them" and "them" is defined numerous times as those who do not serve God. This would include ungodly bureaucrats with a hidden agenda, even when we may enjoy some temporary personal benefit from a government program and it would include political parties that continually lie to get our votes and do not labor to institute Godly policies when in office.

We cannot "come out from among them" and leave our children at the mercy of their educational system or submit ourselves to their financial system. We have strategically been taught to think politics should not be our focus. In truth, our system of politics affords us the promise of blessings or curses but only if we are involved. History teaches us that curses are always the result when Godly people don't demand Godly government.

We have come out of their political system and left ourselves victims in all they do. Coming out from among them sounds good if we had a place to go. We must live here and it is self-defeating to allow them total authority when this is not what God wishes or the proper way for our government system to operate.

We have the duty of coming out from among them by forcing them out of that which is rightfully ours to possess and we have the Godly authority as well as the patriotic authority to do this. They can either leave or submit to the Godly system that is the law in The

United States. Let them go where they will but if they would stay, they must respect the laws of the land and those laws are based on Godly principles, or used to be and need to be restored.

We are under no bondage where we are forced to submit to their evil without a choice. It is only due to ignorance and poor leadership that we have submitted to their will and this can be changed. No deal with the devil is binding for those who would serve God! I have heard often that "satan's greatest trick was to convince the world that he doesn't exist". I disagree. The world doesn't care if Satan exists. Those that do believe he exists don't consider him as a problem and everyone is indoctrinated with the idea that God couldn't possibly "send" people to hell, so why worry? It is no trick to convince apathetic people to be apathetic.

Satan's greatest trick was to fool God's people into serving his agenda, if by no other means than not opposing it. It was not necessary for Christians to make Satan a god, it was only necessary for us to stand aside and let him make this claim without opposition. We are the ones that know Satan exists and what his agenda is but we do nothing to stop him so we serve him by our apathy. We are the ones that know God is love and Satan is hate, yet we tolerate (even promote) the teachings that all the evil that happens is ordained of God.

We are the ones that have been told in The Bible what Satan's agenda is but when we see it coming to pass we don't expose it or warn people. We are the ones that have been told in The Bible what God would have us doing but we reject God's word and listen to those that tell us to do nothing. So whom do we serve? Serving Satan is easy; all we have to do is nothing. In doing nothing we let the lies persist that God is the author of evil.

We tell others that it is God who sends natural disasters, sickness and death upon someone we love. I wonder just exactly what some Christians think Satan does since they blame God for everything. If all evil comes from God, what does He have against Satan? Yet the church doesn't think through this foolishness! We don't know who our enemy is! Satan has successfully convinced the church to carry the message that God is evil and keep silent about Satan completely. It's time we did what God told us to. If the church is going to serve God it needs to fight Satan and that means Satan's strategies. We need to get into the fight and stop this unnecessary growth of government and turn men toward God.

Coming out from among them is having done with this world system. Daniel and the three Hebrew children would not partake with the Babylonians and were blessed for keeping themselves separate. They didn't leave Babylon or act as simple submissive slaves; they influenced the King and introduced him to the one true God. We have a God that is able to meet our needs and we need to start believing that and living it like we believe it! We are at war but we eat at the enemy's table and carry the enemy's message to the world. Why should the world want to serve God whom they associate with a lot of rules, when they recognize that Christians seek their blessings from the government?

Christians are lining up to benefit from the government programs even when the programs are contrary to God's word. Why should God bless us when we don't ask Him to? We ask government to bless us through some program when we should trust in God. Our country depends on bringing our government "out from among" the evil forces controlling it because it is we, the church that knows Satan has set a trap. The world will not recognize this until it's too late. God sent us to warn them and we have a duty to perform what He's asked.

When this is mentioned to current church leaders we are told that "it is a spiritual battle and prayer is our warfare". Scripture tells us frequently to "pray always" but never does it say to "pray only". Galatians 1:4 says "that Christ might deliver us from this present evil world according to the will of God." Read it again, it is the will of God to deliver us from the evil of this world! To receive that deliverance requires a commitment to stop fraternizing with the enemy.

We're led to believe that we can wage this war from the comfort of our homes by prayer alone. We're promised a comfortable warfare with no hassles or dangers. If you consider warfare and analyze this strategy you recognize something interesting; for this strategy to work warfare has to exclude any involvement or contact with the enemy! Who aside from modern day Christians has ever heard of such a war? Any warfare where the enemy is fought will include discomforts, hassles and dangers.

This makes it rather obvious who planned this strategy for us. What is our warfare? If it is "prayer" and only "prayer" why not say that? Why use the word "warfare" if you mean pray? This "pray only" teaching does not bespeak people involved in or prepared for "warfare" but rather people running from the battle making an excuse as they run.

Prayer is an extensive and needful study in its own right and certainly should be studied and properly employed but prayer does not replace our responsibilities. I firmly believe in prayer but we cannot pray for money while refusing to work. We cannot pray for a fulfilling relationship and not put effort into a relationship. We cannot pray for someone to come to know Christ and never broach the subject with them. We cannot pray for our country and not exercise our authority when some arrogant politician violates his position and promotes some ungodly law.

We cannot ask God to bless America if we are only willing to make some half-hearted gesture in the battle to restore Godly government. We cannot ask God to bless America if we are willing to tolerate some evil agenda simply because the battle to set things right will be a long hard fight. These are not the proper way to employ prayer. Yet on the matter of our country's future, we're told prayer is sufficient. So we pray for America while we support bad policies and bad politicians and wonder why God doesn't answer our prayers.

Again, 2nd Corinthians 10:5-6 describe our warfare, "casting down imaginations and every high thing that exalteth itself against the knowledge of God and bringing into captivity every thought to the obedience of Christ; and having in readiness to revenge all disobedience, when your obedience is fulfilled". We will not be perfectly obedient while we're on this earth. If we have been "obedient to accept Christ" our battle is spelled out. Satan and his minions in the new world order are ever creating imaginations that there is no God and we don't need one because if we empower government sufficiently it will meet our needs. It is our battle to expose this satanic lie and we cannot justify abandoning it.

Everything you can potentially do emanates from what you are. "Ye are the salt of the earth and the light of the world". We can't "be" a Christian and not "be" salt and light. You can only fail to live up to your Godly potential and calling. If we oppose Satan we have no way of knowing what we can accomplish because we are certain to have God's help. If we don't oppose him, we have surrendered already (know ye not, to whom ye yield yourselves servants to obey, his servants ye are...Romans 6:16). If we fail to oppose him, we serve him by allowing him to prosper while we have the power, authority and duty to stop him.

The second half of The Book of Acts has detailed how Paul battled people with their own agenda and there is no record that he went home to pray about them. Christians realize freedom exists in this country because Godly men stepped out, putting their lives and fortunes on the line. Today the church wants its freedom for free. It is unlikely that the church would be prevented from fighting Satan through intimidation. Yet confusion about the application of certain scriptures could be a perfect plan. Just convince the church that it's not their fight and they don't have to worry about the consequences of inaction.

We're told to just trust church leadership who may indeed be Godly people but they no longer have any understanding of Satan's battle plan. You can't lead an organized resistance against an enemy you don't know or understand. Church leaders that don't know or understand the new world order may be wonderful pastors and teachers but they are not qualified to interpret or advise on current events.

It is good to recognize that The Bible does not say Satan can appear as an angel of light. It indicates he always appears as an angel of light (2nd Corinthians 11:14). If he appeared in his true evil, vile self, who would have anything to do with him? Satan will only pursue his agenda while hiding behind what appears as some good work or worthwhile cause. This is why we must question the motives and goals of movements that claim to be Godly or seemingly a Godly purpose.

When the very church of the living God starts approaching government for help and solutions we cannot doubt that our spiritual leaders are not qualified to lead or guide!

Finally, of all the battles abandoned by Christians, the battle over religion deserves some consideration. At America's founding Christianity was the only recognized religion under the law. Today the church does nothing as any group with vile or evil intent simply declares themselves an official religion and receives more protection than what the true church of God is afforded. We sit idle as we are associated with ritualistic evil and inconsequential nonsense.

Much of this is because we no longer hold our own accountable under scripture. What well-known pastor or evangelist today fits the definition of Titus 5:7-8? The media does all they can to discredit Bible believing Christians but I know of no one who has earned wide spread respect for integrity and this makes it easy to assume peoples of all religions have only doctrinal differences.

It was once said, "the price of not being involved in politics is to be ruled by your inferiors." From a Christian perspective, the price of not being involved in politics is to be ruled by Satan's agents. The commitment level to work for change is greater among those promoting an evil agenda (from a Biblical perspective) than the commitment level from Christians and this is wrong! This is the reason we see them accomplishing so much, not because God willed. They simply work for what they believe in while we have been taught it's not our fight.

Either we stand up for righteousness, which means we fight to come out of Satan's system and expose it for what it really is or we continue to be drawn in deeper with our complacency. No one can serve God by being complacent. This is a quote from Dietrich Bonhoeffer, a Lutheran Pastor. "Silence in the face of evil is itself evil; God will not hold us guiltless. Not to speak is to speak. Not to act is to act." Although he was safe in London, he returned to Germany in order to teach at an underground seminary at Finkenwald out of dismay for the state church. He was imprisoned in 1943 for opposing Hitler and spent the last two years of his life ministering to those in the prison camp. He was hung on April 9, 1945. No doubt he was a man of prayer but he understood the need to take action.

We have abandoned too many battles and today we are paying a high price in our family relationships, family finances, education and morality of our children, loss of our businesses and business opportunities, loss of property rights and the list would fill pages. Simply stated, we have abandoned God's plan for a harmonious society and we are embracing the corruption that is Satan's system.

From the first civilizations certain types of men have sought to replace God's system. These are men who will not labor to meet their own needs but steal the hard work of those who do strive to produce.

This theft is called taxation and it has ever been a vexation established by man upon his fellow man. Little of the money that we are taxed actually goes to the betterment of our community. Much of it goes to buy votes and curry favor. Much of it goes to build fine monuments to men who deserve no acknowledgment. Much of it goes to build palaces where the self-important meet to determine our future to the full measure we will permit them.

At this writing we are faced with scores of battles and we must ask ourselves one difficult question; is our government limited by anything or are we subjects to be dictated to? Who can now doubt that we are ruled by judges? People pass an amendment to their state constitutions and judges throw it out. People endeavor to pass a law by ballot initiative and a judge throws it out. Congress passes a law and judges throw it out. Did we lose a war? How was this revolution accomplished? Society needs us now and we must return to the fight.

It is important to note that these battles have not been lost! They have been abandoned. The enemy has deceived us into surrendering the field when the victory was ours for the claiming. We have the authority but we lack the resolve to use it. This must change. Perhaps the best way to make this point clear is a historical review of Christians in politics so let's do that now.

HISTORY OF CHRISTIANS IN POLITICS

*2nd Timothy 2:13 "all scripture is profitable for
doctrine..."*

Question: What is the most passionate debate over history that you
are familiar with? I suspect those that give this some thought will
agree that the most passionate debate over history is the question of
whether or not The United States was founded as a Christian nation
or a secular one. There are many disagreements over history, of course,
but the passion is noticeably different. On other matters, both sides
share their opinion, discuss their beliefs and leave it at that. On the
topic of whether America was founded as a Christian nation or not the
argument is pursued with a religious vigor as if both sides view this as
a way to win something larger than the argument itself.

It would be easy to dismiss all of this by saying one side has
religious zeal and the other side has contempt for religious zeal and this
stimulates passion. This is obviously true but religious zeal is a term
that applies more to the strength of one's conviction than it does to any
spiritual beliefs. Many disputes exist that pale in zealous dogmatism
to the debate over America's Christian heritage. On this topic we see
a ferocious dispute where one side insists our founding fathers were
devout Christians and the other side insists, with equal vigor, that the
evidence exposes them as deists. There is a subtle point here, by the
way. We know the founders were not deists because deists do not
believe in a personal God or Devine intervention, hence, they would
not have asked God for any guidance or blessings. Deism is not a "type"
of Christianity or a somewhat clouded offshoot; it is diametrically
opposed although this point is frequently convoluted by some.[43]

The point here is that if you don't seek God's guidance or
blessings, particularly for our country's future, the new world order

crowd will be strangely satisfied with that. We should consider what they're thinking here! This is really what they're fighting about. They have an agenda and want to set the course for our country's future and they don't want God or Christians interfering. Thus it becomes necessary to rewrite history and create the doctrine that our founding fathers accomplished what they did without God and so must we.

Here again we see the need they had to get Christians out of politics but equally important, we see the need they have to win this debate. Their agenda depends on alienating people from God. These are historical matters and the records can be reviewed and the matter settled but they know they would lose if the truth were known. They cannot afford to concern themselves with facts and they never lets the truth get in the way of achieving their goals.

In a situation where emotional arguments will not end the debate, it becomes necessary for them to substitute their propaganda for the facts. I'm not referring to simply telling a lie here. I'm talking about creating an industry to sell these lies as truth. Specifically, I'm referring to the known practice of "history revisionism" which is simply ignoring that which actually happened and documenting that which you want taught as the truth. Once again, to quote George Orwell:

"Whoever controls the past controls the future; whoever controls the present controls the past".

The new world order would have us believe that modern day historians are honest and hardworking with no personal agenda or values aside from making truth known. At the same time we're told that the historians of previous generations have "tainted the historical record" with their personal (Christian) beliefs, thus the greater reliability is afforded the more recent "discoveries".

Here we see a common new world order tactic of "accuse your opponent of fraud before he can accuse you". A common standard for historians (or any researcher) has long been that the most reliable documents are originals and secondarily would be the documents closest to the original. This standard is abandoned by the new world order on all topics but most importantly on scripture and of America being founded as a Christian nation.

We increasingly see the writings of The Bible being called into question by "other writings" which we are told are as original as those we've long accepted but these were rejected by prejudice. It would be an easy matter to refer back to these documents and settle the debate but Satan is a liar and so are his minions. They do not want the debate settled; they want to fabricate lies to deceive.

It is worthwhile to ponder what would motivate a historian to spend years in review of all the documentation and abandon all of their training in terms of research to promote an agenda they know to be totally false. One reason is that they realize it is the only way to get published. The new world order has a virtual strangle hold on the publishing, marketing and distribution of books. Books that defy their interests are difficult to get published, are ridiculed in the media to hurt sales and are not promoted by the major distribution outlets.

A second need to destroy any belief that America was founded as a Christian nation lies in the matter of evolution, which enters the debate from the perspective that if we are evolving we must be constantly gaining knowledge. For this to be a viable point, we cannot admit that these men of two centuries past had knowledge that far exceeded our own. To admit they knew better than we about concepts in good government is contrary to the very core of evolutionary thought. This type of thinking is responsible for a host of legal decisions breaking with "precedent" because "we now know better" than previous generations.

We are "enlightened" but if our founders were Christians, and if The Bible is true, then they had a source for knowledge that may be worthy of consideration today. It is a scriptural truth that "it is not in man to direct his own steps", Jeremiah 10:23. If man cannot direct his own steps he is incapable of governing himself or a nation. The idea of a nation of self-governing people may sound appealing but according to The Bible, man is not up to the task. It has worked until recently because Christians have had a strong influence on our government and Christians used The Bible for guidance. Man can only govern himself with God's help and by using God's word for guidance. It is breaking the connection between God's word and good government that is vital to the new world order because they know the result will be chaos which is their goal.

The chapter on "Satan's view of Government" deals with Satan's objective of creating chaos. Here we need to recognize that in order to create chaos Satan must break the reliance men have on using Godly concepts in government. As long as we revere God's word we have standards to govern ourselves and will avoid the chaos Satan desires. So the gain for the new world order in this debate is obvious; don't look to history or scripture for wisdom, look to us – your newly and self-appointed ruling elite.

Satan needs people to believe that our founders were not Christians to prove that America was not founded as a Christian nation. If we can be made to believe this we will attribute none of America's former greatness to Biblical guidance in establishing and maintaining government. We will not cry out to God as previous generations have done because we will lack the knowledge that they did this. We will accept the deceptions and leave all government in their evil hands while we both ignored God and blame Him for all the ensuing horrors.

The point to be remembered is that the new world order does not care whether America was founded as a Christian nation or not, they know with certainty that it was! Their objective is to control the future and their agenda would be identical if the fact was universally established that Christians founded America. If our founders had several scriptures included within The Constitution itself it would have no impact on them or their agenda. To achieve success they must remove Christians from politics and destroy any belief that Christianity offers something superior to what they desire to force on the world.

Christian history is one of God intervening in the affairs of men and stopping Satan in his tracks. The new world order cannot afford to have God intervene so they must devise a strategy to exclude God. It's simple; God works through people so infiltrate the churches, water down the message, drop teaching on authority and replace them with teachings promoting complacency and tolerance and the people are lost for lack of knowledge.

The historical record and a true interpretation of scripture would expose their lies and their agenda. In this debate, the argument is kept on a level of what the founders believed and not why they believed them. These were highly educated men who saw miracle after miracle when they prayed in faith expecting divine intervention. It would be disastrous to have this known by Christians today.

Since it is not in man to order his own steps, once Christians withdrew from leadership Satan and his minions moved in to lead. Inevitably America faced increasing problems in quantity and severity. The truth of America's past greatness must be hidden and distorted or concerned patriots would demand America return to its Godly heritage as our only hope to survive. By denying our Christian heritage there are many among us, even in the churches, who do not consider the key to restoring quality of life as a return to Christian principles of good government. You cannot desire to return to a Godly heritage if you are unaware that you have a Godly heritage. You can't want what you don't know.

Thus we accept the lie that Christians should not be involved in politics since we no longer understand that this is our heritage and the reason for our country's former greatness. Most important of all, however, is the matter of God. America's founding history is, for a Christian, a parade of fascinating events, which declare incontrovertibly that God delights in blessing those who diligently seek Him! This is a history that would spark some of the greatest praise and worship services known to our modern age if only the story were told! If the church embraced this knowledge and attitude Satan wouldn't stand a chance!

We know America is in its death throws but we do nothing, why? Obviously there are two reasons. The first is that we don't know what to do and the second is we're not convinced that we should do anything. We don't know what to do because principles of sound economics and good government have been removed from our educational system and we're not sure if we should do anything because we have been completely indoctrinated with confusion and false leadership. Satan has accomplished this. God is the same yesterday, today and forever.

What would happen if Christians of today acted like Christians of two hundred years ago? What would our country be like if Christians acted like Christians? Satan's lies would be exposed, we would hunger after truth and seek to understand good government principles, sound economics, spiritual principles and those in the occult would see that their god is a liar.

It can be argued that two groups with radically different agendas founded America. One was the mercantilists who were solely profit oriented. This too is a valuable part of our history and there is nothing morally wrong with investors receiving a profit. The second group is those seeking religious freedom and their history is American history as much as is the history of the mercantilists.

Businessmen have traveled the globe in search of profit and opportunity but only in America do we have the rich history of freedom and liberty that we all know. This liberty cannot be attributed to the mercantilists, as it can't be shown that they seeded this liberty in any other land. It developed here due to the Christian's commitment to Godly principles, which had no conflict with the beliefs of mercantilism. This is important because we see still today where businessmen are moving globally in search of profit but no where in their travels are they promoting the cause of liberty.

Our founding fathers were not just in pursuit of religious freedom. They knew their religious oppression came from the state sanctioned church and from their governments. They wanted freedom from oppression by both and they sought God that they might receive this freedom. In America, those that hunger to control other men lost two chains with which to bind the masses.

We do not read an American history of men being freed from the bondage of religious overseers and with their new found freedom they embrace the lusts of the flesh and give God no concern. Rather we read of an America that was colonized by one religious group after another. Then we enter a period history records as "the great awakening". "The second great awakening" shortly follows this. Then we read about the religious fervor of the civil war period followed by what some call "the third great awakening".

By the time our founding fathers signed The Declaration of Independence America had existed as a society largely free to pursue relationship with God for 150 years. During that time government was completely dominated by devout Christians.

Predictably there were variations. The Anglican Church worked to establish controls in Virginia as it had in England. Promoters of Calvinist doctrine worked hard to establish control in the colonies. The Puritans arguably had the greatest success in establishing doctrine but in the end, Americans had a passion for freedom and this extended to their passion to worship God freely.

This passion, combined with the fact that America was vast and unsettled, created problems the dominant denominations could not overcome. Farms spread far and wide and sometimes deep into the wilderness. Any type of constant contact between a clergyman and individuals was quite difficult on any type of ongoing basis and certainly financially burdensome.

One would consider that with the loss of regular contact with any clergy the passion for scriptural study lessened with each passing generation. This would not seem to be verifiable by the historic records, however. Massachusetts broke into revivals that began in 1679 and there are records of other revivals taking place across the land and throughout the years. Probably the freedom from Calvinism played a large role here, as when one is free to form a relationship with God it becomes more meaningful than obligatory church requirements. What we can take note of is that during this period the large controlling denominations lost ground to those that encouraged the independent pursuit of personal relationship.

Calvinism played a large role in America's founding era but as total freedom of religion was exercised Satan took advantage to spread much false doctrine through what would come to be called "Deism" and "Unitarianism". Dealing with people on an individual basis is not Satan's first choice. He much prefers to deal with large groups of people at one time such as creating false religious doctrines and forcing these teachings on the masses. Individually takes more time and effort. It was concerning this apostasy that devout servants of God spoke forth most adamantly and launched The Great Awakening in 1735. Some estimate this fantastic time of revival lasted into the 1770's, an entire generation! It was from this passion for freedom, all types of freedom, that our founding fathers sprang.

It should be noted that one of these new freedoms was in education. Previous generations were harnessed to an educational system that was run by a controlled religious environment or the state itself. As America grew it established new institutions of learning which had nothing to fear in asking the hard questions of history, questions governments and denominations might not approve of, as the answers were embarrassing and revealing. Writers from the old world were welcomed into the new and their political manuscripts were welcomed and studied.

The Bible was cited more frequently as a reference document than any other source by our founding fathers so it is understandably curious how modern Christians fail to consider political involvement as a duty.[44] The Bible, used to the extent it was at the Constitutional Convention and in other writings is something most modern historians are very uncomfortable with yet they have no records to bring forth and argue that our founders cited Voltaire or Rousseau.

Clearly our laws and institutions were established with the belief that man has a sinful nature that must be accountable to the laws of society. Those who serve society were required to swear a belief in a Divine judgment. These men were required to acknowledge God would judge them for any violation of their oath.

They believed Christians have a duty to resist tyranny.[45] From the persecution against Lutherans and Calvinists our founders learned the lesson well, that no religious freedom can exist without a limited government. Virtually all of the documents of the time cite some reference to God as "Creator" or as the "Supreme Being". It was from this recognition of God's authority and providential rule that the arguments of "God given rights" evolved. The right to religious freedom was considered absolute by the time of our nation's formal beginning.

Those that held different beliefs were not persecuted but neither were they considered worthy to serve in government. Furthermore, there was no nonsense about all religions being equal. The term religion in any variation was reserved exclusively for Christianity. All other beliefs were considered equal; equally wrong! Freedom was considered to be dependent on Christianity.

Perhaps the most significant aspect of The United States government is the aspect of a covenant between the people and the leadership. Men or governments were never considered to be without accountability and no government was unlimited in its power. Rather, all were limited by God's word and what it revealed about the proper role of government. The covenant, or Constitution, was written down at both the state and federal level. The duties and powers of government were established and made available for all to see, read, understand and amend.

With the changes that have taken place in government over the last few years, we see that we no longer have a covenant. Our constitution is ignored and there is no limit to the authority current leadership assumes unto themselves. Neither is there any outcry from the churches about the immorality of this ungodly use of power.

By attacking the integrity of the founders and arguing they were seeking financial gain derides the fact that many of them suffered significant financial damage in the fulfillment of doing their duty. This is clear evidence that it was their Christian values that motivated them, not the pursuit of wealth as we're told today. They understood God's law and they understood the motivation of tyrants to destroy God's law. With this understanding they could not sit idle. They believed a Christian has a duty to God and his fellow man that transcends other considerations.

They believed the writing of a Constitution to be the strongest means of equipping themselves and future generations with a tool few have had in human history. A tool to deal with tyranny before it started and certainly before it amassed any serious power. A tool to deal with tyranny at its source where power is most easily used for corruption – the government level. This was a Christian belief in a written law that all men are subject to, even those in government.

The state was regarded as an organizational structure to serve the people. It was not viewed, as in history past, as some divine entity worthy of service and devotion. If God is not the standard then government becomes the standard since it will inevitably define the standard. This is why the new world order cannot afford to lose the debate. Everything we are as a nation and everything we aspire to be centers on Christianity. Everything the new world order desires and pursues is satanic and will end in destruction.

Such a basic distinction cannot be debated on an ideological level since only the deranged would invite destruction upon themselves. This debate can only be controlled by burying the truth so deep it cannot be ferreted out and anyone who tries must be discouraged. It is truth that must be told and Christians that know America was founded as a Christian nation have no excuse not to demand history be taught truthfully.

Here are a few pages of history no longer taught in America:

The Mayflower would have been lost at sea from a storm, which struck the ship so violently that the main beam supporting the center of the ship was severely damaged and surely would have caused the ship to break apart. In the Pilgrims ambition to print Bibles and other religious tracts, they'd brought with them a printing press. Positioning this machine under the cracked beam and extending the giant main screw from the press to force the beam back into place saved the ship. This somewhat haphazard but emergency fix, miraculously, held firm during the remaining storm and saw the Mayflower safely to America. The Pilgrims faithfully taught this incident as providential and Divine intervention for generations but it is not taught today.[46]

For years historians have debated if the Captain of the Mayflower, a Dutchman, sailed off course intentionally. He'd insisted that the winds blew the ship off course, which caused their landing at Cape Cod rather than at a specific natural harbor, which is what the Pilgrims had contracted with him. This dispute is based on accusations that Dutch businessmen bribed him since they desired this natural harbor for themselves. This natural harbor is what we know today as Manhattan but was settled as New Amsterdam four years after the Pilgrims sailed. There exists, however, an intriguing bit of history on this question. Had they landed at Manhattan they would almost certainly been destroyed by local tribes which were quite formidable and hostile at the time. The tribes of the Cape Cod region had suffered from disease about 1619, which had severely weakened them and diminished their numbers. They were in no condition to constitute a serious threat in 1620 when the Pilgrims landed.[47]

It was the repeated teaching of these incredible stories that so imbedded the name "Mayflower" in the minds of Americans. Who can name a ship that brought over any of the other many colonists? If that fails to imply Divine providence, consider the incredible story of "Squanto". Admittedly the kidnapping of this boy by sailors was cruel and unjustifiable but one must consider Divine intervention when we realize he was kidnapped twice!

"The first time he was brought to England and taught the language so that he could be used for a guide and interpreter on future expeditions. When on one such expedition he spotted his village, the kindly captain gave him back his freedom. He was home only a short while when he spotted what he thought were English ships in the harbor. Believing them to be friendly he approached with no hesitation and even brought several fellow tribesmen with him. Sadly, it was a Spanish slaving ship. One can easily believe God intervened in this young man's life as a kindly monk paid the price the slavers demanded and set young Squanto free again. Having no place to go and no means of travel, Squanto stayed at the monastery where he witnessed first hand the kindness of these men who used all of their available funding to free slaves.

During these years Squanto learned the valuable lesson that, while all Europeans couldn't be trusted, neither were they all evil and selfish. During these years the monks also educated Squanto about Jesus and the gospel, which, reportedly, had quite an impact on him. Finally he was able to obtain passage back to England where he was able to contact his former explorer friends. He worked with them for years before he, once again, located his old village. As sad as this account is, it was during the years of his absence that illness struck this region and virtually wiped out his entire tribe. With his family gone, Squanto moved to another tribe with a childhood friend named "Samoset".

Only a few months went by before they, once again, saw sails in the harbor. This time Squanto was apprehensive and used all caution before making himself known to the settlers. Ironically, they determined to build their homes upon the very piece of land where his village had sat but he silently watched from the forest until his intervention was needed.

Several other tribesmen were curious and wanted to meet these settlers. Accounts vary but suffice to say the pilgrims were uncomfortable with so many natives approaching and had their muskets ready. Rather than wait for matters to get out of hand, Squanto decided it was best to communicate with these people and assure them the natives meant them no harm.

Understandably, an English-speaking native was a greater shock than the approaching tribesmen. With Christian compassion toward the pilgrims, for the number of them who had died in the bitter cold, Squanto decided to stay with them and assist them in hunting throughout the winter. Satisfied that they could trust this young man, from his confession of Jesus that he'd learned from the monks, the pilgrims gratefully welcomed his much needed assistance. On the first Thanksgiving the pilgrims publicly thanked God for Squanto whom they called "God's special instrument to save us from hunger".[48]

The story of "Bunker Hill" reads like something out of the Old Testament. Few people realize that the battle was actually fought on "Breed's Hill". This recounting of providence is known to history as the battle of Bunker Hill because of the prayers of Chaplain David Avery who had positioned himself on Bunker Hill. Those who fought that day were so convinced that his prayers and bravery shifted the battle that history has recorded the fight on the wrong hill".[49]

Today history students are no longer taught that when Paul Revere rode to Lexington to warn Sam Adams and John Hancock that the British were coming, he also addressed Pastor Jonas Clark. Pastor Clark was one of many area pastors who had taught the men in his parish the need for public service, which meant opposing evil, when and where it presented itself. At that time he did not hesitate to assure the men present that his parishioners would stand against the British. His men did not disappoint him or anyone. They had been trained well. He'd taught them that defense of their liberty was part of their covenant with God. Out numbered ten to one on the Lexington green these men stood firm and Pastor Clark stood with them.[50]

Again it was Pastor Jonathan Mayhew who preached "if all Scripture is profitable for doctrine, reproof, correction and instruction in righteousness, why are verses on civil government not examined and explained as well as others", 2nd Tim 3:16. He too had trained his parishioners about covenant relationships and a Christian's duty to oppose tyranny. These men and their associates were never found to preach a sermon that Christians should not be involved in politics. They didn't believe that.

What has American Christianity done for global Christianity? Our spirit of freedom most certainly translated into our passion to worship and seek God independent of organized religion and oppressive rules. Subsequently the stranglehold that mainline denominations had on knowledge and scripture has been broken. Peoples of all classes in all parts of the globe have access to God's word and subsequently they can act upon this knowledge and build a true relationship with Jesus Christ.

This mighty freedom to spread the gospel could not have blossomed into the global evangelizing activity we are familiar with today had men of history past sat idle and let tyrants tell them their duty. Freedom to spread the gospel takes freedom. Satan is determined to destroy freedom. He will tell us anything, he will sell us anything, he will manipulate, divide and raise up armies against us. Our response should be the same as our forbearers; we will serve the Lord our God and in Him only will we trust!

I'll not argue if America was founded as a Christian nation. More important is, are we a Christian nation now? I don't think we are and we won't be until increasing numbers of people rise up and live righteously but it starts with each one of us. We have a duty and we should be willing to serve, first by understanding, then by being willing to commit ourselves and last we must be willing to organize.

We do not read a history of God intervening on a daily basis and fighting the battles for those who desired freedom. We read a history of those who desired a Godly country fighting for it. We read a history of those who desired a Godly country seeking God when they had nowhere else to turn and no other place to hope. We read a history of God intervening with a "national course correction" that brought victory to those who were willing to fight for it. It is America's history of Christians involved in politics.

PROPHECY AND POLITICS

Matthew 5:13: "if the salt have lost his savor ... it is thenceforth good for nothing but to be cast out and to be trodden under foot of men."

It is doubtful if any single subject has served to neutralize the church as much as teachings on prophecy have. When it is suggested to Christians that they should get involved and fight the evil new world order the overwhelming response is "why? It's prophesied, we can't do anything to stop it" and we do nothing. Since prophecy teachings have been so beneficial for the advancement of evil we should examine God's purpose in giving prophecy. We should immediately recognize that God would not desire His word to advance evil or stifle good works.

Then too, we should question how the new world order could take advantage of prophecy teachings. We can recognize that they are aware of it and have factored prophetic teachings into their strategy. One scripture we must consider is Matthew 5:13: "if the salt have lost his savor ... it is thenceforth good for nothing but to be cast out and to be trodden under foot of men." A Christian loses his/her saltiness when they no longer confront evil but just meet it with tolerance or a feeling of inevitability. This must be considered as a reasonable interpretation of this verse because salt is universally recognized as a preservative.

This too is a valuable point to those who still argue that a Christian's sole duty is to spread the gospel. Why then did Jesus call us salt? Spreading the gospel is typically verbalized in the expression "bearing fruit" but salt is no benefit to fruit growth. It is a preservative and a spice and we are to bear fruit and work to preserve that fruit as it's maturing.

We do not work to preserve anything spiritual anymore. In many cases we do not work to preserve our own spiritual lives due to apathy. Nothing causes apathy like prophecy. No single body of teaching has been so embraced by the church as a license to wait out events in idleness. We do not hear the teaching from Isaiah 46 where God explained His purpose for giving the church prophecy was to prove that He is God, not so that Christians would develop an acceptance toward evil.

Isaiah 46:9-10 "I am God ... declaring the end from the beginning and from ancient times the things that are not yet done, saying My counsel shall stand." Verse 11, "I have spoken it, I will also bring it to pass ..." God makes it clear that His purpose in giving prophecy was to prove that He is God.

He can tell us the future when no one else can, therefore He is the one we can and should trust with our future and our salvation. No other religion has a god that can do this; this is the standard. If your god can't tell the future he's not really a god worthy of being trusted or capable of providing salvation. Yet this purpose for prophecy has been twisted and we now ascribe an entirely new purpose for prophecy – a license to stand idle while evil prospers on the earth.

What God meant for good Satan has twisted into apathy and complacency towards evil. Evil has reached such a degree today that it is beyond what earlier generations of non-Christians would have tolerated, yet we do nothing. To our own peril we ignore the fact that the new world order studies prophecy and has an incredible opportunity to influence events. These people have started global wars, global pandemics and global starvation. They have been directly responsible for billions of unnecessary deaths throughout history and they feed on human suffering. Today they have achieved such a degree of global control it is, admittedly, hard to believe. Proof exists but only for those who desire to know it.

God has given us incredible insights into Satan's plan yet we refuse to believe these events are coordinated and find it difficult to accept the argument that there is a plan. All of this was made possible by the subtlety of patient gradualism and by deceiving Christians into attributing all events as being "God's will". This has been part of the new world order's strategy for centuries.

Voltaire had a vision and a desire to rebuild Solomon's Temple as far back as 1763 and approached Catherine of Russia to finance it.[51]

The concept is simple; Christians believe in prophecy, control events to create the impression that they are prophetic and you will have enormous influence on the activity (or lack of activity) of Christians.

Chapters two and three of Revelation are seldom taught. When studies of Revelation are offered these two chapters are typically just touched on hastily and the real study begins in chapter four. Reviewing these two chapters we note that Jesus told all seven churches that He "knows thy works". Looking at Revelation 2:2 we read where Jesus compliments the church of Ephesus because "thou canst not bear them which are evil ..." It goes on to say "thou hast tried them which say they are apostles and are not and hast found them liars ..."

To the church at Pergamos Jesus really had nothing good to say except they "hold fast my name and hast not denied my faith ..." They are told they dwell where Satan dwells, "even where Satan's seat is". There is an obvious comparison between these two. Jesus was pleased with those who did more than just "hold fast". Pergamos had the opportunity to do much more. It is pointed out to them that Satan has set up shop and grown very comfortable in their midst but that didn't concern them.

Sardis is told "thou hast a name that thou livest and art dead." Can you imagine having to be told you're dead? I don't care how complacent we've become, that has to come as a surprise! What a sad commentary on a life to hear these words from Jesus. What can we conclude here except that they were idle? They are commanded to be "watchful and strengthen the things which remain that are ready to die". This is confirmation that they were idle. There clearly was something dying in their midst that Jesus wanted preserved. They were told to get to work rather than complacently existing.

There cannot be a long list of things that Jesus was concerned about. We shall see later that there are only four things, at least in the context of His message to the churches.

The harshest words were reserved for the Laodiceans. They were told they are neither "cold nor hot ... thou sayest I am rich and increased with goods and have need of nothing ..." Because they were tolerant of evil and complacent with their lives and possessions Jesus said He would "spue them out of My mouth". They are also called "wretched, miserable, poor, blind and naked". There is no room for confusion here! Jesus is not happy with them at all. One would almost prefer to be called dead than have this to look forward to!

Smyrna was told just the opposite as Jesus acknowledged their tribulation and poverty but assured them they are rich. Knowing what made them rich is revealed when they are told not to fear what Satan would do to them. This is an important statement. Satan doesn't waste time on people that are no threat to him! Clearly they were in the battle and Jesus encouraged them.

Thyatira was acknowledged for their service, faith, patience and works but Jesus faulted them for tolerating a false prophetess who taught them to be tolerant of fornication.

The seventh church listed is Philadelphia, which is acknowledged for having a little strength and using it to keep God's word. Not one of the other six churches is acknowledged for keeping God's word.

Let's examine this further. The seven churches are faulted for four things; lack of faithfulness, eating things sacrificed to idols, fornication and tolerating false leadership. This fourth point is elaborated on when we read that Ephesus is told it is good they hate the "Nicolaitans" and Pergamos is told it is bad they tolerate the "Nicolaitans" as well as those with the doctrine of "Balaam".

There are two theories of who the Nicolaitans were. The most common teaching is that they were tolerant of sexual immorality. This seems difficult to believe for a number of reasons. First of all, Jesus admonished Pergamos specifically for committing fornication. He didn't repeat Himself when addressing the other churches so we should not conclude He repeated Himself concerning Pergamos. He also admonished Thyatira for fornication and made no mention of Nicolaitans. It seems reasonable that He said what He meant and was speaking of something completely different than fornication when He speaks of Nicolaitans.

Secondly, this idea of the Nicolaitans being a sexually perverse cult stems from suspicious theology. Nicolas was one of the seven men of good report chosen along with Stephen in Acts 6:5 to share in the church leadership. The specific accusations against Nicolas that create this teaching of Nicolaitans as a sexually perverse cult are too vulgar and disgusting to be repeated here but one question concerning this teaching is reasonable. If you were a man of good report and respected among the fellowship, then grew away from the fellowship and embraced extreme depravity, would any reasonable person return to the church and hope to recruit and practice this vulgarity there?

I think it far more likely that such a person would be too ashamed to come back to the church or would simply recognize the futility in attempting to proselytize there. The idea of Nicolaitans being a sexual cult seems ridiculous as well as insulting and not supported by sound history.

This brings us back to what I believe to be the far more accurate interpretation of what Jesus referred to here. Furthermore, we need do no creative interpretation here. We simply need return to the Greek. In Greek "Niko" means "conquer" or "triumph". The implication is to dominate or defeat an individual or a group. "Laos" means "people" and we occasionally still here this word used today in churches as "the laity" in reference to the membership. Thus what Jesus said He hates is for the people to be dominated, conquered, oppressed or misled.[52]

This is witnessed by numerous other teachings of Jesus such as when He told the disciples to beware of the leaven of the Pharisees and in Matthew 20:27 He told the disciples "Whosoever will be chief among you, let him be your servant" and many other verses. This is not to disparage church leadership but there is a significant difference in attitude between one who truly desires to serve and help people, verses one who enjoys having others serve them in some capacity. Recognizing that Jesus made this point directly to His disciples makes it far more logical that this is the matter He was addressing in Revelation.

The final two subjects raised here are "the doctrine of Balaam" and "the spirit of Jezebel". We are all too frequently told that the doctrine of Balaam has to do with sexual immorality and Jezebel is a controlling spirit usually attributed to a woman that is manipulative.

The doctrine of Balaam has many points that should be considered. The first and most obvious is a desire for personal profit more than abide by God's word. In Numbers 22:12 God had told Balaam to reject Balak's offer but Balaam couldn't be content with that decision. God then allowed Balaam to go which led to some interesting events.

First of all, why did God change His mind? Secondly, if God truly planned to kill Balaam on the road why did He give the donkey power to speak? This donkey could not have spoken without this divine intervention so the donkey was empowered by God to save Balaam's life. Thirdly, God allowed Balaam to continue, even when he offered to go home. This passage is also a rather strong confirmation of free will!

The obvious point here is that God knew He could not trust Balaam when there was profit to be made and went to extremes to caution him. This may raise the question of why God allowed Balaam to be a prophet in the first place. We do not know what relationship Balaam originally had with God. By the time we're introduced to him he's already living comfortably among idolaters.

Romans 11:29 "The gifts and calling of God are without repentance." Micah 3:11 says "... the priests thereof teach for hire and the prophets thereof divine for money ..." This is something we're very familiar with today and something familiar to God but He does not recall His gifts even when we rebel. It was not God's desire to use Balaam as a prophet with a message for Balak at this point; it was Balak who sought him out.

Our modern theology, as we read these passages in Revelation, is to interpret all references to Balaam, Jezebel and the Nicolaitans as referring to sexual sin. This is largely due to the knowledge we have that God hates sexual sin. Still, Jesus speaks directly against fornication and in judging His own church it is highly unlikely He would be unclear. Neither is it reasonable to assume He is repeating Himself.

Numbers 31:16 says that the Midianite women caused the sons of Israel to trespass against the Lord through the counsel of Balaam. Numbers 25:1 very clearly states that Israel committed sexual sin with the women of Moab after Balaam left. Yet we read in 31:8 that Balaam was slain by the Israelites so he obviously returned on his own.

Jesus said "the doctrine of Balaam". A doctrine is "a guiding principle" or a "statement of governing principle". Hence the doctrine of Balaam would be the law or principle concerning Balaam. This is clearly defined in 2nd Peter 2:15-22 "... Balaam ... who loved the wages of unrighteousness ... they speak great swelling words of vanity, they allure through the lusts of the flesh, through much wantonness those that were clean escaped from them who live in error. While they promise them liberty they themselves are the servants of corruption

..." and in Jude 11 "... they ... ran greedily after the error of Balaam for reward ..."

Getting back to Revelation 2:14 we read, "thou hast there them that hold the doctrine of Balaam, who taught Balak to cast a stumbling block before the children of Israel..." Read in context this identifies Balaam as the one who taught Balak to cast a stumbling block before Israel. We need to focus on this. We are quick to conclude that this stumbling block referred to is fornication. Surely we can agree that Balak had as much knowledge of fornication and eating things sacrificed to idols as had Balaam. It can be argued that this means that it was Balaam who suggested to Balak that Israel could be defeated by using the women to seduce them and cause them to grow cold towards God. This is supportable by other scriptures but it is scripturally inconsistent with the doctrine of Balaam as defined in 2nd Peter.

Balak was afraid of Israel. We need not assume he made a single effort to defeat Israel. We cannot doubt he tried everything he could think of. Sexual seduction was just one effort and scripture is clear that he used it. We must examine the scriptures and learn what Balaam specifically taught him to do.

It is to our benefit to recall that the first generations of Christians did not have the access to scripture that we have. It is reasonable to conclude that earlier generations did not know Balaam by name or reputation, especially gentile converts. Four things are mentioned here in Revelation:

1) Thou hast there them that hold the doctrine of Balaam
2) Who taught Balak to cast a stumbling block before the children of Israel
3) To eat things sacrificed to idols
4) To commit fornication

We must hold on to the definition of the doctrine of Balaam given in 2nd Peter 2:15. We can't abandon it for expediency. The subject of this passage is the doctrine of Balaam, which Jesus hates. Since the definition is given in 2nd Peter, we know exactly what that doctrine is. Therefore we must conclude that these additional comments were added, not for the purpose of adding to the doctrine, but for clarity in identifying who Balaam was. Yes, these too are things that Jesus hates but to be true to scripture we cannot include them in the doctrine of

Balaam. Others may reject this statement and argue another reason for this list but we must accept the definition given in 2nd Peter. It is not logical to assume Balaam taught Balak to do things he already knew well.

The Book of Numbers does not document implementation of this doctrine just as it does not document the implementation of eating things sacrificed to idols. It does document the sexual sin and this has led to the linking of the doctrine to sexual sin but 2nd Peter clarifies this. We must conclude that the topic of this passage is the first thing listed, those that hold the doctrine of Balaam tolerate prophets who are focused on money. To add these three things to the doctrine of Balaam is not a point worth arguing. We can agree that Jesus hates them all and therefore they should all be purged from the church.

The greater point is to insure that the doctrine is taught properly as defined in 2nd Peter, which is not done today. The doctrine of Balaam is a doctrine that creates personal profit from sharing supposed truths from God's word. While those making the profit may be sharing actual truths from The Bible, they are not discipling people as Jesus wanted but are making profit from what they teach. We should not deny a reasonable living to those who have committed their lives to work in the church. This speaks of those who withhold Godly truths unless paid, not those simply trying to make a living by serving God and discipling a group of local believers.

There is a natural out growth of the doctrine of Balaam, which is a mighty stumbling block to the church today. 2nd Peter 2:15 speaks of those who "have forsaken the right way". The "right way" according to the teachings of Jesus is discipleship and faithfulness to God's word. Today we have massive television ministries and many highly revered evangelists who travel and have made quite a name for themselves and subsequently became quite affluent. Virtually all of these use God's word to some extent but none of them are helping build the church according to discipleship principles that Jesus taught. Few, if any, sitting under their ministries grows spiritually the way God wants.

Scores of Christians should be involved locally in discipling people, either independently or working under competent leadership. Yet they attend some "mega-church" or send money to some television ministry and don't understand the difference. The word of God is substituted for a motivational speech or emotional appeal and the profits are enormous. We have a form of Godliness in what we say and some of our beliefs but our lives don't command respect among our peers and we have no evidence that what we practice is real, powerful and life changing.

It is interesting that after Jesus told the church of Sardis they were dead He told them "Remember therefore how thou hast received and heard and hold fast and repent." The system that Jesus instituted was one of discipleship and this is how they received and heard and were to continue. This is how Jesus told them to deal with their "death". This is a stumbling block the church must address, this idea that those who are on television or making the big money are competent spiritual leaders. If they can't help you grow spiritually and recognizably, they should be abandoned.

This brings us to Jezebel who calls herself a "prophetess". The story of Jezebel from 1st Kings is very well known but taught rather strangely. First of all, who among us read this story the first several times and didn't come away astonished. Here we have Elijah, great man of God, who just went "toe to toe" with all the prophets of baal and witnessed the awesome power of God first hand. 1st Kings 18:27 says that Elijah "mocked them"; he was truly having a great time. By verse 40 he is giving orders to the King and Priests and fearsome orders at that.

Yet a half of chapter later (verse 19:3) we see Elijah so afraid of Jezebel that he ran for his life and in verse 4 he tells God he would rather die (than face Jezebel presumably). What made this woman more ferocious than all of the prophets of baal combined? Today we're taught that this "Jezebel Spirit" is a formidable spirit. We're told it is the spirit of witchcraft, feminism, Diana of the Ephesians, the great harlot of Revelation 17 and every female occult presence from Semiramis to Isis all rolled into one with the very power of Satan at their immediate disposal.

It is used to describe every woman who challenges authority or speaks her mind in a fashion deemed inappropriate by church leaders. It is also identified as the cause behind the gross promiscuousness of our age. There is only one big problem with this teaching; there is nothing in The Bible to support it. Attempts are made to support this theology by using Revelation 2:20 which talks of Jezebel in the present and future tense. Still, if we compare Revelation 2:20 with 2:14 we don't find Jezebel significantly worse than Balaam. We can note that Jesus elaborates on her judgment in verses 22-23 but it cannot be said that her judgment is worse than any unbeliever's. The point is we do ourselves a grave disservice when we add to scripture. When we build these ferocious adversaries from a verse here and a verse there, we too are putting stumbling blocks before the church.

Let's talk about Jezebel for a moment and let's begin with Ahab. It is universally agreed that Jezebel was a forceful, manipulative, evil woman. It should be equally recognized that Ahab was a whining, stupid coward. We read beginning in 1st Kings 16:30 that Ahab "did evil in sight of the Lord above all that were before him ... as if it were a light thing for him to walk in the sins of Jeroboam ... that he took to wife Jezebel the daughter of Ethbaal king of the Zidonians".

We read in 20:4 that Ahab was willing to give his wives and children and all his wealth to the Syrian king out of fear but then he stupidly made a covenant with him (20:34) after God intervened and soundly delivered him into Ahab's hands.

1st Kings 18:13 tells us it was Jezebel that "cut off all the prophets of the Lord" and is later made clear that she had virtually all of them killed with a sword. It was this murderous Jezebel that Elijah feared – not some powerful demonic spirit similar to what the church refers to today. As one reads the various passages we read where Elijah had no fear of Ahab or of the demons of Baal.

Elijah knew this woman to be what she was and she was a threat. This is a powerful lesson for Christians today. As stated earlier, we battle three enemies: spiritual, our own flesh and those who oppose us physically. Elijah knew Jezebel fit into the third category and was a threat that could not be ignored because she had the power of government behind her.

It was after he'd traveled into the wilderness with no food or drink that he considered he was no better than all of the prophets killed by Jezebel. God intervened but it took Him several weeks to build up Elijah's strength and courage as well as a sort of physical manifestation of His presence before Elijah was ready to return to the battle. After

Ahab died and Jezebel was left without her power source the new king had eunuchs cast her out a window to her death.

This still begs the question of why Elijah ran and this is all the more curious because he ran just after seeing the most powerful move of God associated with his ministry. One reason is that he thought he was all alone. Another reason is he recognized Jezebel had the power of government behind her and she'd used this power to kill some 400 prophets. He was in his comfort zone fighting spiritual battles but ran from physical ones. Today the church is again running from physical battles. What God wanted done with Jezebel is revealed in 2nd Kings 9:30-37. There is much to be said here about what would have happened if Elijah had not ran in the first place. There is a powerful message here about Christian authority to stand up to evil in government.

In the end she was no ferocious power, just an evil manipulative woman who easily took advantage of a milk toast husband and grossly misused the power of government for her selfish desires. Theologians have researched Jezebel sufficiently to determine she was the daughter of a king whose kingdom was deeply immersed in baal worship. It has also been learned that in Hebrew the name Jezebel means "without cohabitation".

Tremendous meaning is ascribed to her name. What purpose is served with all of this talk aside from creating a formidable enemy for ourselves, which then becomes too intimidating to face? I repeat, in the end she was no ferocious power! We are left to wonder if any one of the four hundred prophets could not have stepped up and cast her to her death, saving a great many lives.

This is not an attempt to discredit the work of those dealing with demonic spirits, witchcraft or manipulative and controlling personalities. It is simply an argument that we must be true to God's word and not add false teachings to the church. These teachings of a Jezebel spirit are widely held and taught because the personality traits described by this title are legitimate threats to a smooth running assembly and need to be addressed. As reasonable as it may be to give a name to the spirit of witchcraft, manipulation or dominance of unlawful authority the fact remains that Revelation 2:20 is used as a foundation scripture for a host of teachings where it does not apply.

Theologians have revived Jezebel from the dead and ascribed her with so much power and authority she is widely viewed as the mother of all false prophecy, manipulation and witchcraft. We have made her so powerful that she is widely regarded as a sort of "bride of Satan" with the skills to usurp his power like she did Ahab's. If Revelation 2:20 could support all of these teachings Jesus would have specified more than being a false prophetess, seducing His servants, fornication and eating things sacrificed to idols.

The attempts to link Jezebel to the great harlot of Revelation 17 along with attempts to make Jezebel into the queen of heaven sited in other verses are examples of the misapplication that has become associated with the name Jezebel.

There simply is no scriptural support for these arguments. False prophecy, manipulation and witchcraft existed before Jezebel and they continue among us today. Eating food sacrificed to idols is offensive to God as eating this food is typically done in ceremonial fashion. This may possibly be patterned after the eating of the Passover meal as a counterfeit or an unholy communion (1st Corinthians 11:27), which would also explain why God is offended by this practice in addition to ceremonial worship that is part of the meal and strictly forbidden by God.

So we read in Revelation 2 and 3 that God hates unfaithfulness, idol worship, false prophets who mislead and oppress Christians and fornication. Look at that list again. The four things Jesus hates directly deal with the relationship He desires with each one of us. All four of the things Jesus hates are dealing with whether we will be totally sold out to Him and His word or if we will allow interferences between us. Let's put all of this back into the context of this book and consider how the new world order can take advantage of this information.

Discipleship as taught by Jesus is one person who understands spiritual truths helping (approximately) twelve disciples learn the spiritual principles and applications to live in the abundant life Jesus promised. I say "approximately" as other factors are involved such as personal leadership skills, personal knowledge and time availability. Then too, a church support network would be of great assistance. We see more implementation of this type of system outside the church today than in. It is not uncommon to see a host of programs dealing with addiction teaming people up for support. This is nothing different than one who had struggled with a problem helping one who is currently struggling. This is a type of what Jesus called discipleship but it stops short of the vital spiritual truths needed for salvation.

Confusion enters from the book of Acts where Peter spoke to the crowd and thousands were saved. When we read the gospels we read where Jesus spoke to thousands as well but He discipled twelve. This is the difference between the office of evangelist, pastor and teacher. The word "disciple" was interpreted to mean, "be transformed" which is to say that one who embraced another worldview was transformed into one who walked in Biblical truths and practices. One had to be saved before one could be discipled and one had to be approved and willing before one could disciple others.

There were Christians who were never discipled and each was free to make this choice. It was a question of whether or not they were willing to submit to a teacher. The point is that pastors, evangelists and teachers had studied and proved themselves worthy to lead in the church and to instruct others in the truth. This is the great tragedy of Alexandria; those who humbly served Christ were abandoned in favor of the "intellectuals" with their own agenda.

This is where the new world order had succeeded. They replaced God's system with a counterfeit which they controlled and through which they could work to build an ever more powerful system under their control while giving the appearance of "doing the Lord's work". In time even those who didn't directly submit and accept this system adopted many of its teachings and strategies.

It is this system that Jesus hates and He states this in The Book of Revelation. He hates anyone or system that oppresses the people, gives false leadership to create apathy, tolerance of sin, ceremony over application and leniency of idol worship. Today government fits the description of an idol because we have made it a false god. An idol is a false god, which has been empowered by you through giving it authority that belongs to God.

Authority to define your moral laws, deceptively answer your prayers to meet your needs, falsely promise to take care of you and your family and falsely give you assurances of eternity. God hates idols because they lead men to damnation. Prophets no longer sound the alarm exposing this idol but instead they eat at its table and cooperate with this system because of the profit to be made. They are worth the expense to the new world order because they assure the people that this false god is a good thing.

The unfaithful, false prophets have established a formal system to replace the one Jesus had established. Satan needed to corrupt the system that Jesus established or his plans were finished. He has always been at war with God and that means he has always been at war with the church. To control the church to any significant degree he first needed to replace the discipleship system with a formal system that would allow him to teach his students what he desired them to know (which isn't much) instead of what Jesus taught. He then promoted those instructed in such a way to make them the respected leaders of Christianity.

Religions based on some variation of salvation by knowledge are numerous. Christianity was not supposed to be one of these. To create a substitute system and maintain control Satan had to duplicate Christianity. He needed false pastors, teachers and prophets. These people would lead a church that would be no threat to Satan and what he intended to do. Much was accomplished by doing away with discipleship and replacing it with formalized, ritualized religion. Much more was accomplished with stolen credibility. By making people believe they are dependant on his system for salvation they develop an emotional attachment to the very system that is enslaving them and robbing them of true salvation. Once this attachment is established it is difficult to break.

Credibility is further established by controlling the educational system and the sciences. It is said that we live in the age of "check-book" science. Where science used to be the search for facts it is now simply the search. Studies are published simply because some organization with an agenda is willing to pay for them.

Where a scientist was typically an individual of humble circumstances many have now become quite affluent. The same can be said for education and journalism. With the churches, media, education and science working for him Satan has the ability to create the illusion that what he's creating is good for mankind. With Christians believing God is in control of everything their defenses are down. With the threat of global warming, aliens attacking from another planet and shortages of everything from food to energy few stand up to protest the growth of government, indeed many misled Christians welcome it.

All of this gives quite a platform to false prophets. There are those who constantly predict pandemics, world hunger and the planet disintegrating beneath our feet. Their purpose is to keep people afraid and anxiously hoping that government will intercede and alleviate all fears. This keeps government growing in power and size. Christians have been neutralized through a combination of being overwhelmed by the evil in our world and the hope promised in The Bible of the second coming of Christ. We don't accept the real problems of society as our responsibility. With a clear conscience we watch as things grow worse and feel no obligation to engage the enemy in battle.

Like Elijah we run and hide and pray for the end. He had the power and authority to cast Jezebel down. Today we are assured that the church will be raptured any moment. We are told that the end of the world is prophesied in the Mayan calendar that supposedly offers proof that our current "cycle" will end on December 21, 2012. On this date some theorize that all life will end, others theorize a new cycle will begin – a new age. We too could cast Jezebel down; we have the power and authority but we have grown complacent and tolerant. We believe the false prophets and no longer hold to scripture as our guide.

The information we are given ranges between outright manipulation and fraud from the sources that follow Satan. If we dare to examine it, we see that the information we receive from the church is also largely manipulative. Each person will need to consider for themselves how receptive they are to this argument. This book is purposed to prove from The Bible that these four lies are part of a master plan of deception to neutralize the church. Another book could easily be written concerning how the new world order has infiltrated "prophecy" teachings and corrupted God's word. Many Christians have become such followers of modern day "Bible prophecy teachers" that they will (by design) abandon all hope if things do not work out the way they've been led to believe.

We, as a people, have stopped studying God's word and we now grasp teachings and hold them as scriptural truth simply because the teacher has sited a verse here and a verse there. If we examine these teachings thoroughly we recognize they are not so iron clad in scripture as those in the prophecy industry insist. We can believe what they say as long as we don't return to the word and challenge it. If we do we note they raise as many questions as they answer.

Again, I'm not attacking their character, I'm simply pointing out that if you are unfamiliar with the new world order then you have made yourself unable to factor their efforts into your beliefs. They are very familiar with prophecy and they are very able to manipulate facts. We, as Christians, must put prophecy back into its scriptural place. We can trust in prophecy but we cannot use it as the whole of our moral compass in either Christian service to God or civic duty to America.

Those that believe in the rapture as it's currently taught are notorious for a common response when they are told of the new world order threat. The response is always, "I don't care; I don't plan to be here". You can't plan something that's beyond your control! People don't plan to have an accident or catch a disease. You can only fail to plan concerning that which you do control. These people would not react this way, with such indifference, if they had not been trained to react this way. They do not have the slightest idea of how they are being manipulated. We have power, authority and God on our side. All of which does nothing for us if we sit idle because we're convinced to sit idle.

The Thessalonians were concerned that they missed "the day of the Lord". We have come full circle. Today we are so overconfident that we will not miss it, and will be accepted with no effort, we take little interest in any issue facing our lives. We need to take a hard look at our beliefs from a scriptural perspective. We need to affirm that what we believe as prophetic is clearly spelled out in God's word and not simply someone's interpretation that sounds pleasing to us. We have too much at stake and we see society degenerating on our watch. We have a duty to be sure of our facts.

PART FOUR

LEGISLATING MORALITY

AUTHORITY TO LEGISLATE MORALITY

Acts 5:29: "we should obey God rather then men"

Working our way through the list of lies the church has adopted, we come now to the third "you can't legislate morality". The irony of this fallacy is that if the word of God is revered properly we would recognize that "we can't legislate morality" because God already has! It is, however, our responsibility to live and teach God's standards of morality and insure that this is the standard society adheres to. To neutralize the church and remove Christians from having a Godly influence on society we are (or were) constantly admonished with this slogan until the seed took root and was adopted by religious leaders who echoed the sentiment. Finally it was accepted by significant numbers of Christians and idleness became the standard of conduct as evil abounded.

The word "you" is used in a generic sense; "you can't legislate morality" or "we can't legislate morality" but the pronoun implication is always Christians. It is Christians to whom God gave the duty of holding society to the standards He revealed but it is now Christians whom this world tells "can't" legislate morality and should remove themselves from the discussion. The obvious objective is the abandonment of a Godly standard at which time "morality" becomes what each individual determines is right for themselves. This will result in chaos. To bring about "order" the government will then need to intercede and start dictating proper standards for all. Does this teaching sound scriptural or do we see an agenda at work here?

Let's begin with some definitions. Most people are aware that to legislate is to enact laws. Legislation means "the exercising of power and functions of making rules that have the force of authority by virtue of their promulgation by an official organ of a state or organization". Morality is defines as "relating to principles of right or wrong in behavior and standards of conduct". No part of this process should exclude Christians, from a Biblical perspective or a legislative one. Indeed if we look at the terms we can note that every person should have a vested interest in the standards of behavior for society. This begs the question "why can't we legislate right standards of conduct" and equally important, "who says we can't and under what authority"?

Clearly there is an objective here of removing Godly standards. To argue we can't legislate right standards of conduct is to question the purpose of lawmaking power or need for government at all. Virtually every law falls into this category. The real issue is about who will set the acceptable standards of behavior for society if Biblical standards are abandoned? It has been common to western civilization, sometimes referred to as Christian civilization, to adopt a Biblical standard of conduct and this has proven to be superior to any other.

This, however, is not conducive to Satan's agenda or to his servants that promote the new world order. This lie is just another attempt by Satan's minions to destroy Christianity and eliminate the proper influence Christians should have on society. We have no scriptural instruction to support their assertion. The first five books of The Bible are commonly referred to as "the law" and are heavily focused on crimes and punishments. Most of the laws given by God fit the definition of legislating morality. Some laws were given for symbolic purposes but most are to promote Biblical morality.

A study of Roman law has classified all laws under two fields. In Latin they are "mala in se" and "Mala prohibita".[53] "Mala in se" laws are the types of laws that we as a society desire our government to punish so that our families and communities will be safe. It is these "mala in se" laws that are also God's laws and would rightly be considered moral laws as they deal with the conduct and standards of behavior. These are morally wrong and are listed in The Bible along with what God directs as the appropriate punishment.

These types of crimes include such things as murder, theft/robbery and rape. West's Encyclopedia of American Law actually defines this term as "acts morally wrong". In Latin this is a phrase (malum in se, or the plural mala in se) that means "evil in itself".[54]

"Mala prohibita", Latin for "wrongs prohibited" are laws that are not evil but prohibit personal actions by statute.[55] Examples would be speed laws, seat belt laws, helmet laws, don't kill the king's deer (without a license), etc. As you can note, there is a defined limit to the number of moral laws and as such, a limit on the laws that government needs to recognize as necessary. By extension this creates a limit on the government's power to control the people.

This is certainly not true with regard to prohibitive laws. All laws limit behavior and by extension limit freedom. Too the extent we have no laws we have freedom. For example, if you have no speed limit in your town you are free to drive as fast as you choose. If we as a society have agreed among ourselves to not tolerate this particular behavior for the greater safety of the community we pass a law limiting the speed. The action we have taken is to remove the freedom of the people to drive as fast as they choose.

Understanding this principle, we can see the hollowness of our courts as judge after judge serves the new world order by denying the people their rightful authority to govern themselves and pass the laws they desire to have in their states or communities. The judges always desire to be seen as protecting the rights of a certain group of people against whom the law was past. Reality is, however, that any and all laws take away the rights of someone. These judges are taking away the right of the people to govern themselves but they do not concern themselves with this truth as they serve an agenda and not the public.

If we as a society allow our leaders to pass laws continually, they are by affect of their actions, continually removing our freedoms. This is why we must stop elected leaders from passing any law they choose.

A significant example to consider was the "Religious Freedom Amendment" proposed a few years ago. Currently our Constitution reads, "Congress shall pass no law respecting the establishment of religion or prohibiting the free exercise thereof …" Here it is written that our government has no authority to pass laws regarding religion. In the absence of law making authority the people possess total freedom. While the promoters of this amendment may have good intentions their actions open the door to government's involvement in religion.

Once authority is delegated to Congress to legislate in the arena of religion total freedom is lost. Specific legislation, no matter how it is phrased, will necessarily limit the total freedom we now enjoy. Then we must consider what the courts (and religiously contemptuous judges) would do once they are legally free to attack religious beliefs.

Total freedom is the absence of law. As a society we need certain laws to maintain order but we must stop politicians from passing any law they choose. By removing Christians from the political debate they were effectively removed from the legislative process.

Many Godly legislators have fought bravely and struggled for Godly principles and laws over the years but with their constituency base abandoning them their efforts became increasingly futile. New legislation increasingly failed to hold a Biblical standard of conduct for society. The new standard stifled the freedom of the people as it increasingly prohibited harmless behavior.

There are the additional arguments dealing with the incentive government has for passing laws that are not outlined in scripture. To the extent morality breaks down in society there is need of more government and subsequently more pay and power for those holding office. As crime rises we need more government protection. As the work ethic deteriorates we need more government programs. As our foreign policies stimulate hatred for our country we need a larger military and so forth.

Politics is the arena where failure is its own reward and subsequently its own incentive! Politicians can insist that they are powerless to solve problem in spite of their best efforts but in reality when they fail to resolve the problems they spoke of during campaigns they have secured for themselves an ever-increasing growth of their power. As these specific problems grow in terms of the people's needs and security, so does the need for more government involvement and programs.

Additionally, laws that prohibit behavior are usually punished by fines instead of imprisonment. This means the lawmakers have established for themselves a steady source of revenue through fines imposed upon those who violate their regulations. As their greed affects their thinking we find we have less and less freedom of movement and generally less opportunity to function in our daily routines without continual harassment by the state.

Increasingly it becomes the duty of a local policeman to raise revenue rather than protect lives and property and the courts share this incentive. We can recognize too that under "the Mosaic law", one who committed a crime had to pay restitution directly to the victim. Government did not prosper from lawbreakers and had no incentive to promote lawlessness. If you stole someone's property you were required under the law to repay that person directly including punitive damages.

Today the victim is twice victimized, the first being the actual crime against them or their property. If caught and prosecuted successfully the most the victim can hope for is restoration of what remains of their property. Any fines go to the government to support the system. The victim is left without restitution and if the criminal is sentenced to a lengthy prison term the victim is taxes to support their incarceration.

All of this is quite different from the system we read about in scripture and is a result of Christians believing the lies they are told. Let me phrase this "you can't legislate morality" statement another way, "Christians are free to recognize problems in society but they are not free to address these problems". Does that sound like a Godly statement? God works through people and His people, who are called to His service, are the ones that He expects to enforce the moral standards that He has given.

As Christians have withdrawn from the process, the punishments for immoral crimes have been reduced and fear of punishment are no longer an incentive upon moral behavior. Rape is a horrific example of this point and not that many years ago this type of crime would not be tolerated in our society. The Bible is very clear that rapists are to be punished by death but this is not the current standard in our society.

The FBI estimates that only thirty-seven percent of all rapes are reported and the U.S. Department of Justice speculates that only twenty-six percent are reported. Among those that are reported, there is only a sixteen percent chance that a rapist will go to jail. If the statistics for unreported cases are factored in, there is only a six percent chance that a rapist will ever see a day in jail let alone pay for his crime with his life as required by God's standard. God is not willing to tolerate this outrage but the church is.

The Bible gives the standards we are to observe and the church is failing in its duty to enforce this standard. God works thru people and for the purpose of maintaining a Godly society He has delegated authority to specific entities so that society will function organizationally in such a way that good works will be rewarded and evil works will be punished and thus society will prosper. When society functions in a Godly manner, men are introduced to God and free to pursue a relationship with Him if they desire.

It is the desire of Satan to squelch contact between God and man and replace it with a relationship between Satan and man. Only a small percentage would desire a relationship with Satan so he must achieve his goals through deception. The deception includes creating a government with enough power to seemingly meet the needs of the people so they do not recognize an immediate need to seek God.

Next, remove moral restriction and attitudes against base behavior because without Jesus Christ men can always be counted on to pursue their base lusts. Finally, remove all consequences of base behavior. What have you created? A society that does not seek God is deeply mired in sin and does not see any need for repentance. The payoff for Satan comes in step three.

The consequences of sin cannot be removed. They can, seemingly, be diverted away from the individual to society as a whole. An unplanned pregnancy can be aborted, the child can be adopted or a tolerance for single parents promoted. Those lacking a work ethic are supported by welfare. Criminals have little or nothing to fear of the justice system.

All of this requires a large number of government programs and the growth of these programs gives Satan the power base he needs to form his world government. The agenda is to stop society from functioning organizationally the way God has ordained and pervert the system. While government is seemingly a blessing to the people in need of the programs it is actually amassing ever increasing control over society. To accomplish all of this Christians had to be removed from the process.

This was done by replacing functions of the church with government programs and telling Christians to stay out of politics. Perhaps the most insidious aspect of this lie emanates from the fact that it is Christians who have the authority in Christ to legislate morality. Look at the definition of legislate again; "the exercising of power and functions of making rules that have the force of authority by virtue of their promulgation by an official organ of a state or organization." God is the "official organ" who made the rules. He gave Christians the authority to enforce His rules and He expects us to do that.

The subject of authority has been abandoned by the 21st century church and must be addressed again. Authority means to have "power to influence, or command thought, opinion or behavior." These sound like things Satan would desire very much and subsequently these are things Christians must diligently insure that he is never successful in gaining. In the study of authority you can see that one must have a greater authority to "command behavior" than to "influence". This is what Satan is after.

He has had the authority to influence since the Garden of Eden but he desires the authority to command behavior and he needs the power of government to achieve that goal. If the church is not exercising greater authority in the world than Satan is, his authority will grow from simply being able to influence to the point where he can command behavior.

God gave man authority, "dominion", over the earth. For Satan to have authority as defined above, he must both confuse men into doubting their God given authority and deceive men into believing he (Satan) has legitimate authority. Once he has accomplished the first part he can successfully remove Christians from any arena that will threaten his goals. Accomplishing the second part requires that he be totally covert until all resistance is futile. It is highly unlikely that non-Christians would be attentive to Satan or his agenda. This requires people who know he exists, are committed to exposing him and have the authority in Christ to do the job.

This battle is whether Christians will act on their God given authority and strip Satan of his false authority or if Christians will, either by ignorance or apathy, stand silent while Satan amasses enough authority to "command behavior" on the entire earth. No Christian can desire to see Satan succeed. We have a duty to expose him because God gave us the authority. If we do not exercise it, we're in Satan's service by allowing him to prosper when we have the ability to stop him.

The first important consideration on the subject of authority is that it's only valid if coming from a superior source. This is the point of Luke 7:8. The Centurion understood Jesus was a superior force to disease and disease must submit. The Centurion understood that, as a Centurion, he was backed by the "superior source" of his superiors all the way up to Caesar. He could use his authority to command the behavior, and submission to Roman law, of all under his command and the entire regional population.

Caesar was his source and the Roman army had enough force to overcome any opposing force. Whether or not the Centurion knew Jesus as God (the ultimate source) he knew Jesus had access to the force greater than disease.

This is the essence of authority but it is only formidable in the hands of one determined to use it, not among those who stand idle. Authority from a superior source will accomplish nothing if we don't exercise the force aspect. That is to say, enforce God's laws. The fact that our source is superior will never diminish but is irrelevant if we don't call upon that source. If we don't draw upon that source and use the force we have been authorized we will suffer the consequences.

With our superior source, and if we bother to learn and understand the specifics of the battle in which we are to be engaged, we can meet the enemy and overcome. The same logic can be seen in our world today. We give local police departments the authority to enforce the laws and ordinances of the city. Private security firms or a police impersonator have no such authority. They can look the same and even know the same information but the source of the authority makes the difference. The police department has the authority of the city officials and ultimately the people living in that city to back them up. This is the superior source of their authority. It's not their knowledge, appearance or ambitions that give them power. It's the superior source of the authority behind them.

Satan wants authority to control the behavior of men but he knows he's not going to get it from God; therefore he needs to get it from men. This makes the study of authority vital to the church.

Some misconceptions abound that Satan accomplished some type of one time massive transfer of power from Adam and now he is much to be feared. This is not how authority works. Satan is a liar and he knows how authority works. He knows to steal the authority God gave to men he must accomplish it by deception. Not a one time trick but an on going and expanding deception that will keep men ignorant on the subject of authority or his plan will ultimately fail. We must review what scripture reveals actually happened.

It's true that Satan deceived Eve but we do ourselves a disservice when we believe that this deception was anything more than a deception. It was a single event where Satan influenced Eve's thinking and got her to disregard God's word. He did not have the authority to command behavior and he did not gain that authority with this one time lie. Theologians put so much emphasis on blaming Eve for disobeying God's word that they lose sight of the fact that when Adam and Eve ate of the tree they gained knowledge of evil.

Yes they violated God's word but Genesis 3:22-23 says that it was because "the man is become as one of us, to know good and evil; and now, lest he put forth his hand and take also of the tree of life and eat and live forever: therefore The Lord God sent him forth from the garden of Eden …" The text reveals that as serious of an act as it is to disobey God's word, the unforeseen consequences was that they gained the knowledge of evil that God did not want them to have. This is because if you don't know about evil, you won't think about evil things and Satan will not be able to abuse your imagination.

Moving ahead to Genesis 4:7 we read "If thou doest well, shalt thou not be accepted? And if thou doest not well, sin lieth at the door. And unto thee shall be his desire and thou shalt rule over him." Some theologians have challenged the word sin in this context. Some argue that the word used is actually "sin offering". The same word is used for sin offering in more than a hundred places in The Old Testament. The same word is used in 2nd Corinthians 5:21 "For He hath made him to be sin for us, who knew no sin; that we might be made the righteousness of God in Him." The passage can read that Jesus was made our "sin offering".[56]

The significance of this is that man has always had authority over Satan but we don't exercise it because we've been taught that we lost it in the Garden of Eden. That is to say man has the authority to stop Satan from influencing us or commanding our behavior to act in an ungodly manner. What God was actually telling Cain in verse 7 is "if you do right you will be accepted and if you don't do right you have a sin offering available right outside your front door that you can make and be forgiven". In other words God was not willing that Satan ever come between Him and His creation for any short or extended period of time.[57]

In Genesis 3:3 we read that Eve actually added to what God had said with "...neither shall ye touch it ..." Arguments have gone back and forth over the significance of this addition however the fact is that Adam was given this command in Genesis 2:17 and Eve was not created until verse 2:22. There are theological arguments that deny that it was Adam who added to what God had said, however Eve's addition could be attributed to resolve or her understanding from the stern instructions she'd heard from Adam.

One clear fact we can take away from these verses is that Adam and Eve did not exercise their authority but rather allowed Satan to influence them. It works very much to Satan's advantage if we read into this passage some huge transfer of power and to do so we are as guilty of adding to God's word, as was Eve.

I suppose I should explain for clarity that in Genesis 4:7 "... unto thee shall be his desire and thou shalt rule over him" is not talking about sin. Many Jewish theologians agree this is a reference to Cain's birthright and that God was assuring him he would not lose his birthright to Abel.[57] In modern language it would read, "your brother still respects you and you are still the firstborn". This teaching claims that this was an effort by God to bring peace between the two brothers and deal with the envy Cain felt.

Back to our topic, by promoting this big power transfer deception Satan has gained enormous influence in our society and control of many of our institutions because we have not resisted him in the way we are commanded in scripture. God is our source and He is a "superior source". That is to say, we can stand on our relationship with God and exercise our full, Godly authority any time we want to!

God did not ordain, consent or approve of this "authority transfer". God still desires men to have and exercise the authority He gave them. It's still ours and we can still use it. Further evidence of this is revealed in the fact that Satan's influence and control over our institutions is all recent.

Satan's trick is to deceive all people into believing all authority is exercised through governments and then empower him over the government. The lie is strengthened with the dual and conflicting arguments that all government is of God and that there is a separation between church and state. For his authority to be sufficient to "command behavior" he needs a superior source/force of government.

He had to convince Christians that "all government is of God" and without searching scripture for a definition of Godly government we accept an increase of government authority. There are differences between a Godly government, verses a satanic government as well as differences between a Christians view of government verses a non-Christians view.

Currently we're taught that government has authority over people but we never question who has authority over the government. This is not the American system! The American system is a free people who cannot be oppressed by any government as the people retain authority over their leaders. The daily affairs of the nation are managed by Representatives of the people who are sworn to accept the limitations of our Constitution. They are to "represent" our interests, not govern us.

The American system recognizes "authorities" greater than government. The authority of God for one, and another would be the authority of the citizens. As we allow our authority to be robbed we grant Satan's ancient wish of a world government under his control. If the church doesn't exercise the authority God gave us, Satan will. He effectively steals the authority because Christians are allowing him to. Recognize Eve gave Satan something tangible in the garden. When Satan asked, "hath God really said..." she should have responded with a resounding "Thus saith the Lord..." and have quoted God. This would have ended the fruit discussion permanently and stopped Satan from influencing her!

Eve gave Satan the authority to influence her thoughts and behavior. She listened to him and, in turn, influenced Adam. Specifically, the power or authority exercised here was the power to argue and cause doubt about God's word. Satan had the power to argue but Eve gave him the power to influence her when she entertained his arguments even though she possessed the greater authority.

The second important consideration on authority is that it is given for a purpose and must be exercised or it's of no value. Just as a police officer is of no value to the city when he is negligent in his duties so is the Christian of no value as salt and light when we allow evil to prosper. Satan and his servants have worked hard to impress upon the church that the authority of government is supreme and absolute. This is a deception to cause us to doubt our Godly authority. If successful we will not use the authority God gave us, in effect yielding that authority to Satan.

Arguments persist as to what mankind lost at the fall and the extreme view is that Satan, through this one deception, gained all power over the earth. We add to scripture when we make this claim. It is true that due to this rebellion mankind suddenly needed a Savior but salvation and authority are two separate subjects! There is no scriptural evidence that God revoked Adam's authority. There is no scriptural evidence that Adam ever let Satan influence him again. It may well be true that Satan thought he would accomplish more than he actually did but he failed to consider the love of God and God's heart to forgive. One thing he certainly accomplished was to introduce evil into God's creation.

We read of evil continually in Genesis but we don't read anymore about Satan. Apparently he gained so little at the immediate fall that he had to allow evil to germinate in the hearts and minds of men as he worked to influence them over several generations. Consider Genesis 6:5 "And God saw that the wickedness of man was great in the earth, and that every imagination of the thoughts of his heart was only evil continually".

We know that God, being Just, punishes the guilty. We see in Genesis 3:14 that when God found Satan to be at fault He punished

Satan. In Genesis 4:11 when God found Cain to be at fault He punished Cain. Here in 6:5 we see God holding men guilty, not Satan. He didn't destroy Satan at that point or punish him in any way recorded in scripture. Man had the authority to rule over Satan but weren't exercising it and all men suffered for it. The people before the flood chose not to.

There is no mention of Satan in the "Tower of Babel" story in chapter 11. We can certainly agree that he was responsible through his influence but God clearly held men accountable for what they had allowed their world to become.

There is substantial scriptural evidence that men throughout history have increasingly rejected God's influence in lieu of Satan's. We read in Romans 11:29 that "the gifts and callings of God are without repentance". He doesn't take back what He's given and He didn't take back the authority He gave to Adam! Neither could Satan steal it because the superior source (God) would not permit the authority to be transferred by theft anymore than a city would permit a police impersonator to perform an arrest.

Romans 11:29 reveals a truth about God that we need to apply! There is no evidence Satan gained any authority he didn't already have - to argue, cause doubt, etc. Satan has been amassing unlawful authority by deception for thousands of years. He has been impersonating an authority over mankind.

It is not a third principle of authority that it can be stolen but the belief it can be stolen is widely taught. Authority is given by a superior source to a designated force (police force, military force, etc) for a defined purpose. To imply it could be stolen is to imply the superior source is incapable of foreseeing or preventing that result. Rather, we see a situation where the designated recipient of the authority is not utilizing the delegated authority and fulfilling the defined purpose for which the authority was provided, while an unlawful force with unlawful authority is, through deception and intimidation, accomplishing their own purpose.

It is perfectly acceptable to question authority. Godly authority recognizes no threat in proving its legitimacy. We all have a duty to insure those we allow to influence us and control our behavior are serving God's purpose. We see in Matthew 4 when Satan attempted to influence Jesus he was met with one who knew and understood authority. Jesus didn't yield a syllable! He didn't let Satan influence Him at all. Acts 26:16-18 Paul is re-telling what Jesus said to him. This is why Jesus came to earth, so they "can turn ... from the power of Satan to God".

Satan had created so much confusion and his influence was so dominant on the earth by that time it's doubtful if very many people concerned themselves with God's influence. This is not to diminish the need for salvation but the church understands salvation. It is the subject of authority we have completely misunderstood under deception. There is no justification for the church not using its authority to influence our world. We must use authority and not submit just because the new world order tells us to.

As defined beyond "influence", authority extends to "commanding behavior" and in many ways this is the goal. Satan's goal is to make "government" a "superior source" under his control, which by virtue of military, police, control of the currency, etc. he can "command behavior" upon all mankind. If he succeeds in making government a superior source, he can then delegate authority to all of these entities to control the behavior of all mankind. As we allow his strategy to succeed we see an all-powerful government taking shape that does indeed have power to command behavior. It is the duty of Christians and patriots to stop this from happening.

We read in Luke 10 that Jesus gave authority to His followers over Satan and when the seventy returned (vs. 17) they were astonished that devils had to submit to them. The authority Christians have over Satan and his forces will always be superior because our "source" is superior to his. We too can "command behavior" over devils and demons, not due to ourselves but because of who our superior source is. Still, our authority to command behavior is limited to devils. It is important to remember, we were not given authority from God to command behavior of other people. Neither was Satan, he just deceives. There are those who have willingly submitted to him but this was their choice. With regard to other people, our authority is limited to "influencing".

This reveals what spirit we're dealing with, both in the church and the world, when others attempt to control our behavior. We can willingly give another authority over us in an employment situation, for example, or if we are truly being discipled but we as a church need to examine those who claim to have authority in our life. What is their source for this claim? Is it Godly or not? Why should we submit and can we hold them accountable? Neither the government nor the church has the rightful claim of authority over the people that they are exercising. Our government and its various entities have grown powerful in their ability to command behavior but the greater "source" is still ours!

The title verse for this chapter is Acts 5:29 which says "we should obey God rather then men". So should governments! With the withdrawal of Christians from the political arena there is no influence upon government to pursue Godliness. We have wrongfully yielded to Satan's deception. The difference between authority and power must me considered. Jesus said in Matthew 28:18 that "all authority in heaven and on earth has been given to Me". This means Satan must "takeover" the Godly entities and institutions God has ordained to promote a Godly society. As he takes over these entities he can exercise power over them and through them but his authority is still illegitimate and we can exercise our proper authority and dispossess him at any time.

At this point it becomes something of a "power struggle" (warfare) since Satan will not easily relinquish that which he's stolen. Plus people around the globe have become extremely reliant of Satan's governmental system and very much so in our own land. They do not understand what they are committed to and must be educated. As noted, Satan's plan is revealed in an agenda referred to as "the new world order" and is being implemented by those in Satan's service. Christians are their targets not simply due to the hate they have for all Godliness but they also recognize it was to Christians that Christ delegated authority to overcome Satan and his agenda. We do God a grave disservice to easily submit the authority He gave us to His revealed enemy.

In The United States, our government is one of "delegated authority". Government has the rightful authority to enact laws only in the specific areas where authority has been delegated. Any attempt to exercise authority where it has not been specifically authorized by the people or the states is an abuse of power and an encroachment on our freedoms whether it be by a judge, police officer, Congress or The President.

If we can't "legislate" morality then we cannot "delegate" authority to legislate morality but if we agree the primary cause for government is upholding moral (Mala en se) laws then we must accept the truth that we can demand and promote moral laws as our founders did when they first drafted state and local laws which listed certain behaviors as intolerable for society. This entire debate is a satanic deception and its time for Christians to stop listening to Satan. This system of control and intimidation is not a Godly system and it has come into being because Christians have abandoned the responsibilities that come with Godly authority.

God has legislated the standards of proper conduct for a society that desires to live in peace and prosperity. Salt has the duty of preserving society to insure the various cancers of evil do not erode and destroy our quality of life and our children's future. Light has the duty to shine on the evil in the land and expose it for what it is.

It is now time to shine some light on Romans 13. This chapter and Romans 13:1, in particular, have been altered and misquoted as much as any verse in The Bible.

AUTHORITY TO LEGISLATE IMMORALITY

Romans 13:1 "Let every soul be subject to the higher powers... powers that be are ordained of God"

There is one matter of vital importance to the new world order; that Christians become totally convinced that it is they (the nwo) that are the "powers" that God has "ordained" and they should be obeyed. They pursue their agenda of amassing power by expanding government. They focus their energies on convincing all people that their power, the power of government, is unlimited and unaccountable to men and they strive to convince Christians that this is a Godly concept.

In The United States this is a hard sell because the ignorance of the people is not so widespread to readily accept this. Never the less we can easily recognize that our Congress and President no longer feel any obligation to listen to the people. The people pressure Congress concerning an issue or grab for power and may be heard but the same issue is shortly revisited in another bill or in some reformed version and the fact that the majority of people oppose it is disregarded.

They mechanically pursue their agenda and view any set back as very temporary. They operate as if they are unaccountable to their constituents and have unlimited powers to interfere in our lives and, sadly, they frequently succeed.

To silence Christians they are quick to quote Romans 13:1. Their self-serving interpretation of this verse places "government" in this passage as the "higher power". Then they insist we have a duty to obey whatever laws they pass. Some new translations of The Bible even substitute "government" for "higher powers". As Christians we have a responsibility to be true to God's word and not tolerate anyone corrupting it for their own purposes. The translation of Romans 13:1 is the center battleground on the question if Christians must blindly cooperate with government dictates. If the new world order is successful in deceiving Christians with this verse they will be free to pursue their agenda without opposition or accountability. By studying this verse we will see that they have corrupted what God had given in His word and our duty is to oppose them.

In Romans 13:1 the Greek word "exousia" was translated "higher powers". It is significant that Strong's Greek Dictionary does not define this word as "government", which is the translation promoted by the new world order. According to Strong's this word actually has a lengthy, detailed definition. The closest my 1980 version comes to any reference to "government" is a single listing of "magistrate". One listing among many other options includes "jurisdictional authority".[58]

If God had meant "government" He would have said "government". The word is used many times in scripture in many contexts. We have a duty as Christians to study the entire word of God and to know it rather than making doctrine out of a single scripture. The section of this book titled "God's view of government" highlights from scripture that God does not have a favorable view of the governments of men and no small part of that is due to the promotion of ungodliness by government.

If our desire is to serve God then our commitment is to follow His word and not a self-serving corruption of His word, given us by His enemies. God's view on government and service should be highly significant to all Christians.

A more accurate translation of "higher powers" from Romans 13:1 is "jurisdictions" and the best translation would read "jurisdictional authority". God has delegated three areas of "jurisdictional authority" as pertains to Romans 13:1. Satan's authority is beyond these three as it was not delegated by God and is unlawful authority.

The three jurisdictional authorities God has delegated are:
1) Priesthood
2) Patriarch
3) Civil

Christians should know that God would not give total and irrevocable power for men to rule the earth and Christians should know that God would never give authority for ungodly men to rule over the church! God has appointed duties and responsibilities to each jurisdiction, which gives them full authority to function as God intends. This is the limit of Godly authority for each entity.

Let's begin with the third jurisdiction, which is civil government. Today the new world order is diligently laboring to create acceptance of the belief that they are the only legitimate authority. Immediately we recognize this means they must literally declare war on the other two entities to steal their authority. Their best tactic would be to foster ignorance that no such authority exists in these other areas. It is vital that Christians and patriots understand both The Biblical System of civil government and The American system of civil government. In these two systems, civil government is limited and designed to be a weaker entity than the church and family. This is what God ordained and this is what our founders understood.

Romans 13:4 describes the absolute and complete authority that God ascribed for civil government. Twice the Greek word "diakonos" is used from which we get our words "deacon" and "servant". It reads "Ministers of God" or "God's Minister" in most modern translations. Hence we get the terms "Prime Minister", "Foreign Minister", "etc". Read it for yourself: "Minister of God". Men serving in these positions are not to represent themselves or their personal ambitions and they are not to represent other men, not even a king. The implication is that they are God's Minister(s) to the people. Even though their immediate duties are to government they are accountable to God and obligated to serve according to His standards.

The authority to represent God is not unlimited or unaccountable power but delegated power and the civil government is but a single jurisdiction. All three jurisdictions are to respect each other's jurisdiction and be held accountable by the other two jurisdictions. Romans 13:4 states that authority is given to civil government for a mere two purposes, to reward good works and "…to execute wrath upon he who doeth evil". This is the sole purpose of a Godly civil government. They do not possess Godly authority to rob (or tax) one to "feed" another. They do not possess Godly authority to create massive public works programs from which they can dispense political favors upon loyal party members and competitively weaken privately owned business in the market place, businesses that may oppose their agenda or support their competition.

Government has no Godly authority to pursue any number of efforts we witness them mastering control of today. Their sole responsibility is to keep civil order by protecting lives and property from enemies foreign and domestic by punishing those who disrespect lives and property. In history we seldom have seen lives and property more disrespected than they are by governments today. Perhaps the king only awarded property to cohorts but once awarded he respected their ownership.

Destroying private property rights is the agenda of every government. We can note that protecting lives has ceased to be a priority as well. Crime is high and yet our prisons have revolving doors and wars are fought simply to serve corporate greed.

Furthermore, the term "he who doeth evil" is used in scripture. God did not even give government the authority to define evil. By government's definition, anyone who opposes their agenda is evil. Those who must die to further their agenda are inconsequential and those who stand for Godly standards are the most hated of all. God defined what is evil and thereby hindered government from expanding it's own authority but for God's system to work, Godly people must labor to insure God's word is revered and applied.

Today Christians are taught to yield complete obedience to whoever occupies The White House or any government office. Any student of history knows this philosophy is new in our country. The reader can recognize how this deception is a self-serving effort by the new world order to grab control of government and destroy God's system. We can recognize that this lie has had enormous success for the new world order.

This teaching that "Christians must obey government" cannot be true as a blanket statement. Our system of government does not make us subjects under the will of rulers. We are a free people and if politicians fail to recognize this than it is a failure on our part to hold them to their jurisdictional limit. In The United States government is to obey citizens. Satan has been too successful in switching this around. Government's only authority exists when people violate the lives or property of another. Christian leaders of years past held their government leaders to a high accountability but since modern day

Christians have abandoned the process government has grown out of control and increasingly evil.

Our founding fathers knew better than to trust men and they understood scripture. They had witnessed first hand what the power of government had become in other countries and they struggled to institute a system that would ever revere the system that God had ordained. Thus they wrestled with the challenges of creating the world's first civil government that would be limited to the authority outlined in Romans 13:4.

With tremendous consideration our founding fathers brilliantly determined that the civil government of The United States would be empowered by a written Constitution. So little was their trust of their fellow man, they determined to write down exactly what power a government official could exercise. Citizens of this country do not stand before any leader and pledge obedience. Rather, we force our "leader" to stand before us and (with his hand on scripture) swear, "to preserve, protect and defend The Constitution ..."

This is to say we require our leaders to pledge obedience to The Constitution and acknowledge that their power is limited to only that defined there in. The hand on scripture signifies they recognize God Himself will hold them accountable on how honorably they execute their duties. The whole concept of having your hand on The Bible when taking that oath is acknowledgement that the God of The Bible will hold you accountable which is the God our founding fathers recognized and expected future generations to recognize.

Another telling consideration is that the limitations we put on our leaders is so complete that we reserve the right to "impeach" them. What right would we have to remove them from office if we truly believed that God put them in power? Indeed, as a Christian nation, what right would we have to declare war on another country and remove their leaders if we believed God placed their leaders in power? Christians support this because they believe our President is "Godly" and other leaders are not. This is a deception by the new world order while getting support for wars. God did not appoint or ordain The United States as the "world police".

Another scripture the new world order promotes to silence Christians is 1st Peter 2:13 "Submit yourselves to every ordinance of man … whether to kings or to governors…" Let me first address this by calling attention to the fact that read in context this passage does an excellent job of reinforcing Romans 13:4. Again we read in 2:14 "they are sent by Him for the punishment of evil doers…"

To understand this passage, it is best to return to the original Greek. Now if the word "ordinances" were in fact what we think of by "ordinances" today an argument could be made that we are required to obey every whim and fancy of every government bureaucrat. As mentioned earlier, however, God would never give men that much authority.

The Greek "ktisis" is translated "ordinances" here. This has more to do with "art of founding" or "type" than specifically dealing with heads of state.[59] Peter was talking about the various types (or levels) of governments "kings or governors". The Authorized Version, King James reads "whether it be to the king, as supreme; or unto governors, as unto them that are sent by him (by the king) for the punishment of evil…" In other words, "respect the lesser offices of government, even a police officer as one who was sent by the government because he was sent to punish evil doers and it's God's will that in so doing we silence foolish provocateurs and use our liberty honorably".

This does not declare or imply that we are subjects of the police and theirs to command. Just as the local police officer or city councilman has a responsibility, so too do we as Christians and patriots have a responsibility to hold them accountable. We have a great responsibility to future generations to insure that the limited government that God has ordained and past generations have delivered to us be passed on to them. We have a great responsibility to God to insure our leaders abide by His word.

By the way, even though kings, monarchs, etc, were the only known forms of government at the times scripture was written, nowhere does scripture endorse these as the only accepted forms of government. Our Constitutional Republic has proven to be much more Godly even though these ideas in government hadn't been developed at the time The Bible was written.

Our Founding Fathers understood a Biblical principle that kings had a covenant with the people as well as a covenant with God. This is a concept the new world order has completely stifled today. They desire to be viewed as in complete control with no accountability and if it furthers their cause by representing themselves as God's servants they falsely do so. There are several scriptural examples of this covenant.

2nd Kings 11:17 spells it out in absolute terms and 17b spells out a Godly covenant between the king and the people. Again, God did not desire one man to have rule over another, "and Jehoiada made a covenant between The Lord and the king and the people that they should be the Lord's people; between the king also and the people."

2nd Samuel 5:3 is another example. Here King David made a covenant with the elders of Israel before they anointed him king, "So all the elders of Israel came to the king to Hebron and king David made a league with them in Hebron before the Lord; and they anointed David king over Israel". 2nd Chronicles 10:3 illustrates the people forming a new government after Rehoboam would not agree to a covenant.

We should remember that The Apostle Paul, who wrote Romans 13, was frequently in trouble with the civil authorities and wrote four epistles from jail. He obviously would not accept modern interpretations to his writings. Scripturally and at the time of our nations founding, Godly men understood tyranny results when a tyrant is left to amass power. This would seemingly be an obvious statement but today we don't see any alarm from people over the size and scope our government is becoming and the church needs to recognize this is not a Biblical concept. Our founding fathers had a Biblical concept of civil government and what they gave us was limited to protecting the rights and property of the people. Plus they made it accountable to the people at all times.

First and foremost among the delegated jurisdictional authorities is the priesthood. God did not put the priesthood under the jurisdiction of the civil government, except in a situation where the priests were doing evil works and needed to be punished, and neither did our nations founders. There are examples in scripture of the king doing evil and needing to be punished and it fell to the priests to hold him accountable. God expects these jurisdictions to be respected and adhered too and each to do their duty.

1st Samuel 15 illustrates how the priest exercised authority over the king when he disobeyed God's word. The story is about King Saul who neglected to kill the Amalek King Agag and all their possessions as God had instructed.

2nd Chronicles 26:17-18 is very specific example. Azariah the Priest and eighty of his assistants forbade King Uzziah from violating their jurisdictional authority, "and they withstood Uzziah the king and said unto him it appertaineth not unto thee, Uzziah, to burn incense unto the Lord but to the priests the sons of Aaron ... go out of the sanctuary for thou hast trespassed ..."

Numbers 25 illustrates a priest enforcing the laws to avoid judgment when the community embraced immorality. Here the Israelites committed a variety of sins and began worshipping idols.

2nd Samuel 24 is an example of the nation being judged because the priests did not call the civil leader to account when they knew the king was doing evil.

1st Chronicles 21:1 states that it was Satan who moved, "influenced", David to number Israel. This is not the only example of the nation being judged when the priests remained silent and tolerated an evil king. Israel was conquered for this very reason. 1st Kings has numerous examples of Elijah holding King Ahab accountable for his ungodliness.

Christians have the same delegated jurisdictional authority from God and the same responsibilities to speak up and expose evil in the land even when it's promoted by government. Ours is the priesthood with all of its responsibilities and authorities. Our nation depends on Christians utilizing the authority they have and fulfilling God's purpose. It is Christians that are Christ's ambassadors on earth, not government or politicians.

The effort the new world order has made in robbing the priesthood of its authority is the particular focus of the chapter on "501c3". This area of research needs to be studied by all Christians and church leaders in particular. This deception was a subtle satanic trick to steal the authority of the church and it has worked brilliantly.

It can be stated here that the governments of the world today do not respect the priesthood as equal in authority or service to the community. The section on "God's view of Government" outlines how government has, for self-serving purposes, attempted to replace the church with benevolent programs supervised thru the state.

The priesthood being the first jurisdictional authority that God has ordained, the second delegated jurisdictional authority is the patriarch or as we would define it the head of the family. Parents have Godly authority in their home and both the civil government and the church need to respect that. The attack on the home from all levels of government today has reached frightening proportions. This authority pertains to a number of things. There is obviously the authority in raising and educating children. Then there is the authority of the family's finances. Another consideration is over the family assets or private property. God intended that the family own property so it could provide for all new additions to the family. All of these areas are seriously under attack by the new world order today.

Then there is the issue of "birthright" which is a part of the patriarchal system. The concept is that the oldest son receives a double portion inheritance. The logic here is that the oldest son is in line to become the next patriarch and has a duty to insure all siblings and their offspring are provided for. This is no longer an option under the inheritance laws of today (yet another violation of authority).

Aside from the basic needs of life, the greatest responsibility of the patriarch was enforcing a moral code in the family. The loss of a Biblical moral code has destroyed any possibility of a Godly society. This has led to increased lawbreakers and the need for government involvement. It is the responsibility and duty of parents to "raise up your children in Godly knowledge" but we have abdicated that to a local church or Sunday school. If we cannot teach morality in the home, we cannot enforce it. If we cannot enforce a moral code in the home we cannot enforce a moral code in society. This moral code usually included a work ethic.

Not so many years ago a family member receiving some type of public assistance embarrassed a family. It has become accepted since the break down of the family. Naturally with no extended family network there is no system in place for mutual support. A father is not considered any major authority in the home.

No thought is given to a family patriarch, which would be the oldest son of the oldest son and would have a duty towards the basic needs of the family unit, which is why God declared they should receive the larger portion. Ultimate responsibility rested with them to insure no one went cold or hungry. We read in The Old Testament where families hired their own priest, which illustrates their commitment to ensure every member of the family properly understood God and had opportunity to develop a relationship with Him.

There is the added argument of the priest as an "intercessor" which was important in an agricultural environment. If God was not blessing a family for any reason they had to know what this reason was quickly and get right with God. This system shared the burden of raising children in duties ranging from education to basic sustenance, providing for the elderly with due respect for their wisdom and kept each member of the family accountable to each other.

It is obvious, what the new world order had to gain by destroying the family. It is a simple and old strategy. To the extent a Godly home functions – there is no need for government involvement and subsequently no need for the government to grow. When a father is working to provide for the family and the mother is focused on the children the goal is two people united in raising children with a moral and respectful attitude as well as a strong work ethic and love of God.

When you remove one of the parents from the home you can expect some of the vital instruction God wanted children raised with to be missed. If the children are raised without morality or a strong work ethic society starts to break down and there is an increase in need for government involvement.

Problems were seeded as children grew to adulthood under a new system that taught that the church, or priest's, authority was secondary behind the authority of government. The priests were targeted for deception, as were parents. The changes came in a subtle manner and sounded reasonable. In time, so many priests were compliant with this change that it largely went unchallenged by the very ones charged by God with protecting their jurisdictional authority.

From one generation of "priests" to the next, each generation simply accepted a role of "The priesthood" being subservient to government authority. The new world order was successful in promoting the concept that the state "has an obligation" in broken homes. With so many broken homes the church was overwhelmed and further deceived. Rather than turning to God, that is a Godly definition and commitment of marriage and morality, the church accepted the help of government and surrendered their authority. The problem has only increased.

We didn't turn to God and we didn't fight to solve the problem at its core. The church stood idle as "no-fault" divorce laws destroyed the sanctity of marriage and this was an absolute violation of jurisdictional authority. Actually, creating marriage laws was a violation of jurisdictional authority. Most people have long forgotten that marriage laws were originally instituted to prohibit mixing of the races. God had made no such restriction but government seized an opportunity by fermenting hate. God defined "marriage" and the church should have enforced their jurisdictional authority and kept government out of this area. Today we see special interest groups clamoring for "the right" to get married.

The church can no longer deny them this right because we abdicated authority over marriage to government. Government has a duty to treat all people equally and it is now government who sets the terms on marriage. This is unscriptural. Had we demanded our jurisdiction be respected, these arguments would not be attempted. Had the church held fast to God's law that marriage is a covenant relationship between a man and a woman we would be in a position to deny marriage to anyone who is not willing or able to make that covenant commitment.

Today society recognizes that a man has a more binding commitment to his automobile finance company than to his wife. The courts will enforce a finance companies contract but if one spouse wants to terminate the commitment of marriage the courts will accommodate the request with no reason required. This is not the Godly home scripture refers to.

Scriptural marriage is a "blood covenant". This is the highest type of commitment that a person can make to God or to another individual and no court or man made laws have the authority to break a blood covenant. With our promiscuous society, marriage can no longer be considered a blood covenant and these commitments are broken multiple times hourly.

The church did nothing as welfare laws destroyed God's design for the man to be the provider to his family and tax laws were passed which placed an enormous burden upon the families finances, which frequently required a second income. These too are violations of jurisdictional authority. The church was also not to be found defending the sanctity of motherhood as the new world order launched a propaganda campaign to convince Godly women that a "stay at home mom" was a wasted life. We have paid a terrible price for getting uninvolved in politics.

It is essential to the agenda of the new world order to get children away from the authority (influence) of their parents. Parents have yielded in the defense of the home. It was a strategy of the new world order to get mothers out of the home so the state would be the greater influence on the children. The state, frequently represented by a "school teacher", has now replaced a loving mother. Mom is the chauffer who runs the kids from soccer practice to band practice. This too is designed. Even when the kids are not scheduled to attend school their time has demands on it. From a new world order perspective, the less time a child spends with its parents the better to break down the family unit and destroy parental influences.

Now as never before, America has God size problems. The fight is now! The fight is OURS, not our children's. As intimidating as these problems may sound, the fact remains that we have the authority to solve these problems. God did not leave or change, the church did. It's time to get back to church and start focusing on the things that are really important. Frequently we are quoted Matthew 22:21 "render unto Caesar the things which are Caesar's" but we do not so frequently hear the second half of the verse quoted "render unto God the things which are God's". The government has no more Godly authority today than it did in 1789, which is when our current Constitution was ratified. Parents must take a stand for the sake of their children.

We must oppose this ungodliness no matter what the personal sacrifice. Churches have a responsibility to take a stand. No church should be content to stand silent with all of the abuses of God's delegated authority in today's world. This is a clear call for each one to decide whom will we serve, God or government.

We need to mindful that simply because government grew in power, it did not grow in authority. The authority it exercises is unlawful and rightfully belongs to the patriarchs and priests. If we decide we want to reestablish Godliness we can exercise the authority because it is ours and since God is the source of our authority, we can expect God to act on our behalf. It is we who abandoned our authority, not God who revoked it. It was never God's idea that we fail to use it.

By usurping the authority of the patriarch and the priesthood the government has positioned itself as the only recognizable authority. The only hope we have, as a nation, is to recognize God's plan is the only one that will work. Government will not easily relinquish the power it has gained. It was once the weakest of three delegated powers. It is now the strongest.

The fight to get government back within its Godly parameters will take all of us but it's a fight long overdue. Christians need to understand that they are very much involved in this fight. They have simply been taught to surrender rather than take a stand. There is a strategy being used against us but we have Godly authority to take back what is ours.

All efforts put forth by government strategically exacerbate the problems. Much purpose is served by creating ever more dysfunctional homes and a society of illiterate, lazy, immoral people. The government has moved in to fill the void from where the church has retreated. This chaos is leading to destruction and the responsibility is ours for permitting this to happen.

If God is our God then we owe Him allegiance and duty. Adam was commanded to take "dominion". Today we stand idle as the enemies of God and Godliness take all dominion from us. If Matthew 22:21 means anything it is another reference to the fact that God did not intend for government to be "the higher power" of Romans 13:1. The "things which are Caesar's" are limited to the jurisdictional authority of government and the things that are God's, in this context, must be limited to the jurisdictional authority of the priesthood. Otherwise this passage would conflict with Psalms 50:12 "the world is mine and the fullness thereof".

We can argue that everything belongs to God but that would miss the point of this passage. Obviously, in context, Jesus was talking about the obligation of paying taxes. We can conclude that He had some purpose in adding the second half of the statement. His only purpose could be that we have duty to both God and country, not just country and not just God.

We are taught blind submission to the government except when it is in direct conflict with God's word. Unfortunately far too many Americans and clergy do not study the principles of government. We are not to submit to government with a few exceptions, we are to submit to God and abide by His word. We are to walk and serve in the authority He has given us. We are to make government submit to God's word. This is the system our founders gave us.

To render unto God the things that are God's we must revere His word, which includes a moral standard and responsibilities for civil government. Hence, the government is in direct conflict with the word of God whenever it usurps the jurisdictional authority of the priesthood or the family and Christians have a responsibility to step up and stop the unlawful usurpation of authority and render unto God the things that are God's.

It is curious how the church in America ever got to a place where we believe God created a system where evil politicians could dominate the church. It is singularly due to our ignoring the warning in Romans 13:11. We have been lulled into a complacency under which we tolerate everything.

Recently the suggestion was floated that The U.S. Congress investigates a variety of ministries for fraud and malfeasance. Most people would readily agree that if any entity should be investigated for these crimes it should be The U.S. Congress. Why doesn't the church investigate Congress? Simply put, we don't believe we have the authority. How did we come to a place where we fail to recognize that God's ambassadors on earth have authority? It was by evil design.

Today Christians and clergy consider themselves without duty. These four lies have so neutralized the church that we cannot site an example of when Christian duty requires intervention. We do nothing when our country goes to war without cause, rewards crime and debauches the currency. Recently we have seen it suggested that the state has authority to take a child away from its parents if they refuse state recommended vaccinations.

What is the point of having God's word if we're not going to stand on it. We have the God given authority to stand on it, we simply lack the will and resolve. As Christians increasingly refuse to get involved in the political responsibilities that belong to all citizens of this country Satan's government will continue to grow more ungodly. All Christians are aware that Jesus is King of Kings. They have not stopped to consider that this is a political title. Lord of Lords is a Priestly title. He is both and we should serve both duties, that of being a Christian and that of being a citizen.

Pastors that have chosen to submit their ministries to the IRS have bound themselves but they have no authority to bind anyone else. This will be the focus of a later chapter but it is not the IRS that has created this illusion that Christians should not get involved in politics, it is the new world order. In today's definition of good citizenship Christians are free to recognize what is wrong. We are just not free to do anything about the problem. Christians, like non-Christians need leadership. Today our leadership is leading us from pasture to pasture, not into battle. All of this may seem pleasant for the moment but will come at a high price when the battle overtakes us. There really is no wonder why the world does not respect Christianity or the church today. We have run from the fight in a strange fashion.

Typically when anyone holds a religious commitment they are viewed as being "zealous". This is a word that would apply to few Christians today. We fail to recognize that this ineffectiveness is hurting our ability to draw new converts, even among our own family members. We are no longer a blessing to society. Society is blessed by a host of government programs. We are no longer salt and light. We have withdrawn from the fight into our church buildings.

The divorce rate in the church, the covetousness for material wealth, the financial struggles, the dependence on the medical profession instead of seeing people healed in the church all go to illustrate that being a Christian doesn't really mean anything anymore. We now hear a strange thing. Have you heard it said, "The difference between a Christian and a non-Christian is that Christians are forgiven"? If this is the only difference, it is a sad commentary on what we have become and what we think we are capable of. I don't think this would be a slogan God would prefer for His church ...

AUTHORITY TO BIND THE CHURCH

*Matthew 22:21 "render therefore unto Caesar the things
that are Caesar's..."*

This chapter is going to deal with the church being legally neutralized
and prohibited by law from performing both it's civic duty and fulfilling
it's cultural mandate. Specifically we will focus on two bodies of laws,
which are "501c3", and "incorporation" laws. 501c3 is clear evidence
that Satan is involved in politics and has successfully maneuvered into
a position of power over the churches.

There are many great deceptions that have neutralized the
church but none more powerful than the 501c3 regulations. This has
done more than neutralize the church; it has enslaved it. This is a point
Christians need to consider; if the church is enslaved by Satan than it
is in his service, not God's.

Pastors and other church leaders, even lawyers that specialize in
helping churches, should be aware that under our system, government
has absolutely no authority to make demands or dictates to the church.
This very statement will probably astonish scores of readers because
we are so indoctrinated with the teaching that government is the final
authority, even if we don't want to use the word sovereign, that we
no longer consider that there are other forces that can be equal with
government or beyond its control.

An all-powerful government is the deception that the new
world order desires us to embrace, however, our country was founded
on Christian principles and our founders understood the fallen nature
of man. They desired that the church be beyond government control
as it was established by God and is immediately accountable to Him.

It is true that if men who are employed through some ministry
violate the law they can and should be brought before the law but

government was given no authority over the church itself. Atheists and others who hate the church may not recognize that the church has a greater authority than government but they must be made to realize that the authority is equal. The greater challenge is to get Christians and church leaders to understand our authority and role.

What our founding fathers established in 1772 (Articles of Confederation) was new in world events. They created the first ever "limited government", at least the first in modern times. The government they created was one of "delegated powers". This is quite different from the government we have to deal with today. The point here is that they did not delegate any power for the government to influence or control the church.

When The First Amendment was drafted and ratified in 1791 it expressly forbid the government or elected leaders from even trying. The First Amendment of The Constitution is clear; "Congress shall pass NO LAW respecting the establishment of religion, or prohibiting the free exercise there of;" There it is as plain and simply as it needs to be, Congress has no authority over the church. The control government exercises in our country are done by legislation, not military might. The area where government is forbidden to legislate is an area where they have never been granted authority to legislate. The people and the states have simply not given them authority to legislate in these areas and so they have none.

We see the system of delegated powers violated today by every session of Congress. They pass laws to control the education of children, regulation of food and drugs, ownership of property and just about everything else we can think of. The government recognizes no limit to its authority because the people and the states have stood idle for decades and allowed federal encroachment of power and authority. Idleness aside, the government has no authority to pass laws regarding the church.

The church has a responsibility to maintain a Biblical moral standard and the government has a responsibility to protect lives and property. The moral standard must be maintained or the government has no hope of accomplishing its purpose and the only moral standard that has proven reliable over the test of time is a Biblical moral standard. The only enmity between the church and government stems from a jealousy to usurp the other's authority but any argument that the church has lesser authority is wrong and must be reproved!

All of this changes, however, when a church applies for and is given 501c3 status or incorporates. At this point the individual church that takes this step voluntarily places itself under the authority of the IRS in the case of 501c3, and the state in the case of incorporation. Once you place yourself under their jurisdiction they own you and there is no easy escape! The IRS doesn't seem to be behind this deception. The church is doing it on it's own with the help of "church lawyers".

The IRS acknowledges taxing churches is against The First Amendment and all contributions are deductible. Churches voluntarily seek 501c3 status at their founding either through ignorance or bad advice from a lawyer. In exchange for 501c3 status churches are legally bound to "not be contrary to the settled public policy"[60]

Have you wondered why the far left may have any speaker at any church with no threat of IRS retaliation? Topics promoting homosexuality or abortion are government policy (settled public policy) and therefore not contrary to the IRS code. A church that opposes abortion or homosexuality is no longer free to voice their beliefs because they have now become "an agent" of the government. The IRS is simply the government agency responsible to insure the agents' carry out government policy.

This is much like The Department of Defense is the agency to see government policy is carried out in the military and The Department of Education insures government policy is carried out in the schools. If the topic were a military action we would not tolerate a branch of our armed forces to independently set a new policy. For example, if The Marine Corps decided it didn't want to go half way around the world and fight a dangerous war in a muddy hostile environment and they just took it upon themselves to move to Kansas City Missouri and police the streets their actions would be stopped and leaders would be disciplined. If a teacher or a local school superintendent decided to abandon the federally required curriculum and developed their own, they would be stopped.

These examples illustrate that if you are under the authority of the U.S. Government you have a specific agency/department holding you accountable. When a person joins the military, they voluntarily give up certain freedoms. They cannot take the assets of the military (including themselves) and simply choose an agenda. When a person becomes a teacher in a government school they are required to use the approved material. They have given up the freedom to teach what they regard as important, including their personal values. They must submit to the laws of the department with authority over them.

What far too many Pastors fail to understand is that when they apply to the IRS for 501c3 status they are giving up their religious freedom, freedom of speech and their First Amendment rights. They must commit to the requirements dictated by the IRS as an agency of the government.

From the time their 501c3 status is approved they are agents of the U.S. Government and no longer free to dispute government policy or adopt their own. If a 501c3 Pastor decided to challenge a government policy and speak according to their personal beliefs the governing agency, which is the IRS, is perfectly legitimate to step in just as the governing agency would step in with the other examples I gave. The IRS is not a business partner or even a "co-pastor"; they are the governing authority. You will abide by their dictates or they have authority to take action against you because you signed away your rights. If you are a "rebellious federal agent" they can assume control by taking the property, fire the agent and dispose of the property as they choose.

Obviously no Christian pastor would voluntarily relinquish their pulpit away from God's service to government service if they knew what they were doing. This is a tremendous and unnecessary deception. This is blatant fraud that Satan has used to stifle the message of the Bible from being preached in America's churches.

You cannot even argue they "sell" their pulpit for privileges that save them a few dollars in taxes. When they become 501c3 they jeopardize paying taxes and penalties in ways they would never have to concern themselves had they remained free from IRS jurisdiction, it's all a fraud! Once a church is deceived into 501c3 status they are no longer legally allowed to influence legislation even when it's church related. [61]

At this point it becomes impossible for a church to maintain a Biblically based moral standard in society. Attempting to do so violates their contractual designation as an agency of the government.

We have Lyndon Johnson to thank for this travesty. Senator Johnson had a history that was not well hidden from moral and patriotic Texans. After a great deal of embarrassing information was made public by dedicated pastors in his 1954 Senatorial campaign, Senator Johnson took steps to insure his reelections would not be similarly jeopardized in the future. He had churches added to the 501c3 code.[62] Still, this was only voluntary.

As corrupt as LBJ was, he knew he had no authority to place demands or requirements on the churches. Christian lawyers and misinformation tricked them into voluntarily submitting to this unnecessary and damaging commitment.

A few concerned Congressmen became so alarmed over this trend and it's predictable repercussions that in 1969 they spearheaded Congress passing public law 91-172 reaffirming churches have no need to apply for 501c3 status.[63]

Churches are so uninformed that this law has had no impact. Christian lawyers have been of no help in ending this trend and arguable have hurt many churches by promoting this un-American agenda. Indeed, we read in the forward of The IRS's "*tax guide for Churches and Religious Organizations:*

"Congress has enacted special tax laws applicable to churches, religious organizations and ministers in recognition of their unique status in American society and their rights guaranteed by the First Amendment..."[64]

How can you go from "Congress shall make no law ..." (First Amendment) to "Congress has enacted special tax laws applicable to the churches"? By seduction, deception and brazen fraud! This publication goes on for 32 pages outlining the "special tax laws" that Congress has benevolently passed. Under the heading "Tax-Exempt Status" we are warned,

"No substantial part of its activity may be attempting to influence legislation".

The significance of this issue cannot be overstated. Here we see a blatant and successful attempt by politicians and bureaucrats to dictate to the church and remove them from the process that should involve all Americans. We are told in very specific terms under "Political Campaign Activity"

"Under the Internal Revenue Code, all IRC section 501(c)(3) organization, including churches and religious organizations are absolutely prohibited from directly or indirectly participating in, or intervening in, any political campaign on behalf of (or in opposition to) any candidate for elective office..."[65]

So here we see the reason why Christians "should not be in politics." It is not from scripture and never was. It is from politicians. Remember, The IRS does not write it's own code, the politicians do. Politicians with their own agenda have followed LBJ's lead and promoted a strategy to disenfranchise the portion of their constituency that was the most judgmental and demanding on matters of personal integrity as well as the most contrary concerning growth of power via more government programs. Now we are "absolutely forbidden"!

Other factors with regard to this portion of their constituency; this group offered the least financial assistance toward supporting a politicians bid for reelection while frequently demanded popular legislation be defeated. That is to say Christians frequently fought the popular agenda (promoted by major media) while offering little assistance to a Congressman or legislator's bid for reelection.

There are a number of reasons for this but paramount on the list is the fact that Christians do not have the available funding of large eastern foundations with millions of dollars to throw around to achieve their political agenda. Typically Christians would find themselves at odds with eastern foundations. Christians were appreciative of our system of government and our God given freedoms and their agenda was to keep government small and honest.

According to the IRS political activities and legislative activities are two different things and are subject to two sets of rules. Once again this appears to be done for the sole purpose of keeping Christians out of politics. According to The IRS web site, the purpose served in separating these topics allows private foundations, of 501c3 declaration, to enjoy the full benefit of tax free status, just like a church, when, in fact, they are not a church but at the same time engage in politics.[66] So they are welcome to participate but Christians are not!

Not only is this a clear double standard but also is evidence of the war we're in. You submit yourself to the devil and he says "OK, serve God by sitting over there and shut up" but if you will serve Satan, "feel free to scream from the roof tops"!

501c3 also requires virtually all of its assignees to file an annual report declaring gross receipts.[67] This information is of no concern to the government - it's church business. You can see the one-sidedness of forbidding churches to assist physically or financially, for or against a candidate for office while allowing other types of 501c3 organizations, such as foundations, to assist fully. This arrangement simply assured the attrition of devout Christians being cycled out of office as those with better funding and backing are cycled in.

501c3 laws literally mean churches are prohibited to battle proposed laws that may specifically hinder them when, Constitutionally, Congress has no authority to be passing laws upon the church at all! All the while we have the propaganda preached its God's will and we shouldn't worry about getting involved because God has it all under control. As a result we never stop to consider that we are fully cooperating with Satan's system.

In this manner, it was purely a matter of time before all ambitious politicians learned that the financing for their campaigns was going to come from people with an agenda such as pro-abortion, pro-homosexual, pro-government education, etc. As they learned they could not get any assistance from the church, the church simply lost representation in both Congress and state legislatures. Devout Christians who desired to serve in government couldn't raise the money for the campaigns and could not compete. Additionally they were forbidden from turning to the church for help (or even exposure).

The church could no longer speak vital truths about ungodly candidates and issues. Christians increasingly failed to grasp the importance of getting these people elected. The big eastern foundations had any number of candidates to choose from and as Christians quit they were able to win more elections.

Then when Christians independently bought the lie that they should not get involved in politics our national course was set in the direction Satan and his minions desired. They were free to move in, where we moved out and institute their policies with military precision. How many millions of Christians have tolerated this injustice for fifty plus years now? Do you yet doubt that the church has been neutralized?

It is no small point that "churches" are hardly mentioned in Section 501c3 of the IRC (Internal Revenue Code); only "religious organizations".

Churches are mentioned in The IRC Title 26 Section 508c (1) (A) that states, "a church, its integrated auxiliaries and conventions and associations of the church are excluded from taxation".[68]

IRS Publication 557 states:

"Some organizations are not required to file form 1024. These include churches, interchurch organizations of local units of a church, conventions or associations of churches or integrated auxiliaries of a church ..."

There is no U.S. law requiring churches to submit to the IRS and any law attempted would be unconstitutional under The First Amendment.

Then there is the problem of pastors as "employee agents" of 501c3 organizations who are required to sign an agreement prohibiting them from "carrying on propaganda..." The code reads:

"No substantial part of the activities of which is carrying on propaganda or otherwise attempting to influence legislation (except as otherwise proved in subsection H) and which does not participate in or intervene in (including the publishing or distributing of statements) any political campaign on behalf of (or in opposition to) a candidate for public office".[69]

Those that think the sole purpose of the church is to "spread the gospel" need to take this to heart. The word propaganda has its roots in missionary work and evangelism. Being bound by this agreement simply insures legal entanglements when the government decides it is no longer in its best interest to allow churches to spread the gospel. They have a signed agreement with which to begin stifling pastors and the entire 501c3 body of laws to afford them jurisdiction and authority to determine what can be preached and what cannot be preached. They simply need to define what propaganda is and what it is not.

We can see that this teaching "our only job is to spread the gospel" is only a short-term deception and the government is free to "reassign" our duties at any time, which they did, in a manner of speaking, in 1984.

This is when the 501c3 regulations were changed to demand a service of all pastors. Thus there are no more disputes as to who's in charge. In 1984 pastors were charged to become both tax collectors and IRS informants on church employees. Statutes were changed requiring churches to withhold income taxes, payroll taxes and report income of all employees.[70]

If all of this sounds harmless to you, you simply do not grasp that in our country the government or its agents have been denied authority over churches. The church of Jesus Christ was accountable directly to Him and given its mission by Him. No part of our mission from Jesus is to be tax collectors for the government.

Rather than being bound by the limitations of law (The Constitution), government has "cast away their cords from us" (Psalms 2) and has steadily worked to gain complete control of the church and those working in the ministry of God. There is no reason why Christians should stand idle and permit this theft.

The government simply lacks the authority to hold the unlawful possession of the church but they do hold it because Christians lack the resolve to take it back. On occasion a Godly Pastor will take a valiant stand. Through the illegal use of power government typically destroys him in some manner. Hence no viable movement has successfully challenged the new world order. 501c (3) laws have put pastors in a position where they have abdicated their authority and can no longer perform their duties to the full extent done by previous generations.

Consequently we can only anticipate that the government will continue to expand its unlawful authority over the church.

In United States Code, Title 26, section 508c1a it is recognized that churches are not required to apply for 501c3 status in order to be exempt from federal taxation or to receive tax-deductible contributions. Individual contributions to churches are deductible under Section 26 USC 170-B and churches are automatically exempt.[71]

The IRS does offer publication 557 which suggests churches may find it advantageous to apply for 501c3 status, however, if 557 is reviewed carefully, it will be noted they offer no advantages that are not afforded without 501c3 status. This is important as it creates the illusion that churches can "obtain an advantage". In truth, churches are immune to begin with. No advantage can be obtained and the offer itself is simply the arrogance of an inferior (or equal) authority attempting to entice an equal (or superior) authority into legal entanglements that ultimately accomplish the submission of the one to the other when no submission was necessary. Indeed submission of the church to government is contrary to the very principles of freedom of religion that this country was founded upon.

This is a diabolical plan – a satanic plan to muzzle pastors in their pulpits from exposing Satan's evil agenda. The fact churches desire 501c3 status without the IRS promoting the program is an indication that our churches falsely recognize the government as having authority and it is proof that our clergy and our citizens no longer hold significant understanding of the principles this country was founded on. This thinking needs to be changed and the truth promoted.

Now with "Faith Based initiatives" we see churches lining up for government revenue. The Supreme Court has consistently ruled that what the government finances it can control. As churches increasingly get sucked into this program they will bring upon themselves even greater bondage. We are well on our way to "state churches" and its time to re-establish Houses of God that speak the truth and expose lies. Churches that are fiscally liable to the state and preach the message approved by the state are state churches.

Another deception many ignorant pastors are signing up for is a new Federal program called "The Clergy Response Team". This is a program through The Federal Emergency Management Administration allowing FEMA to control churches if a national emergency is declared. Pastors who have agreed to this program are bound to cooperate fully and help FEMA control their parishioners during a declared crisis. This is done because sociologists firmly believe that people will submit to the clergy and cooperate with them to an extent far beyond the level of cooperation and submission they would afford bureaucrats. Therefore it was decided to make the pastors bureaucrats.

Those alarmed by this program are assured it's a harmless remake of the 1950's Civil Defense Program that also sought the cooperation of the clergy. This has few similarities. Nothing in the old Civil Defense agenda suggested pastors help disarm their parishioners or encourage them to voluntarily surrender their private property. Neither was Romans 13 misquoted and misapplied under the old civil defense program. The program was explained to the clergy and they were free to weigh the benefits to their congregations. No deception was involved and the benefit was to the people, not the government. This is quite different than The Clergy Response Teams.

Another mechanism in place to harness and gag the churches is the belief that churches need to incorporate. This is typically sold to the pastor and elders as a way of protecting themselves from lawsuits. While it may be prudent to protect yourself in some fashion, incorporation defeats the purpose of establishing a church to begin with. Sadly, insufficient research is done so church leaders are not aware of what they are sacrificing or what other options (such as insurance) would be preferable if they have a desire to preach freely.

A "corporation" by definition is an entity that has obtained "a charter of incorporation" from its respective state. Legally this charter is permission to exist and do business as the designated entity. Corporation status is awarded by the state in order for the business to function as a legal "personality" apart from its members.[72] It is sought out by the businessmen to achieve certain protections against personal harm including financial liabilities.

In business this may be reasonable as a manufactured product could conceivable do someone some unforeseen harm. An accident that was determined to have resulted from negligence or a host of other unforeseen problems could easily destroy the business and bankrupt all investors. Confusion is wide spread on this topic as the entire process of incorporating is highly abused in our society today. Additionally, unscrupulous business people have protection, once incorporated, which creates an incentive for the immoral to seek this status.

These are not good reasons for a pastor to seek corporation status. The church can purchase insurance to protect themselves against liability suits so there is nothing to be gained. To be lost is the religious freedom under The First Amendment. Once incorporated you operate at the pleasure of the state that has granted you permission to incorporate and they can revoke your status and shut you down.[73]

The church should not be seeking protection of the state for immoral business practices or be concerned with its favor. The idea of churches being incorporated was bad and unnecessary from the beginning. Once incorporated the church must comply with the specified conditions of the incorporation agreement. It derives its power to function from the state at that point and has only the power that the state has granted to it.

The concept of "granting of corporate status" is another example of the state thinking it has the power to grant some privilege to the church. It is not illegal or immoral to preach the gospel of Jesus Christ in this country and churches need no permission from the state in fulfill their calling. Neither are they free to fulfill their purpose of being salt and light once they have contractually agreed to submit.

A corporation is an "artificial person" created by law and is subject to the laws of the state of its creation. Its powers and authorities are limited to its charter and can make no claim, promise or contract not authorized by its charter under penalty of law. Its authority to function is preserved to it only so long as it abides by the charter of its creation. No part of this should sound remotely appealing.

Much of this deception has been accepted because of the lie that all religions are equal before the law. Reasonable people consider that some control or oversight is desirable when you have religions like witchcraft and satanism in the market place. Hence we see why government promotes false religions like witchcraft and satanism. When you must treat all religions equally and you have religions that engage in personal harm or destructive tendencies, people want the government involved in religion because they want protections against any religious practices harming themselves or their property.

All religions are not equal before the law and The United States was founded as a Christian nation. It is well documented that whenever our founding fathers spoke of religion they singularly had Christianity in mind. They did not recognize any other so-called religion as viable and many writings exist that they regarded Christianity as the only system that would support the type of government that they instituted.

The fraud against the church and against Christians is staggering. Its satanic and its something we can do something about if we desire to. We do not need to suffer from these lies any longer.

The church must stand its ground and return to founding principles which declare a Godly nation is a Christian nation. The Bible is very clear on this point. Religions that promote satanism, witchcraft, humanism, idolatry, polytheism or astrology are not to be tolerated but are to be cast out of the land.

Yet under 501c3 all are welcome and some are more welcome than others. From the outset of this writing I have argued that the churches have been infiltrated and led away from the purpose God had intended for us. This is highly insulting to a great many people, I'm sure. Yet when we read Revelation 13 we see the church in the service of Satan and his system. Admittedly there will be many individual Christians who will not submit. Neither should we find ourselves submitting to this system in our time. We can and should recognize the deception that is enslaving the pulpits of God. This system is how Satan got control of the churches and we all have a duty to oppose this.

The information in this chapter is extremely detrimental from the perspective that the IRS will not casually end its ability to exert authority over any church. I caution each church to seek out the best legal assistance they can find before proceeding. The emphasis here would be on the experience and success they have in dealing with the IRS.

Additionally I would like to caution all readers and church leaders against taking action based on generic advise from organizations or individuals who will attempt to convince you it is they that can assist you by selling you the necessary paperwork to file (and their books with corresponding instructions) to end your obligations but offer no assistance if problems ensue. Be warned! There exists the very real question of legal authority and laws that must be adhered to for your own protection.

Protect yourself to insure the advice you accept is from (or verified by) attorneys versed on 501c3 and laws of "incorporation" and who have had success in dealing with The IRS, not just experience. I would also recommend you verify they have experience in IRS courts and are familiar with the associated rules of evidence and acceptable defenses. Dealing with The IRS requires you be accurate with your facts.

Finally there is the question of spiritual authority. You have voluntarily submitted to the IRS and abdicated your authority. God holds people to contracts and covenants and He expects you to honorably administer yours. Do not let anyone convince you that you can simply break this agreement and expect Divine intervention. Make sure that your choices satisfy your legal obligations.

WITHOUT MORALITY

Psalms 1:1 "Walk not in the counsel of the ungodly..."

One great advantage held by proponents of the new world order is the inability of the average American to comprehend pure evil. It is something few in this country have had to confront. The best effort that can be made by most people is an awareness of some psychotic serial killer especially if children are involved. The idea of business professionals openly engaging in occult activities such as Satan worship, child sacrifices, any type of blood sacrifices, black masses, any number of rituals or the many types of crimes that are necessary to support this type of activity is quickly rejected as unbelievable by most people, including Christians.

Then there are the sexual aspects of it all. Most people still believe in monogamy on some level. Ideas of "open marriages" or "wife swapping" are still rejected and judged as immoral by the majority of Americans and simply a lifestyle they want no part of. This leads them to assume that these activities are quite limited and to the small extent they are practiced would only include the very dregs of humanity. The same attitudes are held to varying degrees for pornography, recreational drug usage, and a host of other activities that society, as a whole has never embraced.

These arguments support the statement that the average American cannot comprehend absolute evil. We can conclude, then that the average person cannot comprehend seemingly respectable people who would choose evil as a lifestyle choice. This is a decided strength of the new world order as it affords them the freedom to function and grow without fear of exposure. Those that happen upon some truth of their agenda or existence will be quick to dismiss it as a misunderstanding or an isolated event.

Here, as perhaps under no other topic, is it vital for Christians to accept the duty and responsibilities of being salt and light and to remind our fellow citizens that Satan appears as an angel of light. We see a public side to immorality that is tearing down the very fabric of society. Illicit sex is the forerunner in this parade and this is why no effort is ever permitted to diminish the promotion of unbridled sex. We as a society see a need to "counsel" those addicted to drugs, alcohol and even tobacco but none of these vices have the detrimental effects of illicit sex.

Some in society wish to control the behavior of other people regarding their ability to eat certain foods, drink too much soda and movements exist to restrict the dosage of vitamins purchased over the counter. No such movement exists to limit casual, flagrant sex. The very few who still dare suggest abstinence are ridiculed and mocked as old fashioned, naive and self-deceived.

We can address any other ill that can be defined in society but sexual immorality is a "sacred cow" that cannot be limited or stifled in any small way. The cost to society of this single evil is staggering and growing but we are told we are helpless to prevent illicit sex and must focus our energies on after the fact solutions such as abortion, aid to single mothers, adoption and foster care and treatments for sexually transmitted diseases.

On any other topic the "cost" to society is argued as the greater need to justify government intrusion and regulation but on this topic the costs to society are gleefully absorbed without complaint. We are told that it's a private, personal choice. The major media and Hollywood preach that it is natural and must therefore be acceptable. This message is always followed with the slogan "you're not going to stop it anyway".

This was no unavoidable circumstance; it was carefully planned. It was also strictly forbidden in God's word. God knew where this type of attitude would lead us and what it would do to society. This is the point we must now address, where this attitude is taking us. We were put on this course for a purpose and we have not yet arrived at our destination.

The purpose is not profit although the profit making in abortion and pornography is enormous. The course and the purpose are much deeper than profit. The purpose is to attract innocent people into an immoral lifestyle in the confidence that the majority of them will embrace it. Once they have embraced it, it becomes their new standard. Few will come to a place where they question it and turn back to a higher moral standard.

Here is where we must take a hard look at the strategists. Many innocent people have difficulty in grasping the evil in the hearts of those who would promote the abandonment of all sexual standards simply for a self-serving purpose. Even the majority of abortion protestors fail to consider the root causes of this problem. They focus only on the act of abortion one case at a time with little or no regard to the core agenda. The occasional woman who is counseled into changing her mind does not threaten the agenda. Neither is it threatened by the occasional attempt to pass legislation forbidding abortions in full or in part.

The agenda is not about abortion, or pornography. Illicit sex is the most wide spread opportunity to debase the morality of the masses because we all have a natural sex drive but this too is not the real agenda. There are evil people who desire that the morality of society be debased, therefore illicit sex must never be hindered. With illicit sex comes abortion and pornography, which are very profitable.

Mass numbers of people do not have a natural drive to engage in any other vice that is capable of destroying the social makeup of society. Working towards any agenda will generate either positive or negative reactions from every effort. These reactions spawn opportunities for profit making. The opportunity to make money serves to draw many others into supporting the agenda without questioning it. The more people that support the agenda the more rapidly it grows. The strategists need not control these people. They have already influenced them and now through their greed and immorality they will continue to support the agenda.

The agenda is a new world order, which is a global satanic tyranny. Immorality is a vital tool necessary for the success of this agenda. As immorality tears down the fabric of society and erodes all of societies various strengths, chaos ensues. To address the chaos the masses of people demand more government intervention. The promotion of immorality in all its aspects simply benefits those who desire to expand government. Thus we see the strategy at work.

The promotion of immorality for any purpose achieves tremendous results toward the success of their agenda and they never risk exposure because they are viewed as benefactors aiding those who are in need of some government program. The actual agenda of a new world order is not debated or challenged, only the amount of spending for new government programs.

One truth the strategists understood is that people who have embraced immorality are not likely to hold others accountable to a higher moral standard either. Few are likely to become activists promoting a higher moral standard than they live personally. Many will remain silent while they secretly favor new and lower standards of morality for society as a whole. This also appeases their conscience because their own behavior is more bearable if it is deemed tolerable or acceptable by society. It becomes a mechanism to deal with their guilt because so many people are engaged in similar activity.

Sex as a tool is simply an opportunity to influence and spread immorality among more people than other forms of immorality. Again, all people have basic biological urges that are sexual in nature but not all people have a basic biological urge to use drugs, steal, kill or any number of listable immoral actions.

So abortion, as one example, becomes a means to promote immorality. It relieves the individual of living with the result of their actions. This promotes freedom to pursue base human behavior free from concern over the consequences. Those who make a profit in the abortion business further advance the agenda. This is how the larger agenda is kept hidden.

The purpose of this chapter is to call the reader's attention to the world being planned for us. That is to say, what all of this immorality is going to cost us in the long run and who stands to benefit. It is vital for the reader to understand that while sex may be the most attractive doorway for the strategist of the new world order to use in the corruption of the greatest number of people, it is a small matter towards what they stand to gain. They plan to enslave the whole of mankind and openly destroy all that will not bow and worship them.

Their blood lust will not be pacified by any number of abortions. They feed on human suffering and their own sexual proclivities are so perverse that no reasonable person desires to even know more about what they do. Paul cautions us in Ephesians 5:12 "it is a shame even to speak of those things which are done of them in secret". It is not necessary or beneficial that we know of the sick and perverted practices of those in Satan's service. It is necessary and beneficial that we understand a Godly duty we have to stop them from taking over society.

Toward this end it is necessary to recognize the unbridled evil that many will embrace for their own perceived benefit, the strategies they intend to use against us and the very nature of the battle in which we find ourselves. This is why the reader must look past the nice clothes, handsome faces and warm smiles of those employed in the business of promoting this agenda. They are there for a purpose.

Their purpose is not to inform or educate. Contrarily their purpose is to deceive outright and mislead constantly. A well-educated public would do much to stop the agenda Satan plans for this world. Those that have dedicated decades to Satan's service have contemptuous attitudes towards God, people not in allegiance with them and any agenda that is contrary to their own such as thoughts of nationalism, family or personal freedoms.

Unchecked base human behavior will destroy any society and sexual immorality simply has the greatest appeal to the greatest number of people. Once they have been seduced down this path, it will take a life-changing event to call these people out of this lifestyle and back to a Godly standard. With the church neutralized, few will have a truly life-changing experience. Society will continue to deteriorate as more and more types of conduct become tolerable.

Finally, the only conduct that is intolerable is that which the government has outlawed and they will have small incentive to harshly punish the outlaws. This will all end in chaos and society will collapse from the lawlessness and lack of basic values from which one person normally cares for another as it becomes an "every man for himself" situation.

This is inevitable because lack of production is inevitable from a lack of work ethic. As food and warm clothing become scarce crime and selfishness will reign. People should hear from our pulpits that high government taxes and aid programs to the unemployed are destroying our country's work ethic. Unfortunately this book cannot entertain all of the valuable arguments concerning government policies, which have created such high unemployment, but this too should be known and spoken from our pulpits.

Since we do not hear this we can expect the people to turn to the same government that has caused the problem and demand "rationing" and "redistribution" which will give government ultimate control over who eats and who goes hungry.

One of their greater strengths is that the very people they plan to destroy trust them. Developing that trust simply took an expensive suit, a make up artist, a loud microphone and significant self-promotion. Maintaining that trust is done by using the same formula as making rat poison, ninety-nine percent food (truth) and one percent poison (misinformation). Of course the truth portion can be trivia and entertainment but the formula works. Many have a favorite news anchor that they listen to regularly. They will not easily be convinced to challenge the patriotism, credibility or sincerity of the anchor in whom they've placed their trust.

Another aspect that makes this so successful is in what information they choose not to share with their listeners. They promote UN food drives, for example, but say nothing of The UN removing an earnest leader of some third world country in order to install a new world order puppet. They promote the economy in China and may air an occasional story about newly authorized religious freedom but say nothing about forced abortions, work camps and devout Christians jailed for speaking spiritual truths that yet remain unauthorized.

Even large Christian ministries in America have fallen victim to this propaganda campaign. They may air stories of the collapse of communism in the former USSR but will not give airtime to those who predicted this turn of events and work to expose it as nothing more than a plot to escalate their agenda. They may air a story about failures in public education only to conclude the reason for this failure is inadequate funding. Never do they allow the suggestion that a better solution would be to decentralize government.

Frequently those chosen to voice opposing views on controversial subjects are poorly qualified and unaccustomed to public speaking. Sincere, though these people may be, they are chosen to create the impression that those who oppose the networks position are poorly educated and limited in their knowledge of the facts. Better spokesmen could be easily had for any number of issues but they are rejected simply because they are the better representatives of the opposing view.

Once the doorway to immorality was thrust open and the access to truth was sufficiently centralized, the ability to destroy society was far more attainable. Without the destruction of society they could not achieve the chaos from which they hope to build their new world order.

A moral people virtually unanimously recognize the God of The Bible as the One who sets moral standards. Those who may not fully embrace the God of The Bible still embrace the monotheistic beliefs which had largely become universal until the influences of the new world order became so wide spread. A moral people would not tolerate subtle attacks on God and what we are witnessing today is far from subtle.

In their planning, the new world order has long made known their desire to destroy God. Godly people typically stand for personal humility and frequently give some consideration to the welfare of other people. They also consider an existence beyond this life that is greater and subsequently more important. It is also true that they are not as easily misled by Satan's media, entertainment or educational system as they are typically grounded in The Bible to varying extents.

It is also typical for them to be in contact with a local spiritual advisor who is also grounded properly in The Bible. This is why it became so vital to their agenda to infiltrate the churches, install their own leadership and gain control of the message.

Some of Satan's followers have been led to believe that there will come a final fateful confrontation known as Armageddon but Satan will prevail. They have been taught to understand scripture accordingly. Others have been taught that Armageddon is no deception, but rather, when they achieve the ability to enforce total power they will install their messiah on his throne as king of the world. This will be accompanied by the total destruction of those who oppose their will.

The most effective strategy towards achieving their goals is to not deal with any concept of a final confrontation. Satan's servants are clueless so deception here is quite simple.

Additionally, they have achieved much in tearing down the morality of individual church members and clergy. There is benefit in publicizing this as it not only discredits the church but also weakens the morals of those fighting temptation. God is destroyed, not in fact, but in purpose as His people no longer follow His teaching and are not sold out to promoting His agenda. With this form of Godliness many have no real relationship with God and don't even realize it.

Without a sincere commitment to a Godly standard Christians, as well as non-Christians are victim to a constant onslaught of temptations that will eventually wear them down and prove effective on some level.

Another primary temptation that is quite successful in America is greed. Without morality one decreasingly considers the welfare of other people and increasingly considers satisfying his own wants and desires. He is motivated to consider the "now" and not the "future". As he increases in wealth the next step is a feeling of superiority. He develops the belief that he's better or smarter than other people and deserves his wealth and what it buys. Satan can easily exploit the selfishness of one so conceited.

One tactic to exploit such people is based on the fact that arrogant people do not deal well with criticism. They like to feel superior and tend to be unwilling to discuss topics that they are unfamiliar with like politics and religion. Yes they have an opinion and are quick to share it but they will not be taught. They will not discuss such important matters and learn truth from someone they regards as inferior. They do not embrace absolutes because they do not want to be judged. They have found it far more expedient to just ignore those who try to make them aware of any potential crisis. They consider themselves intellectual, well informed and superior so when someone broaches a subject with which they are unfamiliar they confidently convince themselves they have superior information and are sufficiently aware of current events.

Indeed many conceited people have been recruited into Satan's service simply by a manipulator playing with their ego. As their ego grows their feeling of superiority develops into contempt and even to hate of those who oppose them. In this fashion Satan has very successfully turned many patriotic Americans against the very people that work arduously to insure no government program will ever rob them of the wealth they have worked for.

We hear much about tolerance but we must recognize the immorality of tolerance. It is immoral because tolerance is no substitute for love. It is certainly no substitute for Godly love. I can tolerate my neighbors but have no concern when they suffer a personal tragedy or are in need of help. The promotion of tolerance needs to be placed in the perspective of what it's costing us as a society.

It's costing us real relationships, personal tragedies, horrors and sufferings too vast to be numbered and all for the benefit of a select few which have no concern for the greater welfare of society themselves. They have become too consumed with selfishness in the pursuit of satisfying their personal lusts. It is illogical to both "tolerate" someone and intercede with compassion when you fear for their welfare. You either tolerate or have compassion. They are mutually exclusive.

There are those that argue that we are civilized because most metropolitan areas have police officers for every five hundred citizens or because we have so many laws and investigatory tools that anyone who commits a crime will surely be found out and held accountable in the courts. This does not describe a civilization; it describes a police state, which, itself, is a threat to civilization.

No civilization can exist when the weak are so easily victimized by the callous. This is where the immorality of tolerance has brought us. The morality of Godly standards would never have tolerated the majority of what we view on the evening news. Love and morality would have interceded. Tolerance shrugs and walks away. In the end, tolerance, itself, breeds poor character as it breeds a failure to hold anyone to a standard or accountable for their actions.

It is in this environment that the youth of America grow to adulthood and learn standards of conduct and interaction with their fellow man. This environment is strategically designed to corrupt the youth of America. They are taught to tolerate but nothing else and this is not a standard. Without a moral standard or concern for one's neighbors, selfishness is bred among the populous. A nation of people who are immoral in the sense that they do not recognize Godly standards will not judge the behavior of other people or judge it's impact on society from a Godly standard. We have become a people believing in evolution as a fact and subsequently taught to follow our own instincts and desires.

It is no mystery what end we face as a society and where this road will take us. There is never a shortage of those who covet power. We, as a society, have tolerated the constant and strategic erosions of our moral base to such an extent that casual sex is no longer regarded as wicked and in some circles its not even considered ungodly. Our prisons have revolving doors and those guilty of the most vile crimes frequently get paroled back into the community with a minimum amount of time served.

Government is now in the theft business, just taking what it wants from rightful owners. The size of government is still growing and to cover the costs the debt ceiling is raised on a regular basis. Our military serves corporate interests instead of national interests. This list could continue for several pages.

Can there yet exist people who fail to grasp the basic truth that all of this is happening by design? Can there yet be people who refuse to believe that Satan has taken the simple and basic steps of organizing his efforts in order to achieve his goals. Where, in the annals of man, is it written that man is so incompetent that he cannot structure a monetary system, educations system or conducts his international business honorably?

All of history cries out to be heard and if we listen, history proves man is capable of founding institutions that function ably. We had the finest, most respected and most free country the world had ever known. We had a nation with a sound monetary system, the finest educational system in the world, a quality food supply and citizens who honored and respected each other. By permitting the abandonment of common decency we see all vice practiced as acceptable behavior and if this is the standard of the people, why should the standard of government be higher?

Numerous scriptures will argue that God will respond to people who humble themselves and seek Him. We don't humble ourselves and ask because we have grown tolerant of immorality and no longer consider it evil. True to man's nature, as we have embraced a low moral standard we tolerate a low moral standard in other people and in our government. Perhaps the worst is that we have allowed ourselves to be convinced that these circumstances are inevitable. With this erroneous mindset we don't even try God's way, we just tolerate Satan's way.

We do not count the cost of inactivity or of losing our Godly system. Never do we ponder our responsibilities as salt and light. Never do we admit that getting out of politics is the most monstrous decision we have made because we have abandoned our society to Satan. Let's stop and consider some reality before we proceed. The system that Satan would foist upon us is sufficiently visible that we may draw some reasonable conclusions.

I keep going back to the educational system because this is extremely vital. Satan's system currently requires children to spend a minimum of ten years immersed in their educational system by law. This would be from the age of six to sixteen. Ideally they prefer children to begin preschool at age three (day care prior to this) and remain in a university until twenty-three or so. We can see the impact they have had on the current generation with ten to fourteen years of influence. We can deduce that adding an additional ten years will increase their impact accordingly.

Similarly we have noted the growth of government over the last two generations and we recognize the growth rate is increasing in speed. We see government taking over private corporations by declaration and not even a pretence of any legal authority. We see politicians brazenly ignoring the stated will of the people and forcing controls upon society with vigor and determination. We see the federal government funding local police departments with military style weaponry and increasingly federalizing many laws. Increasingly we see the authority of law enforcement privatized and employees of agencies that previously had very limited authority are increasingly empowered with full police authority.

We see our nations entire economic structure being altered. Under NAFTA we are taxed and the money sent to Mexico (now Central and South America too) to build factories. With no capital investment, no minimum wage laws and no prohibitive regulations, there is simply no way for U.S. manufacturers to compete in the market place so we watch helplessly as our manufacturing jobs are eliminated. We have roughly the same problems increasing in agriculture, as foreign producers are not burdened with the strict regulations and fees that U.S. ranchers are forced to accommodate, under penalty of law.

NAFTA aside, under "Most Favored Nation Trade Status" laws China, Vietnam and several other "third world countries" are negotiating similar agreements to "take our money so they can take our jobs" where we give them ridiculously low interest loans to build factories and buy the equipment necessary to put our factories out of business.

Seldom a day goes by when we don't learn of some atrocity in our food supply and the days of a compassionate, caring family physician are either gone or will be very soon. Our money literally isn't worth the paper its printed on and countries that formerly held our currency with the confidence of gold are now demanding hard assets for debt instead of currency.

What can be said about our churches? Aside from an exceptional few, they are oblivious to all of this and many refuse to consider the importance of these matters or regard that Christians have a responsibility. To conduct ourselves with morality is a Christian responsibility. We have failed in promoting God's standard to society but we neither must live with this failure not accept the abandonment of standards upon ourselves. There is a single issue here that should be promoted on two battlefronts, morality in our personal lives and morality in our government. We can ponder Bible prophecy but we should do our reasonable service and not cooperate with Satan to any degree including preoccupying our minds with rhetoric that we have a destiny to fail. This simply gives him an ungodly influence on us.

We can ponder the new world order and choose to conclude what we will but this too does not give us license to give Satan place in our government due to a lack of concern. The future is satanic if we do not get involved. The educational system has destroyed the individualism and spirit of independence of future generations. Also shattered is a reverence for family, country and God. To a dangerously large extent future generations are overmedicated, manipulated, overindulged, entertainment junkies. They are told what to demand and pushed into a voting booth to demand it.

Government is not conducive to morality. It never was. Government affords all the allures that evil covets; power, greed, the ability to manipulate, the ability to intimidate, the ability to violate, fame and prestige. As we consider our fellow man we note that few know how to use freedom with moderation. This then is what we can expect from those we seat in government office. Politics has no more in common with morality that rhetoric has to reality. In politics might is virtually always right. These are all matters a moral people would not tolerate.

Immorality will destroy us and this is why God gave us authority to set and hold a moral standard. It is time to count the cost of idleness. There is the obvious; lives ruined, destroyed homes, starvation, disease, crime and any number of personal abuses that we will suffer. I question if the average American can truly accept the possibility that these horrors will affect them right here in our nation. We are listening to the counsel of the ungodly. They tell us all will be well if we trust them. They tell us it is not our fight.

Proverbs 14:34 assures us "righteousness exalteth a nation but sin is a reproach to any people". As Christians have left the arena of politics the unrighteous have taken over. No longer is there any standard. There is only ambition and the requirements necessary to satisfy ambition. Once the ambitions are satisfied there remains only the need for entertainment and the satisfying of base lusts. No nation can survive under such a system. No nation can survive without observing a Godly standard of morality because all conduct is based on a moral code and all need for government is based on personal conduct.

Godly government requires a moral people. This fact was never before questioned in history and it should not be questioned by our generation now. We have seen what happens to society when Christians abandon their civic responsibilities. The price is too high and the arguments are wrong. It is not sufficient to dabble and make mediocre gestures. We have been assigned a responsibility and we have a duty. We as Christians, parents and citizens cannot afford to abandon our nation to the forces of evil that lust to shed innocent blood and enslave all who draw breath.

It is only due to deception that we would consider such actions. We have one lie yet to examine, that Government is of God. We will see that the deception is deep and all encompassing. But it is not final.

PART
FIVE

GOVERNMENT
IS OF
GOD

GOD'S VIEW OF GOVERNMENT

Romans 13:11 "it is high time to awake out of sleep…"

We come now to the fourth and final lie addressed in this book but it is far from the final lie accepted by the church. Satan is a liar and only the return of Christ will put a final end to his efforts.

It seems to go unnoticed by Christians that whenever God referred to government in scripture He seemed to be warning us. God made it absolutely clear in 1st Samuel 8:7 "they have rejected Me; that I might not rule over them". God wanted to rule Israel as their King; yet they wanted a man to serve as their king like the other nations had. It also escapes the notice of most Christians that God had a system in mind – a government system that He'd planned to use to govern the nation of Israel. Surely this is worthy of study and replication.

The government of God's choice was patriarchal with judges and priests, each having their responsibilities to God and the community. This system placed responsibility on the head of each family to insure all in his family were fed, educated, healthy, housed, disciplined, taught a work ethic, polite, respectful, moral, raised in the knowledge of God and employed in the family business.

Priests were central in the community to teach Godly principles and maintain the moral code set down by our creator. Lastly, there were judges to settle disputes, oversee legal transactions and determine from "The Law" the appropriate punishment when an "evil doer" had to be dealt with.

It was from this beginning that all men of all nations rejected God as their King by rejecting His word and His system and sought a corrupt system. This corrupt system centered on "man" and had allure to those who lust for the power of being able to "rule over other men". God knew what power would do to men. He knew those that taste power constantly crave for more. He knew that men were not capable of ruling in a just and moral manner. He also knew that there exists an enemy of God and man who desires to destroy all the good that God desires for people. It is this perversion of God's system that we know today as "government".

Christians believe (because they are taught) that God established governments. To the extent described above, He did. Satan has been corrupting God's plan for man from the beginning and he has used government as the primary vehicle to gain influence and power. Today he is largely able to use government to new extremes and his primary use for government is to promote all of his deceptions in his never-ending quest for power.

The church, which has the responsibility of fighting Satan and revealing truth and exposing his lies, no longer questions anything. We believe what we're told from the politicians, from the media, from the educators, from the scientists and from the preachers. Christians believe incredible foolishness simply because Satan's salesmen insist it's true. In abandoning our duties to be salt and light we have stood idle while God's word has been abandoned in all spheres of society. The sphere with the most repercussions in corrupting God's system is government.

Consider, in Daniel and Revelation, God refers to governments as the vilest beasts describable. He describes them as vicious, evil, ugly and predatorial, frequently enhancing the description of the wild beasts to make them even more vicious than the actual beasts God had created. This too is a message that what God has created can be corrupted and grows more vicious.

Why would he use these "beast descriptions" to illustrate government aside from trying to make the point that governments are beastly? One has but to briefly consider history and can easily recognize the vicious and predatorial nature that is common to government. The more powerful a government is, the more this statement has proven true.

The final government described in Daniel and Revelation is so vile that God had never made a beast He could accurately use in depicting just how dangerous this government would be. This government would be more evil than all the previous governments combined. Yet Christians disregard this truth and accept the teaching that government is of God and therefore what ever the government determines to do is Godly and we have a duty to submit to government's will.

Aside from using vicious beasts to describe governments, God warns us of their nature in other verses. Psalms 2 makes His point, the question in verse 1: "Why do the heathen rage and the people imagine a vain thing?" The answer: "The kings of the earth set themselves, and the rulers take counsel together against the Lord, and against His anointed saying let us break their bands asunder and cast away their cords from us". How can we believe that governments are of God when scripture clearly tells us they are "against the Lord"?

We must recognize that if governments are "against the Lord" they are "against the church and Christians"! If they are against the church and Christians we find ourselves involved in warfare simply due to the fact that an enemy has designed to be against us. We know the hate and the desire to destroy that this enemy has, therefore we can conclude he will attack. To conclude otherwise we are guilty of underestimating our enemy and the determination he has to act on his hate.

It's worth pause to consider our individual beliefs. Christians have been taught to trust government and in this country few Christians fear the government but these are dangerous attitudes. These are not truths born out in scripture and this is not the clear message God has given us concerning government. We must consider government from a scriptural perspective. When we study how ungodly government has become and how hostile toward Christianity in particular, we should immediately recognize this government is not of God.

As Christians we are to be salt and light. As patriots we have a civic duty to pass on to future generations, that which was passed to us. If we consider this matter we are left with one conclusion. If government is against the Lord and we are for Him we are naturally enemies, at least to the extent our government is against God. We may not desire that this be so but if we have chosen to take a stand for righteousness and others have chosen to stamp out righteousness on the earth we have a difference that some are committed to fight for.

The question then becomes what will we do? We can pretend everything is fine but this is getting increasingly difficult, as we must endure ever increasing government intrusion into our homes and lives along with increasing hostility to our beliefs. The reverse of this is to note that everything is not fine but then what?

We can convince ourselves to forget about patriotism or any duty as salt and light; that the Godly way to handle this is to be the first on our block to surrender. We can busy ourselves with a local church to such an extent that we convince ourselves we don't have time to take on another project. We can do many different things but one option to consider is that we can also address the problem.

Our founding fathers gave us an awesome and Godly system and the struggle over deciding what we should do is no more difficult than learning what they did for us. We should require government function as they directed. This must become a passion for us. We cannot vote our problems away; we cannot elect someone who will right all wrongs. Satan has conquered that arena. It is not scriptural that we stand idle and do nothing or busy ourselves with anything except the task at hand. We cannot expect that if we join some local organization with a half-hearted commitment that it will affect those who have organized against us.

We are to be warriors and watchmen. This is not to say that our options include some wild, violent scheme. Neither is a wild, violent scheme necessary. We have a system and the system is sufficient if we get informed and take advantage of the tools we have available but step one is a commitment to do something and stop this tolerance of all ungodliness.

It is the nature of man to embrace power. It is the nature of Satan to take advantage of man's fallen nature and use us in his war against God. Our founding fathers understood this and devised a brilliant restraint on the nature of man as well as any influence Satan may have to "break their bands asunder and cast their cords away from us". They required our leaders to be "bound by the chains of a Constitution". They instituted "checks and balances" against anyone or group amassing more power. They gave us a system to insure Godly people could install Godly leadership. They divided power to keep government limited and accountable.

Still, from the beginning many politicians have worked to "break their bands asunder" by twisting the wording of the Constitution, redefining words, generally working to cause confusion and a lack of respect for our Constitution by convincing people it's "outdated". They have created organizations, institutions and publications to deceive the masses while working to stifle truth. They have infiltrated the church and brought us false leadership with false solutions to promote idleness. They have even fought wars – both overt and subtle to amass power. Scripture is very clear on this point; "it is their nature".

We have a nature too. We have a nature to promote Godliness, a strong family, honesty and integrity in government. Note also that in Psalms 2:1 "the heathen rage and the people imagine a vain thing". What do the heathen rage about in our day and what vain things do they imagine? They rage against what they are told to rage against because they have no standard or moral compass.

Currently the words used in rage are about "healthcare, education, war and the economy". The demands change from time to time but the demands themselves are manipulated by the new world order and are always and only an excuse for them to grasp more power. When the heathen rage, it is a demand that government "take care of us, provide us good health, give our children a future, protect us, house us, feed us, entertain us, peace and safety"!

They have been given the ability to imagine a vain thing. The vain thing that Satan wants them to imagine is that these blessings can be had without God. They desire the blessings of God but their nature is not to turn to God so they turn to government. They fail to realize that what they are doing is turning to Satan. They would not do this if they had not been manipulated and deceived into believing this is a viable solution. The manipulation is to reject God (1st Samuel 8:7) and the deception is "you don't need God, we can provide for ourselves" and as we entertain this deception Satan increases his power.

We should not wonder then why God described governments as predatory beasts. The end of this will be the consumption and destruction of those whom God loves. No one who loves God should be content to stand silent and allow this travesty to succeed! This was Satan's manipulation of Eve, "you shall be as gods"; "you won't need Him anymore"! In man's fallen state the lie is enticing.

Another area of scripture where the church completely ignores this fact is the story of Nimrod told in Genesis 10:9. It describes him as "a mighty hunter" before the Lord. We realize that there is nothing wrong with being a "hunter". The word "hunter" here implies "provider". Nimrod began amassing power by hunting and providing for the people so that they didn't need to seek God anymore. He would feed them and clothe them and protect them if they would follow him (or so he promised). This has been a strategy of Satan's from the beginning.

Next scripture moves on to the tower of Babel. The church has a host of teachings on the verses concerning the tower. One is that the reason this tower was built so high was to provide confidence that the people could never be destroyed by flood (by God) again. Another is that the tower was built so high above the clouds so as to foster a false religion, star worship. Enough is known about ancient Babylon to believe there is significant truth to both of these arguments but scripture also gives more information.

In Genesis 1:28 God commands Adam and Eve to "replenish the earth" and this is repeated in Genesis 9:1. In Genesis 11:4 the people said, "let us build a city and a tower ... lest we be scattered abroad upon the face of the earth". In 11:8 scattering them upon the whole earth is exactly what God did. Here we have a cause for study. The people apparently knew what God wanted and built the tower in defiance. The significant part to all of this is the question of government.

God wanted men to be dispersed across the planet. He wanted each to be self sufficient and free, needing only Him and free to seek Him. God and Nimrod knew that both self-sufficiency and freedom are abated by urbanization. We need to develop this thought, as it's quite contrary to our thinking today. Many people in our industrialized world of today would not relish the idea of an agricultural existence on a small farm. Remember, first and foremost, God wants us to be happy, content, in communion with Him and have our basic needs for life met.

It is a strange system that we embrace today in lieu of what God wanted for us. We have hectic schedules, merciless demands on our time, unfulfilling jobs, and educational needs to make our skills competitive in the marketplace. We have come to accept these stresses along with high crime, shallow family relationships, the constant threat of an insufficient income and exorbitant controls over our daily activities. Few of us are self employed and opportunities for self-employment are constantly shrinking. The Bible views employment as a type of slavery but we regard it as necessary in today's world without question.

Any joy or contentment we achieve is through toys and entertainment not relationships or accomplishments. Godly property rights are no longer respected in this country. Owning a piece of property in a Biblical sense means no authority can tax it. This is because if they can tax it they can take it from you for failure to pay whatever tax they assess. If they can take it from you, you don't own it. You simply think you own it until you learn someone can legally take it from you.

Thinking you own it is very important because why would you pay the taxes if you don't own it. In a Godly system the land is yours. You're free to use it to produce and provide for your family. The family works as a single unit and the work is divided. The land yields healthy food and water and the home yields happiness and contentment, as there is abundant time for relaxation and relationships.

In growing crops, God's creation does most of the work. The seeds regenerate and the land produces. All man has to do is plant, harvest, store and varying degrees of cultivation. This is all work to be sure but far less labor intensive than the schedules we maintain today. Those families who desire or have needs for more land can purchase it. We can see what God had intended. By comparison, many would relish a remote, self-sufficient agricultural existence.

The system depended on a dispersion of the population. Their means of supporting themselves and their families was limited to hunting, farming, ranching, fishing and little else. With all the people congregated in one region there would not be an adequate food supply. Additionally, there would not have been sufficient landmass for each to own property. This would require some to be in the employ (control) of those who do own property to support their families. One who controls another is in a position to stifle or hinder that person's relationship with God and God is totally opposed to any system like this.

Nimrod wanted the people to stay in one spot so he could control them. Towards this purpose he was deceiving them by promises he would "provide" for them. He had no real desire to care for them or he would have listened to God and promoted God's will. His desire was to have control over them and his strategy was the deception of concern for their welfare. With the people congregated and both trusting Nimrod and needing him he could, over time, build an army and use this to further increase his control. As his power grew he could afford to reduce his provision for the people and openly create a class of abject slaves forcing them to meet all of his desires and man's system of government was born.

God did not create anyone to suffer this fate and we should be warning people and teaching them these principles today. There was plenty of land but the choice was to trust God, strike out and spread upon the earth or trust those who promised to take care of you. This not only takes God out of the personal relationship He wants but creates an environment for people to be abused, misled and manipulated.

By enticing the people to stay in one area Satan and his agents created an ability to control them. God's heart is to provide the things Satan promises. It's not to God the heathen pray, it's to government and they believe their prayers will be answered with a conviction the church should emulate! As the churches now turn to government for help, those working in government are elated. To satisfy the people government must amass more ungodly power and power over the church is highly coveted!

What further proof do we need that the church has been neutralized than to see the church joining the rage and imagining a vain thing? As stated before, this "vain thing" is that "we don't need God. We'll be just fine on our own". Only Satan could seduce the church into believing we don't need God! We too are now "praying" to the god of this world to solve our problems. This is why God told Samuel, "They have not rejected you, but Me". When you reject God's system you are rejecting God.

Many pastors preach of "tithes and offerings" but when someone in the church is in need, does the local church meet the need or send them to the government? How many people in these churches are on some welfare program and what is the church doing about it? How many people in the church are receiving money from some government program? How can the church stand against the world system when they rely on it? If they are doing nothing they have rejected God and are trusting government to meet the needs of the people. God IS God. He is able to meet the needs of His people without the help of a satanic world system.

Even our tithes and offerings are given to Satan's system. I don't begrudge a pastor a reasonable salary and I realize many pastors don't get one but aside from a reasonable salary, what does the church do with its money? Many times people tithe to a church and their money goes to service the debt from some monstrous building program. There is no money left in the local church to help meet the needs of local members.

Money is spent on items to make the services more entertaining or enticing to a crowd and the membership turns to government for assistance. Then there are the churches that send substantial sums of money to some third world missions program but don't take responsibility to meet the needs of their members because the local members "can take advantage of some government program".

The churches have not done their duty and now don't understand the mess we're in. As long as the churches remain uninvolved politically, it will continue in confusion. With no life changing church to turn to, where shall the world turn but government? Jeremiah 2:11 asks, "Hath a nation changed their Gods"? Verse 12 indicates God is astonished by this, "be astonished oh ye heavens and be afraid … for my people have forsaken me..." We may not wish to admit we have forsaken God but as we look around us we can see we're in a relationship with government. It is government that makes our laws, sets our standards and has the greater influence on our behavior.

Romans 13:11 states "… that now it is high time to awake out of sleep …" This word "sleep in Greek is "hypnos" from which we get the word "hypnosis" so this verse is telling us to "come out of a hypnotic trance".[74] Verse 12 says "The night is far spent, the day is at hand: let us therefore cast off the works of darkness and let us put on the armor of light".

Here we (Christians) are told to "cast off the works of darkness". How was it that we put on these works to begin with? We were hypnotized/seduced by a slow steady diet of compromise that would lull His people into complacency and false dependence on a government that promised to meet needs and does it fairly well.

What God expects of government hasn't changed over the years. What has changed is the commitment God's people have to His word and His service. We have become very quick to accept platitudes that defy God's word simply because they lessen our burden of responsibility. We are paying for this lightened load with too high a price. It's time "to cast off the works of darkness". It's time to have done with this vain deception that society doesn't need God. It's time to cast off these false teachings that government is not accountable to God or that government is free to rob from one to buy votes from another. It's time to cast off all the lies of the enemy. It is time "put on the light" which is the truth of God.

It's time to be alert, equipped with Godly understanding and ready to do battle in the authority of the Lord. We have been hypnotized by a steady diet of platitudes and promises. God's view of government is one that reflects God's heart; a government that serves the people not oppresses them. Government has a very small role in a Godly society and has no role in interfering in a family or the church. Neither the church nor government is to be subservient to each other but rather they are both to be in submission to God.

A church has authority in its own right and is not accountable to government; it is accountable to God. If politicians fail to recognize the significance of this fact it becomes our Christian duty to hold them accountable by holding them within the proper limits of their own role. Indeed, the church has authority to demand accountability in its own right.

Christians are warned about the consequences of abusive government. We will become the focus of an abusive government because what we stand for is what the government hates. We have already seen laws passed banning prayer in public places, The Bible is banned in public buildings, crosses are banned on public property and this is only the beginning. There is an old axiom that says, "People ultimately get the government they deserve". This too is a deception. Nobody deserves what this satanic world government will institute.

This idea that we should not insist our voices be heard, our beliefs respected or our Godly standards be universally held by our elected leadership is a satanic lie the new world order has promoted for its own benefit. Only as free people are we free to pursue God's will. God has told us in scripture what His view of government is. Scripture also documents what the people face when they abandon God's view of government.

Aside from scripture, others have documented what the people face when they abandon God's view of government. History books are filled with the documentation of people who died at the hands of their own government. The facts reflect that many were coerced into doing the killing because the government successfully perpetuated a deception upon the people. They were manipulated into believing the government's aspirations were the will of God and this concept is no longer foreign in our society.

2nd Thessalonians 2:10-12 says "with all deceivableness of unrighteousness…for this cause God shall send them strong delusion that they should believe the lie…but had pleasure in unrighteousness". Scripture does not reveal this "strong delusion" but I see a mighty delusion being birthed in our midst and the church is embracing it. This delusion is: "government is good, government will provide for our needs, government is of God, whatever government does must be God's will".

1st Thessalonians 5:3 says "when they shall say peace and safety, then shall come upon them sudden destruction". Scripture doesn't say in what context "they shall say peace and safety" but we hear that phrase commonly today. We're told we must fight a war against terrorism so the government can provide us with peace and safety. We are told we must have national I.D. cards so government can provide us with peace and safety. We are told we must have new levels of government authority (Home Land Security and Transportation Safety Administration, etc.) even though we're required to give up our freedoms but we're promised government will provide peace and safety so we give up many freedoms. Who can deny our government has "pleasure in unrighteousness"?

We always fail to recognize that governments never yield power back to the people once it's been forfeited. Thus we surrender our children to slavery and consider it the right thing to do because we were promised peace and safety. Under this deception we're not alarmed when the government moves to take away our God given rights. We believe its Godly because we believe God wants government to protect us. We're told our government is taking bold moves promoting "peace and safety" but we fail to recognize all its really doing is forcing governmental authority over free people in a fashion never before attempted in this country.

Christians are familiar with Matthew 24:6 which speaks of "wars and rumors of wars". In our apathy we no longer investigate if war is necessary or legitimate. We have grown accustomed to the rumors. We think of wars as soldiers on a battlefield but the enemy is not hindered by small thinking or preconceived notions. War is a means to an end and only partially involves actual battlefields.

Much of war is deception and deception by definition is "miss" leading. To "mislead" is "to lead in a wrong direction or belief frequently with deliberate intent". We are deceived into believing there is a need so we tolerate government intrusion and the loss of freedom.

We are deceived into believing we are fighting wars on poverty, illiteracy, drugs, saving the environment, crime, hate and now terrorism! We have a duty to question if we are really fighting "wars". We see no visible results aside from having to surrender our freedom. Without investigation we have no way of knowing if these are truly wars or simply rumors told to manipulate the public.

Many reasonable questions have been raised about this war on terrorism. As one example, your primary step in protecting your home is locking your doors yet our nation makes no effort to seal our borders. We're told this is because our borders are too expansive yet China and Russia have more border miles to patrol and they manage to do it quite efficiently to hold their people captive. We have made no effort to locate those who may be in this country illegally, not even to certify they have no hostile motives.

Quite the opposite, we continue to expand federal programs that offer all types of assistance to those who are here illegally. It is widely known that simply halting these benefit programs would send a considerable percentage of them home on their own volition. The point is that The U.S. Border Patrol publishes a statistic called "OTM's" (Other Than Mexican's). This figure is largely Middle Eastern men and women who come into Guatemala and from there into Mexico. They spend enough time there to learn the language and mannerisms and slip into The United States with other illegal immigrants as they cross our border.

This is known but nothing is done about it. Yet we are told you and I must abandon our God given freedoms for our children and ourselves because we are engaged in a war against "terrorists". We have witnessed incredible expansion in law enforcement with a decided change in police procedures against innocent citizens, which are to be presumed and treated as innocent until proven guilty, since this war was declared.

We have witnessed the courts upholding "government's right" to violate the rights of a free people so long as they make a claim it is in the interests of "national security". Property is seized from people in complete violation of The Fifth Amendment under the disguise of a war on drugs yet with the borders unprotected we have no way of halting drug flow across the border. We can't close the border but we can seize the property and businesses of any American without due process of law under the authority of the war on drugs but we're not supposed to conclude that there is a hidden motivation or agenda.

By the same token there is an obvious agenda to get as many kids trained to "pop pills" to solve problems. Not too many years ago if you didn't pay attention in school you stayed after school. Now the school gives you a pill. There is no concern whether this helps the child achieve higher grades or not, only that they take the pill.

Government policies have fought the home schooling movement, which has proven a far more successful educational strategy over public schools. This would certainly call into question this so called war on illiteracy.

The three common denominators in all of these wars are:
1. The constant expansion of government making it stronger and more controlling over our daily lives
2. The constant loss of our individual freedoms and privacy

3. The problems sited for the needs of government growth are never solved or abated with any proven results but the programs are continually expanded

We are told that the answer is more government – always more government and even the church has now embraced this idea. Perhaps the saddest argument is that Christians no longer promote God as a solution either.

We have suffered the consequences of not understanding this warfare for so long that we are now lost at what to believe or how to pursue change. 1st Thessalonians says "Prove all things; hold fast that which is good". We have a duty to investigate all arguments before we tolerate an expansion of government.

Christians should know that God would never have them submit to evil and this would include government. Satan has accomplished quite a deception convincing the church that his government is of God. It is time to awake out of sleep. It's time to stop being manipulated and stop believing that everything the government does is God's will. It's time to stand for righteousness and have done with Satan's evil system.

I have asked, "If it is true, would you want to know?" This deception is not a new one. It is one that was birthed millenniums ago and nurtured carefully to insure its effectiveness and thus requires study to comprehend. We did not get in this mess because of some casual, easily exposed lie. Those who desire knowledge and understanding of what's going on in this country politically must make the commitment to study.

The truth is frequently offensive. Those who desire to know the truth must be willing to be offended and willing to put that offense aside. We have all been fooled because Satan has designed a deception to engulf the masses. It has been a process for all of us to come to the knowledge of how Satan is working to fulfill his dream of a one-world government. The truth can be known but not without taking into consideration that many of the beliefs we have grown comfortable with are but satanic illusions. Failing to recognize this truth will hinder us from understanding how vast a deception Satan has employed to achieve his goal. Prove all things.

We now leave a focused study of scripture regarding the lies Satan has nurtured in the church. We now examine what Satan has done from a historical perspective in terms of what he was able to accomplish once he had successfully neutralized the church. Prepare to be offended.

Satan's View Of Government

Isaiah 14:16 "Is this the man that made the earth to tremble, that did shake the kingdoms"

We have covered specifics regarding the four lies including God being in control, God's view of government and Godly authority, legislating morality and Christian duties and opportunities politically. It is time to take a look at Satan's view of government, which can best be described as "the mechanism necessary for him to achieve his goals".

Perhaps the best definition of Satan's concepts in government came from one who understood government well, George Washington. He said, "government is not reason; it is not eloquent; it is force. Like fire, it is a dangerous servant and a fearful master".

This definition would not be valid if man had embraced and held fast to God's ordained authority for government. Man has not embraced what God had ordained and so we must reflect that President Washington's definition of government is reasonable and accurate. His statement also gives us a good definition of Satan's view of government. He tells us why Satan desires to control government, how he intends to use it and what we can expect life to be like under his system.

Using President Washington's definition we can begin a list of particulars, which can be identified and expected concerning Satan's view of government. These are matters that Christians should reflect upon before they allow Satan to build his one world government. It is worth our consideration to ask ourselves if we really want to permit him this success, even to a degree. With each success, numerous lives are ruined.

First is the capacity to force. Force is such a small word to have sufficient meaning in this context! It is final; there is no appeal. It is complete; there is no negotiation. It is fatal; those who won't submit will be destroyed. It can be cruel and may act as it's own judge on cruelty. It can be evil; I add this as a reminder that most among us cannot comprehend evil but I remind the reader that force is always God's last resort. We cannot comprehend those who desire to see others suffer for nothing more than their own greed, amusement and an absolute lack of compassion towards other human beings. To say they are selfish and self-serving does not address the fact that they have pleasure in creating the suffering that others must endure.

Mao Tse Tung said, "Political force comes out of the barrel of a gun".

You may think this can be summed up as "submit or die" but there is another matter. Once they have achieved the power they desire they must still be entertained. To those who feed on human suffering, the end of human suffering means only boredom. Suffering may be viewed as a means to an end but they enjoy their work. To those who love power force means people are tools and toys. They will do with you as they please. Their desire is the only consideration.

As we move on, the next consideration is the government as a fearful master. Here we have two points to consider, government as master and the concept of fearing our government. The concept of government as our master is new in this country but not altogether unpleasant for a great many people. Many have come to feel protected and secure through government programs they perceive to be beneficial and they enjoy having agencies to turn to when they are in need of assistance. For this they are willing that government grows to a size and exercises more power than previous generations would tolerate.

As yet government is not so intrusive and abusive that it is viewed as a threat but, instead, through all of these programs it is viewed as benevolent and necessary to meet the needs of the people. Additionally we are constantly assured through the propaganda mechanisms that we are the most free people on earth. The combination of these helpful programs and the assurances that we are not sacrificing our freedom has lead to a trust and appreciation of government. We dismiss those who warn us that, as government grows, it is adopting unconstitutional and detrimental powers since we see no visible evidence.

Still, in a nation where the people are to be masters and government the servant, it cannot be disputed that a reversal of authority has come into being! This reversal was only possible because we have been convinced that governments, primarily "our" government, can be trusted.

Our founding fathers didn't trust government so why do we? We must consider what caused this paradigm shift in American thinking and what it's costing us. Satan needs the power and appearance of authority that is government. If we don't trust government our suspicions and concerns will make his work difficult, as people will naturally be more apprehensive of what government wants.

By the same token, if we do trust government we won't challenge what we're told and all that we know will be what government tells us. All we look to in terms of solutions will be what government proposes. The belief that government wants to protect us largely comes from politicians constantly telling us they want to pass a particular law to protect us from a particular threat or go to war with some country "for our protection". We see the need for protection as we note the increase in crime but we haven't taken the time to learn the enemy's tactics so we are unfamiliar with how we're being manipulated.

We wouldn't know if the threats are real or if the threats are exaggerated. When we are approached by someone who tries to explain that all of this trust may well be misplaced we are skeptical at best. We note that all of the increase in government seems to serve no good purpose as the threats are never eliminated and the problems always persist yet with no foundation of knowledge we know of no alternatives so we submit to more government controls.

We may even suspect the flow of information is heavily controlled and we're not told the whole story yet most people are not willing to research for themselves.

Yet one more reason why we now trust government is because we are trained to do so from our youth. Once again I encourage Christians to seriously consider the plight of American children and must revisit some points made in other chapters.

Kids begin their toddler years with a diet of cartoons that very frequently deal in magic, magic crystals, magical rainbows, super human powers, mother earth, goddess's, spells, witches, warlocks and such occult themes such as telepathy, reincarnation and spirit guides. They then move into elementary school where they are encouraged to read books like "Harry Potter" among others to intrigue them about witchcraft. In subtle manner, many occult topics are worked into the curriculum inviting the children to explore finding a "spirit guide" as they are warmly nurtured into a belief that "witchcraft" is "just another religion".

Then moving on to their formidable teenage years they are not prohibited from listening to the most vile, evil "death music" they can find. They watch a parade of "horror" movies that desensitize them to death as well as demonology.

While the curriculum in government schools is reason enough to oppose public schools, the real harm is done to a child's view of individualism. No more do we teach individuality (rugged or otherwise) but instead teach each child they are not an individual, they are part of a group.

Then there are sports. This too is an arena where the church has been seduced and deceived. We are told "sports build character". Where is a scripture making this argument? My Bible teaches that character comes from a personal relationship with Jesus Christ. Sports have become a dominant influence in our lives, a far greater influence than the church. We fail to recognize that sports reinforce the "group think" of the new world order. Sports are singularly about the flesh; competition instead of compassion, worldly accomplishment instead of Godly humility, team instead of individual achievement and winning instead of sacrifice.

All of this over what used to be called childish entertainment. Paul said in 1st Corinthians 13:11 "when I became a man I put away childish things." Now we often here it said "he who dies with the most toys wins..." Children have been trained to play as a group, eat as a group, study as a group, think as a group and act as a group. Anyone who is not part of the group is looked down upon. This teaches and reinforces the "conformist" mentality.

By the time a child completes twelve years of government "education" he/she has been taught that they are socially acceptable only when part of a group. After twelve years of routinely eating when the group eats, studying math when the group studies math, even going to the restroom as a group these children have been taught to think of him/her self as part of the group and no longer as an individual.

The group is important, not the individual. The individual is either part of the group or unacceptable. This is important when we reflect upon the fact that an individual relationship is what God desires with each of us and an individual decision to accept Jesus is difficult for one who has been trained from their youth to look to the group for guidance.

While these are the things our children are taught, what are they taught about Jesus? What child wants to pursue a personal relationship with Jesus Christ when the group doesn't approve? Is it a coincidence that so much sports takes place on Sunday? How many Christians race out of church (if they come at all) to get to the golf course? Estimates consistently claim that by the time a child reaches eighteen he/she has seen over twenty thousand hours of television. He/she has been exposed to twelve years of government school indoctrination and countless hours of movies/DVDs/music dealing with the occult.

It is true that a comparative handful have had at least thirty minutes of Bible instruction in some sort of "Sunday School Class". Yet (Sunday school or not) they have all been exposed to a church that is totally impotent by comparison. Very few fights are fought against evil and those are lost.

God intends that children be raised in an environment of loving parents prioritizing nothing more than their children's future and well-being. He made no provision for government to have any involvement with the raising of a child. Through patriarchs and priests a child would grow to adulthood knowing Godly standards and responsibilities. Satan knew this alone would defeat him and must be altered to serve his purpose.

Through a systematic strategy that involved ever weakening the message of the gospel, getting the mothers out of the home in order that the state became the primary influence on the child and then using that influence to firmly establish a fascination with the occult in the receptive minds of children Satan has been able to insure his new world order is the primary influence on the child. This influence says that all good things come from government. There is a predictable end to children who are raised with no particular respect for family or religion but are raised with reverent respect for government; they welcome more government.

This is Satan's goal, that people choose his system over that given by God. Thus it became part of the strategy to work on the children so each new generation would come to adulthood with an increasing reliance on, and complete trust of, government.

Washington also commented "experience teaches us that it is much easier to prevent an enemy from posting themselves than it is to dislodge them after they have got possession." This is as true about Satan as any enemy and he has been invited into our homes, churches and institutions. Now we have the burden of dislodging him and this is made difficult by the ignorance of those who have welcomed him and fear life without a "government safety net". While some may challenge the claim that government is our "master" it can hardly be disputed that our government exercises more control over our lives today than ever before in our country's history and the power grabs continue!

We have options, of course. That is, if we choose to get involved politically. This mastery is illegitimate and unlawful by The Constitution but through a strategy of patient gradualism over generations and by building a relationship of trust we find ourselves with a very powerful government today.

Our next focus is fear. President Washington well understood that unrestrained government is a threat to happiness. He warned us against allowing government to become unaccountable or powerful, as it would certainly use its full access to power to abuse the masses and satisfy the lusts and whims of those in power. His context of a "fearful master" was in keeping with the argument that power surrendered is power forever lost.

There is a different application to fear, however, that we should consider. Fear is, arguably, the most powerful manipulator known to man short of mind-altering drugs. When government is unaccountable it can use this very powerful tactic as a tool of manipulation against the masses. Government has much to gain by keeping the people afraid.

In our world, today, we are encouraged to be afraid of everything: diseases, different religious beliefs, quality of food, healthcare, the economy, etc. If government actually solved these problems, what need would we have for all of the government programs that "address" these problems?

In keeping with the topic of fear we can add a third word that well defines Satan's view of government, albeit an addition to President Washington's definition. That word is deceiver. Satan is, of course, the greatest deceiver in history but no entity can maintain the power of deception like government. This is especially true once the population has been disarmed from suspicion of government and regards it as benevolent.

Deception on this magnitude requires that the traditional sources of information (media, church, schools) have been dominated and their agenda controlled. We can recognize it is futile for Satan to lay his agenda on the table and submit to a vote. He knows he must deceive mankind into embracing his plan over God's.

The most effective way for him to do that is to create chaos and use the chaos to create fear at which point the masses demand government intervention to solve (or address) whatever they are afraid of. Chaos is Satan's plan for mankind and chaos is the plan promoted by the new world order. Indeed, the slogan of the new world order is "order out of chaos". When the veil is lifted we can recognize the concept of "order out of chaos" revealed as "the new world order" out of "chaos".

The necessary part of the equation that we must grasp is that those in Satan's service stage the chaos. Satan has excelled in two important regions of our minds, which makes the grasping of this truth all the more difficult. First, he has deceived the nations into buying the lie of all chaos being circumstantial. Good people, Christian and non-Christian have a very difficult time grasping this truth that the chaos is staged. Most people firmly believe the chaos in our world today comes from any number of zealous people who are independent from any master plan.

Many cannot accept the premise that the chaos is staged because of the layers of trust the government has built in their minds. Yet proof exists for those willing to examine it. There is an interesting quote in an interesting book worthy of note. The book is George Orwell's "1984". Although fiction, the book cannot easily be dismissed as it was written in 1949 and much of it has come true and the rest is now quite easily visible on our horizon. In this book Mr. Orwell documents the initiation ceremony of a secret society called "The Brotherhood". The candidate is asked,

"Are you prepared to give your life? Are you prepared to commit murder? Are you prepared to commit acts of sabotage which may cause the death of hundreds of innocent people? Are you prepared to betray your country to foreign powers? Are you prepared to cheat, to forge, to blackmail, to corrupt the minds of children, to distribute habit forming drugs, to encourage prostitution, to disseminate venereal diseases, to do anything which is likely to cause demoralization and weaken the power of the party (opposition)?" (Pg 142)

A work of fiction cannot be construed as proof but with all of the accuracies of this work and with what we witness in our world today, is it not reasonable to consider the content of this book? For those who say "no", fine, there is no shortage of sources that are not fiction that quote this oath and oaths more vile and bloodthirsty than this one. Many are now aware that in 1776 Adam Weishaupt founded The Bavarian Illuminatti. It was he who wrote (after specifying they could only achieve success through secret associations) that they

"Will by degrees, and in silence, possess themselves of the governments of the States" (countries).

As Satan deceives the nations through the fear of chaos he promotes his solution that is always bigger and stronger government. Christians are encouraged to leave government as Satan assimilates his people in. This is what is known as "the Hegelian dialectic" and is occasionally phrased as "the poison and the antidote are made in the same laboratory". The point is, as Satan expands chaos people will grow afraid and demand protection. Government is expanded to provide that protection. As Satan achieves more toward his goals, we can expect to see an increase in the implementation of this strategy. Chaos will increase, people will grow ever more afraid and demand protection and government will be expanded beyond conceivable levels not to provide any relief from the chaos but to satisfy the goal and purpose which is total government control.

We have given place to Satan and allowed him to "post" and "possess" far too many of our greater institutions, government departments and he has entirely too much influence on the church. Today we are faced with the task of "dispossessing" him and there is much at stake.

We can witness the next steps in his agenda as government is now well advanced in destroying laws of property rights, property seizure laws, the use of no-knock warrants and an ever increasing burden of new regulations that all must abide by. Child protective services have become the single biggest threat to the sanctity of the home yet. Evidence suggests that control of the family diet will soon become another battlefront via health care laws and vaccination laws.

If this proves nothing else, it proves government's insatiable appetite for power and control. Once they have this degree of power they will surely use it; "cradle to grave" care has become government deciding who gets a cradle and who gets a grave.

Psalms 1:1 says, "Blessed is the man who walketh not in the counsel of the ungodly". 1st Thessalonians says "Prove all things; hold fast that which is good". Scripture does not tell us to guess, we are to prove. Above all else we should prove a truth when our children are concerned. We don't "prove all things"; we just accept these lies without considering that they are told for a purpose. We don't consider what the agenda is; we don't even suspect there is one. We have grown comfortable with this idea that government is good but it has been abusing our trust for a long time now.

Our system of government never gave the state authority to forcibly draft boys into the military regardless of the parent's support or willingness. Yet over the years many parents sent their sons off to war simply because the government deceitfully told them they had to. This is a violation of a Godly jurisdiction. What was so important to Christians that they were silent during this assault on the home? Nothing; it is simply a jurisdictional trespass that took place gradually over several generations so it went unnoticed.

The church did not stop compulsory state supervised education either. Many books have been written about compulsory education, not just of substantial evidence that it was never needed but the overwhelming evidence that state sponsored education is corrupt and inferior to home schooling. The literacy rate in this country was higher and the curriculum far more educational and challenging prior to when the current system was made mandatory.

The state sponsored curriculum is offensive even to non-Christian parents yet today very few challenge it. This state sponsored schooling is vital to the agenda of the new world order so that the young can be trained up in the ways of the new order. Christian views are forbidden in schools but all other religious teachings are welcome yet the church will not even take a stand on this issue. So what is left for our children if we continue to stay out of politics? Satan's evil empire! We can view precisely what this will mean to our children as we examine nations who have fully embraced the concepts promoted by the new world order.

In Russia (USSR) the number of people killed by Stalin's maniacal ambitions has ever been adjusted upward. Just since the publication of his book "Democide" (a term he coined meaning death by government) Dr. R. J. Rummel has now raised the number of deaths in The USSR to just under sixty-two million. In China he has raised the figure to just under seventy-seven million. Dr. Rummel now estimates that two hundred and sixty-two million people were killed by their own government in the twentieth century.[75]

War was a primary tool, as was disease. This is a lot of chaos and throughout all of this we have seen each of the worst offenders grow in power individually as well as in their commitment to global totalitarian government.

We have been warned. Scripture has left no doubt of Satan's plans or ambitions. One would think that Christians would need no further warning but we have had many that are ignored. Scores of people from all walks of life have sounded the alarm; a list that includes Presidents, Prime Ministers, High Ranking Military Officials, Historians, Clergymen, Educators, Statesmen, Journalists, Businessmen and yes we have been warned by those who have first hand knowledge of this agenda in significant detail.

Yet many still dismiss even the possibility that it is true. Many people who have never been exposed to truths about the new world order have awareness that all is not what it seems. Many recognize government is out of control and never delivers on its promises yet they remain idle.

No part of the new world order would be possible if they had not first laid a foundation of trust. Satan well understood what God had done and why. He also understood that he could only destroy what God had made by eroding it. To promote an alternate system that could be compared with the system God had ordained would bring him swift defeat. He had to raise up a system within the system God had ordained as the only means of hiding himself and his agenda.

Repeatedly scripture illustrates that if a nation abandons Godliness it will suffer the consequences. History has taught us nothing if we fail to recognize that without a strong family, society has no core.

Finally we have but to view the daily news to note that chaos reigns in a world with out the rule of law. Even doctors are coming to play a larger role in the agenda. The ultimate power over another human being is the power of life and death. With the same control over the medical schools as over teachers colleges it became possible to promote those within the medical profession who ascribed to this agenda while stifling those who do not.

The focus and target of this strategy is, and always has been children. Satan has no illusions of drawing mass converts away from a people who are firmly grounded in God's word and have a personal relationship with Him. Satan's work must be done before someone gets grounded in The Bible and develops a personal relationship with God. Hence, all of this effort to gain control over the flow of information is strategically designed to keep children ignorant of Godly truths.

It may well sound ridiculous but it is scriptural and the evidence is all around us. It is this skepticism in spite of scripture and in spite of the existing evidence all around us that makes it possible. Satan's success hinged on stopping the church from exposing him and all he had to do was build skepticism into our minds.

By controlling the major elements within the media and controlling the educational system so as to control the majority of information Satan successfully controls "foundational knowledge ". This is the basic information everyone is exposed to through education and media. Satan is able to insure that no one will learn of him and his plans through basic information sources. Additionally he can encourage people to be contemptuous toward those of differing beliefs.

Thus no one would have the basic knowledge to properly consider new information if they heard some information Satan didn't want them to believe. It may be some very credible and revealing piece of information but if it sounds crazy to you (because you have no foundational knowledge to judge the information on its merit) you will readily dismiss it as too crazy to be true. As long as people continue to reject information without research they will never build a foundation of knowledge and understanding to build on. The path to global government hinged on the flow of information, which must be controlled.

With the control of information few will grasp the fact that the chaos is staged. Most will submit to the ever-increasing government controls and abuses because they are afraid. Christians, who have a Godly duty to fight evil, overwhelmingly accept satanic government but not out of fear. It is accepted as inevitable yet we do not "prove" this by God's word. We simply use the verses on prophecy as if we had full knowledge and understanding.

We do not study the verses on government and embrace their truths with the same resolve as verses on prophecy. We do not study the verses on fighting evil or commandments to be salt and light. We do not warn the world of what Satan is plotting and planning and we do not listen when we are warned.

Now we are told of a great "war on terror". Predictably we are asked to tolerate mammoth new programs and departments. Predictably we are told to "trust" government that the threat is real and the enemy dangerous but we are not permitted to view any proof. Predictably we are told that our protection will cost us freedom. Predictably we are told by those "on the right" that "the right has the answers" and those on "the left" tell us "the left has the answers" but they offer the same answer – more government.

Satan's view of government is government as a tool to destroy. To force full and merciless surrender from those who refuse any dictate. Satan's view of government is to destroy everything sacred and anything Godlike, to elevate the unfeeling, unknowing bureaucrat because of their service to the state. Satan's view of government is to break every promise made when the need for deception is no longer a consideration. In time he will ignore the suffering and heartache because there is no longer a purpose served in satisfying these needs.

Whom do we serve? The day may be far spent and the end may be near but we still have time and in that small span of time, whom shall we serve? In the title verse of Isaiah 14:16, when Satan was viewed in the truth of what he is, the spectators seemed surprised. "Is this *the man* that made the earth to tremble, that did shake kingdoms"?

Note here that it was Satan that accomplished this and not "God". Why were they so shocked? Possibly it is because they bought the Hollywood lie that Satan is far more powerful than he really is. Perhaps they were shocked to learn that Satan is not all-powerful. Perhaps they were amazed in recognizing the one they thought was too formidable for them to combat was all deception.

We have allowed Satan to have place in our government and we have a duty to dispossess him. We have a duty to God and to all future generations to rectify the error of our apathy. To "occupy" in a military sense of the word is to possess. Satan occupies our government but it is not his by authority. To dispossess him will take strategies and determination.

First we must understand a bit more of his strategy and how he maneuvered himself into the position he is in. We can learn the historic specifics of what he has done but, essentially, he has created chaos and offered more government as the solution. He has put forward counterfeit leaders to deceive his opposition and built the necessary organization to keep the public ignorant of what was happening. It will be hard to believe but we must face reasonable suspicions.

GOVERNMENT AND PARTY POLITICS

2nd Kings 18:20 "whom dost thou trust, that thou rebel against Me?"

The extent that most Christians get involved in politics is limited to their aligning with one of the two parties and simply voting for their candidate. Frequently we embrace a party because a candidate is promoted as "conservative" or "Christian" in the media and many are led to believe "their" party represents "Christian values" more than the other. Christians are seduced into supporting a political party by a deception designed to convince us that there are substantial differences between the two parties on major issues. Many Christians have been tricked into supporting those in Satan's service. We have been beguiled into trusting those unworthy of trust and the deception is still strong today.

In this chapter we must take a hard look at this concept of a two party system to examine if, in fact, there are any differences between the two parties and why no major policy changes occur when a new party is voted in. Neither is there any investigations exploring the corruption of the previous administrations.

We must also examine both parties in terms of how they truly embrace God's word, not simply how they voice homage for it. We still have the obligation to judge a candidate by a Biblical standard and not simply by the party he belongs to. We have an obligation to hold every candidate accountable for his actions.

Again, I'm not opposed to voting or encouraging anyone not to participate in this effort. The point needs to be made, however, that voting was intended to be a means to an end. The concept of voting was to install leadership that would represent the desires and the agenda of the majority of people in their districts under the powers delegated for their specific office. Voting was never to be the whole of one's political involvement. Those that believe voting is an end unto itself or the whole of our obligation fail to recognize that when voting fails to deliver the necessary results other means must be pursued.

Voting has become a sedative in our society that keeps people believing they're doing something to meet their civic responsibilities. We have this sense that we've fulfilled our obligation when we vote but we do not rise up and take Godly authority over those we install in office when they clearly reveal they lied to get votes or otherwise violate their office. Since we are sedated we have learned to live with poor performance by deceiving ourselves into thinking we can affect change in the next election and we're prepared to suffer abuses until then.

With this passive mindset we have come to accept outrageous conduct by our government and we do nothing about it. Many do not vote because they recognize the futility of trying to affect change in this manner but they have been convinced that to get involved to a greater degree is "ungodly".

We need to question the irony of believing "government is of God" but "politics is not a realm for Christians". Godly government will only come from Godly people introducing Godly values into the process and holding their elected representatives accountable to these Godly standards. Godliness cannot be established so easily and conveniently as a mere few minutes every couple of years. To simply vote isn't enough and voting should not be based on "whom dost thou trust". It should be based on absolute standards.

I find 2nd Kings 18 an interesting parallel to our situation today. Fresh from his victory over the northern kingdom, the king of Assyria sent three ambassadors to Jerusalem. Their message was (vs. 30-31 paraphrased) "don't trust your God, pay me homage and taxes and I will give you peace and safety and you will even prosper". In their arrogance they presumed God was on their side. In their vanity they placed their trust in military might and dared declare they were doing God's will. In their ignorance they failed to seek God and therefore had no understanding that Hezekiah did right in the eyes of God when he tore down the high places of idol worship.

It is reasonable for Christians to ask why our country is rotting before our eyes. We are to be salt and light and we cannot doubt our lack of effectiveness. We're not preserving anything Godly in our nation today and Christian input is rejected and ridiculed. This obvious truth has led many to simply quit which is not a scriptural option. The scriptural option is to be salt and light. This means we take a stand for Godliness and refuse to compromise.

Satan has pushed the concept of "compromise" as necessary to maintain civility in politics. Yet if ever we see the new world order compromise it is very temporary. Invariably they are back in a short span of time, not simply wanting to gain what they've compromised but four times that. Yes, they will "compromise" and settle for twice what they failed to gain with their previous effort.

For a Godly people who are raising children and working productively there are not vast amounts of time to spend on politics. Therefore when compromise becomes, not the end of a debate but rather an interlude and a strategic effort to deceive one side to abandon their values incrementally, we have a duty to stop further compromise in spite of our schedules.

The first compromise we have made is accepting the limitation of two political parties. This has led to this acceptance of the need to "vote for the lesser of two evils" and is nothing short of self-destruction! Indeed if we are limited to two there is no real competition or need for someone to take a moral stand. America was founded under the premise that all views could and should be represented and the popular view would succeed.

Forcing all to abandon most of their beliefs and submit to the agenda of a mere two parties has afforded the new world order the opportunity to control both parties from behind the scenes, something impossible to do with a greater number of parties and a well informed electorate. Now this siren song of promised prosperity and safety through political loyalty has become the theme music of both political parties. Both pay lip service to Christians in pursuit of votes but make no confession of a need to trust God or follow His teachings.

They are not shy about claiming Godly motives in the pursuit of their agenda whether it be a military campaign or some new benefit program. They would have us believe that God will bless America if we simply allow them to assemble more bureaucratic control over our lives as if this were God's plan all along. We need a solid understanding of the principles of good government as well as understanding of the principles of economics. These matters used to be taught in our school system and it is no coincidence that they are taught no more. Some knowledge of history would also be helpful.

I will offer more evidence of duplicity in Part 6 but in this chapter I must do a harsh overview of both parties. This concept of political parties came after the founding of our nation as political alignments were made for political gain. Essentially the "Federalists" debated the "Anti-Federalists" over the ratification of The Constitution (without a "Bill of Rights") and after the ratification many had come to recognize these associations as beneficial in the promotion of their agenda.

Soon the era of Andrew Jackson came which introduced "nominating conventions" from which point forward gaining the party nomination became increasing costly and necessary in mounting a successful campaign.

Many Christians consistently vote Republican believing that it is the more Godly of the two parties. Many Democrats feel the same way. Many in each camp recognize their party has had numerous opportunities to promote Godliness when in the majority. Others in each party have such a passionate commitment that they quickly take offense when the subject is broached that "their party is really not substantively better than the other". It is precisely this thinking we must address if we are going to understand the new world order. We should begin by questioning where this thinking comes from.

For previous generations of Christians to be told they must suffer "the lesser of two evils" would have been a hard sell and many non-Christians would have questioned it as well. We find ourselves back at the two points "the paradigm of trust" and "the teach-ability index". We are constantly assured we can trust the system and we can trust our government but these concepts are not Biblical and are relatively new in America.

To peer through the darkness effectively we must be willing to consider facts that will offend many. The point is that Satan is about his business and if we are to understand him and his wiles we must be willing to face the uncomfortable truth. He is a deceiver and he could not achieve his ends without a massive deception that "if possible they shall deceive the very elect" (Mathew 24:24).

One effective deception used to sustain patriotic Republicans from leaving this party when it supports the new world order is using the term "Republicans in name only" (RINO's) and ascribes to them all blame for the party's failures. If these RINO's are the real problem, what is the party (or what are we) doing to get them removed from the party leadership? If they don't represent the majority of the party position on issues, why are they so successful in getting their agenda passed where the majority fails? If nothing is being done about these "RINO's" then what is our hope or purpose in voting for a party which admits its agenda is controlled by a core group and not the majority of supporters of the party?

The harsh truth of the matter is that The Republican Party is The "RINO" Party. That is to say that from its founding The Republican Party has been controlled by "The Eastern Establishment" which is who we refer to as "RINO's". Their agenda is virtually the opposite of what the voters are promised but they continue to promise what they must to get elected, and then pursue their own agenda after the election. This is the deception and it's worked brilliantly to neutralize the church.

The Republican Party was founded by a variety of political parties that had failed consistently to win mass approval from the electorate. The largest of these was "The Whig" party. The agenda of the Whig Party was what we would label today as "tax and spend" and "a strong central government". Predictably, it was not voiced this way to the voters. Rather, they used slogans based on "internal improvements" which meant they would aggressively tax and use the money on roads, rails, bridges, schools, etc.[76] This agenda did not appeal to many people.

At the time The Democrat Party was the party of small central government, states rights, individual liberty and Constitutional government. As a number of small parties combined (some of which were genuinely conservative) the agenda of The Whigs was maintained but more covertly. The Whigs, having the financial backing in addition to having been the most successful of the combined parties, had learned from experience that there was not mass appeal for their agenda. They needed to be deceptive to get elected.

With the founding of the new Republican Party the platform was "God, family and country"; just what the American people wanted to hear. Of course after getting elected the agenda of The Whigs was pursued. It should be pointed out that previously The Whigs did, in fact, win The Presidential election twice but in both cases they were somewhat deceptive and their victory certainly didn't come from an endorsement for strong central government by the voters.

William Henry Harrison was not just the first Whig to win The Presidency but their first candidate for national politics. They were newly formed in 1836 to oppose the agenda of The Democrats and specifically the policies of Andrew Jackson.[77] Sources differ; some indicate Henry Clay ran as a Whig in 1832. He ran as a Whig in 1844 but in 1832 he ran as a "National Republican" which, essentially, adopted the name "Whig Party" as it had been used in American politics earlier.[78] Harrison was a candidate best known for his military service but he had good name recognition as the Secretary to the "Northwest Territory" (Ohio and Indiana), their first delegate to Congress and later appointed first Governor of the Indiana Territory that included present day Indiana, Illinois, Wisconsin, Michigan and Minnesota. His previous political history was viewed as "non-committed" to any party and this too was viewed as beneficial to The Whigs.[79]

John Tyler, a life long Democrat, was selected as his running mate and the party adopted no platform choosing instead to run on a single issue; defeat Martin Van Buren. Whigs won the election of 1840 by swimming deep into Democrat water, claiming similar positions on the issues and capitalizing on an unpopular President. After thirty days in office, President Harrison passed away and John Tyler did nothing to actually promote The Whig agenda. With desire to regain The Presidency in the 1848 election and have a candidate that would pursue their real objectives, The Whigs used the same formula. They ran a candidate best known for his military service and no record affiliating him with any political party.[80]

Indeed Zachary Taylor had nothing, aside from ambition, in common with The Whig Party. Taylor was raised on a Kentucky plantation and was a slave owner. His daughter married Jefferson

Davis who later became President of The Confederate States of America (she died a few months into the marriage) and his only son became a lieutenant general in the confederate army.[81] Many regard Taylor's death as suspicious and "The Compromise of 1850" is believed to have only been possible due to his death sixteen months into his term.

All of this history may seem to be off topic but the issue is the neutralized church and the immediate chapter is on the deception of party politics. Christians are to be "lovers of the truth" and we have been seduced into tolerating dishonesty from our chosen party. This has been a rigged game from the beginning and one Christians should never have fallen victim to.

Now we come to what may be the most difficult few lines in this book for some to accept. What can I say about "Honest Abe" and how can I say it so as to encourage the reader to abandon every preconceived belief you have been embedded with about this man and do some research?

Perhaps a good verse is Luke 6:26 "Woe unto you when all men shall speak well of you! For so did their fathers to the false prophets". Then too we can site John 15:18-19 "If the world hates you, ye know that it hated me before it hated you. If ye were of the world, the world would love his own but because ye are not of the world but I have chosen you out of the world, therefore the world hates you". No man falls into this category as much as Abraham Lincoln. He is possibly the most loved man in U.S. history. Whether he was a willing pawn of this new world order or greatly deceived by the master of deception is not important to us. It can't be. What is important to us is the question whether his impact on government was Godly or Satanic.

Recognizing Abraham Lincoln is at least as highly revered in our nation as is Jesus Christ (certainly this is true among non-Christians) should be sufficient for Christians to suspect they are being deceived regarding this man's life! If he truly were a Godly man, the world would despise him! "History is written by the winners" is an old proverb.[82] It refers to the fact that those who win wars write the history of those wars and always write for themselves the morally superior justification for starting the war.

The new world order has been in charge of writing history for a long time now. It is in the power to write history that they are able to

327

hide their existence. If actual history were widely known there would be no doubt that they exist and what their agenda is but then secret societies would no longer be secret and Satan would be revealed.

It should come as no surprise that Presidents are, necessarily, the most lied about individuals in their generation. This is because they are the visible leader promoting the agenda of the new world order. If the truth were told of these men the entire illusion of "two" parties would be exposed and the agenda for global government would be visible to all.

Research will show that no President is as lied about as Abraham Lincoln. This is a key point because we don't do research. We just believe what we're told. It is vital that Christians understand how they are being deceived. This deception runs deep and has been formulated over a much longer period of time than many will accept without personal study to confirm the evidence.

Our founding fathers believed in individual freedom and they knew the key for this was a limited government hindered from amassing illegitimate power. They also knew through history that governments traditionally grow due to the lust for power that is a constant among those who choose government "service" for their careers. Therefore they employed a number of "safeguards" (checks and balances) to insure those in government service in The U.S. would be hindered from growing the power of government without the consent of the governed.

The first was to bind them down from mischief by the chains of the Constitution. Additionally they instituted several "checks and balances" to keep law making difficult and arduous which would hinder growth. Best known among these were dividing power among three branches of government.

A good argument can be made that the most powerful "check" on preventing excessive growth, which would create a strong central government, was the right of a state to secede from "the Union".

The federal government was created by the states with limited authority and no power exists in the federal government to dictate to the states on any issue unless it is power delegated in The U.S. Constitution. The states came into being at various times before the war for independence. It was the states that sent delegates to create a federal government by writing a Constitution, which was ratified in 1789, long after the thirteen states were created. The right to secede was recognized as the ultimate check on federal power. If this new federal government grew burdensome and oppressive the various states could simply leave without the violence of a war.

Of course this concept was strongly opposed by those who covet absolute power but the subject of secession was not new in 1861. It had been raised several times and debated at "The Hartford Convention" in 1813.[83] South Carolina had threatened to secede so frequently President Jackson publicly threatened to "hang John Calhoun."[84] The right to secede from the Union was used very effectively between 1800 and 1861 to pressure the federal Congress into respecting the rights of the various states.

> Lincoln is viewed as the U.S.'s greatest President for "saving the Union". If the term "The Union" is used geographically to describe territory, and the land is what's important, he is due this credit.[85]

When considering the system that our founding fathers instituted, one of a limited central government, Lincoln removed the strongest check against unlawful usurpation of power and this has severe repercussions for us today. Lincoln is also praised for "freeing the slaves". This is the moral cause that the new world order historians have taught was the purpose for this war. Other historians who find much cause to question this teaching argue that the cause of the war was tariffs. There is a much stronger case for this argument as the states that seceded were sustaining eighty percent of the nation's budget through tariff as the larger northern populations had better representation in the Congress. This all came about because the southern representatives to The Constitutional Convention were unable to convince representatives from the northern states to allow black people to be counted as full citizens. This distorted accurate population figures and gave the north a substantial advantage in The House of Representatives. It was not the south that denied blacks this distinction.[86]

No-doubt tariffs were an incentive for many but this too does not address the interests of the new world order. The most vital incentive of the new world order was amassing power, which they simply couldn't do under The Constitution that our brilliant founders wrote. A casual reading of our Constitution (about 24 pages with Amendments) will reveal something significant. Our Constitution has been amended twenty-seven times, twelve times before this war and fifteen times after. Concerning the twelve Amendments before, two were administrative changes and ten were used to further clarify the limitations on federal powers.

Everything changed after this war. Of the fifteen times The Constitution has been amended after the war nine increased the power of the central government at the expense of state's rights and six were administrative. Amid the administrative Amendments we find The Seventeenth and to those who understand the new world order agenda, this Amendment also seriously increased federal power.

The concept our founders had was that each state would have two Senators appointed by their legislatures. The reason they were appointed in such a way was because their primary duty was to represent the interests of the state legislatures at the federal level just as a representative is to represent the individual people in a district at the federal level. This was to insure against the encroachment on states rights by the federal government.

Since the seventeenth amendment was ratified in 1913 there has been no effective body working to protect states rights and standing against federal encroachment on these rights. The federal government has worked to become an all-powerful central government ever since; one that the states could no longer peacefully secede from. So we see that this war completely changed the system our founding fathers instituted and replaced it with the type of government our founding fathers seceded against in 1776.

In 1868 came The Fourteenth Amendment, which is widely believed to be a complete transfer of power making the states subordinate to the national government. This was the objective of the new world order in creating this war and this is the service provided for them by Abraham Lincoln and they do indeed love him for it! The agenda of The Whig Party was widely opposed by Democrats and all patriotic American's as they recognized the strategy of high taxes to be spent on internal improvements as an obvious method for the party in power to buy political favor.

It is little remembered that, once in power in, The Republicans in Congress passed legislation for the transcontinental railroad. This "internal improvement" had nothing to do with the war, as it spanned from Omaha Nebraska to San Francisco California, not north to south.[87] It generated fortunes for many shrewd investors. Railroads were also the excuse needed to expand federal bureaucracy through agencies like The Interstate Commerce Commission. This strategy proved so successful at holding power that there were only two Democrats elected as President between 1860 and 1932, serving a mere sixteen years out of seventy-two, three elections out of eighteen! The ability to tax and spend on "internal improvements" proved to be a very formidable hold on political office.

Republicans passed "The Morrill Act" in 1861 creating the first federal funding for (and subsequently control over) education.[88] Lincoln signed the National Bank act of 1863 that returned centralized money power to Wall Street.[89] Prior to this banking had been handled Constitutionally and had grown where it was needed.

More change came after the south had been beaten into submission. The Republican controlled Congress turned its sites on the western half of the continent. Perhaps even greater brutality and viciousness than that used to conquer the south was loosed on those in the west that were next to be conquered.

The evil, greed, shamelessness and brazenness in the minds of men at this stage of our country's history can scares be believed today.

The very states that The Union government (Lincoln) said could not secede in 1861 were kicked out of The Union unceremoniously in 1866 as a form of blackmail. They were told they would not be allowed to seat Representatives in Congress until they ratified The Fourteenth Amendment.[90] The insidiousness of this becomes obvious when you note that these same states must have been part of the Union in 1865 because they ratified The Thirteenth Amendment! If you review when each state ratified The Thirteenth Amendment you will notice that some southern states ratified The Thirteenth rapidly upon the secession of hostilities.[91]

They were still free to consider the issue and decide for themselves to ratify or decline as evidenced by the states that did decline. Then came The Fourteenth Amendment and states which would not ratify this transfer of power to Washington DC were treated as conquered territory until they did consent to this transfer of power. This program was called "Reconstruction".

We are still on the topic of "Party Politics" and the illusion that one party subscribes to Godly values more than the other. The Republicans held office during these years but those behind the scenes set the agenda and had no loyalty to God or country. Over the next fifty-two years The Republican Party worked consistently to expand government and establish the precedent that what Washington chose to control, they could declare unto themselves a "right" to control it. The only rule now was the obligatory phrase "for the people's good".

With the south conquered the Republicans went west and then international. Theodore Roosevelt, who was instrumental in starting The Spanish American War as well as U.S. involvement in Panama, also expanded government to include "The Department of Labor and Commerce which was the first bureau to investigate the behavior of private corporations.[92] His belief, that the federal government should be empowered to regulate corporations, would be called "fascism" today. He opened the door for federal involvement in a host of areas such as an income tax, inheritance tax and minimum wage. He spearheaded most of the socialist ideas later implemented by his distant cousin.

Many who consider themselves well informed Americans blame President Wilson for The Sixteenth Amendment (income tax) but it was first proposed by Taft in 1909 and passed by Congress that year and sent to the states for ratification.[93] The Sixteenth Amendment was proclaimed ratified on February 25th 1913 and Wilson didn't take office until March 4th.

Additionally, The Seventeenth Amendment was proposed in 1911 and ratified on April 8, 1913, just a month after Wilson took office.[94] Taft also grew The Federal Government by dividing The Labor Department and The Commerce Department into two.[95] Neither Department is authorized by The Constitution and is used as tools promoting the globalist agenda.

Commerce (international trade) is the strategy most favored by the globalists today to destroy national sovereignty. Karl Marx is on record as early as 1847 promoting free trade. He delivered a speech in 1848 saying

"... The free trade system works destructively. It breaks up old nationalities and carries antagonism... the free trade system hastens the social revolution... I am in favor of free trade".[96]

The Labor Department does nothing about the jobs being "outsourced" and hurts wage rates by permitting entirely too many work visas in a bad economy.

Taft was also significant in convincing Congress to build The Supreme Court their own headquarters, which was decidedly against the vision our founders had for The Court. They desired that it meet infrequently and hear few cases only those which had specific Constitutional ramifications. With it's own headquarters it rapidly grew to a full-fledged arm of government and began this "legislative fiat" that we must battle today.

By 1955 The Supreme Court was legislating and making arbitrary rulings. By 1912 The Democrat Party too had been taken over by those who had no commitment to The United States or to our Constitution. The Wilson Administration showed a complete break with the historical patriotism of The Democrat Party in exchange for the globalist agenda.

Few are aware of the circumstances that launched The United States into World War I and it is all intriguing, however, the sinking of the Lusitanian is a case of clear duplicity![97] Secretary of State William Jennings Bryan was so disturbed by the affair that he resigned his office in disgust. One of the many goals sought by those who envisioned that war was "The League of Nations", however our Senate refused to join.

Unquestionably, one of the greatest horrors in American history had its roots sown during the Wilson era, the founding of The Federal Reserve Bank. Right under the nose of the American people control of our currency and credit was privatized.

The Eighteenth Amendment (Prohibition) established an enormous need for the growth of the Federal Government for the purpose of law enforcement. Previously there was no such need. Federal involvement in local law enforcement continued even after the Twenty First Amendment repealed The Eighteenth Amendment in 1933. Today we see an agenda to federalize all laws and create a national police.

Originally, The United States only had three federal laws. They were piracy, counterfeiting and treason. Now who could know how many there are? How many people even question why all laws suddenly need to be federalized? The local police, as members of the community, are every bit as dedicated to law enforcement as any federal officer.

Resources do not need to be an issue. Our history is one of local law enforcement calling upon the local citizenry for aid when it was needed. Why has this changed? Thousands of physically able citizens would gladly make themselves available to assist law enforcement, if for no other reason than to lower tax rates. If the local police wanted them trained many would gladly submit to a training regiment. The problem with this thinking, from the new world order perspective, is that these people would be committed to the local community.

They want law enforcement officers who have a primary commitment to them and their agenda. In a bad economy, a lot of dedication can be purchased with a good paycheck. Additional dedication can be had by creating issues that turn local people against the police and vice versa, such as altering the mission of the police department from protecting lives and property to writing tickets and making petty arrests. In this manner the public rapidly looses respect for the police.

The police lose respect for the public when criminals are not detained and punished justly but simply "slapped on the wrist" or not prosecuted due to some technicality in the law and released back into the community. The public stood idle while the courts were corrupted in just this way. This has frustrated many dedicated police officers. If they can't count on the public to demand justice when a lenient judge and a fancy talking lawyer turn some violent criminal loose again, why should they think they could count on us for attempting to catch the criminals in the first place? It was Christians who were charged by God to hold the standards for society and we let this happen.

As stated earlier, Presidents are the most lied about members of their generations. Another case-in-point is Herbert Hoover. History revisionists talk and write incessantly about how conservative this President was. The agenda is to paint his administration as a failure while painting him as a conservative to create the impression that conservatism doesn't work. Hoover was not a conservative by any reasonable definition of the word! Historians work to blame Hoover for the great depression but he shared the new world order agenda.

> Prior to Hoover the government had a consistent policy of cutting expenditures during a depression and as a result all depressions were reasonable short and not widely severe. Hoover abandoned this policy in favor of what economist Dr. Benjamin Anderson calls "Hoover's New Deal". This included extensive government intervention in the labor market, propping up weak businesses, increased spending including public works and artificially expanding credit.[98]

All of this federal spending didn't help the economy for Hoover anymore than it later would for Roosevelt because socialism does not work. Another war would be necessary to build the economy and advance the globalist agenda. Many books have been written theorizing the cause of "The Great Depression", many simply to create confusion. This is necessary as the great depression would be a conclusive case study exposing the absolute futility of socialism and deficit spending.

The socialism and deficit spending of the era must be convoluted or it would not be tolerated today, yet it is the only solution offered today. What the reader must understand is that proponents of the new world order have no allegiance to their country or national sovereignty.

> All throughout the twenties, while "silent Cal" was President, the head of The Bank of England made numerous trips to The United States to meet with

Benjamin Strong, the Chairman of The Federal Reserve Bank of The United States. He had been inflating The British Pound and needed The U.S. currency inflated equally to protect the pound. Strong had no dispute with this easy money policy.

The obvious and completely predictable problem was that the easy money and credit policies led to overproduction. This strategy was sold to American bankers and politicians as a means to "help" Britain return to the gold standard which was an absolute lie. They had no intention or desire to do that. This deception was accomplished by creating "a gold bullion standard" which allowed for paper currency to be redeemed for gold but only in very large amounts by banks and governments, not businesses and certainly not ordinary citizens.[99]

What followed under FDR was an expansion of Hoover's policies, not a reversal. The teaching that Hoover was a conservative is relative to FDR at best.

The FDR years were opportunity for the federal government's to strengthen the "power grab" which they began in 1861.

Their first action was a virtual "take-over" of banks as newly authorized federal inspectors were given authority to close banks simply by the examiner making a determination they were insolvent. These were private businesses that were the least guilty among those involved in a corrupt system. The parties of most guilt were never held accountable and added to their fortunes.

The Emergency Banking Act gave The Treasury Department authority to confiscate gold owned by private citizens and private companies. They were forced to accept $20.00 per ounce and immediately after the confiscation was complete the value was set at $35.00 per ounce – cheating them all out of $15.00 per ounce.[100]

Roosevelt implemented the Agricultural Adjustment Administration. For the first time in our history farmers were told how much of their land they could plant. It was voluntary, of course. Of course, farmers who failed to volunteer had a fifty percent sales tax imposed on them. A majority of the public opposed this assault on freedom and private property but The New Deal abandoned the old system of a representative government. The National Recover Administration imposed production standards and price controls on a variety of goods and services. This absolutely fascist attack on freedom involved the government in the ability of every American to buy or sell![101]

Truman continued the socialist policies of Roosevelt by signing the treaty joining The United States into the United Nations. By dropping two atomic bombs he is guilty of the two greatest terrorist attacks in history. It is no coincidence that Nagasaki is believed to have been the largest Christian community in Japan and was a debatable military target at best.[102]

Here again we have the new world order media working overtime justifying this horrific and unnecessary decision. Japan had been attempting to surrender since January of 1945 but The U.S. would not consider their reasonable terms.[103] Truman also presided over the creation of The Department of Defense and The National Security Act that created The CIA and The NSA.

Scores of books have been written revealing that The CIA is, among other things, a private military for the new world order involved in a parade of evil activities largely at the expense of The U.S. taxpayer. This organization has been exposed for involvement in assassinations of duly elected leaders of other countries, drug smuggling to raise revenue for "black ops", starting wars and fermenting revolutions.

The NSA is a domestic spy organization that consistently stands accused for completely disregarding the rights of the American people. Under the banner of national security the health and welfare of every American is threatened by this largely secret organization.[104]

Eisenhower did nothing to retract the fantastic and unconstitutional growth of federal power under the Roosevelt and Truman administrations. Eisenhower expanded government to include The Department of Health, Education and Welfare. He dropped The Monroe Doctrine allowing communist governments to seed movements in Central and South America that includes Cuba. He ran a deficit of $8 Billion in two years, compared to $5.5 Billion in the seven Truman years. Eisenhower nominated Earl Warren as Chief Justice of the Supreme Court (as political payoff), a politician with no judicial experience.[105] It was, in turn, The Warren Court that "ruled" prayer and the Bible out of public schools.

We hear the argument concerning the importance of voting "conservative" so we will get conservative judges. It's worth noting that Eisenhower appointed five judges to the Supreme Court - a voting majority. Yet The Warren Court was as unconstitutional as any court in our nation's history. Had there been any truth to this deception regarding Republicans nominating good judges, Eisenhower could have ended judicial activism but his appointments included some of the most liberal that ever sat on the court.

The Kennedy-Johnson years brought "the military industrial complex" into a mainstream investment sphere. War had always been profitable for certain investors but now it was considered an acceptable form of profit making and the profits were enormous and far above any previous era! The Johnson years brought an incredible amount of federal intrusion into the daily affairs of most Americans and he attempted to do much more. Federal spending exploded under President Johnson. He is attributed with starting an incredible 435 social welfare programs.

Not a single one of these programs was halted under President Nixon. Rather he worked to expand each one of these intrusive, unconstitutional and immoral programs. Nixon asked Congress to create "The Commission on Population Growth" in 1970. Here are some of its recommendations:

➤ Abortion services made available to all Americans (married or single)
➤ Abortion be specifically included in "comprehensive health care benefits" public and private

- ➤ Federal, State and local funding be provided for abortion services
- ➤ Minors be given access to abortion without the consent of a parent or guardian

It was Richard Nixon who appointed Chief Justice Berger. It was "the Berger Court" who "ruled" "Roe vs. Wade" and it was Nixon also nominated Justice Black who wrote that decision fabricating this "right to choose".

It was Nixon who started "The National Petroleum Board" which ultimately grew into "The Department of Energy" which now stands accused of more wasteful spending than The Department of Defense and is one of the most intrusive into daily life. Nixon's labor department was the first to introduce affirmative action regulations, created OSHA and the EPA as well as The Consumer Product Safety Commission and school "busing". Let us never forget the debacle of "The Paris Peace Accords" which surrendered South Vietnam to the communists and left almost 2500 American POW's behind.

Richard Nixon's commitment to the new world order was quite extensive and his association with several of it's known players were indisputable. His original campaign for The House of Representatives was designed to unseat a patriotic Congressman named Jerry Voorhis who wanted (in 1946) to investigate The Federal Reserve Bank and make a full determination of its ownership, investors, loyalties and assets. Nixon found fundraising during the campaign to be a breeze and seriously outspent Voorhis who had been a popular Congressman.[106]

Congressman Nixon's reputation of opposing communism was highly suspect as are several of his political associations. One such association was with "The Atlantic Union". Former president of "The Atlantic Union Committee" Elmo Roper published a book titled "The Goal is Government of all the World" in which he wrote, "Our objective in this committee is to have the Congress pass a resolution supporting the call of a Constitutional Convention..." Nixon co-sponsored this resolution in 1949 and sponsored it in the Senate in 1951.[107]

As Vice President Richard Nixon was known to have worked diligently to defeat the "Bricker Amendment" which would have insured treaties would not supercede The Constitution of The United States.

As President Richard Nixon broke all of his campaign promises about spending, he successfully pressured numerous Republican Congressmen to support foreign aid who had opposed it previously. He increased spending for "the war on poverty" (another broken campaign promise) even though he had the votes to kill it and in 1967 Mr. Nixon wrote an article for "Foreign Affairs" magazine openly calling for "a new world order" by name.[108]

The Carter year's elevated "The Department of Education and The Department of Energy to Cabinet level and signed the treaty giving away the Panama Canal.

The Reagan years gave us record deficits creating a horrifying national debt, numerous tax increases and absolutely no cut in the size of the government. Not one agency was eliminated during his eight years. Prior to The Reagan Administration The Department of Education, Energy and the size of many other Cabinet level Departments were debated as unnecessary. Reagan ended those debates and enlarged all departments.

President H. W. Bush gave us "The American's with Disabilities Act" and the 1st Iraq war. H. W. Bush's background would have exposed a liberal agenda to any investigator. He voted for the 1968 "Gun Control Act", in 1969 he introduced "the Family Planning Services and Population Research Act" in Congress which was later sited as authority for taxpayer funded abortions. This was the first time The U.S. Government funded abortion. He supported the "Roe" decision, The ERA and was the first President to formally welcome homosexuals to The White House for a bill signing, the 1990 "Hate Crimes Statistics Act" which wrote "sexual orientation" into law for the first time.[109] NAFTA was passed by Congress only with the aide of three fourths of The Republicans in both Houses supporting it, which they did due to pressure from Bush. This was a major advance of the globalist Free Trade agenda.

President Clinton signed NAFTA into law in addition to The GATT Treaty, which created The World Trade Organization. This gave The United Nations authority to dictate to our Congress on trade issues and had been a desire of the globalists since 1945. Clinton's high priority was a failed attempt at creating a government health care program.

The G. W. Bush Administration has given us the 2nd Gulf war, The Department of Homeland Security, The Patriot Act, Patriot 2, CAFTA (and a host of additional 'free trade' agreements), TSA, doubled the amount of money for research on "fetal stem cells", has never addressed legitimate questions about 9-11 and claimed his bloated budgets are the result of his "war on terror" but he has increased spending in every department. President Bush worked to merge The U.S. into both a Free Trade Area of The America's, which would have created a European Union type government in this hemisphere, and a North American Union when The FTAA failed. This was a scaled down version of The FTAA.[110]

Listing such historical events without commentary disallows the opportunity to explain their individual promotion of the new world order. Never-the-less had you no preconceived notion of which party is "the more conservative" you probably would not have guessed such action on the part of Republicans.

The point is that Christians should never put their faith or allegiance into a political party. Our job is to insure both (or all) parties promote Godliness. We have not done this. This is only a "short list" but every one of these issues should be of vital interest to Christians. What would the last fifty years have been like if Christians would have been doing their civic duties? God expects us to abide by His standard, not that of a political party.

We are told nine times in scripture "not to be ignorant of the enemies devises". Political parties are one of his "devises". How can we believe Satan (or the new world order) is so stupid they would allow themselves to be voted out of power? They wouldn't, so we must make an effort to be informed and we must use The Bible as the standard when voting. This is an argument that people must get informed and get involved in such a way as to effectively fulfill a Christian's "cultural mandate".

The point to all of this history is that we must trust God. The deception of trusting a political party has played right into the hands of the new world order. Party politics is a fool's game. This idea that voting in and of itself is some solution is a deception. Never in the history of freedom has freedom been that cheap. It does no good to vote if you don't understand principles of good government, one of which is to be involved!

James 4:8 speaks of being double minded. The same term is used in James 1:8 but in a completely different context. 1:8 has more to do with being easily influenced, indecisive, lacking faith and wisdom while 4:8 is dealing much more firmly with evil influences in our lives that we have allowed to take root. This goes beyond a battle over some unresolved sin in our life. 4:8 deals with a stronghold we have given Satan in our life.

This is relevant to "the two party system" when we understand that the occult has a form of manipulation frequently called "the Janus mind". This is best described as "control by fear of opposites". When limited to two choices, causing fear of "A" will force people to side with "B". It is important to recognize there may be no ideology here, just manipulation. If we prefer to vote for a "pro-life" candidate, we are manipulated into believing party A is aggressively pro-abortion and this manipulates us to vote for party B.

After we vote we don't stay informed and involved to insure that the party we have empowered with our vote has solved the problem. This type of manipulation is the essence of modern elections and it survives on a lack of vigilance on our part. Another example would be government welfare programs. If we benefit from a program we are told party B will end this program and this manipulates us to vote for A. Those that fail to recognize that both parties are controlled by the same interest groups will fail to understand the strategic approach of this type of manipulation.

Well-informed people understand that neither party promotes Godliness and both are directing us toward global government at the expense of national independence.

Christians have grown apathetic, as they have put their trust in politicians and parties who have told them what they wanted to hear but did nothing to solve our problems. The inevitable frustration and confusion has led to more apathy, a direct result of not understanding how the new world order plays the game they have instituted. As a result of our apathy, we don't insist on good Godly candidates, we're pacified with the "lesser of two evils"; a strategy that guarantees Satan and his new world order will rule.

PART
SIX

THE
WORLD
DECEIVED

INTRODUCTION TO PART 6

Numbers 32:6 "shall your brothers go to war and shall you sit here?"

Previously we have dealt with Satan's efforts to neutralize the church so that he could pursue his dream of world government without opposition. Now we must look at his strategy from a different perspective. While it was needful for him to neutralize the church he must also have a strategy to deal with non-Christians. Simply because one has not become a Christian does not mean one would embrace satanism or a satanic agenda. Satan is fighting a war and war requires strategy. The Bible makes this point clear and Christians need to get back into the fight.

The concept of an all-powerful government in The United States is a new idea and not an easy sell. Americans have always embraced ideas of liberty and we love the idea of being free to make our own choices. Therefore Satan's agenda must be pursued by stealth and created under the deception of being advantageous for people. Satan has devised a seduction for America.

He promises a Utopia where all needs are met and all desires are realized; a global harmony of no war, no envy, no suffering and no want. Those that study history have irrefutable evidence that what he delivers is quite the opposite!

History absolutely reveals that when God is abandoned and Satan is permitted to govern the results are horrors in the forms of famine, hopelessness, disease, war, violence and death. This truth is obvious to researchers but it does not hinder Satan. He simply casts blame for this devastation upon a lack of power to take sufficient action to meet needs. We are led to believe that what's needed is always a more powerful government. He assures the world that the failure lies in the rebellion of those who will not submit and that once he has been afforded complete control the paradise promised will be delivered.

In the Garden of Eden Satan promised Eve she could be "as God". In Isaiah 14:14 we read Satan telling himself "I will be like the most high". [2] This is his goal. He may never have the creative power that God has but he believes he can obtain Godlike control. This is the allure to those who serve him. It is the control that his minions are after, the power of determining life or death and total subjugation of those they control. Those who will not submit to every vile demand are to be destroyed.

To win we need not go toe to toe with Satan in some holy war. Jesus will take care of Satan in His own good time. We need only expose him as a liar and fraud. We need only expose the truth of what he has done, how he is doing it and the results if we refuse to oppose him. This is the duty of salt and light and what scripture commands us to do and we should reject any excuse to permit Satan victory.

If the American people are educated concerning this threat they will see that the short-term help is not worth the long-term price. The various government programs which the American people are taking advantage of are not worth the enslavement and death of their children. If they are not warned they cannot be expected to know the truth. Satan's plan for a one-world government with excessive controls over each individual is being accomplished by purchasing their dependence. This is what people must be made aware of.

The point of this introduction is that the reader needs to understand one very important truth concerning part 6 of this book; it is all a lie. Satan is a liar, of course, but unfortunately he is not stupid. A lie so elaborate to enslave mankind and build a global satanic tyranny must have layers, strengths and credibility. It must be both hidden and able to withstand scrutiny of the few who investigate. It must have purpose, structure and organization. Even though Satan is the father of chaos, chaos is but the first part of the strategy. It must have goals with the strategic planning to achieve those goals, yet not visible to those being enslaved.

---

2   +Fn2 this as Lucifer. Most people agree that Lucifer and Satan are the same being; some disagree.

In this section we will examine the lies that have deceived non-Christians to complete his strategy. Continuity of government requires organization and cooperation and this requires a written set of plans and rules that all parties at all levels can rely upon and refer back to. The Constitution had to be abandoned since no part of the new world order is permissible under The Constitution. This meant that The Constitution had to be covertly replaced with a new set of government policies and guidelines.

Satan's problem was how to do this since the American people are not about to allow government to trash this revered document. The answer is clever spin, word usage, apathy, a convincing alternative and (at the right times) intimidation.

An example of this is in the preamble of The Constitution. The Preamble to The Constitution of The United States reads "We the people of The United States, in order to form a more perfect union, establish justice, insure domestic tranquility, provide for the common defense, promote the general welfare …" These words have cleverly been switched in their interpretation to read "provide for the general welfare, promote the common defense …" which has opened the door to unlimited federal intrusion into our lives which was previously prohibited.

What you will read in this section is unbelievable and many are quick to dismiss it because it's unbelievable; I was. It's not my purpose to convince you to believe it, quite the contrary, as I don't want you to believe it. My goal is to make you aware of what many in government have come to believe. Only then can you understand what's going on in this country and why our government is so far removed from that authorized in The Constitution. Equally, I have no interest in convincing anyone to fight these lies one at a time. My argument is that truth must be our guiding force. If we stand for truth and work to establish the truth as common knowledge the lies will die and we will not suffer the growth of new lies in their place. Never the less I must encourage you to take these lies seriously. Those promoting them have accomplished much.

These people are serious about their agenda and they are deadly. It seems rather ridiculous to point out that anyone or organization that has killed approximately two-hundred million people must be taken seriously and viewed as a threat! Yet this must be pointed out because people (Christians and non-Christians) do not view the new world order as a threat but readily trust those in government, education, medicine, industry, etc and seldom stop to consider that, perhaps, people in these positions serve a hidden agenda.

Consider the paradigm of trust. That is to say, who have you learned to trust in your life? The new world order has spent trillions of dollars convincing the masses of people to trust their agents while they keep their existence hidden. Doctors, lawyers, politicians, TV anchors, school teachers, pharmaceutical companies, bankers and virtually anyone else who affects some aspect of your life have all been educated in the new world order's schools and universities.

They have been taught only what was decided they should know. Few have ventured into independent research. A concept has been nurtured that they care about you and have only the agenda of your welfare. Sure, they're human and make mistakes and sometimes fall victim to "the law of unintended consequences" but we are assured there is no hidden agenda. Yes, these people may have some personal ambitions and character failures but they would never betray humanity so they deserve unlimited trust.

Most of these people have no idea that they have been educated with a predetermined curriculum that was designed by those with an evil agenda. They, in their turn, have been taught to trust their trade journals for continuing education with no idea that the publishers are part of the same strategy. Few people look "behind the curtain". Few people research for themselves outside of the approved material. They see no need and probably don't have the time.

Therefore, when the subject is opened that there is valuable information contrary to the approved curriculum the normal reaction is dismissive. When one lives the whole of their life being taught who to trust and someone raises the argument that this trust may be misplaced, it is an attack on other people's entire value and belief system. In the end, this brings us back to the question, "if it were true would you want to know?" All of the evidence that exists is worthless to those who will not examine the facts.

With this in mind, it is frequently more advantageous to those who are unscrupulous to be excessive. The more outrageous they are the less likely the masses are to believe those who work to expose the evil. They will just be dismissed as ridiculous. Those who have never researched or considered the evidence have no foundational information to draw upon except the trust that has been cultivated. We have work to do, there is a war going on. I have never heard it more eloquently put than that said by Patrick Henry on March 23, 1775. I have presumed to use a portion of his comments with the liberty of slightly altering his statements in order to bring his astute sentiments into our current battle.

"It is natural to man to indulge in the illusion of hope. We are apt to shut our eyes against a painful truth and listen to the song of that siren until she transforms us into helpless slaves. Are we disposed to be of the number of those who, having eyes see not, and having ears hear not, the things which so nearly concern their temporal salvation? For my part, whatever anguish of spirit it may cost, I am willing to know the whole truth – to know the worst and to provide for it. I have but one lamp by which my feet are guided; that is the lamp of experience. I know of no way of judging the future but by the past. Judging by the past, I wish to know what there has been in the conduct of the government for the last fifty years to justify the hopes with which people have been pleased to solace themselves.

If we wish to be free - we must fight! Shall we acquire the means of effectual resistance by lying supinely on our backs and hugging the delusive phantom of hope, until our enemies shall have bound us hand and foot? We are not weak, if we make a proper use of the means that the God of nature hath placed in our power. Millions of people, armed in the holy cause of liberty and in such a country as that which we possess are invincible by any force which our enemy can send against us. Besides, sir, we shall not fight our battles alone. There is a just God who presides over the destinies of nation, who will raise up friends to fight our battles for us.

The battle, sir, is not to the strong alone; it is to the vigilant, the active, the brave. There is no retreat but in submission and slavery! It is in vain, sir, to extenuate the matter. Gentlemen may cry, "Peace! Peace!" – but there is no peace. The war is actually begun! Why stand we here idle? What is it that gentlemen wish? What would they have? Is life so dear, or peace so sweet, as to be purchased at the price of chains and slavery? Forbid it, Almighty God! I know not what course others may take but as for me, give me liberty or give me death"!

There cause is our cause. Tyrants who would have enslaved them in their generation would enslave us in ours. Much of what Patrick Henry voiced on that day affects us today and should be considered. The following are part of the above speech with some commentary.

"Is it that insidious smile with which our petition has been received? Trust it not, sir; it will prove a snare to your feet". All who approach their Congressman are greeted with a smile and a handshake. This is a token strategy promoting the illusion that our concerns will be considered when there is absolutely no intension of doing so. I have witnessed numerous patriots spend their time and money to make various officials aware of threats and hidden clauses in any variety of legislation. Invariably they were warmly thanked for their information but never have I seen a Congressman take them seriously. If you don't bring a bag of money, don't expect results.

"Ask yourselves how this gracious reception of our petition comports with the warlike preparations which cover our land. Are armies necessary to a work of love and reconciliation? Have we shown ourselves so unwilling to be reconciled that force must be called in to win back our love"? Why are we witnessing such an increased military presence across our nation? We see police departments with military type armored vehicles as well as automatic weapons. We see police increasingly showing up in force with their faces covered, no badges or any personal identification of any kind. If one wanted to protest the actions of an officer you have no hope of identifying the one against the hosts that are present.

We see new laws passed constantly federalizing crimes with mandatory sentencing so that no judge can consider extenuating circumstances in a case. We see military bases located in the heartland where they would be poorly located if their objective truly was to protect the nation from foreign attack. We see police officers taser people with no provocation. We see citizen protestors being gassed and arrested with techniques designed to induce pain. We see a steady increase of "no-knock" warrants and the suspension of The Fourth Amendment in attempts to interrogate suspects, ID cards, checkpoints, police cameras at virtually every intersection and a frightening number of new prisons are constantly being built and filled! This is the "peace and safety" we are receiving in exchange for our rights.

"Let us not deceive ourselves, sir. These are the implements of war and subjugation – the last arguments to which kings resort. I ask gentlemen, what means this martial array if its purpose be not to force us to submission? Can the gentlemen assign any other possible motive for it"? Implements of war indeed! In The United States implements of war are not to be used by police departments. Police are to protect lives and property and all suspects are to be considered innocent until proven guilty in a court. The job of the military is quite different; essentially to beat the enemy into submission by whatever means necessary quite a difference! These are excellent questions, then. Why are these implements of war being distributed to police departments, why are police being trained in (and allowed to use) aggressive tactics? Why are military bases situated across America, frequently with foreign troops?

"Has our government enemies in this quarter of the world, to call for this accumulation of armies"? Ah yes... The "war on terror", the "war on drugs", etc. So here we see the infamous "Hegelian dialectic" put to good use. If we were truly fighting a war on terror we would close the borders. If we truly were fighting a war on drugs we not only would close the border but we would take measures against countries and people smuggling drugs into this country. Instead, local police, who can only target small time local dealers or kids who have a small quantity for their personal use, do the bigger effort. National efforts

are frequently nothing more than "photo ops" to give the impression progress is being made, [3]

"No, sir, she has none". Russian revolutionary Vladimir Lenin said, "The best way to control your opposition is to lead them". Another aspect of this is creating your own opposition. For government to increase there must be recognizable threats a majority of people wants eliminated. If no threat exists, unscrupulous politicians can and have created them so that they may increase the size of government and their power with the approval of the public. This has been a constant throughout history.

"They are meant for us; they can be meant for no other. They are sent over to bind and rivet upon us those chains which the government has been so long forging". We must take note of this point. It may be difficult for many to grasp but I repeat; these new laws, military equipment, training and tactics are meant to control you and I. This is the long held objective of the new world order.

"What have we to oppose them? Shall we try argument? Sir, we have been trying that for the last fifty years. Have we anything new to offer of the subject? Nothing". There is nothing to be gained in negotiating with an enemy that covets your destruction and has amassed sufficient power to achieve what they covet but this does not negate our responsibilities.

The point to all of this is that tyrants have always existed and previous generations have always fought these tyrants. Our generation is complacently embracing them. The Declaration of Independence gives a rather alarming illustration of how our generation has complacently

---

[3] This is not to condone drug abuse but rather to call the reader's attention to the classic new world order strategy employed through this perceived war on drugs. While drugs are pouring across our borders property rights are destroyed, police are being made into military units, good kids with a bright future are given criminal records for a relatively minor act, and we have a new (and unnecessary) department of government meddling in the personal lives of the people. An excellent book on the fraud and duplicity of this war on drugs is "Agency of Fear" by Jay Epstein

surrendered the very freedoms our founders fought for. It reads as though it were written in our current era:

"When in the course of human events it becomes necessary for one people to dissolve the political bands which have connected them with another ... to secure these rights governments are instituted among men, deriving their just powers from the consent of the governed ...all experience has shown that mankind are more disposed to suffer, while evils are sufferable than to right themselves by abolishing the forms to which they are accustomed. Let the facts be submitted to ... the world.

... he has refused his assent to laws, the most wholesome and necessary for the public good".

How frequent do we note a judge throwing out some law passed by concerned, patriotic and active citizens at the state or local level. Our system of "consent of the governed" affords us the right to pass laws for ourselves that are going to protect the quality of life we desire in our communities. Laws banning gay marriage, pornography, hindering home schooling and spanking children are among a long list of laws passed by people with every right to pass them and then thrown out by the courts.

"He has forbidden his Governors to pass laws of immediate and pressing importance ... "

All policy is federal now. Water rights, property, education, energy, and transportation are all controlled at the federal level. Governors and Legislatures have only to decide how to implement the federal mandates. Every matter must now be considered in conjunction with a federal bureaucracy and its dictates.

"He has refused to pass other laws for the accommodation of large districts of people, unless those people would relinquish the right of Representation in the Legislature ... "

Staggering numbers of American's are waking up to the fact that their Representatives do not hear their voices any longer. The only opportunity we are offered is to adopt one of the two party positions on issues and this frequently means abandoning our personal core beliefs, at least to some extent. Thomas Jefferson had something different in mind when he penned these words but the fact remains that Congress will not address a host of issues many people are passionate about. Immigration and the border issue is one, the national debt is another and opposition to the new health care bill was high and yet Congress passed it aside from the stated public opposition. Congress staunchly refuses to address the concerns of the people.

"He has called together legislative bodies ...for the sole purpose of fatiguing them into compliance with his measures".

It is relatively new that Congress is in session so much. Originally they met for just a couple months a year. With Congress in session constantly issues that are initially defeated are brought back again and again until the public and all resistance grows weary of fighting the same battles over and over again and they are passed. This strategy causes us to lose by attrition. Then too, Congress is mercilessly pressured to support the globalist agenda.

So it goes. Reading The Declaration of Independence, one could easily believe it was written recently; *"He has made Judges dependent on his will alone ... He has erected a multitude of new offices and sent hither swarms of officers to harass our people and eat out their substance".* IRS, EPA, EEOC, OSHA, ADA, anyone in business can quickly be destroyed by the endless parade of federal bureaucrats that are empowered to fine you for a multitude of offenses.

"He has affected to render the military independent of the ... civil power. He has combined with others to subject us to a jurisdiction foreign to our constitution..." The UN, NAFTA, WTO, UNESCO and a host of trade treaties that have destroyed manufacturing and subsequently hurt employment.

"For imposing taxes without our consent ... depriving us ... of trial by jury ... tried for pretended offences ... establishing arbitrary government

and enlarging its boundaries so as to render it ... instrument for absolute rule ... has declared us out of his protection and waging war against us ... he is at this time transporting large armies of foreign mercenaries to complete the works ..."

Most of this needs no commentary and is obviously as applicable today as in 1776. Still, there is one important issue that far too many patriots are completely unaware of. That is the numbers of foreign military units that are stationed across this country. Everyone needs to investigate this matter and protest it!

There is much, much more that is applicable but the point is made and the point is that we, today, are facing a threat far more grave and dangerous than did America's founding fathers! We are paying a high price for not being involved strategically in politics. This is our future and we're ignoring it. We, at present, have failed shamefully to pass freedom on to our children the way it was passed to us. Each one of us needs to work toward correcting this problem.

Now we need to examine the specifics in how we were robbed of our great heritage. We need to examine how our Constitution was replaced and with what and what this means. Most importantly, we must become the few that "look behind the curtain at the wizard" and work to expose him and his fraud. Just as Satan has worked through kings and government in the past he still works today. Just as patriots of old worked to expose him in the past, the duty is ours today.

The point needs to be stressed; it's all lies. What he has built he has built without proper authority. The authority is God's and He has given it to us. The following is given so that all can understand the wiles of the enemy and know what politicians are led to believe when they get to Washington. It's all lies...

For a complete and original text of Patrick Henry's famous speech, see http://www.historyplace.com/speeches/henry.htm
For a complete text of "The Declaration of Independence" see http://www.ushistory.org/declaration/document/

NEUTRALIZING JESUS

1ˢᵗ John 2:22: "who is a liar but he that denieth that Jesus is the Christ?"

Aside from the variety of tactics and strategies Satan must employ to deceive the nations he is left with one major dilemma, what to do about Jesus. This is high on his priority list as people must be kept ignorant of who Jesus really is and all things Godly must be distorted and be made unappealing. The question has been a constant in the church from the fall of man; does Satan really believe he can win against such an awesome God? We can agree upon part of the answer, he will pursue all means at his disposal in attempting to achieve his success.

As with the previous topics, Satan relies on no single strategy. His strategy for the complacent is that they have time and no urgent decision is needed. He tells the immoral that as long as they're not hurting anyone they will be fine, surely a loving God will not send anyone to hell for a small error in judgment. To the fool he states that there was no Jesus or if He lived at all He was just another man. The whole concept of a virgin birth, holy life and resurrection are ridiculed.

The focus of this book, however, is the neutralized church. This raises the two questions of what Satan tells those who are truly sold out to his service and also what he tells Christians to deceive them out of the service and relationship God would prefer for them. We need not revisit the many lies and arguments that Christians have come to accept over the years. We have examined many in detail throughout the chapters of this book.

This chapter will focus on those who reject God's word and made a conscious decision to serve Satan's agenda in a belief that they are doing the right thing. For one to be so committed and willing to invest the whole of their religious zeal and tangible resources into Satan and his agenda, a complex and incredible lie had to be formulated. A lie that would stand up to scrutiny and merit such devotion.

Again, for the purpose of this book we need not explore the basic lies of "there is no God, a loving God would not send anyone to a hell, the idea of God having a Son is foolish, etc". The deception began in The Garden of Eden with the lie "ye shall not surely die … you shall be as gods knowing good and evil". The lie here concerned death but the promise to know good and evil was true. The temptation was for hidden knowledge. This strategy has proven to work exceedingly well for Satan through out the years. Today there are scores of religions that have rituals based on hidden knowledge or truth revealed in stages as initiates advance through the various degrees.

Once you have convinced an initiate that knowledge is power it becomes small effort to manipulate those coveting power. Relationship with Jesus Christ is power. Knowledge of Him is life changing. Yet Christians and non-Christians alike idle away our time on frivolous entertainment. It serves us well to consider then, that those who have made the necessary pledge to learn these hidden truths (again, these ARE truths, just not Godly truths) are fully committed to the achievement of their agenda.

It serves me no purpose to offend the Christian community but it is reasonable to point out that we have the word of God, we can study over a thousand years of excellent commentaries from students of scripture, The Holy Spirit to teach us and the promise of God that if we ask He will indeed teach us. Yet we find far too many Christians with a vast knowledge of trivia concerning some sports team, who can bowl and golf as well as any semi-pro and are regulars at the movie theater.

The point is that America is in shambles; babies are butchered and abused, children are brought up with a respect for the occult and no knowledge of God as well as a dependence on government rather than God or even themselves, we are on the verge of a massive economic collapse, virtually all major illnesses and diseases are on the rise, just about every other country on earth hates us and the church of the living God is at play as if we were on holiday. Clearly Satan's allies are committed to their agenda and Christians are not!

Learning is always a process that involves layering information on top of knowledge (that which is understood) at a rate mentally digestible by the student. Satan knows this and has developed a system to accomplish his goals. One thing that must be understood, Satan needs people. He cannot accomplish his agenda under his own power, even with his demon army. His arrogance will not permit him to admit it, of course, but common sense will tell you that if Satan could have accomplish his agenda by now, he would have.

He is restrained, 2nd Thessalonians 2:7. It serves Satan's purpose to promote false religion and lies regarding salvation as this serves to keep people from heaven but too, it weakens the church as we are divided and fighting amongst ourselves over petty theological issues. It is also worth mentioning that in this way there would be fewer devout Christians making war on Satan.

Still, Satan's master plan entails the creation of his own religion. Aspects of this religion do include outright Satan worship and Witchcraft, which is what people commonly think of when the subject of Satanism is raised but these practices and beliefs have poor recruiting opportunities among intelligent, professional people who have grown up in a world of some Biblical influence.

The pure evil and horrific plan that Satan desires to visit upon mankind is not easily accepted by people in our modern age. We hear so much about peace, love, compassion, humanity and so forth that we have lost the ability to mentally grasp just how evil Satan is. Furthermore, it is hard for good people to accept the idea that many who use these terms are insincere and have secret ambitions to fulfill Satan's agenda, bringing into existence the most vile, evil and deadly period in history.

It is frequently as difficult for Satan's new converts to embrace these teachings. They must be introduced to them slowly and in such a way that they will be deceived into full cooperation with enthusiasm. So the strategy is "hidden knowledge" revealed to each individual disciple at the pace they individually labor to achieve. As the disciple loses enthusiasm and ambition he is abandoned believing he has attained the highest levels of secret knowledge when he may have only begun to explore these teachings. While the disciple is being taught the "truths" that are approved for his level of understanding, he is being drawn in and rewarded financial for his dedication.

Additionally most of his friends and business associates come from the same group and share beliefs. If he excels he leaves these friends behind as he makes more friends among the higher levels and starts believing himself to be of superior intellect than his former friends due to his advancement over theirs.

Throughout history, the most common name for this type of religion is "Gnosticism"; a Greek word meaning "knowledge" or "to know" but the implication is "secret knowledge" or "revealed knowledge". These beliefs and practices predated the Greeks and arguably go back to The Egyptian Mystery Religions and Babylon itself but the Greek term is still used. Once again we broach a subject that would take volumes to clarify and these study materials are abundant but for our purposes we must do a brief accounting.

Any date set for the formal founding of Gnosticism has been lost to history but it is entirely reasonable to consider it was founded in The Garden of Eden when Satan offered to share the knowledge of hidden truths (evil) with Eve. All other attempts to determine when this thinking was popularized are short lived as further research always proves the pre-existence of these beliefs by some name.

At one point Gnosticism was believed to be a corruption of Christianity but it is now accepted by scholars that this teaching existed long before the time of Christ. One can easily note the similarities in the Gnostic beliefs to Plato and "Platonic Philosophy". I have previously mentioned that it was the Platonic beliefs taught at the Alexandrian School of Christian Theology.

A meeting referred to as "The Fifth Congress of Orientalists" held in Berlin in 1882 had mention of the connection between the ancient Babylonian religion and Gnosticism.[111] Other historians concur although they debate over exactly what the ancient Babylonian religion was. In any event the similarities between Babylonian and Gnostic beliefs are quite obvious in such schools of thought as astrology, the study and usage of numbers and many aspects of the supernatural.[112] While some labor to prove Gnosticism originated in Egypt and others in Babylon it is beyond reasonable dispute that it existed and was taught at the Alexandrian School as "Christian Gnosticism". The objective of

Gnostic thought is to overcome human suffering, disease and death through study and knowledge.

There can be no doubt that Gnostics came in contact with Jewish beliefs prior to the age of Christianity and some forms of Gnostics have adopted what is commonly referred to as a Gnostic "redeemer myth", a Jewish attitude toward a coming "Messiah" or at least a leader of advanced wisdom. Most do not look for a savior, they don't need to; their beliefs dovetail nicely with the concept of a ruling elite.[113]

This brings us back to the topic of this chapter, which is neutralizing Jesus. If Jesus is what He said He is than the debate is over and the pursuit of knowledge begins and ends with the pursuit of knowledge about God. The message taught by Jesus was and is not popular among those who desire to be kings over men with unlimited power. Still, the rapid expansion of Christianity demanded satanic effort to stifle its growth and confusion has always been one of Satan's primary tactics.

Then too, why kill a popular movement when you can assume control over it and redirect it for your own purpose. Gnostic Christianity has very little to do with scripture and nothing to do with the scriptural Jesus. While the Gnostics have seemingly adopted Christian terms they have consistently redefined these words to serve their own purpose. They then teach the "proper terminology" as part of their revealed knowledge to their initiates claiming the uninitiated lack understanding.

They have drafted writings referred to as "the Gnostic Gospels" to support their claims and successfully use these writings to mislead those unfamiliar with scripture. The effort they have put forth is so clever (in a diabolical sense of the word) that they have successfully created an alternative way to interpret scripture.

They can sit and read the same Bible as you and I and with their "hidden" meanings they can take away a message that fully supports their teachings. I choose not to go into too much detail here as their teachings are quite vulgar and offensive to Bible believing Christians but to give a couple examples to prove my point, they have no problem with Jesus as savior if savior means one who has advanced in knowledge to the degree of master and now teaches others the secret mysteries. They believe where Acts 1:9 documents Jesus ascended into heaven to be interpreted as Jesus being initiated into (their) priesthood. The second coming of Christ is the beginning of a new age (a return to "cosmic purity") and a Christ consciousness. Indeed their term "christ" is defined as the global brotherhood of man (the body of christ) defines as those who will embrace the new age.

They have twisted the entire Bible to create alternative meanings. This type of study is a waste of time since there are no sure truths one may debate but only levels of truth that you cannot be expected to grasp since you have not attained the higher levels of understanding. Furthermore one battles the "exoteric" definition of words while there may be as many as seven layers of "esoteric" meanings to each key teaching. You can see how the strategy is designed to keep people committed to their own spiritual advisor and his system.

A greater example of twisting scripture would be in the second paragraph above. A reasonable thinking person would know Jesus could not have been initiated into the priesthood after His crucifixion if His crucifixion were completed. This is a major point, as neutralizing Jesus simply demands that something be done about His death and resurrection. If this much is true then the teaching of Jesus would be indisputable and take on an all knew importance for all, as they have for Christians. All would know salvation does not come by knowledge, secretly revealed or otherwise.

Reading the four gospels, it is absolutely clear that Jesus died and was resurrected. However for those who do not take The Bible literally words can be twisted. One version is that Jesus switched places secretly as another was killed in His place. Another version is that Jesus was hung on the cross but taken down before He died. To those who know the scriptures and believe, these stories are ridiculous. To those who do not know the scriptures and do not care to read them, these stories are far more believable than Biblical accounts of a supernatural Jesus.

Still, to best serve the purpose of those in Satan's service, it is best to tell the story of Jesus on the cross as symbolic. Explain the entire ordeal as an initiation and a "ritual death" rather than anything literal. In this manner it becomes logical that He would be elevated to a "priest" rank in a later ceremony.

In any event, denying the death and resurrection of Jesus and adopting selected teaching to use for selfish purposes has been an enormously successful strategy. In this way, the new world order has long preached that Jesus taught communist/socialist and tolerance. Few are aware that they have also corrupted His teaching to create the illusion that Jesus taught hidden mysteries and degrees of knowledge.

They point out that He had twelve to whom He taught secrets of life but He did not reveal all truths to the masses as evidenced by the seventy or more to whom he didn't explain His parables. Only as others strived for knowledge and proved their devotion could these secret mysteries be revealed, according to Gnostic teaching.

With their false writings and false teachings they were able to expand around the world. When their seditious plans were discovered by governments they were able to argue they were being persecuted for religious beliefs. When their false teachings were discovered by Christians they were able to turn the tables and make themselves appear as the rational legitimate church concerned about people.

Their form of Christianity had no appeal to those who hungered for a real and personal relationship with Jesus Christ but that was of no concern to them. They had an agenda and those who would best serve their agenda had no desire for a real personal relationship with Jesus Christ. They viewed Bible believing Christians as superstitious and unfit for intellectual truth. They viewed themselves as intellectuals and "the elect".

Greek Gnosticism teaches that while all humans have a "divine spark" within them, there are few who will seek all truth and only those striving for all hidden truth may be part of the intellectual elite. Then there are those who believe that only the elect have this "divine spark" to begin with.[114]

Aside from a desire that some people have to possess secret knowledge, Gnosticism contains an element of intrigue based on the sciences. In a time when little was known of the natural sciences they had much with which to entice people. Some of the more occultist groups invited in a variety of pagan magic that added further intrigue for their initiates.[115]

The influence of Gnosticism in our society is quite evident to those who have studied it and understand its objectives. For example

Gnostics have no concept of individual salvation but rather the collective advancement of mankind. To know their Jesus is to be free from the bondage and judgment of a "creator God" and pursue enlightenment and salvation through the pursuit of knowledge.

The Gnostic Jesus is not The Biblical Jesus. To the Gnostic there is no sin but only ignorance. There is no such a thing as a personal relationship with a loving forgiving God but only the advancement of the collective good for the whole of society, as determined by the self appointed intellectual elite.

Being a Gnostic means one pursues knowledge and therefore "knows" more than those who are not Gnostic. Therefore, being the intellectuals, they believe Gnostics are entitled to the authority and power necessary to direct the affairs of men, even control the collective actions of the masses to insure salvation or as they understand it, achieve the collective enlightenment.

The Christian plan where one achieves salvation by recognizing you are guilty of sin and the only one with the power to redeem you from that sin is Jesus Christ is abandoned for a plan where salvation is placed in the hands of the ruling elite because they, supposedly, know what's best for mankind.

If these intellectuals have learned sufficiently they can lead mankind to a new age of enlightenment but we must trust them. All must be made to comply with their every whim, will and commandments. Individually all we can do is cooperate and work helping to stifle any opposition to the collective good as dictated by the intellectual elite. This is our only hope for the survival of the planet; the collective will of humanity to abandon individualism and embrace our anointed intellectuals to lead us to salvation. If this doesn't sound like Satan's dream religion, you're not paying attention!

It is widely believed that Gnosticism died out for the most part some time around the fifth century AD. This is wishful thinking. Satan doesn't abandon a plan that works for him. During the fifth century and since, Gnosticism has largely been promoted by secret societies.

When one attempts to study secret societies one encounters some predictable difficulties. First of all is the obvious fact that the vast majority of what we know about any secret society is what they want us to know about them. Do not assume that because they are secret they waste great effort in hiding their existence. They do not and they recognize the self-defeating aspects of trying. If their energy was spent on hiding their existence one could do them serious damage simply by proving that they do, in fact, exist. They will not allow themselves to be so vulnerable.

Satan appears as an angel of light. You will find him lurking in the shadows behind some benevolent organization or right sounding cause. He is very much in control of these organizations; he simply must keep himself hidden and operate through minions. Throughout history governments and the church have fought valiantly to oppose these societies because, as one writer put it, "there never was a secret society that did not exist except to destroy the cause of Christ".

In our enlightened, information age some people are more inclined to dismiss them out of hand. This is exactly what Satan wants. He cannot achieve his objectives openly and therefore must operate in secret. He must grow organizationally to succeed or he would be defeated by the very chaos he works to build. To grow in secret and organizationally the obvious tool is a secret society.

Satan's network of secret societies exists much like a fishing net with more groups than he would ever need. The key is that they all share the same goals and objectives, even if only to an extent. They are individual but connected by their cause. If one is exposed it is sacrificed and abandoned to create the illusion that "the problem is solved" while the rest of the network proceeds with increased freedom because the public has been disarmed believing the threat has been overcome. They are even free to attack and destroy each other to gain strength so long as they do not expose the master plan.

Their primary vehicle is people who are not even aware of the society they serve. Vladimir Lenin coined a term "useful idiots". Having coined the term, he gave it a definition of "people educated on a matter only to the extent to which they could be emotionally manipulated". Thus useful idiots in all walks of life promote Satan's cause. They demand more government because they know only enough about a matter to be manipulated.

Examples would be, they know only enough of science to believe in global warming. Useful idiots know only enough about health care to demand a government run health care system. They know only enough about education to demand federal guidelines and controls. In this manner we have ended up with The Federal Reserve Bank and The United Nations. We also have a national government that recognizes no Constitutional limits and now seeks to intrude into the daily lives of our citizens in employment, communication, travel and is working hard to control the rest of our affairs. All because one special interest group or another has been molded to demand action.

This all originates and is controlled from behind the scenes but the useful idiots are quite thrilled to deny this fact and take credit for launching a movement or creating some national debate. They do not stop to reflect that these movements and debates all center on creating more government. No movement to limit government ever achieves significant success. They do not question where their financing is coming from or why those promoting the opposing side to the issue lack funding or why they're given favorable treatment and promotion in the major media or have the ability to grow and organize with such speed. They just attribute it all to personal charisma and brilliance. The secret societies are content with this since it permits them the hiding place they need to promote their agenda.

Disinformation is a primary component of any secret society. Rather than deny their own existence, they frequently promote it but under some deception of purpose. They employ the strategy of planting false information about themselves to create confusion. Strategically they occasionally reveal some truth for the purpose of desensitizing the public to their agenda. There are those, however, who have been a party to these organizations and have come forward to reveal the true threat and there are excellent researchers who have spent a lifetime ferreting out information that was intended to be concealed. The truth is frequently revealed but does them no harm without action by concerned people.

The point to all of this is that these secret societies have a plan to sell a different Jesus to the masses. Their Jesus is an enlightened master who advanced through their teachings and taught their message but has had his teaching corrupted by "organized religion" and deified aside from his wishes. The Biblical Jesus is the most mocked and ridiculed person in history. This is but a preliminary step to destroy any truth regarding Jesus or His teachings and create the illusion that those who stubbornly cling to "old fashioned" ideas and concepts are small minded fools. Those with such beliefs are victims of organized religion and need help.

Once Jesus, and those who believe in The Biblical Jesus, is discredited the road forward is prepared since opposition has been neutralized. The next step would be to introduce Jesus "as he really was". One tactic toward this agenda is the Gnostic gospels and another could easily be The Dead Sea Scrolls. Debates already rage over how much and how many of the scrolls have been released.

Then there is the question of accuracy in their interpretation. It should not escape notice that the scrolls were purchased for The Rockefeller Museum in Jerusalem (now The Israel Museum) and have carefully been guarded since their discovery.[116] No one examines them without special permission. These people are carefully screened and it is reasonable to question if they are screened to determine if they hold "old fashioned" values or are interested in "the historical significance" of the scrolls. Very few people have been afforded the ability to examine them first hand. There are no security measures in place to determine if the scrolls examined are legitimately of the original Dead Sea findings or counterfeits. Clearly there is an agenda here that transcends historical research or "protecting the sacred documents from further deterioration".

Why else would a single entity desire to own and control them all? What interest has the Rockefeller family ever shown in Biblical truth or discovery? To date no information released is controversial against The Bible but some scholars argue that a very small percentage of the scrolls have been examined to any extent.

It would be a small matter to approach an ignorant, manipulated world and convince them that "as more scrolls were examined new information was learned". This is my theory on The Knights Templar, although I confess I can't prove it. Consider them for a moment. No one believes the exoteric story that nine men were sent to Jerusalem to guard the three major roads and protect Christian's traveling to Jerusalem. The first layer esoteric story is often accepted as more probable; that they were sent there to find treasure in the Temple of Solomon. I find this equally ridiculous. Sacking and robbing temples is something the Romans had down to a science. They would not have left treasure behind and this was well known.

This brings us to the second layer esoteric story; that they went there to find holy relics with which to blackmail The Catholic Church. The problem with this story, for Christians who take the Bible literally, is that there would be no holy relics in The Jewish Temple that would intimidate the church. Many accept this story as valid since it accounts for the success of The Knights Templar and explains why The Catholic Church tolerated them.

Yet another version of the story goes that the Knights were on a mission to find occult writings believed to be in the temple. These were to disclose deep hidden mysteries of occult power and ceremonies in which tremendous knowledge would be imparted from demonic sources. We are not told why a search for them in the Jewish Temple would be a productive venture or why Rome would have left them behind. To date, major discoveries of this sort are found in Egypt and Babylon so this story too is suspect.

Let's examine the facts from my cynical but Biblically committed perspective. Hugues de Payens, revered for his work in the first crusade, was cousin and vassal to the Comte de Champayne, a very wealthy landowner. It is argued whether all nine of the Knights worked for Champayne but he did fund them and organized them under his cousin Hugues. Now if we consider the wealth of Champayne we can question why, of the hundreds of employees he had, he sent only nine to guard the roads if such were his intent. Similarly, when manpower is abundant, one does not send a mere nine men on a treasure hunt when hundreds are available.

One does, however, limit the manpower to as few as possible when one proposes to perpetuate a fraud. I do not believe these nine men were sent to Jerusalem to guard anything. Nor do I believe they were sent to find anything. I believe they were sent there to fabricate something! I believe these nine men were scribes with historic and Biblical knowledge sufficient to draft writings in Jerusalem that they could later claim were "discovered". I believe it is these writings that are known as the "Gnostic gospels" today.

We are told that these Gnostic gospels date back to the time of Christ but how do we know that for a certainty? We are told they were written by Peter, Mary and Thomas but what can account for such a contrast in these writings verses the known gospels? This argument is answered by blaming the church for selectively choosing writings that promoted that which it wanted to promote but this argument does not address the question of how there could be such disparity in the first place. All of these mentioned walked with Jesus and heard Him first hand.

Equally important, if this fraud is attempted on the church once, why would it not be attempted again through the Dead Sea Scrolls? The message could come forth that new discoveries in The Dead Sea Scrolls substantiates information in the Gnostic gospels and scores of people would fall victim to this insidious lie. The charge has already been made that The Vatican had the scrolls suppressed fearing the scrolls would damage Christianity. If disingenuous leaders at The Vatican came forward and "apologized" for this deception millions would instantly be converted to a new set of beliefs since they have no foundation in scripture and no personal relationship with God. The irony is that scores of people would continue to trust those who then confessed to being involved in a massive deception.

This is not simple speculation. There are those in the Muslim community and the Jewish community who are violently opposed to any reference no matter how small of Jesus being The Messiah or Son of God. Already many fundamentalist Christians have embraced the teaching that Jesus was an Essene. The problem with this, aside from the fact that this labels Jesus in a way scripture does not, is that not much is known of the Essenes. Toward this end, the more we learn of the Essenes, the more we (supposedly) learn of Jesus.

We should question Jesus being an Essene because the Essenes taught scripture in an allegorical manner, were highly legalistic, did not join in temple sacrifices and they washed frequently for "ceremonial purity" which Jesus denounced. While they may not have worshipped the sun, they held it in such high regard that other Jewish sects were offended by their beliefs. It is highly unlikely that any of this could be said of Jesus.[117]

Essenes have much in common with Gnostics including a reverence for secret (or revealed) knowledge, a belief in magic as well as a communistic belief that all property should be held in common.[118]

We should question why the Essenes have received so much attention recently. This is curious because the Essenes were a small Jewish sect at best and very little consideration was afforded them previously. Someone has a purpose in reviving this small, inconsequential sect from the pages of dead history and they are using Jesus for credibility without evidence.

Then there is what may appear as the more ridiculous possibility, that of UFO's. Most Christians would hastily reject any UFO talk and this would create a mighty opportunity for the new world order to formulate tools without close scrutiny. I, personally, am quick to reject information concerning being from other planets, however we should keep in mind that brilliant physicist Nikola Tesla gave lectures to electrical engineers as early as 1891 regarding basic power and lift energies that could be used for flight. His preferred design was "saucer" shape.[119] Even if his efforts failed in application this would explain where the idea of a flying saucer came from in the first place.

In the end, it's a question of what ideas are truly ridiculous verses what are possible through science that is information not yet made available to the public at large. A great many discoveries in many areas are held in silence. Famed Christian author C.S. Lewis wrote (fictitiously) of beings from other planets in the 1940's and 1950's, which was long before this topic was mainstream. From his writings as well as many from the new world order we are introduced to the concept that man was planted on Earth by beings from another planet.

These "enlightened" beings seek to help mankind "evolve" to the place where we can embrace their technology responsibly. Lewis used his talents for writing science fiction to warn Christians that demonic beings can be introduced to humans as "extraterrestrials".[120]

We know that top-secret spy planes with previously unknown speeds and maneuvering capabilities have been tested in the Nevada desert. Many who witnessed these flights assumed they could be interplanetary simply because they had never seen the technology before and didn't believe man was capable of it.

This served the governments purposes as all information from these sources was dismissed as foolishness. We have no way of knowing how far technology has been developed and tested.

Then too we must remember "The Report From Iron Mountain". This was a study done by the new world order in 1964 - 1967 to address a single question. Until this time, war had been the primary threat used strategically in manipulating the public. The threat of war enticed fearful people to give up freedoms and tolerate incredible government growth in the name of security.

The need addressed at Iron Mountain was to determine a "replacement threat" as effective as war since war could not be used to build a "global brotherhood of man". Several options were agreed upon and one of them was to fabricate a threat about beings from another planet. The option used most heavily was the threat of universal environmental calamity but others have been used to lesser degrees.[121]

Beings from another planet don't have to be a threat, necessarily, but a cause that would unite mankind.

Hypothetically, if information was "discovered" in The Dead Sea Scrolls that Jesus was an enlightened master from another universe and The Scrolls were "sealed up" until the time when mankind was better suited to receive this information and the time had come, we see a lie that would serve the new world order quite nicely!

Already we have seen bogus predictions attributed to The Scrolls that a spaceship will land with being from another universe and meet with lawmakers. The Scrolls also predict (supposedly) that Elvis's grave will be found empty and cell phone technology will permit calls between the living and the dead. When no one is permitted to authenticate your work you can afford to be creative!

2nd Thessalonians 2:11 says, "For this cause God shall send them strong delusion, that they should believe a lie". 2nd Thessalonians 2:3 says "that day shall not come except there come a great falling away first …" Mark 13:22 says "false christs and false prophets shall rise and shall shew signs and wonders to seduce, if it were possible, even the elect".

Then there is the fact that sects of Judaism have taught the idea of two Messiahs. This would be the one of Isaiah 53 and a belief held by some that the Messiah would live forever. This teaching is exclusive of any death or resurrection.

The Jesus of The Bible is no part of this new world order and those who hold a belief in Jesus and The Bible will not embrace the lies seeded by this agenda. Something has to be done to neutralize Jesus and break the commitment that so many have on Him and His word. The work of getting people to trust government instead of God is largely complete. The work that remains is dealing with those few who still cling to the teachings of the past.

Much will be accomplished with persecution. Many who have a shallow faith and believe God would never allow them to suffer in such a way will have their faith tested and many are sure to fail. Many have placed their hopes on successful authors who have grown rich with the message that we will be raptured out of here before things get too bad. If this fails to occur according to what they've been taught, large numbers of them will be easily influenced into questioning all of their beliefs and considering some previously unknown "truths".

One thing we can agree on is that Satan will continue to lie about Jesus and the only defense is firm knowledge of The Word (not just prophecy) and a strong relationship with Him. Paul said in Galatians 1:8 "If an angel from heaven (this would include a being from another planet) preach any other gospel ..."

Satan can mount no lie that will overcome the truth to those who are ready for him. Gnosticism is too strongly linked with the current agenda to be abandoned now. It is predictable that Jesus will be reintroduced as an enlightened teacher. It is predictable that new writings will be "discovered" revealing Jesus never claimed to be God and when He defined Himself as "The Son of God" it was in a context referring to himself as part of the "global christ consciousness" where all men are brothers and sons of god when they submit to global needs and serve where and how they are told. His message will be that we should all bow down and submit to the self-ordained global elite.

Jesus will be neutralized because new teachers, carrying a message into our day contrary to the actual teachings of Jesus, will have "documentation and "facts" capable of great deception. Matthew 24:24 "there shall arise false Christs and false prophets and shall shew great signs and wonders ... if it were possible they shall deceive the very elect." Those who lack knowledge will be fooled.

I refer to those who are ignorant of how government leaders lie. I refer to those who are ignorant of how Satan has raised up so-called religious leaders who lie but are highly revered by many Christians today. Here I am NOT talking about some television evangelist who shamelessly begs for money or promises ridiculous returns on a small donation. I am talking about revered LEADERS!

Those who trust a political party, politicians or high profile religious leaders will simply continue to trust them and be led into destruction. Those who have been seduced into believing they will be raptured before they are seriously persecuted will be shocked to their core and confused, to say the least! Many will buy the lies of the religious leaders and these lies must be pondered. These lies will require a complete break with Biblical Christianity and the argument that there was no rapture could easily be used to create the belief that the entire Bible has been taught wrongly over the years.

Even now many refuse to consider that this is a false teaching planted by the new world order to neutralize the church. Many just cling to the few scriptures they have been taught on this subject and reject all other arguments. We know that millions will buy this lie because millions are buying it.

This has been the "secret mystery" of the secret societies for a millennium or more and there is no reason to suspect they will attempt a new lie now, after cementing this one for so many generations. But their plan is much more involved than that. Now we must look behind the curtain and view the mechanics of this incredible deception that has afforded them structure and illicit power to build their evil empire.

OVERWHELMING DECEPTION

Romans 1:25 "Who changed the truth of God into a lie
and worshiped the creature ... "

There is a belief among propagandists that the more outrageous the lie, the more mileage you can achieve from it. This seems to be centered in the benefit liars have from the tendency of people to dismiss outrageous lies without consideration. Hence, they can accomplish much more by being bold than by being subtle. There are constants among the promoters of the new world order and tenacity is a chief characteristic to be found in those they would recruit.

I do not refer to one who is caught conclusively in an embarrassing lie but yet can face the camera and make his excuses convincingly. Such people as these are simply accomplished liars. No, I am referring to those who can face the cameras and "sell" the most outrageous and evil plans that that Satan can devise. Sell them to such an extent the people demand these plans be brought into fruition.

Consider the lies of this scale that have been successfully sold to the American people and are deeply entrenched in our culture today. Among these lies would be America's armed forces being used as a global police force. We have soldiers permanently stationed in over eighty countries. We no longer question if there is any patriotic purpose in this. We do not ask if America has so many enemies to require this or if we do, why? What is it about our foreign policy that causes the world to hate us requiring this presence? We accept lies of phantom enemies and words like "preparedness" but our country was not set up allowing for this and now this change is accepted without question.

Another example would be the so-called oil (or energy) shortage. Scores of reliable sources have documented that we face no oil shortage and people ask no questions about why private companies are forbidden by law to harvest oil from massive deposits if such a shortage were factual.

Yet one more example would be The United Nations. Few people give this organization serious consideration since they regard it as some anemic debating society in New York but they fail to understand that through its subsidiary organizations such as UNESCO, WHO and The World Trade Organization The UN has achieved a tremendous influence upon our society.

These organizations are little known and little understood by the average American but they suffer under their agenda, never the less. These organizations were "sold" to Congress by very accomplished liars and the lie was always how beneficial these organizations would be to mankind.

These liars convinced The Congress and the American people to embrace a good many other organizations that would work to destroy our independence, freedom and Godliness as a nation. The lie was always how these organizations would "serve" the public but with each there was a hidden agenda.

Those unfamiliar with The Federal Reserve Bank are missing out on a fantastic lie that is a major power source for the new world order. The public purpose of The Federal Reserve Bank is to manage the nation's money supply and process checks. The hidden purpose is for the new world order to create money out of nothing that they can use in their diabolical schemes.

Most people fail to realize that The Department of Motor Vehicles has become a national identification bureau responsible to identify and maintain records of all people including those in this country illegally. Christians who feel passionate about never carrying an I.D. Card have been carrying one for years! If you don't believe that, and perhaps have a friend who's a police officer, ask him where the police go first to get a photo I.D. of a suspect whom they do not have in their own files. With the photo comes an address plus additional information the DMV has been tasked to collect. This would include social security number, previous address, next of kin, age, birth date, etc.

The public purpose of education is teaching children to read, write and the basics of mathematics and sciences. The hidden purpose is to make new generations completely dependent and reliant on government for basic needs and protection. Significant here is the open teaching of sexual conduct that would have brought imprisonment to the instructors a generation ago. Education as we know it includes the teaching of evolution, global warming, socialism, globalism, immorality and even Satanism if one knows what, specifically, to look for.

This is true with every agency. Where a public purpose is cited, a hidden purpose is served. These are all major deceptions and indicators of a much larger system that has grown up and exists unknown before us but we do not notice and we do not recognize the old system is gone.

These deceptions did not come into being with a single effort. They were part of a grand strategy that took years of effort and long repetitive battles that ultimately overcame temporary defeats. All of these institutions are very much a part of our society today and there is small effort to remove any one among them. The vast majority of society believes they are essential and serve the greater good.

What shall we say about the church? Who can believe it remains unchanged when Satan and his minions have so cleverly seated themselves in the leadership of so many of our other organizations. It may offend many to say it but the current purpose of the church is to provide "a form of Godliness while denying the power there of" 2nd Timothy 3:5.

Our churches no longer weep for the lost and commit themselves to disciple new converts into spiritual depths and relationship with God that would cause the rest of humanity to covet that which we have. Our churches are about fellowship with each other, entertainment and God is simply to be there in the background, not changing lives but so we don't feel guilty.

Even the purpose of our government has changed. Where once it existed to protect lives and property it now exists to serve Satan and usher in total global obedience to him. All other institutions are subsidiary to government now and all other purposes must conform to government purposes.

We must now address the issue of what exactly must be "conformed" to. It is no longer The Constitution of The United States. It is no longer the will of the people. It is a wholly new agenda that serves the few. All agencies must now submit and conform to the satanic lie that enables Satan to achieve his long sought after goal of control of the government.

Noted in the Foreword to Senate Report 93-549, dated 1973 are the following.

The quoted is an official U.S. Government document:

"Since March 9, 1933 The United States has been in a state of declared national emergency. In fact, there are now in effect four presidentially proclaimed states of national emergency: In addition to the national emergency declared by President Franklin D. Roosevelt in 1933, there are also the national emergency proclaimed by President Harry S. Truman on December 16, 1950, during the Korean conflict, and the states of national emergency declared by President Richard M. Nixon on March 23, 1970, and August 15, 1971.

These proclamations give force to *470 provisions* of Federal law. These hundreds of statutes *delegate to the President extraordinary powers, ordinarily exercised by the Congress*, which affect the lives of American citizens in a host of all-encompassing manners. (Italics mine)

This vast range of powers, taken together, confer enough authority to rule the country without reference to normal Constitutional processes.

Under the powers delegated by these statutes, the President may: seize property; organize and control the means of production; seize commodities; assign military forces abroad; institute martial law; seize and control all transportation and communication; regulate the operation of private enterprise; restrict travel; and, in a plethora of particular ways, control the lives of all American citizens.[122]

(end quote)

Congress did pass a new law regarding The President's future ability to declare national emergencies but they did not revoke the four mentioned.[123] What, then, can we say about a Congress that recognizes (and documents) the above but takes no action to resolve the situation. At best they are worthless and to put things in the worst perspective, they are servants of evil. This is no casual comment. A trap was set for them and through the motivations of greed and power they were ensnared. At the base level the enemy is Satan. It is true, however, that Satan has raised up a network of international investment bankers who are sold out to his service and we can rightly point to them. They respect no nationality, religion or human rights. They are completely self serving.

Stock in these banks make it possible for control to stay with a small number of families. The agenda of these family controled banks make their interests global. These bankers used their fraudulent system to create money out of paper (really out of nothing) and used the ignorance of politicians (and the public) to finance explosive government growth and ultimately indebt the nation to bankruptcy.

Currently, paper is no longer necessary and money is created by a simple electronic entry. With the governments of the world heavily in debt but completely addicted to money, they administer as much influence behind the scenes as needed to amass power unto themselves.

Some politicians were corrupt and welcomed this treachery for their own purposes, others were afraid of what would happen to them if the public learned the truth. There was no official declaration of bankruptcy. Rather an interesting and knew term was coined: "National Security". It was determined that national security would be the determining factor in what the public was permitted to know about their nations business. Then as now "national security" was most frequently an issue of political treachery which must be kept from the people rather than a matter having to do with any viable threats from any enemy to the country.

Again we can read from The Congressional Record dated March 17, 1993 Vol. 33, page H-1303 the following comments by Representative Traficant, Jr.

"Mr. Speaker, we are here now in chapter 11. Members of Congress are official trustees presiding over the greatest reorganization of any bankrupt entity in world history, the U.S. government. We are setting forth hopefully, a blueprint for our future. There are some who say it is a coroner's report that will lead to our demise.

It is an established fact that the United States Federal Government has been dissolved by the Emergency Banking Act, March 9, 1933, 48 Stat. 1, Public Law 89-719; declared by President Roosevelt, being bankrupt and insolvent. H.J.R. 192, 73rd Congressional session, June 5, 1933 - Joint Resolution To Suspend the Gold Standard and Abrogate The Gold Clause dissolved the Sovereign Authority of the United States and the official capacities of all United States Governmental Offices, Officers, and Departments and is further evidence that the United States Federal Government exists today in name only.

The receivers of the United States Bankruptcy are the International Bankers, via the United Nations, the World Bank and the International Monetary Fund. All United States Offices, Officials, and Departments are now operating within a de facto status in name only under Emergency War Powers. With the Constitutional Republican form of Government now dissolved, the receivers of the Bankruptcy have adopted a new form of government for the United States".[124]

This is a very controversial statement and it arguable cost Congressman Traficant his career and seven years in prison. In 2002 Congressman Traficant was indicted on federal charges. During an Ethics Committee hearing, the possibility that the Congressman was being framed was certainly raised sufficiently to justify an investigation. This much was acknowledged by Congressman Strickland of Ohio but no investigation came. On July 24th Congressman Traficant was expelled from Congress. After his conviction, the trial judge refused to set bail and permit the Congressman to exercise the normal appeals process. He was ordered to begin serving his sentence immediately.[125]

He has constantly insisted he was not guilty of the crimes with which he was charged and refused early release. Many will be quick to recognize this is a familiar statement of felons, however this Congressman had a clean record, had won nine elections, had previously worked as a county sheriff, had a very strong pro-family and anti-abortion voting record and had a history of opposing and exposing unconstitutional legislation. The political power brokers came down hard on him for something that (if he was guilty at all) is too commonly done by members of Congress and only selectively prosecuted!

So here, then, is the situation where we currently find ourselves. The government granted monopoly status to private investment firms to print, distribute, charge an arbitrary interest on and manage the credit of the currency of The United States. Yes, they must have consent of Congress to raise the national debt ceiling but this is no hindrance when you control the Congress.

Still, the fact remains that private investment firms own roughly fifty-two percent of The Federal Reserve Bank and since they're private no one knows who owns them. It's not believed that they are American but they certainly have no loyalty to any country or its citizens. Since Congress has never been permitted to audit The Federal Reserve all information about exactly who owns controlling interest is largely speculative. Certain names keep reappearing but the actual owners permit no incontrovertible documentation to be made available and Congress has consistently been prohibited from asking too many questions.

This private financial firm then lent and distributed sufficient money so as to create a debt beyond what the government was (theoretically) able to repay when payment was demanded and subsequently put themselves in the position of lenders being masters of the borrowers. The next step following this arrangement was to make self-serving and treasonous demands upon disingenuous politicians. Many of these key politicians had long been in their pocket and on their payroll so their demands were met.[126]

The specific demands of these bankers were formalized on March 9, 1933. This agreement transferred the wealth of the nation to these bankers in exchange for absolution of the debt. It was further agreed that the labor of all citizens would henceforth be licensed and taxed for the sole benefit of the nations creditors.[127]

If all of this sounds rather ominous, please keep in mind the point stressed in the introduction to part 6 of this book. This is all deception. As covered in the previous chapters on "authority", there is simply no authority on the part of our elected leaders or government to enter into any such agreement. There is no authority to enter into any agreement privatizing the nations money supply and there certainly is no authority to ascribe the nation's labor force to a private entity!

Our Constitution and system of government is one in which the sole powers of the federal government are defined and declared by the states. The power to declare us bankrupt and the citizens subjects of the bankers was never sought or granted and was, therefore, exercised illegally. This means, by the organized effort of an informed electorate, we can reclaim what is ours. Without an organized and well-informed electorate, the problems continue.

It is true that the various states accepted these monies without giving the matter proper contemplation, however ignorance and greed (bad though they be) are not license to enslave the entire people of this nation. Often we find our situation exacerbated by state politicians who are intimidated by demands of the federal government. When one among them learns of this duplicity and seeks to resolve the matter they are told, to be removed from the current system can only be accomplished by the repayment of sums of money they do not have. This is the sum they have "borrowed" over the years. Here we see the federal government functioning as an enforcement agent for the international bankers.

To keep the wheels of government turning smoothly, The Constitution of The United States was quietly ignored and a new document was adopted as the law of the land. Its called "The United States Code". This is a collective listing of all federal laws but any connection to these laws and The Constitution is flimsy at best. The reader will recall that today one frequently hears the rule of law quoted as "Title Nine, Title ten" or whatever section of the U.S.C. that is applicable.[128] The emphasis in court is no longer The Constitution, it's the Code.

The U.S.C. works in conjunction with another document called "The Uniform Commercial Code" (U.C.C.) which was first published as guidelines for businesses in 1952 but has since been adopted by all fifty states with small revision.[129] We increasingly see The U.C.C. cited in building regulations, highway development and other infrastructure. Let us not forget that we commonly see the U.C.C. cited in safety regulations as well. All laws are being standardized and being brought into compliance with international agreements and enforced by such international organizations as The WTO. Such treachery requires tools of deception, of course. Certain members of Congress may accept this change with acquiescence but many more would take some level of offense at The Constitution being abandoned.

The legitimacy of this fraud was sold to Congress by citing Article 1, Section 8, Clause 17 of The Constitution. Here the argument is made that a separate nation exists inside the borders of our country. They determined this separate nation was a "Legislative Democracy" named "The United States" inside the borders of our Constitutional Republic named "The United States of America".[130]

Skeptics will agree that this is a rather shallow and obviously self-serving lie but there are ways to deal with dissenters. The purpose here is to establish a structure around which a new system could be constructed.

This Clause reads "To exercise exclusive legislation in all cases whatsoever over such district (not exceeding ten miles square) as may, by cession of particular States and the acceptance of Congress, become the seat of the Government of the United States and to exercise like authority over all places purchased by the consent of the legislature of the State in which the same shall be, for the erection of forts, magazines, arsenals, dock-yards and other needful buildings".

Our founding fathers had nothing to fear in this paragraph. It seems rather basic and its purpose well outlined. It does, however, afford (to the criminally motivated) the opportunity to build on some select wording. "To *exercise exclusive legislation* in all cases and to *exercise like authority* over all places *purchased* by the consent of the legislature of the State". What constitutes a "purchase"? That is a matter for the courts to decide. The point here is not so much about a transparent abuse of power as it is in exposing the blatant dishonesty upon which our current system is built.

Even though he had declared the federal government bankrupt, in 1933 F.D.R took our nation on a spending spree that overwhelms the mind! Our national debt in 1932 was $19.5 billion. In 1936 it had grown to $33.8 billion. Clearly these bankers are not concerned with the repayment of debt! The sums of money they currently have at their disposal is far beyond any conceivable need. It is power and control that they seek and financing government spending is simply the vehicle of obtaining control.

Many misinformed American's believe this money was spent wisely to assist the unemployed during the depression. In point of fact, government policies did much to exacerbate the unemployment situation, hurt farmers across the board and raised food prices at a time when scores of people hand no income.[131]

With The Federal Reserve Act of 1913 independent banks, and equally important state banks, were forced to use Federal Reserve Notes. The economic panic put state, counties and cities in a desperate financial calamity. With the various states facing substantial chaos due to high numbers of unemployment and no ability to meet the demands of the public, the new world order was able to step in (through elected government officials) and offer a welcome solution to all problems and seemingly help the public at the same time. Their solution was to provide "Federal Reserve Notes" to the states and honor them as money in exchange for the states agreeing to accept their portion of debt owed by the federal government. The states received the benefit of operating capital and the stockholders in the Federal Reserve Bank received the benefit of repayment (or the promise to repay) the national debt.

The states were now as obligated under the new system as was the federal government. With the federal government enforcing the agreement, it then becomes their duty to act as a Board of Directors of the nation or a Legislative Democracy. They then must exercise a primary concern toward their stockholder's (employers/ bankers) interests and no longer prioritize the public interest.

The bankers then quietly, patiently and covertly set forth their demands and gave our elected leaders instructions on what types of legislation they wanted implemented to bring their new world order into existence. Again, it was not repayment they coveted. The secret purpose of this system would be to create new regulations permitting the control of the people in each state. The objectives were:

1) Tax the public at a rate needed to keep them from amassing great wealth and maintain credit policies to constantly keep them in debt

2) Control the public conduct so as to eliminate opposition to the banker's agenda

3) Control national money policies. This is not limited to but includes

   A) Creating wars to, among other reasons, increase the national debt

   B) Create massive government programs

4) Promote certain attitudes in human behavior such as but not limited to:

   A) Create tolerant attitudes toward criminal activity (prison reform, reduced sentences for violent crimes, dismissing cases on technicalities, etc) so as to generate a need for a larger police presence which will ultimately be used to enforce state interests against the public

   B) Promote all strategies to keep the people divided among themselves

   C) Promote all strategies to make the people dependent on the system

   D) Promote all strategies to encourage base behavior and immorality

5) Promote all strategies to disarm the public so that they are defenseless at the point in time when deception is no longer possible in advancing control

6) Create a system of identification for each person (initially Social Security Numbers) and advanced tracking mechanisms added when available to monitor each individual's education, employment, taxes, debt and location so that their earning potential can be determined and subsequently weighed against the cost of their maintenance. This information can also be

maintained for assessing attitudes toward the system and/or their threat potential to the same

7) Regulate the public's ability to buy, hunt, fish, sell, hold gainful employment, operate a business, travel, produce, distribute and consume goods and services through the requirement of licensing

8) Sufficiently control the media so as to keep the public ignorant of this agenda while promoting its overt elements as beneficial to the masses

9) Control the courts and members of the legal profession sufficiently to stifle all serious opposition to the system

10) Control the political processes (parties, elections and serious candidates) to eliminate any potential opposition

11) Control the educational structure so that future generations will not be made aware of the change in systems or the loss of freedom

12) Promote all strategies to obtain control of all property, utilities and transportation

The reader will recognize that all of this has been raised up right under our notice and has shifted us away from the freedoms exercised and enjoyed by previous generations. All of these mechanisms have been instituted through a deceptive promise of being beneficial to the public safety.

The Supreme Court, and all subsidiary courts, no longer consider a matter on its Constitutional merits but rather on its relative impact on public policy, or more accurately stated, the new world order agenda. No longer do we have checks and balances in government but a system where government passes self-serving laws, provides for their own enforcement and leaves the private citizen no recourse against abuse.

A clear example of this is The Internal Revenue Code. No longer do we have a free people with a government at their service to protect lives and property. With The IRC we have the government creating regulations to restrict the behavior of an individual citizen – something previous generations couldn't conceive would happen in this country. In the event the citizen is charged with violation(s) it is he/she with the burden of proof regarding their innocents. This alone is a staggering change in our country and one that we have simply come to accept.

None of this would be possible without a substantial amount of duplicity and corruption on the part of our countries political leaders. Neither would it have been possible if we were permitted an opposition party to vote for, a real one and not just one who lied to get votes. To be fair we must recognize that many politicians of some degree of integrity are frustrated by the system too. The dilemma in which they find themselves stems from the fact that the public is so grossly ignorant of sound government and economic policies that they continue to vote for the candidate who makes promises that can't possibly be kept.

You may recall a wry line, "America's elections are rapidly becoming public auctions of future stolen merchandise". This is the battle they must fight to win an election but once they have achieved that victory they find themselves confronted by an even greater barrier to fulfilling their patriotic ambitions; the battle they must fight with their party leadership.

Here they are briefed on some very cruel realities. They are told what it takes to survive in Washington. The party leadership has their role to play in the system and it is largely to insure that all newly elected officials stay in line and pose no threat. Any ambitious Congressman who threatens the system must be neutralized by whatever means necessary; personal bribery, bribery to his constituents, enticed into some sexual misconduct, destroyed in the media, massive funding of a political opponent, etc.

On the vast majority of issues the new world order couldn't care less how any single Congressman votes. Furthermore, if a Congressman is ideologically conservative he is free to vote conservatively on the vast majority of bills. They simply do not progress that rapidly that they need to be concerned with more than a handful of bills in each Congress. If a vote they have prioritized is on the floor and they are certain of their desires being achieved they still find themselves with no need to interfere with any Congressman's personal decision. In all these cases any Congressman is free to vote how he chooses.

On a close vote that the new world order has prioritized, it is quite a different matter. On occasion even the most conservative

Congressmen can be seen supporting a globalist piece of legislation, when all who observe recognize they could have defeated it by withholding their support. There is a rare exception to this, when there is such a massive public awareness and outcry on a piece of legislation that even Congress listens and the new world order deems it preferable to back away rather than create an irate electorate. Without this massive public involvement even the most patriotic Congressmen are forced into the role of "lackey" for the party bosses when they need every vote on an important bill.

If one makes an enemy of the party bosses you will not receive party money for your reelection campaign, they may choose to run someone against you, you will not get appointments to the significant committees nor will the party assist you with any legislation you draft, all which are factors hurting your chances of reelection. This is a difficult reality for the average American to grasp.

We put trust in a political party and the candidates from that party and are slow to consider that trust is not deserved or well placed. We like what we hear and find it difficult to believe that anyone could successfully mislead the public on such a large scale. We grasp at small evidence to use as proof that our continued support is justified.

Perhaps most self-destructive in all of this is our willingness to accept the platitudes and arguments that keep us on our current course. These range from any idea that supporting a third party "is throwing our vote away" to voting for "the lesser of two evils". What could possibly be a greater waste of our vote than to give it to someone who will support treason, either by ambition or acquiescence, when elected? Then there is the question of how anyone of any moral standard can so tolerantly support evil in government for such an extended period of time while confronted with overwhelming evidence that it is destroying our nation. We have become extraordinarily easy to manipulate.

It is indeed manipulation. We are managed and controlled artfully by masterful and insidious means. Our covert, artful and masterful manipulators are the new world order and they have been revealed. Many significant proofs of their existence and agenda have been revealed and numbered among them is the book by Professor Carroll Quigley. President Clinton honored Professor Quigley as being one of the most influential people in his life while he was a student at

Georgetown University. Professor Quigley is also widely known as the author of a book entitled "Tragedy and Hope". It is in this book that he tells us "I know of the operation of this network because I have studied it for twenty years and was permitted for two years ... to examine its papers and secret records." It is in this work that Professor Quigley reveals many of the strategies and tactics of this global network of bankers who do indeed work to control governments by establishing control over their political mechanisms.

Mr. Quigley writes "The two parties should be almost identical, so that the American people can 'throw the rascals out' at any election without leading to any profound or extensive shifts in policy".[132]

It is this network, known as the new world order, that has corrupted our political systems and put America on its current course to collapse. This collapse, too, is part of the plan. It is not accidental or an inevitable by-product. Professor Quigley tells us their ultimate plan is to rule the world in a "feudalist fashion" where they are the royalty and all other survivors are servant serfs. The aspect Professor Quigley does not address is a spiritual one. Perhaps he was not aware of it or perhaps he chose to keep it hidden but it is very real. These people are evil and they serve an evil master.

Evil, as any mechanism, must have a vehicle in which to travel if it plans to grow organizationally. The current vehicle that serves its purposes best is the illusion of democracy. Democracy does not threaten those who are already secretly in control of the major centers of influence such as mediums of communication, all practical political parties and all significant financing.

Russian revolutionist Vladimir Lenin once said, "Democracy is indispensable to socialism". He also said, "It is impossible to have a revolution without a revolutionary situation" and "freedom is precious, so precious it must be rationed".

Another quote attributed to Lenin comes from a journalist who knew "Marxism/ Leninism" for what it is; that is to say a "revolutionary" system and not a governmental system. Marxism may be used to destroy a nation but it does not necessarily reveal how the nation would be governed after its destruction. When this intrepid journalist persisted in his question of "how will you rule?" he finally got Lenin to respond.

Through pierced lips the undaunted Lenis replied, "We shall rule by terror".

Explaining this point is, perhaps, best done by a former Black Panther who had suffered for many years in Castro's prison system. Tony Bryant had hijacked an airplane to Havana but made the mistake of robbing the passengers in route. Expecting a hero's welcome upon his arrival in Havana, he was surprised to find himself unceremoniously arrested. One of his robbery victims was a well-connected Cuban.

He spent years in a Cuban prison but was released in 1980 and deported back to The U.S. He went on speaking tour telling of his experience and one issue he stressed was the relentless abuse and seemingly senseless terrorizing of the prisoners. He spoke much about the horrific conditions and his amazement at the high number of prisons per capita and how easily any Cuban citizen could be arrested and find them self with a lengthy prison term. He revealed a great deal about merciless beatings and psychological torment such as mock executions, which were frightening due to the high volume of actual executions. There was simply no way to know if you would live or die.

From all of this he learned what "the system" wanted him to understand and best describes the comment by Lenin. He said *the purpose behind all of this was to break each prisoner mentally and spiritually to such an extent that, if released, they could never again muster the courage to challenge authority.*[133]

Here is the meaning of real terror. To know that there are so many laws and regulations that on any given day you are guilty of any number of violations by simply trying to make a living and support your family. To know that the state has become so powerful that you can be detained and abused at any time for any reason with no accountability; to know that you and your government are enemies simply because you desire to live free while others are determined to enslave you, to know that this is the legacy you have left your children, to know that we here in America have abandoned such a Godly society and let this happen.

We have paid a high price for not being involved in politics but a bill is coming due that we must pay by our involvement or forever be ashamed of what we have done to our children. This chapter has revealed a plan the new world order has been using to institute their system. Simply because they have a plan does not insure our defeat. They have a plan, but they lack authority. We the people have the authority but, unfortunately, we lack the plan.

Or do we? Everything outlined in this chapter (I dare say everything accomplished by the new world order) is illegal and not binding on a free people. We can do something about it.

Author's note: In this chapter I have relied extensively on Internet sources rather than books so the reader can easily verify this information.

The Road We've Traveled

Ecclesiastes 1:11 "There is no remembrance of former things ..."

The road we have traveled, as a nation, is one of deception. It is an old road that we entered over a century ago. It is not the road upon which we first embarked as an infant nation. Perhaps it can be said that all who led us down this path were not of evil intent. It may be they were simply deceived and maliciously used by the ones they chose to trust. We cannot fault them for this; we are as guilty as any and we too are mightily deceived.

Satan lays his plans well and it should come as no surprise when any among us finds we have been seduced by one of his traps. Yet we must be faulted when we refuse to consider the truth or take action when responsibility demands it. Satan could not be considered diabolical if his strategies and plans were so transparent that all, with just a modest coaching, would discover them.

Neither do we serve God or country by becoming gullible and accepting information without demanding proof. There is a reasonable middle ground where we, as Christians, can remain faithful to God's word. We must understand total evil exists in the form of Satan and his legions that are working hard to dominate the earth and we must act responsibly as we learn about any such threat to our country and ourselves. We must use God's word as a standard of whom we trust and not rely on their rhetoric or political party affiliation.

First, however, we must be willing to consider what we have been trained to dismiss. We do society, God and ourselves a grave disservice when we refuse to acknowledge this Biblical truth by rejecting information out of hand for any reason. This has become the traditional reaction among Christians when they have been exposed to this new world order.

America can no longer pretend to be a Godly nation. Our leaders have rejected God completely and the majority of citizens have grown so complacent that they will not commit to anything. This is an important point as those who are non-committal will certainly not consider a commitment that requires sacrifice.

In this chapter we will review the success of Satan's strategy as it grew in size and strength over the years. This will again be difficult for many to believe. One truth that all of us can agree on is that America is in desperate trouble. It then becomes reasonable to ask how we got in this mess. It is difficult for anyone to readily accept that they have long been walking in deception without so much as a suspicion. It is no easier for those who have had suspicions to finally face the real truth that they have hesitated over for so long. What are needed is people willing to embrace the truth no matter how offensive but demanding proof is not unreasonable. The question is, where to start?

Arguments rage over whom among our founding fathers was a willing participant of Satan's agenda as opposed to those who were simply deceived into cooperation. Two that are strongly disputed are Alexander Hamilton and Thomas Jefferson. Evidence is very conclusive that Alexander Hamilton was an agent for the infamous Rothschild family.[134] This is a name that every Christian and patriot should be somewhat familiar with. No name on earth has been so linked with the drive for satanism and world government as this one.[135]

Yet there is reason to defend Alexander Hamilton. He was known to be a very devout Christian and proper in all his financial dealings. He was not perfect and accusations against his character can be made regarding a couple of matters but much can be revealed about a man on how he dies.

Mr. Hamilton was forced into a duel with Aaron Burr, which ultimately caused his death, yet he was such a devout Christian that he had left a letter written the previous evening stating his intention of deliberately firing away from Mr. Burr.[136]

Even devout Christians can be deceived by this satanic conspiracy. Many patriots have come to know The Federal Reserve Bank for the evil it is and consider Mr. Hamilton as one who helped birth this evil in our land. There is no justification to accuse Mr. Hamilton of being as knowledgeable concerning the Rothschild family and banking practices as we are today. We have the benefit of two centuries of history that he did not have and his plan for The First Bank of The United States could hardly be compared to The Federal Reserve Bank.

Satan and his minions do not go about their business by making the entirety of their plans and strategies known to all with whom they affiliate. They simply use people and have become exceptionally adept at manipulation. Patriots who are well educated on banking history hold Andrew Jackson as a hero for his effort in stopping Congress from renewing the charter for The Second Bank of The United States. I share their admiration for President Jackson's brave stand but we must learn that Satan will not be defeated by a piece of legislation.

A letter written by Franklin Roosevelt on November 21, 1933 states: "The real truth of the matter is, as you and I know, that a financial element in the large centers has owned the government ever since the days of Andrew Jackson".[137]

President Jackson was engaged in extreme battle with Rothschild agent and "Second Bank of The United States" President James Biddle over renewal of the bank charter. Rothschild agents were pursuing every effort to intimidate congress and the larger business community into renewing the charter. Other Rothschild agents secretly became the financial agent for the U.S. Department of State to insure no interruption to their agenda.[138]

In the end President Jackson proved successful in ending The Second Bank of The United States but he was unsuccessful at stopping the Rothschild family or Satan's agenda. Aside from banking, Andrew Jackson was involved in other issues that did much to change the course of this nation and change what our founders had instituted.

Andrew Jackson was among the first to trumpet the argument that "The Union derives its authority from the people and not the states".[139] This concept would later serve as the foundation for many arguments in The Congress by those who distained state's rights. They spoke of concern for "the people" and claimed to have their welfare in mind yet in their drive to destroy state's rights they worked to create the total supremacy of the federal government.

The arguments largely entailed the position that anything they desired to do, through the federal government, is permissible, in spite of how the various states feel about it, providing they claim their agenda is "for the good of the people".

In a previous chapter I detailed how the civil war was instrumental in altering the direction of our country away from what our founder's gave us toward the centralization of power. One of the greatest misunderstandings in our land is the belief that The United States is a democracy. America's founders unanimously hated democracy. At the convention in Philadelphia, no member present suggested such a system and many are on record speaking of its many failures.[140]

One has but to consult any encyclopedia to verify that The Unites Sates is, in fact, a Constitutional Republic. Many uninformed politicians who are confronted with this truth ignorantly state that a constitutional republic is a type of democracy. The two are complete opposites.

A democracy is simple majority rule. Whatever the majority determines is what transpires. There are no property rights or individual rights that are safe in a democracy as the majority can rule on anything. The best way to describe a democracy is "two wolves and a sheep voting on what's for dinner". Our founders knew that democracies are always unstable and essentially a transitional government because they do not last long. This fact alone will take numerous Christians by surprise but it is very easy to verify.

A republic is simply rule by law. The new world order loves republican forms of government for two reasons; once in power they make the laws and with an apathetic citizenry they can selectively enforce them. Thus we see "The Union of Soviet Socialist Republics", "The Republic of China", "The Republic of Korea", "The Republic of Cuba" and so forth.

History frequently documents the new world order destroying monarchies and creating republics. Their purpose was to amass power and once a republic had been instituted they simply went about creating laws that would help them amass more power without the inconvenience of a king, dictator or uncontrolled opposition.

Our system, a Constitutional Republic, is different. We are a nation of laws but the powers to make laws are limited. Our federal government was created by the states that had determined that a few matters were best handled by a central authority that represented their collective interests such as treaties, a currency and a military. The various states had written down precisely in what areas Congress has been delegated authority to make laws in their collective interests. This is known as our Constitution. They are prohibited under The Ninth and Tenth Amendments from making laws in areas where they have not been delegated authority to do so.

Additionally our system has checks and balances to insure that all laws are applied equally and hinder any usurpation of authority. This is our history and it is from this foundation we have strayed. From the beginning their have been politicians in the federal government working to usurp the authority of the states, desiring to create an ever more powerful federal government.

One would think the new world order loves democracy because they use the term so frequently. They love two things on this matter; the confusion generated by people thinking we are a democracy (hence we should put all things to a vote) and they love what is perhaps the greatest failure of this type of system, which is frequently called "the paradox of democracy".

Most people have neither the time nor the inclination to be involved in the day-to-day affairs of their government. Most people do not want to read legal documents on the federal level and they don't want to study maps determining where to lay a length of sewer pipe on a local level. This is one of the many important reasons we have created government, so that people who desire to focus on such matters can serve the community in this way and those among us who have no desire to focus on such matters can pursue other interests.

History has taught us that most people choose not get involved in political matters. The paradox of democracy is that the majority never rules! They are busy with their families, jobs and commitments that they have chosen to make. The only ones involved to any degree on a normal basis are the few – the minority.

So the paradox of democracy is that the organized minority always rules the unorganized majority. It has always been so and the new world order knows this. It is their strategy to bring forth a democracy and influence the involved few toward the thinking that will promote their agenda. To do this legally would require a constitutional convention and a complete restructuring of our government. They have tried this several times and failed.

Satan has never been one limited by the rule of law. His efforts continue with the strategy of "patient gradualism". The new world order knows that on any issue where the masses get upset by the proposals and get involved to stop some part of this satanic agenda, they simply need to revisit the issue again and again until the masses get tired or too busy to continue their involvement and they will finally succeed. These delays are no bother to them as they serve the purpose of helping demoralize the public to an even greater degree. Increasing numbers grow tired and frustrated that government will not respond to the will of the people.

The battle is over the will of the people verses the will of the new world order. Until we are prepared to understand the battle in its proper terms and work strategically to defeat those who are committed to systematically destroying our freedom we will continue to lose incrementally.

In 1868 the course of our nation was illegally and unofficially altered mightily from a Constitutional Republic to a Democracy. Gradually the federal government began casting off any Constitutional restraints in favor of what a chosen "minority" wanted. They increasingly began passing legislation in any arena they chose.

With the passage of The Fourteenth Amendment (which is very much in dispute) the states were restricted from any reasonable recourse. They could no longer secede, they could not prevail in the courts, their militias had been taken over by the federal government and The Fourteenth Amendment supposedly authorized all of this. Then in 1913 The Seventeenth Amendment passed so that the states no longer had an official voice at the federal level. The balance of power gradually shifted until more obvious steps could safely be made.

By the time Woodrow Wilson took office it was possible to make vast strides in pursuit of their agenda. Four Presidencies have seen these vast strides: Lincoln, Wilson, Roosevelt and George W. Bush. In each of these cases the federal government grew enormously. Is it a coincidence then, that these four time periods were the most tumultuous in our nation's history? The Civil War, World War I, World War II and The War on "Terror" (9-11 attack) were the identified threats that "required" these new powers to be assumed by the federal government. Other Presidents have their list of horrors but they have always furthered the agenda of globalism by patient gradualism.

Sometimes this was done covertly and sometimes noticeably but always under the "left/right" paradigm. Under these four the advancement of global government made huge and rapid strides. Evidence suggests that one more World War is planned and considered sufficient to reach their goals. Few are aware that Wilson was handpicked for the Presidency while still a professor at Princeton. He was elevated to President of Princeton in 1902, then to New Jersey Governor in 1911 and won election to U.S. President in 1912.[141]

The subject of President Wilson's covert and seditious efforts to draw The U.S. into World War I reveals a great deal about how the new world order operates.[142] Few are aware of the rioting and resistance to his efforts to force a military draft on the American people. It was a difficult matter to convince the people that their government could come into their homes and take their sons by force to send them half way around the world to kill or be killed. These are very important parts of our national history that are largely forgotten today.

It was President Wilson that popularized the idea that The U.S. was a Democracy and that our national interests are best served by our being involved in the politics of other countries. It was under Wilson that The Supreme Court first supported the idea that "treaties" supercede The Constitution.[143] Here is a concept of obvious duplicity. No person of intellectual honesty will argue that the states can delegate specific power to create a federal government and then the federal government can legally assume unlimited power to enter into agreements with other countries – to the detriment of the states!

The next great leaps for globalism came in 1933 when Franklin Roosevelt ushered in yet another major shift, that to fascism. This is a form of government, a type of socialism, with the important difference that under fascism people can own property and businesses. Every piece of property and trade is regulated under strict government control but people have the illusion of believing that their entitlement to "own" makes them free. That they have virtually no control goes unnoticed.

Many are aware that Roosevelt was the first (and only) President to serve more than two terms. This is more of a revelation about political power than most realize. We should touch on the fact that his extreme and un-American economic policies had generated no tangible results by the 1940 election. He had spent seven years in The White House exceeding the legitimate Constitutional powers delegated to the President in a way few had done before him.

Yet he could come to the 1940 election with nothing significant with which to impress the voters. We then have to recognize that his running for a third term was extremely unpopular with many contenders. There were many who aspired to the Presidency who opposed Roosevelt's third nomination, none of whom stepped up and actively campaigned for him after the convention.

Winning the general election was a matter he had resolved in advance through his efforts to nominate his own opposition. The idea that Wendell Wilkie won The Republican nomination is extraordinary! A democrat himself until the previous election (1938), he was a strong supporter of Roosevelt's policies,

It is telling that he raised no serious opposition to any of Roosevelt's policies and even supported his peacetime draft.[144] This single issue, which went into effect on October 29 1940, just prior to the election, could easily have cost Roosevelt victory if he would have had sincere opposition. It certainly should have been a major campaign issue!

What Roosevelt had accomplished with his un-American economic policies in those seven years was to purchase total devotion to himself and the Democrat Party. The depression was in full swing and the money from the Roosevelt administration was taken with few questions, however this had a serious impact on the 1936 election. People were not inclined to vote against the only revenue source available.

The point here is the impact that this had on the ability of the average citizen of this country to influence the thinking of their elected representatives. Every American wants good roads, schools, libraries and so forth but they do not necessarily want to be taxed to pay for these things, especially in bad economic times. Mayors, town councils, county commissioners and state legislators were all forced to balance a budget that provided the required services while not being a financial burden to their constituents.

All of this changed under Roosevelt. With the money provided by Washington D.C., local leaders could provide a host of services with no need to raise the revenue locally. This made them very popular to a public that didn't understand how this miracle of financing was possible and local leaders became quite enamored with this new form of government. They also enjoyed the benefit of putting people back to work building these roads, libraries, schools and everything else that Washington was willing to pay for.

The greater cost, however, cannot be measured in financial terms although this too is a reasonable study. The cost was the loyalty of the local leaders. Previously they had been loyal to their constituents because they were required to "earn" their vote. Hence, if you had an issue with a policy of the local, state or federal government you could approach any one of these leaders and reasonably expect to be listened to. When the money started flowing from Washington, Washington suddenly became every politician's loyal friend.

Suddenly the sense of community, of using the money of your friends and neighbors responsibly, was no longer an issue. The money was available without the approval of your constituency. In time every politician came to appreciate the need to keep the money flowing and that meant cooperating with Washington as well as keeping these people in Washington who promoted these easy money financial policies.

Citizens who had an above average understanding of sound economics and good government policies protested but there was no longer any reason to consider their arguments. Much of the money for reelection came from Washington through the national committees. The Democrat Party had once been conservative while The Republican Party was more liberal. As The Democrats grew more liberal the impression was given that The Republican Party grew more conservative. Many still embrace this belief today but if we stop believing the rhetoric and start taking a hard look at their record we will see that true conservatives seldom have successful careers in The

Republican Party. In a generation this simply became the way modern government works.

The price to be paid for all of this "free" money from Washington D.C. is that politicians feel no sense of accountability to local citizens and simply cooperate with whatever agenda Washington dictates. Citizens lost the ability to protest government policies locally because no local politician wanted to jeopardize the flow of money. They would politely listen, they would patiently sell and defend federal policies but in the end their loyalty was to the money supply.

Some citizens objected and a variety of efforts were made to restore good government but with no results. All business was transacted back in Washington now. You could no longer approach a city councilman, mayor, state legislator or even a Congressman with any serious expectation of changing anything as their loyalty was to Washington. You could expect pleasant, reassuring talk but no action.

Previously, all citizens and local politicians had fairly similar views on the majority of issues. The division came when the loyalty of one switched to Washington's agenda and the loyalty of the other stayed with traditional values. As the two parties united in their thinking on strategies to gain and maintain power the course of our nation was set and not to be altered. A "left/right" paradigm was created to establish an illusion that all "rational views" were represented but in truth there was only one view represented, the view of ever increasing government because only Washington can solve our problems.

This problem was radically intensified in 1929 when Congress passed "The Permanent Apportionment Act" restricting the total number in The U.S. House of Representatives to four-hundred and thirty-five members.[145] In our Constitution Article one, Section two states, "The number of Representatives shall not exceed one for every thirty thousand but each state shall have at least one Representative." There had never before been a limit set on the total number of Representatives. As the population grew, the number of Representatives grew.

Now as the population grows each Representative has an ever-increasing number of people (giving each person less opportunity to be heard) and their "districts" are re-drawn every ten years. With the single change of 1929 each Representative has gone from a constituency base of thirty thousand citizens per Representative to almost six hundred and ninety thousand citizens per Representative! All over America people realize that they have lost their voice in government and this is why! The total number of Representatives hasn't been increased since the 1910 census.

Currently the entire system of Representation is backward. We now have elections which amount to little more than two parties, with no serious dissection on major issues, holding a contest to determine which among their loyal members can become the most popular with voters and raise the most money independent of the party. It's nothing more than a competition over a prestigious job in "public relations". The job requirements do not include honesty, integrity or knowledge of government, history or economics. Neither do the job requirements include any list of personal accomplishments, statesmanship or commitment to the community.

It's all about getting votes and raising money now. The important question is, what is the specific job the party hires these people to do? Previous generations elected someone as their Congressman to go to Washington D.C. and "represent" their interests before the federal government. Now the impression is that we elect a Congressman to "govern" us. That is to say, make rules that we must live by, ration resources such as water and energy without making a case that shortages are legitimate, set educational standards for the raising of our children, etc.

This is quite a change from the government our grandparents knew! When previous generations elected someone to go back to Washington D.C. to represent their concerns, views and desires on all matters before the federal government the person elected was held accountable. The issues would be matters of money such as the debt, foreign aid or military budgets because the citizens had to pay the bill. This would be matters of treaties as it was their sons that would be sent to war to meet treaty obligations. It would be matters of government expansion as it was their freedom sacrificed with each new law.

The candidates would be individuals who lived locally, proved to be worthy of respect in some way such as being successful, perhaps a community conscious businessman who had sufficient knowledge of history, government and economics. This candidate would convince the voters they would manage their affairs with proper concern for the public welfare. All interested applicants would inform the public of what they had to offer and the public made their choice.

Now each candidate works to cultivate favor with the party bosses, learns the policies of their party and proves loyalty by never challenging those policies and spends the bulk of their time promoting legislation desired by the special interest groups who will cut the biggest checks at election time. The candidate who is networking with the most special interest groups is able to raise the most money. If he gets the nod from the party bosses, he can represent the party at the general election. The two parties then have a "face-off" and the one who most impresses the public wins.

The job they are then hired to perform requires they go to Washington D.C. to learn what the party desires the voters be told on each issue. They then return to their district from time to time, not as a Representative of the people, but as a Representative of the party to educate citizens about specifics the party proposes on the various issues.

The citizen's desires are no longer represented in Washington but instead the party now has a representative locally to sell the public on why the legislation they passed was necessary and good. In the case of unpopular legislation the party has a local representative to "blame the other guy" so as to stifle voter outrage. Input is taken but seldom considered.

The new world order believes one "pitch man" for every seven-hundred thousand people is sufficient to their purpose and they can influence four-hundred and thirty-five more successfully than if they permitted the public to have adequate representation as previous generations had so they see no need to expand Congress.

Four-hundred and thirty-five is a number they believe they can control without looking obvious.

While citizens are debating the rhetoric with their party's Representative, The President and the Executive Branch administrators are doing the actual governing. Few American's will face the truth that the candidate they have supported, the candidate whose rhetoric they embraced completely, is actually committed totally to the globalist agenda. As a result the globalist agenda grows with each administration, even if the party in power is changed.

Under The Constitution The President has very little power. This goes back to our founders having a fear of a monarch and not wanting a strong executive. The President is empowered to be Commander in Chief of the military, grant pardons and reprieves, to negotiate treaties and submit them to The Senate for approval and make the appointments of certain federal officers. In the entire U.S. Constitution the powers of the Presidency are outlined in three short paragraphs!

Today the "emergency" powers given to The President are incredible by comparison and all of it illegitimate. Astonishing changes have been made to The Senate and House of Representatives but they pale to the changes in Executive power and State's Rights are gone completely!

Today we are vehemently taught, "Everyone has a right to vote". This is not a principle our country was founded on. Our founding fathers believed you should not be allowed to vote unless you had some investment in the community. The requirement may be that you had to own land before you could vote or perhaps own a business but to vote you had to prove you had a personal investment in the community and subsequently you had a personal investment in the over all welfare of the community. We are taught today that this is offensive and unfair.

Simply put, the power to vote is the power to steal! If I move into a community and have no ties or loyalties, what concerns have I if property taxes are raised? If I choose not to seek gainful employment for my living, what concerns have I if income taxes are raised? If my income is through some welfare program (always adjusted for inflation and cost of living increases) what concern have I if sales taxes are raised? All the more so, if I'm promised some benefit to these new taxes.

Voting was to be the responsibility of those qualified to make informed decisions about candidates for office and committed to the welfare of the community. It was, in turn, the responsibility of those elected to research (at length if necessary) each proposed bill and consider it's far-reaching impacts as well as its merits and faults.

Today we have the most uninformed electorate in our country's history. Having uninformed citizens vote on scores of issues that previously had been considered only through the debating processes of the legislatures exacerbates the problems. This is a recipe for disaster and it is a disaster by design, the design of the new world order. Neither is this unexpected. This is exactly the result that our founders feared when they rejected the concept of democracy and made The United States a Constitutional Republic.

This is why the new world order labors to get every possible person registered to vote, because they don't understand the implications of the issues and will simply vote for more government programs which expands government power. Once again this is done under the pretense of good; everyone has a "right" to vote.

The problems are overwhelming in The Congress as well. Where as these people are elected to carefully and thoughtfully educate themselves and debate the nations business they are now overwhelmed with bills that are purposefully lengthy so that no Congressman, in spite of personal integrity, would have the time to familiarize themselves with the greater portion of any bill. Increasingly we are seeing bills that are drafted by The White House or some special interest group (lobbyists) and only made available to The Congress at the last minute or only in an outline form.

Then there is the added fear of what the courts are going to do with legislation when they get it. There was a time when the whole of a judge's responsibility was to insure that the accused was given opportunity to defend himself, both sides arguing a case presented credible evidence, honest witnesses, be afforded reasonable opportunity to present their case and deliver just punishments against the convicted under the appropriate circumstances. Today, special interest groups have stolen even our courts.

Groups like The American Civil Liberties Union have employed their own strategy sufficiently to alter the purpose of the courts and use them to promote their agenda. The agenda of The ACLU is a very straightforward one; sin with no consequences. Teach sex to children with no consequence. Abort any unwanted baby with the approval of law. Practice any deviant behavior openly and sue for discrimination anyone who dares accost you. Let the criminally guilty out of jail and fill the jails with those who would challenge any man's right to practice decadent behavior.

The ACLU accomplished all of this by simply filing a multitude of lawsuits on every issue. They fail in the majority of these suits but when they have a success they capitalize on it by publishing the court decisions and mailing them to all similar institutions.[146]

Fifty cases may be filed against a prison for failing to afford some inmate a desire. Forty-nine of these suits may be lost but the single victory was all they needed. Letters and copies of the legal ruling were printed and mailed to all prisons, state legislatures and county commissioners. The letter threatened to sue if any prisons under their jurisdiction repeated the offense and the copy of the court decision was used to intimidate by establishing precedent.

The same strategy and formula was used in public schools, private schools, churches, hospitals, cities were sued for celebrating Christmas, cemeteries were sued for displaying crosses and no one was safe from attack. The justice of it all has not been questioned and money wasn't a problem. The battle raged for a few decades but once the ACLU succeeded in getting like-minded judges appointed, victories started coming and opposition started folding like a punctured balloon.

Suddenly (and unbelievably) a judge is permitted to throw out a law passed by an authorized law making entity! Suddenly a single lawsuit no longer has implications for the immediate parties alone. Now we are led to believe that a single court case can determine the law of the land and the decision is based solely on the opinion of a single judge.

Congress, state legislatures, county commissioners and city councilmen are authorized to make laws. Judges can rule in favor (on a case by case basis) in favor of someone harmed under the law but that is the limit of their authority. If a city or state loses a significant lawsuit (or a number of suits) the city council or state legislature may decide to change the law but a judge does not have authority to simply "throw out" the work of the duly elected lawmaking entity. On a federal level, in The U.S. Constitution Article 3 Section 2 specifically gives Congress the authority over courts – including the authority to set the jurisdictional limit of The U.S. Supreme Court yet we commonly see judges dictating to Congress.

Bypassing the proper law making authorities and legislating by activist judges has proven to be a fast track in getting things done for the new world order. When the people get active and get a good law passed it is a simple matter of time before some judge throws it out. This is a very convenient way for the new world order to eliminate problems but it is un-American and we need to understand how the system is supposed to work. We don't even require activist groups to endure the expense of fighting each case. We simply permit them to manipulate a single victory into the equivalent of federal law.

We are moving past fascism now to a dictatorship. The only question remaining is will tyranny follow a dictatorship or will a dictatorship follow tyranny. With the George W. Bush Administration we have a very threatening war on terror. We have seen the institution of The Patriot Act, Patriot 2, The Department of Home Land Security, Transportation Safety Administration, a host of unconstitutional Executive Orders giving The President ridiculous powers he is denied under The Constitution including "Continuity of Government" directives, new powers afforded to FEMA, new powers afforded to The NSA, foreign born citizens hired into our military and Border Patrol Agency, blatant attempts to merge The U.S. into a "European Union" style government in this hemisphere first called "The Free Trade Area of The Americas " and when that failed "The North American Union". All of these centralize power under a dictator.

Perhaps the most frightening aspect to all of this is that it's no longer secret. These matters are done openly and yet few protest. What is to be the barometer of our freedom? How should the new world order gauge the rapidity of their advance if good people yet remain quiet? The strategy has always been "patient gradualism" but the purpose for this was that they remain undiscovered. Now that they are exposed on a dozen fronts and good people react with disinterest they are free to advance with all haste. Why should they fear the complacent or apathetic?

Now that they are exposed they are the most vulnerable they have ever been. Now is the time that each must decide. Will we stand up and be counted with patriots of previous generations or will we turn our back on our God, our children and our country by allowing this satanic tyranny to prevail without a fight?

We have traveled two roads as a nation. The first was of Godly standards and moral commitment. Then the church was neutralized. Since this we have been on a road to tyranny. At times we have traveled this road with difficulty and at times we have raced toward disaster. At all times, the choice was ours. It is ours still. We have a duty and responsibility to correct our course. This is what I will address in the final pages of this book.

PART SEVEN

*OPTIONS
AND
EVIDENCE*

OUR OPTIONS NOW

Hebrews 2:6-7 "What is man that thou art mindful of
him … and set him over the works of Thy hand"

Genesis 1:1 "In the beginning God …" These are among the most important words ever spoken or written. On the subjects of politics or government, most Christians are at a loss what to do. Many believe it's best to do nothing and others do nothing out of confusion. If we simply abided by God's word, confusion would dissipate. We have His word and all we need to add to this is our commitment.

God's word clarifies that He does not desire that any suffer and He does not desire that Satan rob man of that which He gave us. God does not desire that evil prospers on the earth and He does not desire that babies grow to adolescence and then adulthood mired in the perverse environment we have made for them today.

"Jesus Christ the same yesterday, today and forever" Hebrews 13:8. The standards He gave in His word, the promises given, the hope and blessings are all available to us today but they all begin with God. We need a relationship with Him and a commitment to serve if we are going to benefit from these promises and receive the blessings. Sure, we can have a personal relationship with Him and no tangible commitment to serve. This will be of some personal benefit but it is short of what God desires. Society will suffer from our shallowness and eventually the standards we have allowed to fester in society will come back upon us.

God knows, and has warned us, that there is an enemy to God and man. He has told us to teach others of this enemy that the enemy would be stopped in his desire to destroy society but we have opted to ignore this enemy and speak only of God.

God would have no purpose in telling us of this enemy if we were powerless against him. Furthermore, we can ask why He would leave those He loves defenseless to face such a vicious adversary. He did not leave us powerless. He has given us overcoming power in the name of Jesus. (Mark 16:17, Luke 10:19, John 14 entire chapter, John 16:23, to name a few verses) These verses make it clear that Jesus gave us power and authority to overcome Satan and his demon armies. It stands to reason that if we can defeat the devil we can surely defeat his followers. If we don't believe Satan and his followers can be defeated we need to get back into God's word and reaffirm in our mind what Jesus did for us.

Scripture makes it clear we can defeat him and it is simply Satan's propaganda that causes us to question God's word. This is our first option, to quit listening to Satan's media and start studying and applying God's word in our lives and communities. The church is neutralized today and we make no attempt to confront Satan and those in his service that promote his agenda. Scores among us don't even believe there is an agenda to be confronted.

To defeat him we must put forth some effort but he has tricked us into idleness. God has given a structure, an order to things. The choice is ours, if we desire this to be our standard or if we will abandon God's standard and just quietly accept that which is given in its place. To commit to God's standard requires a commitment to know the truth and this requires a willingness to investigate and accept the truth when we find it. If we cannot face the truth, we are doomed and there's no point in denying this fact because we will simply continue to be drawn deeper and deeper into Satan's evil and deceptive system.

We have become a culture that asks nothing of God and expects nothing of Him. We see our society disintegrating beneath our feet and we have become accustomed to watching while taking no action, even expecting things to grow worse. We choose to believe we can do nothing and accept all of these horrors as God's will. We are not even suspicious that this may be a satanic deception. We have no specific scripture to justify our inaction so we use prophecy and ignore all of the promises; indeed, we ignore what we know to be the very nature of God; His love, His desire to bless, His hatred of all things evil.

Even though the self-described prophets we listen to are repeatedly in error and changing their story we choose to believe they are right about their one big promise; that we won't be here to reap the horrors of a satanic government whose seeds we have allowed to thrive.

Those who take issue with this statement must concede one fact; we don't even try anymore. With no effort, what should we expect? With the church neutralized, of course Satan will achieve much. We have a duty to know what God has ordained and be willing to teach it to others. Knowing the truth generates the responsibility of sharing the truth. Out of love for God we should passionately work building truth and understanding under which Satan and his armies cannot prosper or survive. This is the true purpose and calling of salt and light.

Winning souls for Christ is certainly part of the responsibility but recruiting for an army is natural when the army is victorious and on the march. When we make people aware of the clear choice – Godly liberty or global satanic tyranny, people will begin comparing the two. When we sit idle the public doesn't have anything to compare to the only system they know.

What we know of God must be revealed in what we, as Christians, choose for ourselves, as well as what we promote in society. This would include schools, government policies and a host of other issues. This is all lacking today. We are commanded in 2nd Corinthians 6:17 "Wherefore come out from among them and be ye separate saith the Lord".

We have our children in their schools, we are in their economic system, we are in their military and police departments, we work for their corporations, we depend on their system for our retirement and far too many of us attend one of their churches. How, exactly, are we separate? Can it be that we believe we will not suffer from so much association with Satan's system? What then is the application of this verse? All of society is mired in a satanic deception and Christians have not separated themselves. As a result, we are mired in deception as well. We are to know the truth but we don't. We are to expose Satan's lies but we are as quick to accept them as non-Christians. As long as we continue in deception we cannot act as salt and light.

Our second option is to have as little to do with Satan's system as possible. We may have few choices in some areas since they control the currency but we do have choices in many others. In our choices of schooling our children or churches we attend, we have complete authority. Many other ways to separate from their system can be sought out.

The new world order is wholly committed to Satan's agenda and promoting it through out society. We can and should be as committed to promoting God's. They make every effort in teaching his standards and goals for society but we make no effort to teach God's. This lack of commitment on our part is not based on a lack of love but on many deceptions, some of which are designed to neutralize the church. Deceptions are broken by revelations of the truth.

For Christians that begins with God's word, relationship and faith that God will bless those who serve Him, it will not come by continuing to listen to those who work to deceive. It will not come by idleness and deeper immersion into lies.

When we abandon Satan's deceptions we will see that his lies to the world are shallow and vulnerable to exposure. It is then we, salt and light, which can know the truth of Godly government and teach our fellow citizens the error in Satan's lies.

Option number three is the hard one; getting involved and commit to teaching God's standards to society as directed in James 1:22 "be ye doers of the word". The world needs us to hold the standard and teach what we know, whether they want us to or not. The world will not challenge that which it does not find suspicious. Those of the world will not "bite the hand that feeds them". They would not understand if they did challenge and they would be powerless without Jesus anyway. God has given that power, authority and responsibility to Christians. We have God's word. We are to challenge Satan's plan simply because it's contrary to God's word and that should be reason enough.

Here, at the conclusion of this book, we turn to "a must list". A list of matters we must understand, work to enforce upon society and work diligently to help society understand if we will be effective salt and light. In short, we must know the truth and organize to be effective.

A Supreme Court case in 1866 dealt with President Lincoln's unconstitutional decision to suspend Habeas Corpus. The case was called Ex Parte Milligan and is very widely quoted. The decision of the court reads:

"The Constitution of The United States is a law for rulers and people equally in war and in peace ... no doctrine involving more pernicious consequences was ever invented by the writ of man than that any of its provisions can be suspended during any of the great exigencies of government".[147]

Here is proof for whom proof is needed, that no provision in The U.S. Constitution affords politicians the ability to lawfully suspend or replace The Constitution, in full or in part, for any reason.

Additionally, Article I Section 8 requires that it is Congress alone tasked with the responsibility to manage the nations currency and they have no authority to delegate this responsibility to another or sell it for favors. It is, therefore, strictly prohibited that a private investment firm be given the authority and ability to print the nations currency. This is an extremely important point as The Bible makes clear in Proverbs 22:7 "the borrower is servant to the lender".

That these people were permitted to achieve this status is just wrong, morally and spiritually. It affords them the ability to simply manufacture money and use it to buy up the nations of the earth at their leisure and enslave mankind.

Furthermore, all rational parties will recognize that treaties cannot possibly supercede The Constitution. Those that dispute this point simply pursue an agenda that requires they abandon logic. The agenda is to expand government beyond the boundaries set in The Constitution.

These, and many more, are all lies that simply need to be exposed and corrected to bring our government back to its legal jurisdiction. We, as a nation, must not regard any deal with the devil as binding but we, as a nation, didn't consent to these deals. There was no Constitutional Convention or Amendment to the U.S. Constitution authorizing any of this as required by The Constitution. It was all done illegally and we have the authority and opportunity to set things right.

As much as the word "battle" may be unwelcome or intimidating to a majority of people there is nothing to be gained in denying one unpleasant truth; the battle is being waged against us. One has to take small notice of events to arrive at this conclusion. The goal is our enslavement or cruel destruction and short of stopping this insanity, these are our only choices. We can either do the right thing or surrender and there is nothing ungodly about doing the right thing. If we determine to do the right thing we must be strategic in our own planning. This means we must be knowledgeable and willing to commit to the cause.

Strategy requires that we have the ability to take advantage of our enemy's weaknesses. The new world order has three fears that create opportunity for us to capitalize upon; 1) being exposed while they are yet vulnerable, 2) losing the support of the uneducated masses and (3) a resistance movement that is organized sufficiently to challenge their lies and expose their true agenda. This is where they are vulnerable and so this is the logical solution upon which we should focus.

We can do nothing effective if we fail to organize. Only with an organized effort can we expose them with hard facts and conclusive evidence so that the masses will awaken to the horrors designed for them. Any unorganized effort will be destroyed by the satanic organizations that have been designed to protect Satan's system.

Remember, it was not government checks and balances that exposed the fraud of "Watergate" or "Iran-Contra" and a few others. It was the media. Government is now set up to protect it's own interests and when the media cooperates with their agenda the truth will not be told to us. If the media exposes corruption, for whatever reason, they are effective in destroying anyone, including politicians, they choose. If the media does not expose corruption the politicians succeed in their duplicity.

Conversely, the media has successfully shut out a host of important inquiries and stands ready to attack and destroy everyone who seeks to expose that which they are committed to keep hidden from the public. Only by networking organizationally among lovers of truth can we overcome the media and make vital truths known to society.

Since we are under attack, we do not have the luxury of picking and choosing our battles. We have the duty to analyze what is happening to us as a nation and it will take tenacity to meet and overcome these threats. We can know the enemies plan and we can defend ourselves. There are several specific areas where the enemy has brought the battle to us. It is necessary to meet the enemy in all of these areas. This can only be done organizationally. Individually it is futile and dangerous as individuals make easy targets. If we organize we can meet these threats strategically, effectively and meet all threats simultaneously.

The first is the "battle over the empire of our mind". We must stop thinking the way we have been manipulated to think, a way of thinking that singularly benefits our enemies. We must be willing to challenge our own preconceived notions and ideas and be lovers of truth, even when initially offended. We must be willing to be taught and to learn.

We must be prepared to challenge all truths, not just to challenge those who warn us of a new world order but those who would use fear to manipulate us. If there be a pandemic on the horizon, where is the proof? If there be need to go to war, where are the facts that this enemy is a threat? We must not surrender our liberties for the promise of increased government protection.

We must embrace the word of God as truth and as the standard for society and ourselves. We must teach God's word to the young and end this monopoly Satan has to influence their thinking. We must study with a willingness to learn. We must use our intelligence and perspective. That is to say, we must not submit all things to a final vote. That which belongs to God and family is not political. We must end this deception that all things are right when dictated by elected officials or voted on by the majority. We must not be hypnotized or sedated into accepting defeat as final or the ballot box as our only solution or responsibility. We must set our minds on the things of God and remember who and what we are in Christ.

Secondly, we must take back our churches. If the leadership in our churches will not be part of what is necessary we must become leaders so that America has a chance to know God and the desires He has for society and not this milk toast god of tolerance and government programs. We must have a meaningful relationship with God that illustrates love and duty to mankind. If God means anything to us we can surely accomplish this much!

Satan's churches are spewing a social gospel of tolerance and deception. We must build churches that speak standards, truth and responsibility. What we note to be their efforts, we must double in our effort and expose their lies. To control religion they must offer an alternate Christianity and be able to merge it into their system. We must see they fail.

Thirdly, we must take back the areas of power. State Legislatures, Congress, and other seats of government where decisions are made. This is simply unthinkable if we refuse to organize. Satan has invested incredible sums of time and money to organize that he may dominate this arena and he did this for a single purpose. He knew this was the path to his success. So too is it the path to ours.

We must abandon those who have assisted Satan by telling us to flee from these halls. We must abandon those who have made promises and not kept them. We must abandon associations that have had ample opportunity to prove their merit and left us wanting. Our lives and futures are determined in government and we must be present and be heard.

We must learn and fully understand Godly principles in government and economics. Once these principles are understood (and they're not complicated) they are applicable in all the arenas government hopes to dominate such as money and banking, taxing and "internal improvements", education, the food supply, medicine, immigration, military and a host of others. We must talk to our friends and neighbors and we must begin to organize in such a way that we can seat Godly men and women in the necessary offices to restore Godly government and stop this new world order agenda.

An organized body of people can seat their candidates in a variety of local offices such as mayors, town councils, state legislatures and most importantly The U.S. Congress without massive sums of money if they dedicate themselves to educating the people who vote and organize strategically. Communities are already mapped out into state legislative districts. By using these maps and building local bodies of volunteers committed to seating a Godly candidate we can be successful without spending the money the new world order must spend and once we have the voters educated, no amount of money will convince them to vote themselves into slavery.

A Godly church is ideal for this but Satan's system will not permit it. Still, this was common in the churches when America was founded. Satan permits his churches to endeavor into politics today but he prohibits Godly churches from doing the same, precisely because they were so successful in years past.

We must have done with fighting only defensive battles that the enemy foists upon us to distract us. Indeed, we must have done with all distractions. We must end any thinking that it is we who chose our battles. It is the unfortunate reality of war that the one who attacks chooses the time and place for battle. The enemy has begun the attack and these are the arenas we must defend and retake. To make a determination that we will ignore their attack as we launch out on some potentially inconsequential effort is simply a creative way to surrender.

We must have done with complacency about losing. Losing is serious business and we owe it to ourselves and our posterity to win and not consider losing an option. We must be strategic and fight the enemy where we will do him damage, not simply where we would prefer to get involved.

We must hold elected officials accountable to us and remove them if they "sell out" to Satan's system. We must remove politicians from office who prove unfit and remove ourselves from parties that prove corrupt. We must recognize that a standard of "the lesser of two evils" is a standard unacceptable to us as Christians. All of this requires organization and is impossible without it.

As we proceed through this list, remember, number three (organizing) will only work after number one (education) has worked and number two (churches) is the logical place for us to start! Our purpose is a Godly one and only a Godly people will work to destroy the works of darkness and restore Godly government.

Fourth, if we fail to fully take back the arenas of influence we must, at minimum, have an impact with which this world can draw a comparison. Primarily these would be the media, the educational system and the entertainment industry. Truth can certainly overcome lies if the truth be told and we must accept it as our duty to know it and tell it. We cannot hope to accomplish anything if our purpose is to battle Satan issue by issue.

We must get into these arenas of influence and work to create understanding of the ideological realities that differ in the two systems. We must focus on the truth and expose Satan's organizations that work to destroy all things of God. These areas of influence are simply tools for mass education and this is why Satan has chosen them and this is why we need to take them back.

Finally there is the area of money and property. At present there exists much reason to be concerned over our dollar collapsing and that being used to merge The U.S. into a global currency (or at least a regional one). This must absolutely be stopped. We must diligently deny them further power and return America to a solid, reliable monetary system built on tangible assets. Not a phony system built of paper and promises. If we allow the new world order to collapse our economy and merge us into a global currency we will have lost a major stronghold.

We must insist on having an honest currency controlled by The U.S. Congress. We must take back the ability of the new world order to simply print money out of paper and then use that paper to buy all they require to enslave our nation. We must also stop the government takeover of property or we will all be subject to complete control.

The subject of this book is the neutralized church. Christians have abdicated personal responsibility to be salt and light and have followed leadership that was pulled away from what God had ordained. Some were sincere but naïve and made no effort to know their enemy and what their enemy is doing, others were corrupt. The new world order is very well organized and will not be defeated by a loose knit band of well intentioned amateurs guessing as to what might be the best course of action. We must seek out leaders that understand the new world order and are prepared to stand against all that is unholy. The only remaining option is to educate ourselves and become those leaders.

Today prophecy is the big fight. Too many refuse to get involved using prophecy as an excuse. The problem is these prophets don't study the new world order and most of them have never bothered to investigate it. I don't know any of them who are willing to expose any part of it and its questionable if they even know about it. You can't discern information with half the facts.

Bible prophecy is about the new world order. If you don't understand the new world order, you won't understand prophecy. It's like watching a sport and not understanding the rules. If you watch football without knowing each team has four attempts to move the ball ten yards it wouldn't make any sense. This wouldn't necessarily stop you from drawing whatever conclusions you choose but your conclusions would be based on ignorance. The same is true with prophecy. If you don't study the new world order you're missing most of the vital information needed to interpret current events.

Yet America has an entire "prophecy industry" that operates in this fashion. Always the message is "don't worry" but the prophets are ignorant of the enemy and the information he has planted for them. You can bet the new world order knows prophecy better than the average Christian. They have gambled much on their ability to manipulate people and there is no better way to manipulate Christians than through prophecy.

Certainly the three best ways to manipulate Christians are getting them out of God's word, prophecy and poor leadership. The new world order hates the Bible. The only reason they use it is to mislead Christians. They control the information system so they control what we know. The "prophecy industry" has no difficulty in getting their books published, even by known non-Christian publishers. Why the disparity? Why work so arduously to destroy God's word but permit a flood of books to be published concerning prophecy? Because prophecy neutralizes.

What if we have been misled about prophecy? What if we have been tricked into surrendering without a fight? We shouldn't need a reason to fight for what's been stolen from us anyway. If your home were robbed would you want your property returned? If your child was kidnapped you would do everything possible to get them back. Yet we have been robbed of our (and our children's) Godly heritage and liberties and we just accept it without question. We are not even suspicious that this may be a trick or some type of manipulation.

We don't know what we can accomplish unless we remain idle. Idleness has brought us to this current chaos. How have we become so quick to give up on God and believe He now desires to judge America more than bless it? It was accomplished by a false sense of security stemming from a belief that we know our future and God would have us sit back and let evil reign.

Jesus said in Matthew 7:23 "I never knew you: depart from Me ye that work iniquity". Today Christians are wholly convinced church leaders speak for Jesus when He never even knew them. I can make this claim because they are workers of iniquity. They support giving Satan power (illegitimate power through government) when God has warned us to "give him no place".

They support idleness abandoning God's system because Satan's system has redefined their role. They support the destruction of the family by the involvement of government where God has never intended government to be involved and they support the iniquity of government, which God hates. Government is now the great worker of iniquity.

In Matthew 7:22 they claim to have "prophesied in thy name, cast out devils and in thy name done many wonderful works". Jesus makes it clear He is referring to those that falsely prophesize, those who cast out devils falsely and those who do good works falsely. Christians no longer consider that those who interpret prophecy falsely are false prophets.

In 7:21 He says "he that doeth the will of My Father … will see heaven". We have a duty to "do the will of God" and not focus singularly on where we stand prophetically. Matthew 7:15-16 says "Beware of false prophets, which come to you in sheep's clothing but inwardly they are ravening wolves. Ye shall know them by their fruit …" Take a moment and analyze the fruit of Christians not being involved in politics and the fruit of a "pre-tribulation rapture teaching".

These are not bringing forth good fruit and that is proof that they are not good teachings. They have led to untold numbers of deaths and human suffering and bondage. Hosts of Christians are so committed to this teaching that they will not consider other verses from the same Bible such as 2nd Thessalonians 2:3 says "… that day shall not come, except there come a falling away first and that man of sin be revealed" which is clearly one verse among many that challenges this teaching.

Verse 3 begins with "Let no man deceive you by any means…" "Any" would include prophecy and the context of this verse is prophecy. We don't know if we're being deceived or to what extent but we do know that prophecy is being used as argument that we can and should do nothing to fight evil. We must understand that knowing prophecy is important but guessing at prophecy and allowing Satan to prosper from our assumptions is wrong.

Twisting God's word is one of Satan's oldest tricks. Yet today it is the most difficult it has ever been in our country's history to get Christians involved because they have been so immersed in the idea that we should just stand idle and accept all of these satanic changes.

Satan had to neutralize the church. This is a Christian fight. Only those that have a higher purpose will make the higher sacrifice. Far too many among us have made up our mind about what we want to believe and are no longer willing to even consider that we may have been misled. This is true about a great many scriptures, it's true about prophecy and it's true about the daily news we have programmed into us from Satan's system. You can be sure that none of what we're told will jeopardize his plans or strategies. To jeopardize his plans and strategies we must go outside his system for our information and we must go outside his system before we will recognize a call to service. Just because Satan has a plan doesn't mean we must lose. He has no authority and God is on our side.

This is really the cost of all of this prophecy teaching. We have given up on God. We now assume we know His will (through prophecy) and conclude He won't help us so we feel no incentive to get involved. Even with that said many will not question whether there is a satanic deception at work among us. We believe in God for salvation but we do not believe He will bless our efforts to restore morality to society or Godly government to our land. Preconceived notions are killing us and misinformation is as bad.

Christians love Bible prophecy in a box. As long as it teaches we'll be raptured away from here before things get bad, we love it. If the teaching challenges this promise, our interest in prophecy diminishes rapidly! We see how horrific things are getting but we detach the seriousness of the hour from any sense of duty or Christian responsibility. God's system is based on free will, not manipulation, forcing people to do something they prefer not to or overwhelming them with information to the extent that they accept lies as fact. Information overload is manipulation. Christians who want to use prophecy as a reason to remain idle can overload themselves with incredible amounts of information, all affirming that it's perfectly acceptable to remain idle. Prophecy is only one body of scripture and it's the one that is virtually saturated by conjecture.

To be accurate, prophecy teachings must be compatible with all other scripture. Yet what we see from current prophecy teaching is the encouragement to ignore verses on responsibility and duty, salt and light. All teachings should be tested against other verses but when prophecy verses are tested against other verses, the way they're commonly taught today, it just leads to confusion. The more sure way is to go back to The Bible and stand on what it says and have done with picking a few favorite verses and making our theology and beliefs fit these.

We have a duty to fight evil. We need not argue with others about the reality of the new world order. If they refuse to believe and refuse to read we must seek out others with whom to organize. There is nothing to be gained by arguing with people who have no desire to learn or understand. Neither does talking to others about the new world order require over emphasis about "who's" involved. It's about fruit. The great majority of those involved are dupes who know little of the full agenda. We may know them by their fruit.

One who has chosen to affiliate with an organization, which has a clear agenda of building global government at the expense of national sovereignty, has given us the only proof we need to determine their qualifications as a leader or advisor. If they choose not to investigate their affiliations or face reasonable suspicions, that does not require that we abandon what we know to be true. Neither does it burden us with the responsibility of proving the obvious to the ignorant.

It's not about winning; it's about doing the right thing. It's about duty, honor and patriotism from a Christian perspective and from that of a good citizen. Society is crumbling and America needs us now like she's never needed salt and light before!

Soon we will see more war and violence to eliminate large portions of the populations. We will see the increase of deadly diseases and famines for this same purpose. The proposed answer to all of this will be more government. The real point to these efforts will be reducing populations, which will lessen their ability to resist. Soon after this we will see the elimination of "useless eaters". These are those who cannot serve the state. Once society becomes accustomed to this practice they will welcome the next step, which will be eliminating those who will not serve the state. Eventually we will see non-worshipers of the state singled out as the enemies to "progress".

The public will believe all horrors are their fault and eagerly demand they be dealt with. At some point this may become blatant but at first it will probably be subtle such as taxing all churches not members in The World Council of Churches.

Remember, taxing is a form of control. Then too, we will see advancement of the ecumenical movement uniting all churches harmoniously under universal beliefs. The new world order has the advantage of resources. We have the advantages of God and truth if we choose to use them. Things have been bad before in history and Godly people have risen to the occasion. Now it's our turn.

We can do much to stop the disintegration of our society but only if we get involved. To be effective we must know the enemy and his strategies and we must organize strategically. Just joining some group or starting our own is insufficient. We need to know how any group we join plans to halt the new world order and restore Constitutional government. If it has no effective and identifiable plan demonstrating how, exactly, they will accomplish defined goals they lack the strategy to be effective.

Restoring Constitutional government is the key and requires sufficient organizational strength to put a Constitutionally committed public servant in the office of Congressman and state legislator who is willing to stand up to the pressures and temptations that will certainly be used against them. Organizational strength in these districts will be needed to keep a Constitutionalist in office or replace one, if necessary.

This too is a major point. The belief that we can "vote" our problems away is illusion. Part of this is the idea that we will elect a hero and can return to our daily lives. This will not happen. Anyone we elect, we will have to hold accountable.

Plus, to elect someone who is truly a statesman, willing to stand for what's right, is to simply put them on the front lines of frustration and in no small amount of danger! The only way to help them, and protect them, is to insure the new world order is absolutely aware that the electorate in this district is well informed and involved to such an extent that if this person leaves office they will be replaced by one equally or more Constitutional! Therefore the new world order has nothing to gain by this person leaving office for any reason and they have no hope of electing a dupe.

Something of an argument exists as to whether The Preamble to The Constitution of The United States recognizes "people" or "States" as the authority over the government in Washington D.C. It reads "We The People of The United States, in order to form a more perfect union ..." We better hope it is the states!

The government in Washington is totally out of control and in the grip of the new world order. To get it back into control is going to take greater organization and force than they are able to apply. It will take the force of a number of states working simultaneously.

Our focus must be on Congress but we must also prioritize putting solid patriots into state legislatures that will stand up to this new world order and say "no more"! The states created this government in Washington and as its creator they have the authority to exercise control. When a significant number of states tell Washington (and their puppeteers) their illicit rule is over we will have our country back.

This will take an enormous educational effort as the public is overwhelmingly buying the lies of the new world order. Still, this is what must be accomplished. Satan has robbed us of the understanding of good government and good economics and of our true organizational effectiveness, which at one time existed through the churches.

We must ever consider that The Constitution of The United States expressly recognizes two entities beyond the scope of government interference. This is the media and the church. The media is made up of individual businesses and, as such, are available for purchase in the market place with no discrimination based on the agenda of those who choose to make these purchases.

The church, however, was never to be for sale. It was never to be subject to the interference or influence of any force that may choose to dispute the word of God. It was never to be a puppet of a political party. It was to stand, alone if necessary, and hold fast to God's standards. The church has been neutralized. We have been infiltrated, misled, lied to, poorly educated, poorly organized and enticed into idleness with entertainment and diversions.

God still has confidence in us. He still gives us the choice of "occupying until He comes". This has to be true because we still have God's word and the authority to act on it. It is for us to determine that we will stand on God's word and act on the authority we have as Christians. It is time to have done playing Satan's game by his rules. It is time to quit telling ourselves that there is nothing we can do or that time is too short. These statements are made by those who are largely clueless about the new world order and we shouldn't be taking advise from the clueless or following the leadership of those who were first in line to surrender.

Through out this book I have asked, "if it were true, would you want to know?" I come now to a final question; as you close this book, will you open another? This book is purposed to convince you to examine the evidence. It was not designed to be the evidence. There is much available for those who are want to know.

FAMOUS QUOTES ABOUT NWO

Deuteronomy 17:6 "At the mouth of two witnesses …
shall he that is worthy of death be put to death"

Adam Weishaupt founder of The Bavarian Illuminati: "The great strength of our order lies in its concealment; let it never appear in its own name but always covered by another name and another occupation".

Adam Weishaupt: "Nothing can bring this about (the new world order) but hidden societies".

Edmund Burke British Statesman: "When bad men combine, the good must associate; else they will fall one by one, an unpitied sacrifice in a contemptible struggle".

President George Washington: "I have heard much of the nefarious and dangerous plan and doctrines of the Illuminati … It was not my intension to doubt that the doctrine of the Illuminati had not spread in The United States. On the contrary, no one is more satisfied of this fact than I am …"

President Thomas Jefferson: "Single acts of tyranny may be ascribed to the accidental opinion of a day; but a series of oppressions, begun at a distinguished period, and pursued unalterably through every change of ministry, too plainly prove a deliberate, systematical plan of reducing us to slavery".

Benjamin Disraeli Prime Minister of Great Britain: "The world is governed by very different personages from what is imagined by those who are not behind the scenes".

Benjamin Disraeli: "there is ... a power which we seldom mention in this house (Parliament). I mean the secret societies ... it is useless to deny ... that a great part of Europe ... to say nothing of other countries ... is covered with a network of these secret societies ..."

John Hylan, Mayor of New York City: "The real menace of our republic is the invisible government which like a giant octopus sprawls its slimy length over our city, state and nation. At the head is a small group of banking houses generally referred to as 'international bankers'. This little coterie of powerful international bankers virtually runs our government for their own selfish ends".

President Woodrow Wilson: "Some of the biggest men in The United States, in the field of commerce and manufacture, are afraid of something. They know that there is a power so organized, so subtle, so complete, so pervasive, that they had better not speak above their breath when they speak in condemnation of it".

U.S. Congressman Oscar Callaway had the following inserted into "The Congressional Record" in 1917: "In March 1915, the J.P. Morgan interests ... got together 12 men high up in the newspaper world and employed them to select the most influential newspapers in the United States and sufficient number of them to control generally the policy of the daily press of The United States. ... They found it was only necessary to purchase the control of 25 newspapers".

British Prime Minister Winston Churchill: "From the days of ... Weishaupt to those of Karl Marx, to those of Trotsky ... this world-wide conspiracy for the overthrow of civilization ... has been steadily growing".

U.S. Congressman Louis McFadden: "When the Federal Reserve Act was passed, the people of these United States did not perceive that a world banking system was being set up here. A super-state controlled by international bankers and international industrialists acting together to enslave the world for their own pleasure".

Edith Roosevelt Columnist, Granddaughter of former President T. Roosevelt: "The word "Establishment" is a general term for the power elite in international finance, business, the professions and government, largely from the northeast, who wield most of the power regardless of who is in the White House".

President Franklin D. Roosevelt: "The real truth of the matter is, as you and I know, that a financial element in the large centers has owned the government ever since the days of Andrew Jackson ..."

U.S. Senator William Jenner: "We have operating within our government and political system, another body representing another form of government, a bureaucratic elite which believes our Constitution is outmoded and is sure that it is the winning side".

Felix Frankfurter U.S. Supreme Court Justice: "The real rulers in Washington are invisible and exercise power from behind the scenes".

Adolph Hitler: "...national socialism will use its own revolution for the establishment of a new world order".

1953 Report of the California Senate Investigating Committee on Education: "So called modern Communism is apparently the same hypocritical world conspiracy to destroy civilization that was founded by the Illuminati ..."

U.S. Secretary of Defense James Forrestal: "Consistency has never been a mark of stupidity. If the diplomats who have mishandled our relationship with Russia were merely stupid, they would occasionally make a mistake in our favor".

Curtis Roosevelt Grandson of former President F. D. Roosevelt: "... most of his (FDR's) thoughts, his political "ammunition" as it were,

were carefully manufactured for him in advance by the … one world money group".

President John F. Kennedy (at a speech to a Columbia University audience on November 13, 1963) "The high office of President has been used to foment a plot to destroy the American's freedom and before I leave office I must inform the citizens of this plight".

President Richard Nixon: "… to evolve regional approaches to development needs and to the evolution of a new world order".

President Richard Nixon (at his 1972 visit to China toasting Chinese Premier Chou En-lai) "… the hope that each of us has to build a new world order".

Senator Barry Goldwater: "David Rockefeller and Zbigniew Brzezinski found Jimmy Carter to be their ideal candidate. They helped him win the nomination and the Presidency. To accomplish this purpose they mobilized the money power of the Wall Street bankers … and the media controllers represented in the membership of the CFR …"

Richard Gardner Deputy Assistant Secretary of State for International Organizations in the John Kennedy and Lyndon Johnson Administrations: "… we are likely to do better by building our house of world order from the bottom up rather than from the top down … an end run around national sovereignty eroding it piece by piece, is likely to get us to world order faster than the old fashioned assault".

U.S. Senator Jesse Helms: "It is no secret that the international bankers profiteer from sovereign state debt. The New York banks have found important profit centers in the lending to countries plunged into debt by socialist regimes".

President G. H. W. Bush: "This is an historic moment. We have in this past year made great progress in ending the long era of conflict and cold war. We have before us the opportunity to forge for ourselves and for future generations a new world order … when we're successful – and we will be – we have a real chance at this new world order…"

President G. H. W. Bush: "In the gulf, we saw the United Nations playing the role dreamed of by its founders".

President G. H. W. Bush: "Now we can see a new world coming into view A world in which there is the very real prospect of a new world order. In the words of Winston Churchill, a "world order" … The Gulf war put this new world to its first test …"

David Rockefeller (in his autobiography "Memoirs" pg 405) "For more than a century, ideological extremists at either end of the political spectrum have seized upon well-publicized incidents to attack the Rockefeller family for the inordinate influence they claim we wield over American political and economic institutions. Some even believe we are part of a secret cabal working against the best interests of the United States, characterizing my family and me as "internationalists" and of conspiring with others around the world to build a more integrated global political and economic structure – one world, if you will. If that's the charge, I stand guilty and I am proud of it".

In his 1983 book "The Conservators" Elliott Roosevelt (son of FDR) writes: "There are within our world perhaps only a dozen organizations which shape the courses of our various destinies … this unofficial council of the elite …"

In his 1984 book "New Lies for Old" KGB defector Anatoliy Golitsyn documented many events that materialized later in the decade making this book extremely valuable given its 1984 copyright date. This irrefutably proves the events that later took place in The USSR were staged. Mr. Golitsyn exposed plans to liberalize policies of The Soviet Union, Eastern Europe, glasnost, perestroika, the rise to power of more moderate leadership in The Soviet Union, the taking down of The Berlin Wall, the eventual collapse of the Soviet Union, communism and the KGB. This book is still available.

Henry Kissinger Former U.S. Secretary of State, founder and CEO of Kissinger and Associates: "Conflicts across the globe and an international respect for Barack Obama have created the perfect setting for establishment of a new world order".

Pope John Paul II: "there needs to be a new respect for international law and the creation of a "new international order" based on the goals of the United Nations ... an order that is able to give adequate solutions to today's problems".

BBC (in eulogy of Pope John Paul II April 2, 2005) "The Pope was the only one to be a world evangelist; he could visit all faiths - Islam and Judaism. He prepared the way for a religious new world order".

Pope Benedict XVI in his third encyclical called for "rethinking of the global economy, criticizing a growing divide between rich and poor and urging the establishment of a "true world political authority".

Rear Admiral Chester Ward (former Judge Advocate General and member of the CFR) "The main purpose of The Council on Foreign Relations is primarily disarmament of U.S. sovereignty and national independence and submerge us into an all powerful world government".

J. Edgar Hoover: "The individual is handicapped by coming face to face with a conspiracy so monstrous he cannot believe it exists. The American mind has simply not come to a realization of the evil that has been introduced into our midst".

Adam Weishaupt: "You can't imagine what respect and curiosity my priest degree has raised ... a famous Protestant divine, who is now of the order, is persuaded that the religion contained in it is the true sense of Christianity. O man, to what mayest thou not be persuaded! Who would imagine that I was to be the founder of a new religion"?

Rush Limbaugh (on his September 24, 1997 program responding to the question of why President Clinton supported NAFTA) "... there are forces, powerful forces, outside of Washington who are steering this one".

John Leoffler (Radio Host): "Your failure to be informed doesn't make me a nut".

RECOMMENDED READING LIST

1. The King James Bible: I list this first and foremost for two reasons. First, there is corruption in newer Bible translations that should be viewed with all caution. Most of these changes are subtle but do not doubt that the new world order publishes Bibles. Secondly, it is common for people who begin to understand the new world order to become so intrigued with it all that it becomes something of a "feeding frenzy" where they constantly hunger to get their hands on more information. This may be because "truth is stranger than fiction" and it is all intriguing and somewhat sensational. It may be because as people begin to understand what has happened to us as a nation (and to them personally) they find answers to so many questions and feel a freedom as the confusion begins to dissipate. Regardless of the reasons the fact remains there cannot be any substitution for knowing God's word. All the history books, books on economics and any others are not going to replace the one book God saw fit to provide for us.

Books that will give an introduction to the new world order are:

2. The Shadows of Power by James Perloff (history and duplicity)
3. The Insiders by Jack McManus (duplicity)
4. The Creature from Jekyll Island by G. Edward Griffin (Federal Reserve)
5. The New World Order by A. Ralph Epperson (history)
6. The Real Lincoln by Thomas DiLorenzo (history)

Other recommended reading:

7. The Politician by Robert Welch (history and duplicity)
8. None Dare Call it Conspiracy by Gary Allen (history and duplicity)
9. Global Tyranny Step by Step by William Jasper (history and duplicity)
10. The 5000 Year Leap by W. Cleon Skousen (principles in government)
11. America's Secret Establishment by Antony Sutton (duplicity)
12. The Anglo-American Establishment by Carroll Quigley (duplicity)
13. The Illusion of Victory by Thomas Fleming (history)
14. The New Dealers War by Thomas Fleming (history)
15. Economics in One Lesson by Henry Hazlitt (economics)
16. In Caesar's Grip by Peter Kershaw (IRS and Incorporation)

An excellent books on Christian history in America

17. What God Hath Wrought by Dr. William Grady (history)
18. Religion and The American Mind by Alan Heimert (history)

Prophecy and the "Pre-tribulation Rapture"

19. The Coming Epiphany by William Frederick (prophecy)

Excellent books but possibly only available on line:

20. Secret Societies and Subversive Movements by Nesta Webster
21. Wall Street and the Rise of Bolshevism by Antony Sutton
22. Wall Street and the Rise of Hitler by Antony Sutton
23. The Roosevelt Myth by John T. Flynn
24. Collectivism in The Churches by Edgar Bundy

On new world order strategies

25. The Prince by Machiavelli
26. The Art of War by Sun Tzu

For Continued Study

www.jbs.org
www.thenewamerican.org

INDEX

1

1st Peter 2:13,   251

2

2nd Chronicles 7: 14,   139
2nd Corinthians 10: 3-4,   141
2nd Corinthians 10:5,   123, 191, 194
2nd Corinthians 11:14,   155, 195
2nd Timothy 2:4,   143-44

5

501c3,   94, 189, 254, 262, 264-66, 268-72, 275

C

Chazaq,   83
church fathers,   71-72, 74

D

David made a covenant,   253
Dead Sea Scrolls,   366, 368, 370
Democide,   317
doctrine of Balaam,   216-19

E

Ephesians 4:27,	150, 157, 191
Ephesians 6:12,	141-42
Essenes,	368-69, 446
"exousia,"	248
Ex Parte Milligan,	413

G

Genesis 4:7,	74, 239-40

H

hypnos,	301

I

Isaiah 14:16,	308, 320
Isaiah 46: 9,	55, 110, 213

J

Jeremiah 10:23,	200
Jezebel, spirit of,	216
Jezebel spirit,	220, 222
John 18:36,	140-41

K

"ktisis,"	252

M

"mala in se,"	232-33, 443
"mala prohibita,"	232-33, 443
Matthew 5: 39,	140
Matthew 5:13,	133, 138, 212

N

"neither give place to the devil,"	150, 157
New Jerusalem Covenant Project,	126
Nicolaitans,	215-17
Nimrod,	298, 300

O

Orwell, George,	199, 314

P

paradox of democracy,	394-95
predestination,	59-60, 62, 64-65, 68, 70, 76, 78, 84

R

religion,	67
Revelation 2,	214, 218, 221-23
Rockefeller, John D.,	117, 119
Romans 13:1,	246-48, 259-60, 293, 301
Romans 13:11,	260, 293, 301
Romans 9,	75-76

S

SIECUS,	102-3
Squanto,	208-9

U

Uniform Commercial Code,	381
United States Bankruptcy,	378
United States Code, 271,	380
Uzziah,	254

V

Voltaire,   110, 114, 205, 213

W

World Council of Churches,   115, 117-18, 160, 423, 442

BIBLIOGRAPHY

Preface

1 Alice Bailey "The Externalisation of the Hierarchy" pg 514 published by Lucis Trust

Part One

2 Carroll Quigley Tragedy and Hope pgs 1247-1248 Published by The Macmillan Company
3 http://clerk.house.gove/evs/1993/roll575.xml
   See also
   http://www.senate.gove/legislative/LIS/roll_call_lists/roll_call_vote_cfm.cfm?congress=103&session=1&vote=00395

Part Two

4 Catholic Encyclopedias "Religion"
5 http://www.catholic .org/
   See also
   http://www.apuritanmind.com
6 http://www.evangelicaloutreach.org/ashes.htm
   See also
   www.reformed-theology.org/html/issues02/c_vs_s.htm
7 The Original Catholic Encyclopedia article on "Pantaenus"
8 http://www.earlychurch.org.uk/origen.php
9 http://www.sullivan-county.com/id2/augustine.htm
10 http://evangelicalarminians.org/files/On+Mans+Free+Will_What+the+Early+Church+Believed.pdf

11 Strong's Hebrew Dictionary # 2388
12 Strong's Hebrew Dictionary # 3513
13 Strong's Hebrew Dictionary # 7185
14 http://www.jeremiahproject.com/culture/ch_state.html
15 Memoirs Illustrating the History of Jacobinism by A. Barruel 1798 Published by Real View Books 2002 pgs 90-91
16 Collectivism in the churches by Edgar Bundy 1958 Published by The Church League of America
17 World Council of Churches, Financial Report 2009
18 The Interchurch World Movement of 1919 –1920 by Charles E. Harvey
19 Andrew Carnegie by David Nasaw pg 776 published by Penguin Group 2006
20 Thy Will Be Done 1995 by Colby and Dennett Harper Collins Publishers
21 ibid
22 The American Republic: A Nation of Christians by Paul Dienstberger 2000
23 http://tennesseeencyclopedia.net/imagegallery.php?EntryID=S012
24 Collectivism in The Churches by Bundy
25 Industry" semimonthly magazine June 1920 Vol. 2 no 14
26 Keynes at Harvard 1969 by Zygmund Dobbs Published by Probe Research, Inc.

Part Three

27 Proofs of a Conspiracy 1798 by Robison pg 109. Republished by Western Islands
28 The Shadows of Power by James Perloff 1988 Published by Western Islands
29 The New American Magazine "Conspiracy Issue" 1997
30 The Insiders by Jack McManus 2004 Published by The John Birch Society
31 ibid
32 The New American Magazine "Conspiracy Issue" 1997
33 Economic Solutions by Peter Kershaw 1994 Heal Our Land, Boulder, CO
34 The New American Magazine "Conspiracy Issue" 1997

35 The New Dealers War by Tomas Fleming 2001 Published by Basic Books

36 www.globalissues.org/issues/73/arms-trade-a-major-cause-of-suffering

37 www.libertylobby.org/articles/2001/20010318nafta.html

38 http://www.crossroad.to/charts/UNESCO-Goals2000.htm

39 www.unesco.org/education/efa/ed_for_all/dakfram_eng.shtml

40 www.newswithviews.com/DeWeese/tom6.htm

41 ww.natural-health-information-centre.com/codex-alimentarius. html
See also www.healthfreedomusa.org/

42 www.sourcewatch.org/index.php?title=Goliath_and_David_ Monsanto's_Legal_Battles_against_farmers

43 www.deism.com/deism_defined.thm

44 Original Intent by David Barton Published by Wallbuilders Press

45 http://petermarshallministries.com/commentary. cfm?commentary=228

46 What Hath God Wrought! by Dr. William Grady 1996 Published by Grady Publications

47 Voyage of the Mayflower by Blanche McManus Published E.R. Herrick & Co.

48 www.rootsweb.ancestry.com/~mosmd/squanto.htm

49 What Hath God Wrought! By Grady

50 ibid

51 Memoirs Illustrating the History of Jacobinism pg 91 by Barruel

52 http://yahushua.net/nicolaitan.htm

Part Four

53 West's Encyclopedia of American Law > Mala in Se and Mala prohibita

54 http://dictionary.babylon.com see Mala in se and Mala prohibita

55 Clarke's Commentary on The Bible

56 Clarke's Commentary on The Bible "Genesis"

57 ibid

58 Abingdon's Strong's Exhaustive Concordance of The Bible 1980 Gk 1849

59 Strong's Exhaustive Concordance of the Bible #2937

[60] In Caesar's Grip by Peter Kershaw, 2000 (See also www.hushmoney.org)

[61] ibid

[62] A Texan looks at Lyndon by J.Evetts Haley 1964 See also www.bc.edu/bc_org/avp/law/lwsch/journals/bclawr/42_4/01_FMS.htm

[63] In Caesar's Grip

[64] http://www.irs.gov/pub/irs-pdf/p1828.pdf

[65] ibid

[66] http://www.irs.gov/charities/charitable/article/0,,id=120703,00.html

[67] http://www.irs.gov/charities/article/0,,id=152729,00.html

[68] In Caesar's Grip

[69] IRC 501(c)(3)

[70] In Caesar's Grip

[71] ibid

[72] Blackstone's Law Dictionary "Corporation

[73] In Caesar's Grip

Part Five

[74] Strong's Exhaustive Concordance #5258

[75] www.hawaii.edu/powerkills/20TH.HTM

[76] The War Between the States by John Dwyer Published by Bluebonnet Press

[77] The American Presidents by Grolier Incorporated

[78] ibid

[79] ibid

[80] ibid

[81] ibid

[82] See "As I Please" at www.orwelltoday.com/orwellwarwritten.shtml

[83] The War Between the States by Dwyer

[84] www.whitehouse.gov/about/presidents/andrewjackson

[85] The South was Right by Kennedy and Kennedy 1991 Published by Pelican Publishing

[86] The War Between the States

87 The Real Lincoln by Thomas DiLorenzo 2002 Published by Prima Lifestyles

88 www.economicexpert.com/a/Morrill:Land:Grant:Colleges:Act. htm

89 The Coming Battle by M. W. Walbert 1899 Walter Publishing and Research 1997

90 The Real Lincoln

91 www.usconstitution.net/constamrat.html#Am13

92 The American Presidents

93 www.conservapedia.com/William_Howard_Taft#Presidency

94 www.u-s-history.com/pages/h992.html

95 The American Presidents

96 A Discourse on Free Trade by Karl Marx 1888 Published by Lee and Shepard Publishers pg 42

97 The Shadows of Power

98 The Great Depression by Murray Rothbard 1963 Published by Von Mises Institute

99 The Creature from Jekyl Island by G. Edward Griffin 1994 Published by American Media

100 ibid

101 www.conservapedia.com/Agricutural.Adjustment_Administration

102 The New World Encyclopedia / Bombing of Hiroshima and Nagasaki / during WWII

103 http://newsgroups.derkeiler.com/Archive/Soc/culture. japan/2005-08/msg00120.html

104 http://www.govexec.com/dailyfed/0506/051706nj1.htm

105 The Politician by Robert Welch 1964 Belmont Publishing Company

106 Nixon, The Man behind the Mask by Gary Allen 1971 Published by Western Islands

107 ibid

108 ibid

109 The Establishment's Man by James J. Drummey 1991 Pub. Western Islands

110 The New American Magazine See

http://thenewamerican.com/index.php/world-mainmenu-26/
south-america-mainmenu-37/701

Part Six

[111] The Catholic Encyclopedia Volume 6 "The Fifth Congress of Orientalists"
See also
http://www.catholic.org/encyclopedia/view.php?id=5209
[112] http://www.catholic.org/encyclopedia/view.php?id=5209
[113] Christ, The Misunderstood Redeemer lecture by Dr. Stephan Hoeller
See also
http://www.gnosis.org/welcome.html
[114] http://www.thepearl.org/The_Source_of_Gnosis.htm
[115] http://www.paganspath.com/meta/uva/gnosticism.htm
[116] http://www.jewishvirtuallibrary.org/jsource/Society_&_Culture/rockmuseum.html
See also
http://www.gnosis.org/library/dss/dss_timeline.htm
[117] www.newadvent.org/cathen/05546a.htm
See also
Catholic Encyclopedia: "Essenes"
[118] http://www.soul-guidance.com/houseofthesun/gnosticism.htm
[119] http://www.netowne.com/technology/important/
[120] http://www.hearkenthewatchmen.com/article.asp?id=9
[121] Report From Iron Mountain by Dial Press 1967
See also
www.theforbiddenknowledge.com/hardtruth/iron_mountain.htm
[122] http://thecnc.org/documents/sr93549.htm
[123] CRS Report for Congress, National Emergency Powers page 14
See also
http://fpc.state.gov/documents/organization/6216.pdf
[124] http://www.apfn.net/Doc-100_bankruptcy.htm
[125] http://en.wikipedia.org/wiki/James_Traficant
[126] http://www.halexandria.org/dward282.htm
[127] ibid
[128] http://www.gpoaccess.gov/uscode/

129 http://www.law.duke.edu/lib/researchguides/ucc
130 http://www.civil-liberties.com/pages/usax3.html
131 http://mises.org/freemarket_detail.aspx?cotrol=355
132 Tragedy and Hope by Carroll Quigley Published by The Macmillan Company
133 "Message from Hell" an interview with Tony Bryant KHSC Productions
134 The History of the House of Rothschild by Andrew Hitchcock
135 The Satanic Rothschild Dynasty II author unknown
   See also
   "Bloodlines of the Illuminati" by Fritz Springmeier
136 The New York Journal of American History "Dueling as Politics: The Burr-Hamilton Duel" by Joanne Freeman pg 45
137 The Shadows of Power by James Perloff pg 4
138 Secrets of The Federal Reserve by Eustace Mullins
139 Andrew Jackson "Proclamation to the People of South Carolina"
140 http://takeourcountryback-snooper.blogspot.com/2008/12democracy-v-republic-founding-fathers.htm
141 The American Presidents by Grolier Incorporated
142 The Shadows of Power by Perloff
143 1920 Supreme Court decision "Missouri vs. Holland" 1920
144 The New Dealers War Thomas Fleming
145 http://clerk.house.gov/art_history/highlights.html?action=view&intID=200
146 The ACLU on Trial by William H. McIlhany 1976 Published by New Rochelle Arlington House

Part Seven

147 http://www.constitution.org/ussc/071-002a.htm